# The
# Chef's
# Apprentice

# The Chef's Apprentice

## Roy Ackerman

HEADLINE

ACKNOWLEDGEMENTS
Researched, cooked, eaten, written up, drawn, photographed, designed, quantified, computerised and edited by the Alfresco team: Philip Diment, Angela Nicholson and Sally Simpson; assisted by Barbara Baran, Chris Eveleigh, Brian Freeman Simpson and Krystyna Mayer. Thanks also to the Mary Evans Picture Library for the etching of Apicius.

**The Television Series: The Chef's Apprentice**
(A Major Six-Part History of Meals and Manners)
*Presented By:* Roy Ackerman
*Devised By:* Roy Ackerman, Stephen Bankler-Jukes
*Screenplay:* Chris Barlas
*Original Research:* Sarah Lees, Sally Simpson
*Patisserie & Sugar Work:* Michael Nadell
*Directed By:* Jerry Johnson, Ian Lewis
*Series Producer:* Stephen Bankler-Jukes
An SBJ International Production for The Chef's Apprentice Ltd
© The Chef's Apprentice Ltd, 1986

First published in Great Britain in 1988 by
HEADLINE BOOK PUBLISHING PLC
in association with Alfresco Leisure Publications Plc

British Library Cataloguing in Publication Data
Ackerman, Roy
   The chef's apprentice.
   1. Food – Recipes
   641.5

   ISBN 0-7472-0084-X

Edited and produced by Alfresco Leisure Publications plc, London SW10, and
Pilot Productions Ltd, London W1
Designed by Absolute Design
Illustrated by Angela McAllister
Photography by Barry Peake and Leigh Simpson

Made and printed in England by Purnell Book Production Ltd, Paulton, Bristol
Typeset by Dorchester Typesetting Group Ltd, Dorchester, Dorset

# CONTENTS

## FOREWORD

It would take many volumes to cover fully the known history of food, and this selection of recipes has been devised by the Alfresco team especially for this book, using ingredients readily available today, but based upon recipes from the six periods of history. For instance, whereas the Romans might have cooked hare encased in parchment, we have adapted the recipe to modern tastes by cooking baby chickens in paper, illustrating how the same principles are still in use several centuries later. Pigs which would have been fed on dates and figs appear now as rosettes from the loin of pork accompanied by figs. Fish was baked in pastry in the time of the Sun King just as it is today, and the classic recipe for French-style peas is as acceptable today as it was then.

All recipes serve four unless otherwise indicated.

In addition to the recipes, we offer some background detail to the history of each period, in particular relation to food, feasting, personalities and cook-books.

I hope that this gives you a taste of history.

# ROMAN TIMES

## (460BC – AD415)

The Romans dominated Europe for 800 years, and not surprisingly European cuisine still owes much to their influence. Their conquests spread new cooking skills and foods throughout the Roman Empire, every general taking with him his favourite cook. Their armies also created a demand for the specialities of each vanquished country – in Britain's case the oyster particularly appealed to the Roman palate, and plentiful quantities were shipped to the markets in Rome.

In the early days of the Empire, cooking was simple, but by the end it had become highly sophisticated, and 'entertaining' an important part of a Roman's social life. The wealthy middle classes had all the essentials: well-equipped kitchens with servants and slaves to do the work, reliable supplies of food from all over the Empire, and most important of all they had an already established tradition of cooking.

Many authorities accept that this tradition is embodied in *De Re Coquinaria* (*Of Cookery*), which is often cited as the first cookery book. (In fact many others are known to have preceded it, and the earliest is more likely to have been Phagetica of Ennuis' treatise on cooking fish). *De Re Coquinaria* is well organised and attractively laid out despite many subsequent additions to the original manuscript, and its chapter headings have a surprisingly modern ring: 'The Careful Cook', 'The Fisherman', 'Of Birds', 'The Gardener', etc. Its fame was greatly enhanced in the 5th century when a clever publicist attributed authorship to Apicius, a well-known gourmand who when his income was drastically reduced by good living, is supposed to have put an end to his life to avoid the misery of being obliged to live on a plain diet. But its authorship is in doubt, if only because out of some 2,000 titles referred to in *Deipnosophists* (*The Banquet of the Learned*), a splendid combination of learned gossip and recipes written by Athenaus in about AD250, there is no mention at all of the legendary bon viveur as an author.

Many of Athenaus's recipes were very simple. His favourite dish appears to have been cheesecake, and his preparation of steak reads like a modern steak-house order. This simplicity reflects the fact that during this early period most of those who could afford to entertain were either soldiers or farmers whose diet was largely vegetarian. Even the names of some famous Romans at this time supported the trend – Fabius, Cicero and Cato were actually called after beans, peas and cabbages, respectively. Clearly, the accent on vegetables in modern

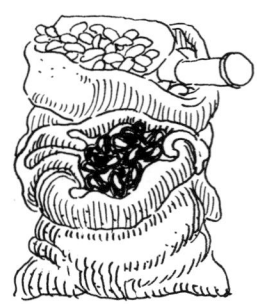

Italian cooking has a rich heritage. Among meats that were eaten, hare and pork were probably the most popular – at least fifty different cuts are recorded for pork alone.

The development from the simple to the exotic in Roman cooking occurred as a direct result of their conquests in Asia, when spices and herbs (as well as Asiatic cooks) were introduced to the West. Pepper, cinnamon, ginger, nutmeg and cloves were imported from India, Ceylon, the Bay of Bengal, the Spice Islands and even from China. And at the hub of the Empire, a person's social status began to rest on the richness and strangeness of the food he displayed. The changing attitude to porridge illustrates well how food and rank became intertwined. In early times porridge formed part of the staple Roman diet; then it became food for slaves; and finally, in later years, it was used as a term of abuse – foreigners were called 'porridge eaters'.

Despite the well-publicised excesses satirised in Petronius's *Trimalchio's Feast*, the Romans did spend much time debating how the art of entertaining could be improved, and their deliberations played at least some part in the development of the conventional 'manners' of the dinner party as we know it today.

*Right:*
*Horn cups were used as*
*drinking vessels.*

*Below:*
*The triclinium, where the host*
*would entertain his guests*
*seated, according to their*
*status, on couches.*

In particular, they considered how many guests should be invited to a properly organised dinner party, and recommended no fewer than three (in honour of the Graces of Greek mythology, the three sister goddesses Aglaia, Euphrosyne and Thalia, givers of charm and beauty) and no more than nine (in honour of the Muses, nine sister goddesses, each regarded as the protrectress of a different art or science). Guests were expected to be properly clothed and shod, and the host would provide slippers if necessary.

At the typical dinner, grace would be said, probably to the goddess Victina, protrectress of food and sovereign of the table. Menu cards would be provided, as would napkins (reports exist of some guests bringing their own napkins and taking home uneaten food in them), and finger bowls, since everyone ate with their fingertips anyway and most people preferred finger bowls to the hair of the nearest slave, as was the way in *Trimalchio's Feast*. There was no need for knives at table since the food was usually cut up by slaves, and forks were not to become common for another thousand years; there would, however, be a selection of spoons provided for specific

*Roman cooks were well respected and highly paid. The Triumvir Antony so enjoyed a meal cooked by Cleopatra's cook that he gave him a house. The kitchens had many slaves, each responsible for particular tasks.*

foods – eggs, snails, etc. At special meals, a gift or 'apophoretae' was provided for each guest – a custom also sometimes encountered today. But, mercifully, another tradition did not survive: it was accepted that guests could bring their 'shadows' with them, hangers-on, people under their patronage who needed a meal.

In wealthy homes, special dining rooms were built, usually with three stone couches, each with seating space for three people to satisfy the suggested limits for guest lists (though in fact larger couches for six, seven or eight people were quite common). If the couch was for three, the centre was deemed to be the place of honour, but if for seven or eight the most important guest would sit at the end, where he would be much less cramped. The dining table itself was often the most precious piece of furniture in the house. When much larger numbers were present, some guests would either be seated at additional, small round tables or food would be passed, buffet-style, from a special serving dresser called a repositorium, later to become a feature of Italian cuisine. Finally, the dining room might also contain a small, portable bronze stove for flambés, or simply for keeping food hot.

Slaves were organised according to how attractive they happened to be: the prettiest would serve the wine, the ugliest would tend the fire. In the larger kitchens they would have had access to a full array of utensils, bowls, moulds and mortars; and they used a wide variety of devices to heat food, ranging from the salamander (a large, red-hot iron ball which would be

passed over the food) to gridirons, chimneys for smoking food (for the table, not just for curing), and the well-authenticated Roman stove made of stone, set above an arched recess in the floor for the fire. Problems of temperature regulation in cooking were solved by having pan stands of varying heights above the fire – those viands requiring least heat on the highest stands.

Roman skills were not restricted to entertaining and cooking, they also included maintaining supplies and preserving food. Each villa would have its own fishponds (there were artificial oyster beds at Baiae near Naples) and pens for rearing and fattening fowl (geese were gorged with green figs to swell their livers), and there would be aviaries and beehives, for honey rather than sugar was a sweetener in Roman cooking.

There existed many recipes for preserving food, and not only fruit and jam – for example, Apicius coated pork with a paste of salt, vinegar and honey, then stored it in sealed vessels. Grapes were covered in barley flour and hermetically sealed in barrels of rainwater, and Varro devoted a whole text-book to preserving apples.

The results of all these skills were represented on Roman tables in a multiplicity of styles, which depended on the individual tastes of professional cooks, since recipes at that time were little more than lists of ingredients – no quantities were mentioned. Cooks enjoyed high status, and guilds or corporations were formed in Sicily, Sardinia and Pompeii, where local candidates were elected to a council.

Because social status was directly related to the richness and bizarre nature of the banquets, in the efforts of each host to try and outdo the other, display and surprise became all-important. The skilled chef tried to ensure, as Apicius boasted, that 'no-one at the table will know what he is eating'. Tastes were disguised by sauces which were important enough to have vintages, as if they were wine. The most written about sauce was a fish pickle called liquamen or garum which, at its simplest, was merely a substitute for a pinch of salt, but at other times appears to have been the principal feature of the meal. Liquamen was concocted from the entrails of mackerel left to rot in brine and oregano (Apicius preferred to use the most expensive red mullet), and there were food factories

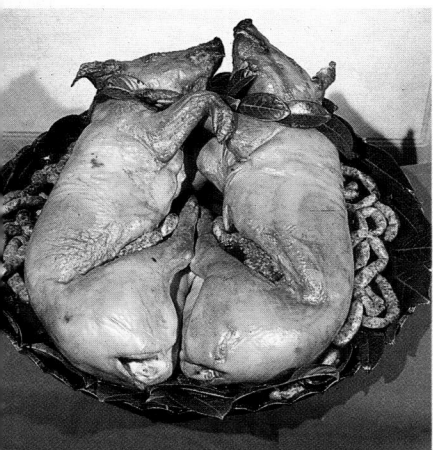

*Suckling pig stuffed with sausages, which fell out of the pig's belly when it was carved open as if they were entrails.*

*Several tasks were performed out of doors, as in many cases the kitchen would be full of smoke, especially if green wood or brushwood was being used to fuel the fires. Some kitchens were, however, quite sophisticated with proper ventilation, painted walls and well-drained floors.*

devoted solely to its production. One bottle, discovered at Pompeii, was labelled, 'Best Strained Liquamen from the Factory of Umbricus Agathopus'.

Roman tastes differed from ours today. While some of the dishes produced, such as ham and figs, or ham boiled with brown sugar and glazed fruits, would be familiar, others such as fattened dormice dipped in honey and coated with poppy seeds, or heels of camel, or ostrich, ass or root of flamingo's tongue, would be less welcome. Again, they liked to eat birds of all kinds - 'from eagle to tom-tit' (cranes and storks were commonplace on Roman menus) – and would not countenance our modern preference for well-hung game (they preferred it freshly killed) or matured cheese. Sometimes, even if the ingredients appear familiar, as in mushrooms cooked in honey or peaches prepared in the same way as jellied eels, their tastes would puzzle a modern palate. One taste familiar both to Romans and us would have been fish – especially tuna and sole, although few people today would relish their pre-prandial practice of watching the fish die under a glass dome before being despatched to the kitchen.

The Roman dinner, 'coena', usually started at the ninth hour - three or four o'clock in the afternoon – and followed the pattern of an hors d'oeuvre, a main course and a dessert; the main course consisted of numerous dishes. It was followed by the 'comissatio', an extended drinking session for which guests were perfumed, garlanded with flowers, provided with thirst-making salty foods, and seated beneath a rose where conversation was privileged (hence the expression 'sub rosa', 'in secret'). The host would decide the proportion of water to wine before it was filtered from a central bowl into the guests' glasses, for only barbarians did not water their wine.

Rome imported fig and date wine from Egypt and raisin wine from North Africa, and also exported Italian wines; wine from Mount Vesuvius was the most highly regarded, and sent to all parts of the Empire. Nor was wine their only export. While Sallust could say of Britain in 50 BC, 'the poor Britons, there is some good in them after all – they produce an oyster,' 500 years later the British could thank the Romans for the introduction of white cattle, snails, rabbits, peacocks, pheasants, doves, beehives and vineyards.

## Food in Roman Times

The ingredients came to Rome from far and wide; there was a bigger selection of food than at any other time. However, to be a successful chef you had to be ostentatious, enthusiastic, and have a good sense of humour; you had to be prepared to show off a bit. There was a sense of competition around, which found expression in all sorts of culinary trickery (a goat's belly might be stuffed with meat and cheese; suckling pigs, fed on dates and figs, would be served up garnished with the same fruits). Cooks found it amusing to disguise what they gave people to eat (the ubiquitous liquamen was used as freely as soy sauce in Chinese cooking) or enjoyed confusing and surprising people's senses by, say, fashioning a fish out of paté of chicken livers.

I invited Robert Carrier to express his culinary views on Roman opulence in the 1st century because his flamboyant and exuberant personality somehow seemed to suit this tradition. He was born in 1924 in New York. As a young man he was an actor, until army service intervened; then, at twenty-two, he moved to Paris to become Director of Dramatic Programmes to North America. There, in the course of a programme for Americans about how the French live, he became involved with leading French restaurateurs, chefs and gourmets, and decided to study the practical side of French cookery. After France, he moved to Italy, another experience which warmed him to our Roman theme. Of course, millions know Robert through his journalism and books, but besides writing about food he has opened restaurants in which to share his creations with the public, first at Carrier's in London's Camden Passage, and then in Suffolk at Hintlesham Hall.

In choosing the recipes for the Roman period there was an obvious problem in that few tastes common amongst Romans would be welcome today. 'First catch your dormouse' might not have proved a very popular instruction. So, while these Roman-inspired recipes do go some way to reflect the innovation, customs and clever tricks of the Roman cooks, and include foods typical of the era, their preparation has been devised to make them acceptable to modern taste.

We have seen how a Roman's status became associated with the food he served, and this was true of even the most basic ingredient of the Roman diet – bread (a recipe for which is included here). It was unheard of for the poorer sections of society to eat the refined white bread of their masters; theirs was, ironically, a more wholesome diet of a coarser brown variety. The artistic cook might be interested to know that for the Romans, bread had other implications too: it was baked into imaginative shapes sometimes symbolic (a sheaf loaf

*Roy Ackerman and Robert Carrier*

signified abundance), sometimes representative of the occasion to be celebrated (linked rings would signify a wedding), or in some way characteristic of the host (a poet might have his bread shaped into a lyre, and so on).

To retain flavour and moisture the Romans would roast hare wrapped in a caul or parchment, and bake chicken in a crust of flour and oil (presaging the modern cook-in-a-bag idea), hence our recipe for baby chickens cooked in paper.

The recipe for country salad reflects the popularity of salads as first courses in Roman times, a habit which of course spread far and wide and is characteristic of contemporary American diets as much as those in Mediterranean countries. But instead of liquamen made from entrails of mackerel rotted in brine, we have used anchovies in the dressing to create a more pleasing effect. If you enjoy oysters you might care to copy the dressing prepared by the Romans for their favourite import from Britain: it was made of chopped borage, cumin, pepper, egg yolks and oil.

Fish, attractive to both Roman and modern tastes, is represented in a characteristically simple trout dish. Freshwater streams and rivers were abundant sources of fish, and important too, because even with the good lines of supply which the Romans enjoyed, there was no guarantee that fish brought inland from the sea would be fresh when it arrived.

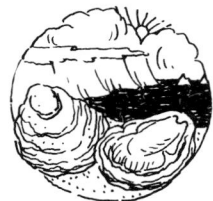

The Romans did not go in for puddings in a big way, although they would eat what they called sweetmeats early on in a meal (these might be marzipan based foods). Something close to cheesecake was known, but by and large they would prefer fresh fruits rather than puddings, and good use has been made of fruit in the two pudding recipes here.

# Country Salad

Salads were popular in Roman times, and this combination of fresh cheese, olives and lettuce is enhanced by the dressing. Anchovies replace the flavour of liquamen or garum, the liquid obtained from fermented fish.

## *Ingredients*

*1 lettuce, or a mixture of salad leaves*

*6oz/170g feta or mozzarella cheese*

*juice of 1 lemon*

*2fl oz/60ml virgin olive oil*

*½ tin anchovies*

*4oz/115g black olives*

*salt and pepper*

## *Method*

Wash and dry the lettuce or leaves, break into suitably sized pieces and cut the cheese into small cubes.

Make a dressing by mixing the lemon juice with the oil, salt and pepper; finely chop the anchovies and add to the dressing.

Arrange the lettuce in a bowl, put the cheese and olives on top, coat with the dressing and turn carefully to mix well without breaking the cheese.

Serve immediately with crusty bread, either as a first course or to accompany a main dish.

# Three Bean Salad

Drying fruit and vegetables was a common method of preserving items which were not to be found growing in the countries which the Romans inhabited. The produce could be stored for the winter when fresh vegetables were scarce and used in many ways to supplement meats. This combination of three beans makes a fine accompaniment to grilled or cold meats, and is also a good vegetarian dish.

## *Ingredients*

*4oz/115g chick peas*

*4oz/115g flageolet beans*

*4oz/115g red beans*

*3 small onions*

*3 small carrots*

*3 sticks celery*

*1½ bay leaves*

*12 parsley stalks*

*3 sprigs thyme*

*3 cloves garlic*

*10fl oz/300ml French dressing (see page 134)*

*chopped parsley for garnishing*

*salt and pepper*

## *Method*

Put the peas and both kinds of beans into separate basins, cover well with cold water and allow to soak overnight.

The next day, drain the pulses and put each kind into a separate saucepan, then cover with fresh cold water and bring to the boil on top of the cooker.

Remove any scum that rises, then add to each pan an onion, a carrot, a stick of celery, ½ a bay leaf, 4 parsley stalks, a sprig of thyme and a clove of garlic. Add a little salt and pepper to each pan.

Simmer until tender. The cooking time will vary for each kind: about 40 minutes for the red beans; about 60 minutes for the flageolets; and about 90 minutes for the chick peas.

When all the peas and beans are cooked, drain them and allow to cool slightly.

While still warm, mix each of the pulses with some of the French dressing.

When all have cooled completely, mix them together in a serving dish and sprinkle with chopped parsley.

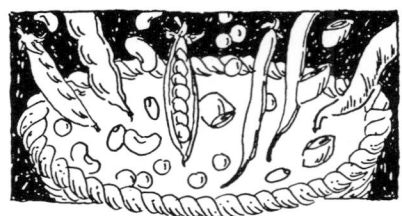

# Snails with Hazelnuts and Herbs

Snails provided an accessible and highly prized dish in Roman times. They were fattened on milk, and in this recipe they are combined with hazelnuts and herbs to create a delicious first course.

## Ingredients

1 tin of 24 snails in brine
2oz/60g butter
1 very finely chopped shallot or small onion
½ finely chopped clove garlic
1½fl oz/45ml brandy
3oz/85g roughly chopped skinned hazelnuts
1tsp chopped parsley
1 sprig fresh thyme leaves
freshly ground black pepper

## Method

Drain the snails, reserving the liquor from the tin.
  Heat a small frying pan and melt the butter.
  Add the chopped shallot or onion and garlic, and stir until softened.
  Add the brandy, and half of the liquor from the tin. Bring to the boil and reduce slightly.
  Add the snails and the hazelnuts, heat through in the sauce, then add the parsley and thyme.
  Season with black pepper.
  Serve piping hot with crusty bread.

## Notes

To skin hazelnuts: put them on a roasting tray and place in a hot oven for a few minutes, or under a hot grill. Take them out and put them on a cloth. Rub with the cloth, and the skins will come away from the kernels.

# Fried Trout with Dill and Coriander

Streams and rivers were an abundant source of good fish, and they were of course less polluted than they are today. Freshwater fish were more convenient to use, especially inland, since the transportation of fish from the sea was far too slow. Good, fresh trout would be simply cooked, as in this recipe where olive oil is used for cooking, and butter and herbs for flavouring.

## Ingredients

4 trout,
weighing 8oz/225g each for starter or
12oz/340g for main

4fl oz/120ml olive oil

6oz/170g butter

a little flour

juice of ½ lemon

1 heaped tsp chopped fresh coriander leaves

1 heaped tsp chopped fresh dill

1 lemon in slices

salt and pepper

## Method

Ask the fishmonger to gut, trim and clean the trout.

Heat the olive oil and 2oz/60g of the butter in a frying pan.

Wash the trout, pat dry and season inside with a little salt and pepper.

Coat the fish evenly with flour, pat to remove excess, then put the fish into the hot oil and butter.

Cook gently for about 4-5 minutes on each side until golden and just cooked through, then transfer to a serving dish and keep warm.

Empty the fat from the pan, clean it and reheat. Add the remaining butter, swirling it round as it melts. Cook to a nut-brown colour, then add the lemon juice and the chopped herbs.

Pour equal quantities of the flavouring over each fish, decorate with lemon slices and serve.

# Baby Chickens cooked in Paper

A common method of cooking game, poultry and fish was to wrap the food in parchment and then to roast it in the embers of the fire. The parchment protected the food from burning, retained its flavour and also prevented the flesh from drying out as it cooked. Today, we can use aluminium foil or greaseproof paper as a substitute for parchment, and the following recipe for baby chickens illustrates the use of this excellent method of cooking.

## Ingredients

*5oz/145g butter*

*4 baby chickens weighing about 12oz/340g each*

*6 sprigs fresh tarragon*

*4 heads chicory*

*a little oil*

*1 finely chopped shallot*

*4fl oz/120ml dry white wine*

*a little cornflour or arrowroot dissolved in cold water*

*salt and pepper*

*greaseproof paper*

## Method

Melt 2oz/60g of the butter and brush the chickens evenly with it, put a sprig of fresh tarragon inside each bird, then tie the birds so that they retain their shape during cooking.

Place in a roasting tin in an oven preheated to 200°C/400°F/gas mark 6, cook for 30 minutes until golden and almost cooked through, then remove from the oven and keep warm.

Meanwhile, wash the chicory and cut into ¼"/5mm slices, melt 2oz/60g butter in a frying pan, add the chicory, season and cook until slightly softened.

Cut 4 circles of greaseproof paper large enough to wrap around each chicken and brush one side of the paper with oil.

Place a quarter of the chicory on the oiled side of each paper circle, put a chicken on top and close the bag by twisting the two edges of the paper tightly together.

Place on a baking tray, taking care not to puncture the bags, and return to the oven for a further 10 minutes.

Meanwhile, melt the remaining butter in a small saucepan, add the shallot and cook until golden.

Add the white wine, boil for a minute, then add the slaked cornflour or arrowroot and heat gently.

Chop the remaining tarragon, add to the sauce, cook slowly for 10 minutes and season.

Remove the chickens from the oven and serve one per person, still in their bags, handing the sauce separately.

# Loin of Pork with Figs

In the earliest known cookery book, *De Re Coquinaria*, which was attributed to Apicius, we find a recipe for Apician ham with figs. Dried fruits, like dried vegetables, provided variety in the cooking of the Roman Empire, and figs make a welcome accompaniment to pork.

## Ingredients

*12 dried figs*

*4fl oz/120ml dry white wine*

*2lb/900g boned loin of pork*

*a little olive oil*

*a little slaked cornflour or arrowroot*

*finely chopped parsley for garnishing*

*salt and pepper*

## Method

Soak the figs overnight in the white wine and sufficient water to cover.

Roll the loin of pork and tie with string, dividing it into 8 equal portions, then refrigerate for a few hours before use.

Simmer the figs slowly in the soaking liquor until tender, then remove from the liquor and reserve both.

Cut the pork into 8 rosettes by slicing between each string, season with salt and pepper and brush with oil.

Fry the rosettes until just cooked, remove from the pan, discard the strings and keep the meat warm.

Pour the excess fat from pan, add the fig liquor, bring to the boil and simmer for 2-3 minutes.

Thicken slightly with slaked cornflour or arrowroot, reboil, adjust the seasoning to taste, then strain.

Arrange the pork rosettes and figs in a serving dish or on individual plates, pour a little of the sauce over, sprinkle with finely chopped parsley and serve immediately.

# Rabbit and Chick Pea Casserole

This recipe is a delicious combination of rabbit, chick peas and spinach, although haricot or flageolet beans could be substituted for the chick peas. The dried pulses provide a nourishing addition to the winter diet.

## Ingredients

12oz/340g dried chick peas (or 2 × 14oz/400g tins chick peas, drained)

2lb/900g rabbit joints

a little flour for dusting

3fl oz/90ml cooking oil

2oz/60g diced carrots

2oz/60g diced onions

2oz/60g diced celery

2oz/60g flour

1oz/30g tomato purée

4fl oz/120ml white wine (optional)

1¾pt/1ltr white stock (see page 133)

1 bay leaf

a few parsley stalks

1 sprig thyme

1 crushed clove garlic

1lb/450g fresh spinach (or 8oz/225g frozen)

salt and pepper

## Method

If using dried chick peas, soak in plenty of cold water overnight.

The next morning drain the chick peas, put them into a saucepan, cover with fresh cold water and add a little salt.

Cover with a lid, bring to the boil, remove any scum that rises to the surface, and cook slowly for about 60-90 minutes until tender.

When cooked, strain and reserve until required.

Trim the rabbit joints, season with salt and pepper and dust with flour.

Heat the oil in a frying pan, add the rabbit joints and fry gently until golden to seal, turning frequently.

Transfer to a casserole or large saucepan.

Fry the carrots, onions and celery in a little fresh oil until they begin to colour, then add them, with the oil, to the casserole.

Add the flour and mix well, add the tomato purée and cook for a few minutes, then add the white wine (if using), stirring gently but continuously to obtain a smooth sauce.

Add the stock a little at a time, stirring continuously to prevent lumps from forming.

When all the stock has been incorporated, tie the bay leaf, parsley stalks and thyme with string to form a bouquet garni and add to the pan with the garlic, salt and pepper. Cover with a lid and cook gently for about 60 minutes, until the rabbit is tender, either on the hob or in an oven preheated to 180°C/350°F/gas mark 4.

If using fresh spinach, remove the stalks and wash the leaves well in several changes of cold water; if using frozen spinach, simply thaw out.

When the rabbit is tender, remove the bouquet garni and add the chick peas and spinach.

Cook for a further 10 minutes, then adjust seasoning to taste.

Serve piping hot in large soup plates.

# Pomegranates and Oranges in Wine

Pomegranates were introduced to Rome from Libya and have remained a popular fruit throughout the centuries. Sweet wine softens the natural acidity of the fruit, and oranges complement their flavour.

## *Ingredients*

*4 ripe pomegranates*

*4 oranges*

*4oz/115g caster sugar*

*10fl oz/300ml sweet wine (Spanish moscatel, Sauternes, Barsac)*

## *Method*

Cut the pomegranates in half and, using a teaspoon, remove all the seeds, collecting them and their juice in a basin.

Peel the oranges, taking care to remove all the pith.

Segment the oranges by cutting with a sharp knife at each side of the membrane separating the segments, and easing out the fruit. Remove any pips.

Add the orange segments to the pomegranates.

Sprinkle with the caster sugar, and pour the wine over.

Stir well, and refrigerate for at least 4 hours.

Stir carefully from time to time during the refrigeration period to ensure that the sugar dissolves completely and that the fruit is well soaked in the wine.

Serve very cold, straight from the refrigerator.

# Baked Stuffed Apples

## Ingredients

*4 medium-sized cooking apples*

*6oz/170g dried dates*

*2oz/60g butter*

*4fl oz/120ml honey*

## Method

Wash the apples, remove the cores with an apple corer, make an incision in the skin around the circumference of each apple and place them in an earthenware dish.

Stone the dates, chop into small pieces and mix with the butter; then fill the centre of each apple with this mixture and pour in the honey.

Barely cover the bottom of the dish with water to a depth of about ⅛″/3mm.

Place in an oven preheated to 190°C/375°F/gas mark 5 and bake for about 30 minutes, until the apples are just soft.

Serve the piping hot apples with the hot fresh custard sauce.

# Bread

'To know the colour of one's bread' was the Roman expression for knowing one's place in society. Bread made from the finest, whitest flour was eaten by the rich whilst coarser, dark bread with a high proportion of bran was the staple food of the poor. How odd that today the reverse is probably true.

Nowadays, it is encouraging to see that bread flours are readily available on supermarket shelves; and when you look at the alternative, ready-baked loaves on some of the other shelves, it is surprising that more people do not bake their own.

Stoneground, wholemeal, malted granary, brown and white strong flours can all be used to produce an interesting variety of loaves and rolls.

Fast-action dried yeast makes the whole process very easy and almost foolproof, as this product is simply added to the flour before the liquid, without having to be dissolved first in warm water.

Most flours have recipes printed on the bags, so that it only seems necessary to reproduce a basic bread recipe in this book. However, we do offer some suggestions for varying that basic loaf recipe:

– prior to baking, sprinkle the bread with poppy seeds, sesame seeds or cumin seeds.

– work some chopped walnuts into the dough (especially granary or wholemeal dough) to make a lovely loaf for serving with cheese.

If you have a freezer, bake a batch of bread once a week and freeze any that you will not use immediately, taking it from the freezer as needed until the next baking day.

The difference in taste between fresh home-made and shop-bought bread is phenomenal, and it really does not take much effort to produce your own.

## Basic White Bread – Fast Method

This quantity yields 5 × 1lb/450g loaves.

### Ingredients

*3lb/1.5kg strong white flour*

*1tbsp salt*

*1½oz/45g lard or margarine*

*2pkts fast-action yeast*

*1½pts/800ml water*

### Method

Sift the flour and salt into a large bowl.

Rub the lard or margarine into the flour.

Mix in the dried yeast.

Add the water, which should be hand-hot, and mix to a dough.

Transfer the dough from the bowl to a work surface, and knead until it takes on a smooth silky texture.

Return the dough to the bowl, cover the bowl with a clean tea towel, and put in a warm place for about an hour, or until the dough has doubled in size.

Take the dough out of the bowl and knead again lightly on the work surface.

Divide the dough according to the size of your bread tins. This quantity makes 5 × 1lb/450g loaves, or fewer larger loaves, or several rolls. For rolls, weigh out the dough at 3oz/85g per roll.

Place the dough in loaf tins or on baking trays, cover again with a tea towel and allow to rise again in a warm place for a further 30 minutes or until doubled in size.

Preheat the oven to 220°C/450°F/gas mark 7.

Before the bread is placed in the oven, it can be brushed with beaten egg or milk; and sprinkled with poppy, sesame or cumin seeds.

Put the bread into the hot oven and bake. According to their size, loaves will take from 15 minutes and rolls about 10 minutes.

Check that the bread is cooked by tapping on the base of the loaf or roll: when properly cooked it will sound hollow.

Transfer the bread from the tins to a wire rack.

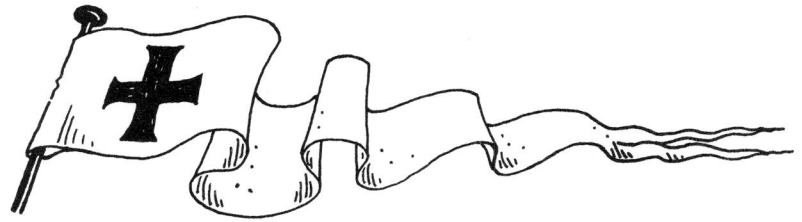

# The Medieval Era

## (1060 – 1453)

By medieval times the feast was much more than the meeting of equals that the patrician banquets of Rome had been. It was now a huge social affair deliberately incorporating every section of society – churchmen, nobles, yeoman farmers, freemen, serfs, merchants and tradesmen. Just as each had a special place at the feast, each played a part in establishing medieval cuisine.

A major source of food was the Church, whose monasteries owned huge tracts of farming land that enabled them to specialise. The Benedictines, for example, would raise sheep on one farm, dairy cattle on another, and beef cattle on a third. They also grew grain and practised viniculture, and their produce earned them large profits in the specialist markets that were springing up throughout England. They used their buildings as hostelries for wealthy travellers, which practice in turn led to the appearance of large kitchens and skilled cooks.

*Below right:*
*Clergymen would invariably be invited to banquets, and they themselves also entertained on a lavish scale. In 1504 at the enthronement of Archbishop Warham of Canterbury, the Duke of Buckingham acted as high steward of the feast, and led in the first course on horseback.*

*Lord of the Manor in full livery.*

Inns did exist, but the monasteries provided whiter bread, softer beds, clearer ale and better lavatories.

The nobles were not slow to recognise farming as a valuable source of income, and encouraged those who leased their lands to pay rents in kind, which not only meant employment for the freemen and serfs but also developed a body of yeoman farmers who were later to become the landed gentry. The nobility, with their country houses, their six or seven servants, a wide, indoor hearth, had an accountant's propensity for keeping records, and these provide most of our knowledge of medieval food and the eating habits of the Middle Ages.

A standard worker's diet in those days was three pounds of bread a day, eaten mainly with cheese and washed down with

a gallon of ale. Hard cheese like cheddar, and spermyse, a cream cheese with herbs, were favourites, and dairy products of this kind were known as white meats. A manorial household could bake 20,000 loaves a year, eaten with 2,000 pounds of cheese. Bread reflected the class structure, just as it had in Roman times, with white bread for the master (who would eat it with two or three pounds of meat a day), brown bread for the yeomen and a rough rye bread for the grooms – who by today's standards, of course, would be considered to have eaten the better bread.

All types of meat were eaten, from rabbits and wild bulls to imported bears that had died after baiting. The demand for beef led to the creation of drovers' roads, which brought cattle

*The architecture and fittings of a hall were designed for the occasions when the Lord would entertain his household and guests at a feast. From the 13th century, the Lord's table was raised on a dais so that it literally became the high table.*

from the north of England to the south-east where, just outside London, they could be fattened in special fields after their long journey. Pork was the poor man's meat and three particular dishes were established at this time: 'collopses and egges' – ham and eggs, brawn (which was regarded in Europe as an English speciality, essential for Christmas celebrations and best made from wild boars), and finally, 'pommes dorées'. These were made after the lord had had the best of the pig and given the remainder, or 'souse', to the workers. They comprised pork balls threaded on a spit, roasted, then dredged either with a mixture of shredded parsley, flour and beaten egg to make them look like green apples, or with saffron to create the appearance of golden ones. The pig's innards, umble, were of course used for 'umble pie'.

Deemed essential for preparing meat dishes was a skilled carver, who could not only 'splat a pike, spoil a hen, unbrace a mallard and barb a lobster', but was also responsible for the correct sauce – mustard for beef, brawn and salted mutton; verjuice for veal and bacon; and ginger for lamb, kid, piglet and fawn.

The Church required meatless days – at this time Wednesday and Saturday, as well as Friday, and this led to huge demands for fish, particularly salted fish. Eels were probably the most commonly eaten fish, and mill rents were often paid in barrels of eels from the mill-pond rather than in sacks of corn. Porpoise, sturgeon and whale were royal fish, and porpoise were often prepared and cooked to look like venison for consumption on fish days. There were extensive fish imports, and by the 15th century Icelandic dried cod, known as ling, was being eaten by the gentry, the common stockfish being reserved for the lower orders. (This particular distinction had disappeared by the time that the guilds of the Saltfishmongers and Stockfishmongers merged to form the Worshipful Company of Fishmongers in 1536.) In addition to the markets, huge fish fairs were held, like the Yarmouth Herring Fair at Martinmass. Sea-fish were caught in many places by the use of hedges of nets at low tides, a practice now associated with third-world countries. Traders were forbidden to sell fish as fresh after the second day, and salted whale was tuppence a pound for the current year's salting but only a

penny a pound if it was over a year old. Spices, fruit and raisins were used to liven up fish pies, which were made with clarified butter to enable them to be kept through the winter. Because fish were often found boring, and too much salt fish 'stopped the pipes', sea-birds including puffins were often treated as though they were fish, barnacle geese being especially favoured since they tasted of meat. The fish family was extended to include many water creatures, so that even beaver tails were eaten on meatless days, with the result that beavers became very rare in England.

An additional food, widely used, was the abundant wild-fowl, and most wealthy families employed a birder. Larks were the favourite, ninepence a dozen as compared to sparrows at a penny-farthing, but cranes, swans, blackbirds and thrushes were also popular. Vegetables were little used except in soup (usually fennel-flavoured), regarded in Europe as an essentially English dish. Salads (largely a mixture of herbs) were rare, and as late as the 16th century Catherine Parr had to send to Holland when she wanted a green salad.

The growth of the towns, especially London, led to increased organisation in food retail, and the growth of the guilds – the Freemen of the Mystery of Grocers, the Pepperers, Vintners, etc., led to specialisation. They set standards, and shops and markets were strictly supervised. When William Sperlyng of West Hamme was found guilty of selling bodies of beef that had died of disease he was put in the stocks, and the putrid and poisonous carcasses were burned beneath him.

A lot of cheap, French wine was imported during this period and to it were added 'starch, grain and sugar to give it body'. When on one occasion the Vintners confiscated it, the seller was forced to drink a large draught and the rest was poured over his head. Many breweries existed to supply the multiplicity of ale houses and to augment home brewing – ale was essential where the water was often foul, but little beer was drunk before the 15th century, as it was regarded as ale adulterated by hops and condemned as the 'proper drink for Dutchmen'. Pie-shops abounded, the McDonalds of their day, and as early as 1378 an ordinance to the Cooks and Pie Bakers of London laid down fixed prices such as 'best capon pie baked in pastry eightpence, 3 roast thrushes tuppence'.

*Wild birds would have been almost the only source of fresh meat for the poor, and for the rich provided variety to the dishes of a large feast. Large birds would be spit-roasted, and smaller ones cooked in pies, set in a creamy egg custard with marrow, dried fruits and spices.*

*An ox is split to reveal a lamb, within that a suckling pig, and finally a dove which, legend would have us believe, had hatched from an egg during the three days taken gradually to roast the meats!*

Whether producing a feast or providing everyday food at the manor, someone had to take charge, and two splendid books of instruction exist. John Russell, who was Marshall to Humphrey, Duke of Gloucester, wrote his *Boke of Nurture* 'to instruct the valet, butler, footman, carver, usher, dinner arranger, and hippocras [wine] maker'. It was part recipe, and part instruction book. Every aspect of his lord's life was covered, including the most intimate details of his physical and spiritual requirements from the moment he arose from his bed until the time that he returned to it. In the section on food he described how 'guests should be arranged, viands carved and his lord's salt smoothed [with a 'planere']; nearly all the birds that fly, the creatures which walk the earth, the fish that swim in the sea are food for the pot; beaver's tail, osprey, brewe, whale, swordfish, seal, torrentyne . . . and gravel of beef'. His feasts were very carefully arranged. He urged that butter and fruit be served before the meal 'as a whet to the appetite', that guests 'do not blow on their food to cool it', and prescribed separate sauces for 'flesh, fish, fowl and the second course'. He would have agreed with Piers Ploughman, who wrote about the 'hodg-poth of one mess – what eye would not loathe, what stomach not abhor such gallemauphrey, yet this is done every day [ie, mixing everything together] and called gallant entertainment'.

A second important book was written in 1392 by the Managier (Goodman) of Paris, and was a treatise on morals and home economy intended by the author to describe 'the art of being a wife, a housewife, and a perfect lady'. The Goodman was of the haute bourgeoisie and close to the king of France, a similar position to that held by many of the up-and-coming gentry in England at the time. The first part was concerned with religious and moral behaviour, and the second with household management. It included sections on gardening, hiring and firing servants, mending and cleaning dresses (especially removing grease spots – clothes were, of course, handed down not only between children but also between generations), six ways to rid one's bed of fleas, how to look after the house, and how to manage the farm. It ended with a cookery section in the usual medieval form, giving a selection of dishes for the menu of a feast or dinner, but uniquely

*Previous page:*
*To have crowds of people continuously coming to the house, to have drink flowing in abundance, to serve up far more food than could be eaten, and to feed the poor with leftovers – all of these were evidence of power, wealth and glory.*

including many simple recipes rarely found in other cook-books – even slops for invalid cookery. It also contained a section on hawking, which was regarded not as a pastime but as an essential means of providing food, the hawk being a far more efficient hunter of birds than the gun. Recipes were included for frogs and snails, and there were almonds with everything (as in China today). There were also measures of time for cooking, based on the number of paternosters or misereres that could be said.

## *TAILLEVENT*

*Taillevent was a nickname which Guillaume Tirel acquired during his apprenticeship in the kitchens of Queen Jeanne of France. Within twenty years he had risen to become chef to King Philip IV de Valois, and subsequently worked for several members of the Royal family. He was soon regarded as the finest chef in France and became 'premier écuyer de cuisine et maistre des garnisons de cuisine' to Charles IV.*

*Taillevent's book,* Le Viandier, *proved to be the authoritative treatise on cookery for almost 200 years, though the dishes of his time bear little resemblance to those of today. He used a wide range of ingredients which were generally puréed to make them easier to eat, and heavily spiced to mask the stale flavours. His recipes were simply lists of ingredients rather than detailed quantities and methods.*

*In addition to his role of cooking, he was also in charge of organising supplies of food for the Royal households, a remarkable task when you consider the lavish scale of entertaining at that time. He employed a large team to assist him, and his importance was reflected in his rank of squire with his own coat-of-arms.*

King and court made the greatest demands, and their chefs needed to be both cooks and household managers. The court in medieval Paris consumed 150 cattle and pigs, 500 sheep, 1,500 goats and 30,000 birds a week. This explains why Taillevent, who rose from spit-boy to king's master chef and was the first professional to publish a cook-book, called his book *Le Viandier* – The Victualler. He had a travel allowance of hay and oats for two horses when he left Paris in search of supplies. For most meals in large households in medieval times, all the ingredients were mixed together in one pot, and pounded and puréed out of all recognition. The food was made to look attractive by colouring with spices, as exotic and expensive as caviar is today. Taillevent used saffron for yellow, sandalwood for red and mulberries for blue. Strong sauces were used to disguise the poor quality of many of the ingredients, and he had his own special all-purpose condiment – poidre fin, similar to curry powder.

During the medieval period methods of cooking and the ingredients used were uniform throughout Europe, only the

*Spices were kept under lock and key by the head cook, who would use them liberally for flavouring, decoration or the addition of colour to an otherwise dull dish.*

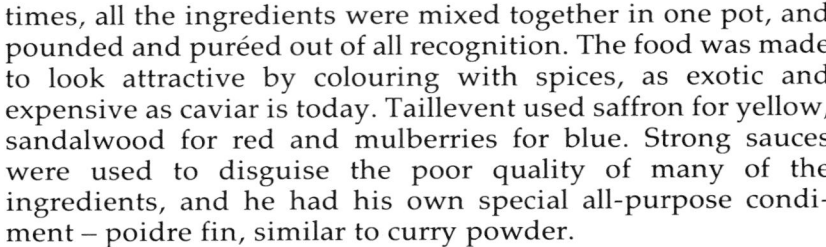

*Most cooking was done on open hearths, with spits for roasting and brick-lined ovens for baking. Earlier kitchens had lofty roofs, with holes to extract smells and heat, but chimneys gradually evolved as stone and brick replaced wattle and daub.*

quality and availability of the food distinguishing countries and classes from each other. And although, by popular consent, England was, at all levels, the best-fed country in Europe and famous for its pies, the English had no distinctive cuisine, rarely ate vegetables except in soup, and distrusted fruit except as a relief from the vapours.

## Food in the Medieval Era

Richard Shepherd is Chef des Cuisines and partner (along with Peter Langan and Michael Caine) of Langan's Brasserie in London, which is one of the busiest restaurants in England (if not *the* busiest), and

*Roy Ackerman and Richard Shepherd*

largely owing to Richard's skill in firing the restaurant with his own personality, it has an atmosphere which buzzes from the moment it opens. In inviting him to tell us about medieval banquets I felt this experience might serve him well. Besides, Richard is a boisterous, forthright character who would have done well in medieval times. He would have fought well for himself and his friends; he's a Taurean and as strong as a bull. You needed to be physically very strong in a medieval kitchen to lift the huge pots and cauldrons, the big sides of pork – it was no place for a woman – and I felt he would have a strong sympathy for the robust, wholesome food that characterised the grandiose tables of the gentry in medieval times.

In fact, at the beginning, medieval banquets were not as boisterous as one might imagine. They followed a fairly strict code of etiquette – for example, there was a correct way to be greeted by your host and be presented to the other guests; and on arrival your hands would be washed because everyone ate with their fingers. But just like dinner parties today, as the meal progressed and people began to relax, etiquette did tend to deteriorate.

Our recipes demonstrate the change that occurred when the Romans left Britain. Little survived of their style of cuisine and by medieval times the food at banquets would have been quite crude and unexciting, although what they lost in inventiveness they most certainly gained in extravagant quantity: quarters of beef and whole sides of mutton and pork were served alongside boar, roebuck, crane, heron and peacock.

The hearty appetites of the time are reflected in the substantial nature of some of our recipes – family hot-pot, lentil soup with sausage, and so on. Salting was an important method of preservation and the recipe for brawn describes a traditionally popular way of preserving the extremities of a pig. In fact all leftover meat would have been utilised in brawn, and on special occasions leftover cooked meat might be shaped, sometimes into small hedgehogs, stuck with almonds to represent quills.

Bread – ideally four days old – was used in place of plates for all but men of high rank. Meat juices would soak into it and presumably make quite a nutritious meal for the lowly human or grateful dog to whom eventually it would be passed. These slabs of bread were known as trenchers, and are the origin of the word, 'trencherman', which means someone who eats well. Here, in pain perdu with honey and pine nuts, we have a delicious recipe and somewhat more acceptable method of using up stale bread. Generally, honey was used in place of sugar as a sweetener because sugar was simply not available in affordable quantity.

The quail with bay leaves and garlic reminds us that people shot or caught and then ate practically anything that could fly – quail would have been just one such morsel in the wild, but today's recipe really *is* something a bit different. Theirs was a diet mainly of meat but we included the recipe for braised cabbage because it satisfies our modern desire for vegetables with meat, and does go very well with any of the meat dishes of their day.

# Lentil Soup with Sausage

Dried lentils flavoured with a ham or bacon bone provided a substantial soup, and the addition of the sausage meat makes a more than adequate meal.

## Ingredients

*12oz/340g lentils*

*2½pt/1.4ltr white stock or water 4oz/115g carrots*

*4oz/115g onions*

*1 clove garlic*

*4oz/115g ham or bacon bone*

*1 bouquet garni*

*6oz/170g sausage meat*

*2fl oz/60ml double cream (optional)*

*chopped parsley for garnishing*

*salt and pepper*

## Method

Put the lentils into a saucepan, cover with the stock or water and bring to the boil, removing any scum which rises to the surface.

Peel and wash the carrots and onions, peel the garlic, and add these to the saucepan together with the bone and the bouquet garni.

Season with a little salt and pepper, taking care not to overseason as the ham or bacon bone will add salt during cooking.

Simmer gently for about 60 minutes, or until the lentils are soft.

Whilst the soup is cooking, divide the sausage meat into 12 equal pieces, and roll into balls; either fry in oil or grill until just cooked and keep warm until required.

Once the lentils are cooked discard the ham bone and bouquet garni, purée the soup in a liquidiser or blender, return to a clean pan, add the cream (if using), reheat and adjust seasoning to taste.

Add the sausage balls, sprinkle with chopped parsley and serve piping hot.

# Brawn

Salting was a common form of preservation and the extremities of the pigs were traditionally preserved in this way. After salting, the head and perhaps the trotters were cooked to prepare a pâté of the type given below. Whilst brawn can be prepared from fresh meats, a day in a brine tub imparts a better flavour to this time-consuming but very worthwhile dish.

## Ingredients

½ pig's head

1 gammon hock

2 pig's trotters

2 large onions

2 large carrots

1 leek

4 celery stalks

1 bay leaf, 2 sprigs of thyme and 6 parsley stalks tied together into a bouquet garni

10 black peppercorns

10fl oz/300ml dry white wine

3 dill cucumbers

## Method

Ask your butcher to leave the pig's head in brine overnight, then soak it in cold water the next day to remove the excess salt.

Soak the hock in cold water overnight.

Put the head, the trotters and the hock into a large pan and over with cold water.

Bring to the boil, remove any white scum that rises to the surface, reduce the heat, cover, and allow to simmer gently for 90 minutes.

Meanwhile, peel and wash the carrots and onions; wash the leek and celery.

Add the prepared vegetables, the bouquet garni and the peppercorns to the meats at the end of 90 minutes, reboil, skim, and simmer for a further 90 minutes.

Remove the head and the hock, and allow them to cool slightly. Whilst the meat is still warm remove the meat from the bones, and discard the skin from the hock.

Cut the meats and the remaining pork skin into roughly ½"/1cm square pieces.

Cut the dill cucumbers into roughly ¼"/5mm square pieces.

Strain 2 pints/1.2l of the stock into a clean saucepan. Add the wine. Bring to the boil, and boil rapidly to reduce by half.

Add the diced meats and the dill cucumber, stir well, then pour into an earthenware mould.

Allow to cool completely, then refrigerate overnight to set properly.

To serve: release the brawn by dipping the mould briefly into hot water to loosen, then turn out. Slice and serve as a first course, or with salad as a main course.

# Eels in White Wine with Herbs

Eels have been fished from rivers and streams for centuries. In medieval times they were probably cooked by boiling, very much like jellied eels are today. We offer a rather more exciting alternative: eels cooked in white wine with herbs and cream.

## Ingredients

*2lb/900g eel fillets*

*2oz/60g butter*

*2oz/60g finely chopped shallots or onions*

*4fl oz/120ml white wine*

*15fl oz/450ml fish velouté (see page 134)*

*2fl oz/60ml double cream*

*1tbsp finely chopped fresh parsley, tarragon or chervil*

*salt and cayenne pepper*

## Method

Unless you feel up to doing battle with live eels, have the fishmonger skin and fillet them for you; but they must be very fresh.

Melt the butter in a small frying pan and soften the chopped shallots or onions until transparent.

Remove the onion from the frying pan, put in the bottom of an ovenproof, earthenware dish and allow to cool.

Season the eel fillets with salt and cayenne pepper, and lay them in the dish on top of the onion.

Moisten with white wine, cover with greaseproof paper or foil, and put into an oven preheated to 180°C/350°F/gas mark 4.

Bake for about 10 minutes, until the eels are just cooked.

Remove the dish from the oven and strain off the cooking liquor into a small saucepan.

Add the fish velouté to the saucepan and boil rapidly for about 5 minutes.

Add the double cream, reboil, then strain the sauce into a clean pan.

Add the chopped herbs, check the seasoning and adjust to taste.

Reheat gently, then pour the sauce over the eels in their serving dish and serve immediately.

# Loin of Pork with Pease Pudding

The onset of winter would bring about the slaughter of domestic beasts, as the cost of feeding them throughout a cold winter would have been too great. In November and December the meat would be preserved by salting, and then hung until needed. It would be cooked in a cauldron, and might be served with a savoury pudding cooked alongside it. The dried peas would be tied in a flaxen cloth suspended in the stock. This recipe still provides an ideal dish for a cold winter's day, although this version will taste rather different from the one made in medieval times, when the cauldron was perhaps only cleaned out during Lent!

## Ingredients

*2lb/900g loin of pork (boned, rolled and salted)*

*2 medium carrots*

*2 medium onions*

*1 leek*

*2 celery stalks*

*3-4 parsley stalks*

*½ bay leaf*

*1 sprig thyme*

*6 peppercorns*

*1lb/450g yellow split peas*

*2oz/60g butter*

*2 egg yolks*

## Method

Ask the butcher to prepare the pork and to salt it for you. Soak overnight in cold water before cooking.

Put the pork into a saucepan and cover with cold water. Bring to the boil and remove any scum that rises to the surface.

Reduce heat and simmer gently for 30 minutes.

Add one carrot, one onion, the leek, celery, herbs and peppercorns.

Continue to simmer for a further hour.

Meanwhile, put the split peas into a separate saucepan with the remaining onion and carrot and cover with cold water.

Bring to the boil, and remove any scum that rises to the surface. Add salt and simmer for about an hour, until tender.

When the peas are soft, remove the carrot and onion and drain the peas. Purée the peas, adding butter and pepper (see notes at end).

In order to mould the purée, beat in the egg yolks, then pour the mixture into individual moulds.

Stand these in a pan and pour hot water into the pan to come about half-way up the sides of the moulds.

Put the pan into an oven preheated to 180°C/350°F/gas mark 4 and bake until firm, about 40 minutes.

To serve: remove the pork from its cooking liquor, carve into slices and serve with a little of the cooking liquor.

Unmould the puddings and serve at the side of the pork slices. (If not moulded, serve the pease pudding separately in a vegetable dish).

Plain boiled vegetables such as carrots, turnips, beans or cabbage can be served as an accompaniment to this dish.

## Notes

To avoid wasting the vegetables – and this also enables you to prepare 2 dishes at the same time – cook an additional 4oz/115g split peas with the peas for this dish. Then purée this extra amount with the carrot, onion and cooking liquor (none of which are needed for this dish) in a blender to give you a delicious soup.

# Roast Duck with Almonds and Raisins

Domestic ducks were a common sight in medieval farmyards, and this simple recipe uses the ubiquitous almond, together with oranges and raisins, for a delicious stuffing.

## *Ingredients*

*1 duckling weighing 4lb/1.8kg*

*1 small onion*

*1 small carrot*

*4oz/115g white breadcrumbs*

*2oz/60g raisins*

*2oz/60g chopped blanched almonds*

*rind and juice of 1 orange*

*1 beaten egg*

*a little olive oil*

*1oz/30g caster sugar*

*a little slaked cornflour or arrowroot*

*1 bunch watercress for garnishing*

*salt and pepper*

## *Method*

Remove the giblets from the duckling and use them to make stock for the gravy: put them in a small saucepan with the whole onion and carrot, cover with cold water, bring to the boil, skim, and simmer gently for an hour.

For the stuffing, mix the breadcrumbs with the raisins, almonds and finely grated orange rind; season, then bind with the beaten egg.

Remove any quills from the duckling, fill the cavity with the stuffing, and tie the bird with string so that it keeps its shape during cooking. Rub a little oil into the skin and season with salt, then put the bird in a roasting tin and place in an oven preheated to 200°C/400°F/gas mark 6.

After 20 minutes reduce the heat to 180°C/350°F/gas mark 4 and cook for a further 60-90 minutes, depending on how well done you like your duck.

During cooking, baste the duck frequently: by the end of cooking, the skin should be well-coloured and crisp.

To make the gravy, put the sugar in a saucepan over a moderate heat and cook gently until caramelised to a golden colour.

Add the orange juice, taking care that it does not splash, then strain the stock from the giblets into the pan and boil rapidly for 10 minutes.

When the duck is cooked, transfer it to a serving dish and keep hot.

Pour the fat from the roasting tin, add the hot gravy, stir to incorporate the cooking juices, then return the gravy to the saucepan.

Thicken with the slaked cornflour or arrowroot, season with salt and pepper, and strain into a sauceboat.

Carve the duck into portions, garnish with watercress and serve with the stuffing and the gravy.

# Family Hot-Pot

The origins of this dish lie in peasant cookery, when a large cauldron would have been put over a fire in the morning and various items of meat, poultry and vegetables added to the pot as the morning progressed. The resulting soup, meat and vegetables, all together in one dish, would provide the sort of nourishment needed during the winter months. This somewhat refined version gives an idea of how flavoursome the so-called tougher (and cheaper) cuts of meat can be when properly cooked, and is an ideal dish for a winter Sunday lunch party. The quantities given serve 8 – it is not really feasible for fewer.

## Ingredients

*3lb/1.25kg piece of beef (shin, silverside, brisket, thick flank or thin flank*

*1 boiling fowl weighing 3lb/1.25kg*

*1 bay leaf, 3-4 parsley stalks and 2 sprigs thyme tied together as a bouquet garni*

*8 black peppercorns*

*1 savoy cabbage*

*8 medium leeks*

*16 small onions*

*1 head celery*

*1lb/450g small carrots, peeled, washed and left whole*

*1lb/450g small turnips, peeled, washed and left whole*

*1 small head garlic*

*salt and pepper*

## Method

You will need a saucepan large enough to hold all the ingredients together.

Tie the beef so that it retains its shape during cooking and truss the boiling fowl.

Put the beef into the saucepan, cover with cold water and bring to the boil on top of the cooker as rapidly as possible.

Remove any scum that rises to the surface, then reduce the heat, add a little salt, and simmer for about 90 minutes.

Add the bouquet garni and the chicken, bring back to the boil, and simmer for a further hour.

Meanwhile, prepare the vegetables.

Keep the cabbage whole, wash thoroughly in cold water, then place in a large pan of boiling water and cook for about 10 minutes, until it begins to soften.

Remove from the pan, allow to cool slightly, then cut into 8 equal segments, ensuring that the stem is intact so that the leaves of each piece will hold together.

Tie each piece loosely with string so that it does not fall apart during subsequent cooking.

Trim and wash the leeks, place in a large pan of boiling water and cook for about 5 minutes until they begin to soften. Remove the leeks from the pan, allow to cool slightly, then tie together in 2 bundles of 4.

Peel the onions, keeping the root ends intact so that they will not break up during cooking.

Trim the top of the celery, place in boiling water, cook for about 10 minutes, cool slightly then tie loosely with string.

When the chicken has been cooking for an hour add the carrots, turnips, celery, onions, leeks and garlic, check the seasoning and add more salt if needed.

Cook for a further 10 minutes, then add the cabbage and simmer for a further 15-20 minutes.

To serve, take the meats from the pot, carve the beef into slices and the chicken into 8 portions.

Remove the strings from the vegetables and cut the celery into 8 pieces. Divide the garlic into 8 servings, if liked.

Arrange the meats on a large platter, surrounded by the vegetables, and serve the soup as a first course followed by the main dish.

Other traditional accompaniments to this dish are gherkins, and coarse salt.

# Rabbit Eger-Douce

As venison was meat for the wealthy, so rabbit was a good alternative for poorer country folk. Sweet-sour sauces were popular in medieval times – vinegar was used extensively and verjuice, the juice of unripe grapes, was another commonly used acid ingredient. Owing to the prohibitive cost of sugar, honey was used to sweeten dishes.

## *Ingredients*

*1 rabbit, cut into joints*

*1 lemon*

*2fl oz/60ml olive oil*

*2oz/60g butter*

*2fl oz/60ml whisky*

*4tbsp clear honey*

*10fl oz/300ml chicken stock (see page 133)*

*10fl oz/300ml jus lié (see page 135)*

*chopped parsley*

*salt and pepper*

*Quail with Bay Leaves and Garlic (recipe on page 42)*

## Method

Season the rabbit pieces with salt and pepper.

Peel the rind thinly from the lemon, avoiding the pith, then shred the zest finely (or use a zester). Drop into boiling water for 1 minute to blanch, drain and reserve.

Squeeze the juice from the lemon.

Heat the oil and butter in a shallow pan, and when it is hot add the rabbit. Turn the pieces around to seal all sides.

Take out the rabbit and keep warm.

Pour off the fat from the pan, add the whisky, lemon juice, honey and chicken stock and bring to the boil.

Return the rabbit to the pan, reduce the heat and simmer until tender, about 40 minutes.

Add the jus lié, reboil, skim, then simmer for a further 10 minutes.

Stir in the strips of lemon zest, and serve sprinkled with chopped parsley.

# Quail with Bay Leaves and Garlic

The smallest European game bird and the only migrating one, quail have always been found in England during the summer months, once they have crossed Europe from Africa. Although still occasionally found in the wild in southern and eastern England, the majority are now bred on farms; and they are as popular today as they were in medieval times.

## Ingredients

*8 dressed quail*

*6 fresh bay leaves (or dried)*

*16 cloves garlic, peeled*

*4oz/115g butter*

*2fl oz/60ml dry sherry*

*15fl oz/450ml jus lié (see page 135)*

*salt and pepper*

## Method

Preheat the oven to 200°C/400°F/gas mark 6.

Season the quail inside and outside with salt and pepper.

Into each cavity put ½ a bay leaf, 1 clove garlic and a knob of butter.

Tie the birds with string to keep their shape, put into a roasting tin and brush with melted butter.

Put into the oven.

Meanwhile put the remaining cloves of garlic into a saucepan of boiling water.

Boil for 2 minutes, drain, discard the water, peel the garlic cloves then bring to the boil again in fresh water with a little salt; simmer until tender, about 10-15 minutes. (The changes of water will reduce the strength of the garlic.)

When the quail are just cooked and golden brown in colour, remove from the roasting tin, set aside and keep warm.

Pour off any fat from the roasting tin, add the sherry and bring to the boil on top of the cooker.

Add the remaining 2 bay leaves, finely chopped, and the jus lié, and simmer for 10 minutes.

Strain, and season to taste with salt and pepper.

Serve the quail garnished with the drained cloves of garlic and the sauce.

# Braised Cabbage

Braising is a somewhat infrequently used method of cooking vegetables which retains natural flavours and provides an attractive accompaniment to roasts or casserole dishes. In medieval times cabbage would probably have been added to the 'pottage', a dish that was subjected to prolonged cooking and included anything and everything that could be used to make a semi-liquid spoonmeat.

## Ingredients

*1 Savoy cabbage weighing 2lb/900g*

*1oz/30g butter*

*2oz/60g sliced carrots*

*2oz/60g sliced onions*

*4 rashers streaky bacon*

*1pt/500ml water or white stock (see page 133)*

*chopped parsley*

*salt and pepper*

## Method

Discard any damaged leaves from the cabbage and take off 4 of the largest leaves, keeping them whole.

Blanch in boiling water, then refresh in cold.

Cut the remaining cabbage into quarters, wash well, then drain to remove excess water.

Place in boiling water and boil gently for 10 minutes, remove, drain well and allow to cool.

Take the 4 large leaves and lay them flat with the best side down; trim the stalk from each of the 4 quarters and place one quarter on each of the 4 large leaves.

Fold the large leaves around the quarters to make parcels, squeezing gently to shape them and to extract excess moisture. Butter the bottom of a small casserole dish and place in it the sliced carrots and onions.

Put the prepared cabbage parcels in the dish, lay the bacon on top and barely cover with hot stock or water.

Season with salt and pepper, and cover with a piece of buttered greaseproof paper or aluminium foil.

Put a lid on the casserole, place in an oven preheated to 180°C/350°F/gas mark 4 and cook until tender, about 45-60 minutes.

Serve with a little of the cooking liquid and a sprinkling of chopped parsley.

# Pain Perdu with Honey and Pine Nuts

The following simple method of using up stale bread to create a delicious pudding (by dipping the bread into milk and egg and then frying it) has been popular for centuries. Make the sauce of honey flavoured with cinnamon and pine nuts, and soak the cooked slices of bread in this and you really have something rather special.

## Ingredients

4 slices stale bread

2 eggs

7fl oz/210ml milk

4oz/115g clear honey

10fl oz/300ml water

½tsp ground cinnamon

2oz/60g pine nuts

4fl oz/120ml vegetable oil

2oz/60g butter

## Method

Cut the crusts from the bread; alternatively, cut shapes from the slices with a pastry cutter.

Beat the eggs and milk in a shallow dish and soak the bread in the mixture, turning occasionally.

Put the honey, water and cinnamon into a saucepan, heat gently, simmer for 5 minutes then add the pine nuts.

Heat the oil and butter in a frying pan, and cook the slices of bread until golden on each side.

Remove the bread from the pan, arrange on a dish, pour the honey sauce over and leave to soak for a little while.

Serve warm.

# THE RENAISSANCE

(1454 – 1605)

The development of an Italian cuisine in the 15th and 16th centuries provides one of the best examples of the characteristic readiness during the Renaissance to combine, imaginatively, ancient and modern ideas.

The Renaissance – a term coined by an Italian in about 1550 – began in Italy in the 13th century, and was fundamentally a change of attitude. Men began to believe that they could control their own destinies and that everything was possible without the spiritual direction of the Church or the temporal protection of the State; and reliance on evidence – inspired by the newly discovered writings of Ancient Greece and Rome – replaced a blind appeal to a higher authority. The decline of both the Papacy and the Holy Roman Empire allowed wealthy Italian families to increase the prestige of their cities, and the ancient idea of the city state was resurrected.

This new self-confidence and desire for a new identity made a distinctive cuisine possible. No longer would food and cooking be uniform throughout Europe (or distinct only between rich and poor).

When Bartolomeo de Sacchi, known as Platina, published

# *BARTOLOMEO DE SACCHI*

*In 1474 de Sacchi was a Vatican librarian and member of the Academicians Club. He studied ancient Roman documents and wrote a book called* De Honesta Voluptate, *which included recipes from the Roman empire together with contemporary Italian ones. Additionally, the book was a guide to healthy eating, proposing a radical change from the heavy style of medieval cookery to more simple foods and more subtle flavours.*

*He advocated the use of fresh vegetables and salads, and his book included many fish dishes. He also included several Spanish recipes, reflecting the growing influence of the Spanish at the Papal court.*

*De Sacchi's recipes were precise. Some specified exact quantities of ingredients, and some described the presentation and garnish, for he realised that display was an important part of appeal.*

*The book was extremely popular, and was reprinted several times in northern Italy as well as being translated into French and German in the early 16th century.*

the first printed cook-book, *De Honesta Voluptate* (*Permissible Pleasures*), in 1474, he was a Vatican librarian and member of the Academicians' Club who studied ancient Roman documents. The book was a combination of ancient Roman recipes and contemporary Italian ones, the latter provided by his friend Martino of Como. It was the first systematic cook-book since that credited to Apicius in the 5th century, the manuscript of which was acquired by the Vatican in 1457.

Like that of Apicius, this book was divided into eight sections – fruit, seasonings, nuts, herbs, salads, meats, sweets and eggs. The Tuscan recipes clearly illustrate that an Italian cuisine existed, not only by the wide range of pasta dishes, but also by the number of provincial dishes – Bologna sausages, Lombardy rice and Venetian crayfish, for example. Most importantly, Martino's recipes were no longer the outmoded messes of the Middle Ages, but sought to highlight the individual flavours and textures of the ingredients by careful seasoning and moderate cooking, using large pieces of meat or whole birds in a sauce, or vegetables cooked whole and then sliced. Soups based on a meat broth and thickened with egg

## *BARTOLOMEO SCAPPI*

*Scappi was cook to many of the influential ecclesiastical families of his time, including Cardinals Campeggio and Capi, and later to Popes Pius IV and Pius V.*

*His amazingly detailed book,* Opera, *followed the style of de Sacchi's* De Honesta Voluptate *but elaborated on many aspects of his art. He described far more sophisticated dishes using marinades and slow cooking methods to tenderise food and make it more palatable. He also described the techniques of sophisticated pastry making which had been learned from Arabia; he acknowledged Italian regional cookery; and he included a chapter on cooking for the sick.*

*The book was illustrated with well detailed drawings showing working kitchens with a vast array of kitchen equipment, some of which has changed little to this day.*

*It was through the writings of these two Italian Renaissance figures that great strides were made in culinary art, though by the early 17th century further development was to be left to the French.*

*When the nobility of Venice married, the bride and bridegroom had probably never met until the day on which they signed the contract. There was general celebration with the finest food, wines and music.*

and breadcrumbs were now substantial dishes, and were to have a profound influence on French cooking as well as on Italian. Martino, too, had his favourite sauce – 'peverata', made from toasted bread, spices and liver, pounded with wine and vinegar – but in his case it was intended to enhance, not disguise.

At the same time as this cuisine had been developing, the city states had established themselves and spread their ideas throughout Europe. Extravagant Florence led the way,

*Despite its price, the availability of sugar combined with Renaissance inventiveness led to the discovery that boiled sugar could be blown in a similar way to glass. These fruits made from blown sugar are very natural in appearance, and are of course edible.*

*A bowl of fruits, entirely sculpted in marzipan and decorated with fresh fruits.*

reaching a peak in 1439 when Cosimo de' Medici held the Council of Florence. From March to July of that year there was the greatest gathering of scholars ever seen in Europe, which led to the founding of the Platonic Academy in 1444. While Florence concentrated on power and display (later to be epitomised in Machiavelli's *Prince* of 1528), the Montefeltro family in Urbino personified the courtliness of the Renaissance, setting a standard of behaviour for 300 years. The concept of the ideal man was portrayed in Baldassare Castiglione's *Courtier* of 1532, which described the perfect character as 'cool, sporting, knowing literature, language, music and poetry, but all done casually with a strong sense of humour, honourable and, above all, loyal'. It was he who took the Renaissance ideas north of the Alps when visiting his friend Francis I, King of France, who not only employed Cellini (as his jeweller), Da Vinci, Raphael and Michelangelo, but also laid the foundations of the Bibliothèque Nationale, the College de France, Fontainebleau and Chambord. Renaissance ideas were also adopted by Charles the Bold, who ruled a separate country at that time and had strong links with both Italy and Flanders, and rivalled Francis I in the grandeur of his feasts.

At this time food was an excuse for display, and one of the most splendid excuses was the 1454 Feast of the Pheasant in Burgundy, organised by Oliver de la Marche. It was a fund-raising exercise for a crusade to recapture Constantinople, and the feast epitomised the Renaissance. It centred on three tables, each as big as a stage, on which were a model church, complete with belfry, containing four musicians; a fully rigged ship with a working crew and pyramids of glass; and a pie containing twenty-eight musicians, all surrounded by jungles where mechanical animals stalked. Living tableaux portrayed the proverbs, food was lowered from the ceiling, and there were sixteen interludes of a kind from which both ballet and opera were later to develop. There was a falcon hunt with living birds, and in the finale a giant, dressed as a Saracen, led an elephant ridden by a lady dressed in mourning, representing the Church.

The development of an Italian cuisine coincided with the influx of foods from the New World and the discovery of new routes to the East. When the spice routes from the Eastern Mediterranean were blocked by the Turks, the Portuguese navigators used the routes they had pioneered to India and the Spice Islands to gain a monopoly on the trade and charge exorbitant prices. Trade with the Americas brought many new foods, including potatoes (a timely gift for those with poor soil), maize, chocolate, peanuts, vanilla, improved tomatoes, pineapples, French beans, red and green peppers, tapioca and turkeys into the expanding ports in the north and west of Europe, especially Spain, Portugal and the Netherlands. This in turn led to a heightened interest in food in northern Europe.

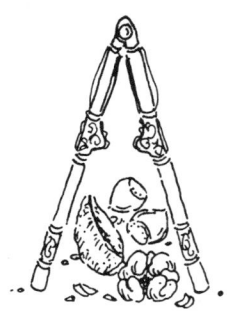

This interest is reflected in a little known cook-book, Lancelot de Casteau's *Ouverture de cuisine* published in Liège in 1604. This was the first cook-book published in French that did not simply re-work medieval recipes, and it provides the best information about what was cooked in the second half of the 16th century in northern Europe. Liège was ideally placed as the meeting-place between Burgundy and the Low Countries, with access to all these new foods through the expanding ports. Lancelot was master chef to three Prince Bishops, and became a member of the Bakers' Guild in 1552, of the Mercers in 1570 and a burgher in 1571. His book was in three parts: the first described daily fare for ladies who liked to cook (it included, together with ravioli and Bologna sausage, some of the earliest pastry recipes, cream puffs and cinnamon buns, followed by lists of vegetables, herbs and pie recipes); the second part described how French kitchens were organised, and included dishes from the cool kitchen (or larder) such as sausages, meat, fish and jellies, as well as stews and foreign recipes for Hungarian capon stew, Dutch Hutspot and Catalan partridges; and the third part gave recipes and menus for a banquet.

The significance of this book is its clarity – specific measurements of weight, cuts of meat – and its greater use of vegetables, half a century before La Varenne. One feature of all cook-books of this period, especially those which were regularly reprinted, was the extension of the sweets section – possibly an Arabic influence. Although sugar was to be sold by apothecaries rather than grocers for the next 300 years, it played an increasingly important part in the creation of new sweets, many of them described in the *Collations of Elizabeth of Austria* in 1571.

Meanwhile, in 1570, the second major Italian Renaissance cook-book had been published. Beginning with a dialogue between the chef and his apprentice, Bartolomeo Scappi's *Opera: cuoco secreto de Papa Pio Quinto* (*Cooking Secrets of Pope Pius V*) contained a wealth of recipes from all over Europe, detailed instructions for these and illustrations of the new Renaissance kitchens. These included fish-tanks, slotted spoons for draining pasta, a ravioli wheel, whisks and waffle irons, and picnic basket saddle-bags. The introduction of the closed stove had led to changes in cooking techniques, and all these were detailed in this beautiful book. The Renaissance approach had brought about a study of the scientific techniques of cooking, which encouraged gentler methods such as the use of a marinade, and cooking by braising and poaching; and Scappi's recipes ranged from Arab pastry, vol-au-vents, Moroccan couscous, German trout, English cod and Spanish pavoni, to such favourites as zabaglione and eggs florentine. The Italian recipes in the book were not particularly new, although Scappi's use of cheese, especially the mixing of different cheeses with parmesan, was an innovation and there

With the increased interest in cooking, kitchens became better organised. One description of a feast describes a sideboard laden with fantasies such as statues of marzipan, castles of turnips, high walls of lemons, candied flowers, and blancmanges in half relief.

The Renaissance saw the use of a wider range of ingredients from around the world. Many were expensive, and would be kept in locked containers to prevent pilferage.

*This ribbon is made from sugar that has been boiled, coloured and pulled, to create an edible decoration.*

*A tart filled with poached pears, coated in different coloured marzipans.*

*Roy Ackerman and Prue Leith*

was a greater *appreciation* of peculiarly Italian dishes.

The Renaissance also brought to the forefront stewards who published their own books on managing the households of the wealthy, in particular how dishes should be served, tables laid and napkins folded – napkin-folding being an art in itself at the time. They highlighted two particularly Italian features of European cuisine: the fork, which made the medieval pottages, stews and purées obsolete, protected the ruff, and made it easier to eat slippery pasta; and the 'credenza', reminiscent of the ancient Roman 'repositorium' and forerunner of the French cold buffet (reputedly introduced to France by a royal cook called Pierre Buffet, who was working in Verona in the 16th century) which not only provided the dishes for the cold courses – pies, sausages, salads and other antipasti – but displayed sugar statues, Venetian glass and silver plate.

When Renaissance Italy created the first national cuisine, it was intended to be enjoyed rather than to display wealth or power. The people studied the *science* of cooking, organised their kitchens, and established clubs with names like Campagnia del Paiolo (The Cauldron) and Campagnia della Cazzuola (The Casserole) where food could be enjoyed for its own sake. Their feasts were still sizeable, but their menus were now carefully planned, ideally comprising six services or courses of eleven dishes each, the first and the last two courses from the credenza, and the three others from the kitchen. No two similar dishes would follow each other, and each guest would taste only one or two dishes from each service. In contrast, at a contemporary German feast the guests ate all seventeen dishes served one after the other, and the meal took four hours. As Marx Rumpolt remarked in his delightful woodcut-illustrated German cook-book *Ein Neu Kochbuch*, published in 1581 (and which contained some of the earliest potato recipes), 'While the Italians were incomparably the best cooks of the Renaissance, the Germans were the greatest eaters.'

The idea of living to eat rather than eating to live was taking hold.

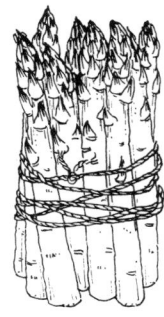

## The Food of the Renaissance

Besides being a well-known radio and television broadcaster, Prue Leith is the author of many cook-books, and has her own restaurant – Leith's – in Kensington Park Road, still a favourite of the London eating scene. Prue is a bit of a Renaissance woman herself, and was the obvious choice to look at the progress of food in this period because she also runs her own School of Food and Wine, and the Renaissance was above all a time of learning. This was the time when the first real cook-books were published, when a person could become a proper apprentice to a chef, and a career in the culinary arts became a real prospect.

Another feature of this period, again so apt for Prue Leith, was a new emphasis on artistry, delicacy, beauty and wit; cooking began to show itself as an art form as well as a science. Food was very often sculpted, and sugar became an important ingredient in this, although it still remained an expensive commodity and was usually kept under lock and key. Sugar was employed in a multitude of ways: blown like glass, it formed baskets of fruit; pulled into ribbons it was used as decoration or might be woven into baskets; as an ingredient in marzipan, it featured in moulded and carved shapes frequently decorated with gold leaf; and it was also used to create crystallised fruits.

Our recipes provide an opportunity to explore dishes typical of the period that are also practical to imitate at home. In place of the wonderful fruit bowl made from spun sugar (which might test the skills of the most experienced cook), we have, for example, oranges with honey and pine nuts, an easier but no less tantalising sweet.

The recipes also reflect the revival of vegetables in the Renaissance diet; vegetables had had no place on medieval tables despite their importance in Roman times, but during the Renaissance people looked far back in time for their inspiration and this aspect of Roman cooking was developed to become, henceforth, an essential feature of Italian cooking.

We have included a soup (lettuce with mushrooms), which would have been delivered to a Renaissance table at the same time as the main course, and of course a pasta dish, for our debt to Renaissance artistry and flair is perhaps best expressed in Italian pasta. Although it originated centuries earlier in the Middle East (and not as legend would have it, in China, a discovery of Marco Polo), pasta was perfected in its myriad forms during this period of Italian cuisine.

Renaissance cooks were innovative in their cooking techniques as well as in their presentation of food. They would, for example, insert strips of fat, or lardons, into the flesh of birds so that they would remain succulent and moist while being roasted on the spit. In our recipe for pigeons and capers, we have provided easy-to-follow modern methods to achieve a similarly successful result.

# Pasta with Parma Ham and Cream

Owing to the Italian influence of the Renaissance, pasta became a popular dish. Here we combine it with cream, Parma ham and Parmesan cheese.

## *Ingredients*

*4oz/115g Parma ham*

*2 sprigs fresh marjoram*

*12oz/340g fresh pasta*
*(or 8oz/225g dried)*

*1oz/30g butter*

*1oz/30g finely chopped onion*

*10fl oz/300ml double cream*

*a little freshly grated nutmeg*

*2oz/60g freshly grated Parmesan cheese*

*salt and pepper*

## *Method*

Cut the Parma ham into strips and chop the marjoram leaves.

Bring to the boil a large pan of salted water with a little oil, add the pasta and boil for just 5 minutes, so that it is still firm (al dente); cook dried pasta according to the manufacturer's instructions.

Melt the butter in a saucepan, add the onion and cook until soft but not coloured; add the cream and bring gradually to the boil.

Drain the cooked pasta, and add it to the cream sauce; add the ham and marjoram and stir well to prevent sticking, then season with salt, pepper and a little grated nutmeg.

When the pasta is well-coated with the sauce, serve immediately on hot plates, handing the Parmesan separately.

# Lettuce Soup with Mushrooms

Renaissance feasts were divided into courses, and it was the custom to serve all the dishes for each course at once, providing an impressive visual display for the guests. Soups were served alongside other hot dishes from the kitchens, and this recipe for lettuce and mushroom soup might have been offered with boiled young calf with parsley, stewed pigeons with mortadella, boiled calves' feet with cheese and egg, and fricasséed breast of goat with fried onions.

## Ingredients

4oz/115g butter

4oz/115g chopped onions

½ clove garlic

8oz/225g peeled raw potatoes, cut into small pieces

2½pt/1.4ltr water or chicken stock (see page 133)

1 sprig thyme

3-4 parsley stalks

1 lettuce

4oz/115g button mushrooms

chopped chives or chopped parsley for garnishing

salt and pepper

## Method

Melt half the butter in a saucepan, add the chopped onions, garlic and potatoes and cook gently for 3-4 minutes, stirring frequently to prevent browning.

Add the stock or water and bring to the boil, then add the thyme, parsley and seasoning, and simmer for 15 minutes.

Meanwhile, wash the lettuce and choose a few leaves from the heart.

Finely shred the reserved leaves and set aside for garnishing.

Wash and slice the mushrooms, then fry gently in the remaining butter until soft.

Add the lettuce leaves to the soup and simmer for a further 10 minutes.

Remove the herb sprigs and liquidise the soup until smooth; return to the pan, reheat, and check seasoning.

Garnish with the shredded lettuce, the cooked mushrooms and the chopped herbs, and serve immediately.

# Braised Lamb with Fennel

Braising is a somewhat neglected form of cookery, which is surprising since it is one of the finest methods of cooking joints of meat, poultry or game. The item to be braised is usually marinaded first and then cooked slowly with liquid in a closed container in the oven. All the flavour is thus retained, and vegetables and herbs are added to enhance the dish further.

## Ingredients

*1 leg of lamb or mutton*

*4oz/115g onions*

*4oz/115g carrots*

*2oz/60g celery*

*2oz/60g leeks*

*1 sprig thyme*

*3-4 parsley stalks*

*½ bay leaf*

*1 clove garlic*

*5fl oz/150ml red wine (optional)*

*a little oil*

*4oz/115g tomato purée*

*2pts/1.2l water or brown stock (see page 133)*

*4 heads fennel*

*a little arrowroot*

*oil for frying*

*salt and pepper*

## Method

Trim excess fat from the meat and tie with string so that it retains its shape during cooking – the butcher may do this for you – then weigh the meat for calculation of the cooking time. Allow 20 minutes per 1lb/450g.

Peel and wash the onions and carrots, wash the celery and leeks and cut them all into slices. Put into a container with the herbs, garlic, red wine (if using) and oil and marinade the leg of lamb overnight.

Heat some oil in a large frying pan, and seal the lamb in the hot fat until golden brown, turning frequently, then transfer to an oval casserole or braising pan.

Fry the vegetables from the marinade in the same oil that was used for the lamb, turning frequently until golden brown, then drain and add to the casserole.

Add the tomato purée, then half cover the meat with brown stock.

Bring to the boil on top of the cooker, carefully removing any scum that rises to the surface, cover with a lid, put into an oven preheated to 350°F/180°C/gas mark 4 and cook for one hour.

Meanwhile, wash and trim the fennel bulbs, then blanch for about 10 minutes in sufficient boiling water to just cover.

Drain, and add to the casserole at the end of the first hour's cooking.

For the last 15 minutes of the cooking period remove the lid, and baste the joint with the cooking juices, allowing the meat to colour – do this twice.

When the meat is cooked, transfer to a serving dish with the fennel and keep hot.

If the flavouring vegetables are to be served with the meat, keep these hot also; otherwise strain the liquor and discard the vegetables.

Slake some arrowroot in cold water, reboil the cooking liquor and gradually whisk in the dissolved arrowroot until the sauce is just thick enough to coat the back of a spoon, then strain into a clean pan.

Carve the lamb into slices, and serve with the fennel and the sauce.

# Partridges with Lemon and Mustard

During the Renaissance, sauces began to be used as accompaniments to dishes, and whilst the very heavy spices of medieval cookery began to be moderated, mustard was still popular as a flavouring.

## *Ingredients*

*4 young dressed partridges*

*4oz/115g melted butter*

*juice and zest of 1 lemon*

*6oz/170g whole grain mustard*

*2fl oz/60ml brandy*

*15fl oz/450ml jus lié (see page 135)*

*salt and pepper*

## *Method*

Make sure that all feathers and quills are removed from the partridges. Season with salt and pepper, tie to keep a good shape, and brush with melted butter.

Place on a roasting tin and put into an oven preheated to 200°C/400°F/gas mark 6.

Cook for 20 minutes, baste with more butter, reduce the oven temperature to 175°C/325°F/gas mark 3 and cook for about a further 30 minutes depending on size.

Meanwhile, put the finely grated lemon rind and juice into a saucepan with the mustard and brandy, heat gently, then add the jus lié.

Bring to the boil, simmer gently for 10-15 minutes, and season to taste with salt.

If you prefer not to leave the mustard grains in the sauce, pass the sauce through a sieve.

When the partridges are cooked, remove them from the oven, discard the string and serve immediately, handing the sauce separately.

# Artichoke Hearts with Nutmeg Butter

By this time, vegetables were becoming popular as dishes in their own right, and the superb globe artichoke offered a wide variety of serving methods. Here, the hearts are cooked and then finished in nut-brown butter, flavoured with a little nutmeg. The dish can be served as a first course, or as a perfect accompaniment to roast chicken, pheasant or partridge.

## Ingredients

*2pts/1.2l cold water, salt, juice of 1 lemon and*
*1oz/30g flour for cooking the artichokes*

*4 large (or 8 small) globe artichokes*

*1 lemon, cut in half*

*5oz/145g butter*

*juice of ½ lemon*

*freshly grated nutmeg*

*chopped fresh coriander leaves*

## Method

The bases or hearts of artichokes will quickly discolour when exposed to air, so artichoke hearts are generally cooked in an acidulated, slightly thickened liquid to prevent discolouration.

Boil the water with a little salt and the lemon juice.

Dissolve the flour in a little cold water, and whisk the paste quickly into the boiling water to prevent lumps from forming.

Simmer gently.

To prepare the artichokes: break off the stalk, remove the outside leaves, and with a sharp knife trim around the base to remove the fibrous parts and give a good shape.

Once half of the leaves have been removed, it is possible to cut the remainder level with the top of the base.

At all times, rub the cut surfaces with half a cut lemon; the acid in the lemon will prevent discolouration.

Place the prepared artichokes in the simmering cooking liquid, and simmer until tender.

The size and age of the artichokes will affect the cooking time: test the flesh for softness with a fine needle, and avoid overcooking.

Once the artichokes are cooked and while they are still warm, remove the fibrous 'choke' from the base and discard – this part is inedible.

Place the artichokes in a basin and just cover with some of the cooking liquor. Allow to cool.

Just before serving, quarter the artichokes and reheat in a frying pan in 2oz/60g of the butter.

Transfer to a serving dish and keep warm.

Clean the frying pan, reheat it and when hot add the remaining 3oz/85g of butter, which will sizzle and melt quickly.

When the butter is golden brown and giving off a 'nutty' smell, add the juice of half a lemon, a little freshly grated nutmeg and the chopped coriander leaves.

Pour the hot butter over the artichokes, and serve immediately.

The artichoke hearts can be served as a vegetable – they are excellent with roast or grilled meats.

# Stuffed Baby Marrows

With the expansion of trade into the Americas, the range of available vegetables increased and vegetables became ever more popular. This colourful dish of baby marrows and tomatoes is a good accompaniment to grilled meats or poultry.

## *Ingredients*

*4 medium courgettes weighing about 1lb/450g in total, washed and trimmed*

*2oz/60g butter*

*2fl oz/60ml olive oil*

*1lb/450g tomatoes*

*2oz/60g finely chopped onions*

*1 crushed clove garlic*

*1oz/30g tomato purée*

*chopped chives for garnishing*

*salt and pepper*

## *Method*

Cut the courgettes in half lengthwise.

Melt half the butter with the oil in a frying pan, gently cook the courgettes on each side until tender but not soft or coloured, then remove and allow to cool.

Place the tomatoes in boiling water for about 10 seconds, then remove the skins.

Cut the tomatoes in half crosswise, remove the juice, seeds and cores, then cut the flesh into rough dice about ¼"/5mm square.

Melt the remaining butter in a saucepan, add the onions and garlic and soften slightly, then add the diced tomatoes and tomato purée.

Season with salt and pepper and cook until the mixture has become drier and more solid.

Using a teaspoon scrape out the central seed section of each courgette half, leaving a recess; fill with the tomato mixture and place on a baking tray.

Bake in an oven preheated to 170°C/325°F/gas mark 3 for about 20 minutes.

Remove from the oven, sprinkle with chopped chives and serve immediately.

# Braised Red Cabbage

Attractive in colour and flavour, red cabbage is perfect with game dishes and as popular today as it would have been during the Renaissance.

## *Ingredients*

*1½lb/680g red cabbage*

*2oz/60g butter*

*2oz/60g sliced onions*

*a little grated nutmeg*

*2fl oz/60ml vinegar*

*6oz/170g cooking apples*

*1oz/30g brown sugar*

*5fl oz/150ml white wine or water*

*salt and pepper*

## *Method*

Discard any blemished leaves from the cabbage, wash, drain and cut into quarters.

Trim off the central white core and slice the cabbage very finely.

Melt the butter in a saucepan, add the cabbage, season with salt and a little nutmeg, and sprinkle with vinegar, stirring well.

Cover with a lid and set over a very low heat, stirring occasionally, for about 10 minutes.

Peel, core and finely chop the apples, then add to the cabbage together with the sugar.

Mix well, transfer to an ovenproof casserole which has a tight-fitting lid and moisten with the wine or water.

Cover the casserole with the lid and cook in an oven preheated to 170°C/325°F/gas mark 3 (or cook on top of the stove) for about 90 minutes, stirring occasionally.

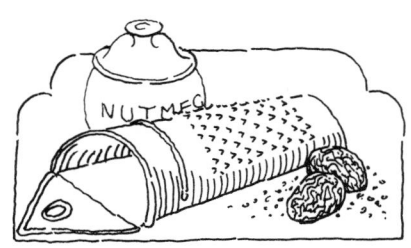

# Pigeons with Capers

It was customary in Renaissance times to spit-roast pigeons, but all except very young birds can become tough when cooked by this method, as they have no fat to render the meat tender while it cooks. Braising the pigeons makes them more succulent while at the same time providing a delicious sauce, to which capers are added for zest.

## Ingredients

*4 pigeons*

*a little oil*

*1 diced large carrot*

*1 diced onion*

*1 diced leek*

*2 diced sticks celery*

*2 peeled cloves garlic (optional)*

*4fl oz/120ml red wine*

*2oz/60g tomato purée*

*3-4 parsley stalks*

*1 sprig thyme*

*½ bay leaf*

*1½pt/800ml water or brown stock (see page 133)*

*a little slaked cornflour or arrowroot*

*2oz/60g capers*

*salt and pepper*

## Method

Clean the pigeons well and tie them so that they retain their shape during cooking.

Heat a little oil in a frying pan, season the pigeons with salt and pepper and fry in the oil, turning frequently to colour and seal, then transfer to a casserole.

In the same pan fry the vegetables (and garlic, if using), turning frequently until golden, then add to the casserole.

Pour the fat from the frying pan, add the red wine, boil to loosen the residue from the pan and add to the casserole.

Add the tomato purée and herbs, cover the pigeons with the stock or water and bring to the boil on top of the stove.

Skim, add a little salt and pepper, cover with a lid and place in an oven preheated to 170°C/325°F/gas mark 3 for about 75 minutes, until tender.

Remove the pigeons from the cooking liquor and keep warm.

Strain the cooking liquor into a clean pan, thicken with the slaked cornflour or arrowroot, boil for 10 minutes and adjust seasoning to taste.

Return the pigeons to the sauce, add the capers, and simmer for a further 5 minutes.

Serve immediately; creamy mashed potatoes would be a good accompaniment to the pigeons.

# Almond Pear Tart

It was during the Renaissance that pastry began to be utilised in more exciting ways, and it was often combined with almonds during this period. A tart of pears in marzipan was served to Pope Pius V at a banquet, and this recipe is an adaptation of the dish.

## Ingredients

*8oz/225g sweet pastry (see page 136)*

*4oz/115g apricot jam*

*12oz/340g frangipane (see page 136)*

*1tbsp eau de vie de poire william (optional)*

*3 poached pears, drained, dried and halved,*
*reserve the cooking liquid*

## Method

Roll out the sweet pastry and use it to line an 8″/20cm flan case.

Spread a thin layer of apricot jam on to the pastry, reserving half for glazing, then two-thirds fill with the frangipane (to which you may wish to add the eau de vie de poire william).

Arrange the pear halves on top of the frangipane, and press lightly into the mixture. (As the tart cooks, the frangipane will rise around the pears.)

Bake for about 20 minutes in an oven preheated to 180°C/350°F/gas mark 4. Remove from the oven when golden, and cool slightly.

Boil the remaining jam with a little syrup from the pears, and strain through a sieve.

Brush the top of the slightly cooled flan with the sieved jam to glaze.

Serve warm with either fresh custard sauce (see page 135) or fresh cream.

*Above:*
*Almond Pear Tart*

*Left:*
*Oranges and Honey and Pine Nuts (recipe on page 66)*

# Oranges with Honey and Pine Nuts

Eating fruit was almost an obsession in Italy during the Renaissance, and was instrumental in overcoming scurvy in Italy earlier than in other European countries. Sweetened with honey and flavoured with crunchy pine nuts, oranges make a simple, refreshing pudding.

## Ingredients

*5fl oz/150ml clear honey*

*juice of 1 lemon*

*2oz/60g pine nuts*

*4-6 oranges, depending on size*

*2oz/60g caster sugar*

*1fl oz/30ml water*

## Method

Put the honey and lemon juice into a saucepan and bring to the boil.

Simmer for 10 minutes, add the pine nuts and allow to cool.

Using a potato peeler, remove strips of peel from 2 of the oranges and cut these into very fine strips.

Put the sugar and water into a saucepan, add the strips of peel and boil until they are almost crystallised; remove from the heat and allow to cool.

Remove the skin and pith from all of the oranges, then cut into slices across the segments and remove any pips.

Lay the segments in a serving dish and cover with the syrup and pine nuts; refrigerate for at least an hour before serving.

Decorate with the orange zest.

## Notes

The flavour will be improved by the addition to the syrup of a little orange liqueur, such as curaçao, Grand Marnier or Cointreau.

# THE SUN KING

## (1643 – 1715)

When Marie de' Medici came to France from her father's kingdom in Tuscany to marry Henry IV in 1600, there was no national French cuisine. The popular cook-books were translations of Platina and Scappi, and no major French cook-book had been published since Taillevent's 250 years earlier. Yet 100 years after that wedding, French cuisine would be admired throughout Europe, and the foundations of haute cuisine had been firmly laid. (In England, however, culinary developments – for which women were largely responsible – centred on the domestic scene.) Undoubtedly, the Italian experience encouraged the French transition, but the basic ingredients for change lay within France itself.

Aresty in *The Delectable Past* summed up this change: 'When Louis XIV came to the throne in 1643, French cooking was as young and unformed as the child king himself. When Louis died in 1715, French cuisine was one of the glories of his dazzling court.' The reasons for the change were threefold. Firstly, in order to weaken the nobles Louis XIV ensnared them in costly rituals of which formal feasting at his palace of Versailles played an essential part. Secondly, he inherited from his father Louis XIII (himself an excellent practical cook) a tradition of formal entertaining and plentiful produce from the royal gardens. Thirdly, and most importantly of all, an experienced chef, La Varenne, recorded every aspect of cookery in France and published it in *Le Cuisinier françois* in 1651.

During the 300 years since Taillevent's cook-book, French cuisine had remained largely medieval, and many of La Varenne's recipes reflect this. However, his sauces were often simpler, consisting only of vinegar, verjuice or lemon juice added to pan drippings and thickened with moistened breadcrumbs or egg yolks; and his poivrade and sauce Robert are still used today. (Sauce Robert illustrates culinary longev-

*The food was prepared for hours by more than 300 staff, and was carried to the royal quarters in procession, headed by two archers, the Lord Steward and other notables. As they made their way through the long corridors they would cry, 'The King's meat'. M Vatel was maître d'hôtel at Chantilly, and on one occasion had ordered fish for a banquet in honour of the King. A purveyor arrived with just two small loads of fish and, thinking that he had ordered an insufficient quantity, Vatel went to his room and ran his sword into his heart. As he lay dying, the rest of his consignment of fish was arriving from all directions...*

ity: although claimed for Robert Viot it was in use long before he was born, and probably relates to the medieval English roebuck sauce, learned by the Normans in England, then brought back to France.) Many of his recipes were half medieval and half modern – for example, a blancmange was a meat broth but was wholly smooth. He was responsible for one important and long-lasting innovation: he listed those ingredients he expected always to be at hand in the kitchen; but basically his work was directed at large households in touch with the latest fashions. Ceramic plates had made more liquid mixtures possible (just as the knife and fork had permitted firmer mixtures) and individual portions, egg-sized pieces of meat or individually stuffed vegetables, were now included. A large part of La Varenne's work relates to armies in the field, so that a recipe is included for chicken in a bottle, and he specialised in stuffed artichokes for meatless days.

That the Italian influence was strong is illustrated by the publication in 1655 of *Le Pastissier françois*, usually credited to La Varenne. Unlike *Le Cuisinier françois*, which assumed basic cookery skills, it is closely related to Scappi's work, giving

## *LA VARENNE*

*François Pierre de la Varenne can be considered one of the founders of French classic cuisine. In 1651 he published a book called* Le Cuisinier françois *which had a profound influence on European cooking. La Varenne was thirty-five when he wrote it, and was working at that time for the Marquis d'Uxelles.*

*The book set out methods of preparation and cooking much as we know them today. He appreciated the differences between various cuts of meat, and suggested the most suitable ways to cook each of them. He realised the value of stocks in cookery, and it was he who devised the method of thickening sauces with a mixture of fat and flour called a roux. Vegetables featured strongly in his recipes, the range of those available increasing in line with discoveries from the New World. Another book called* Le Pâtissier françois *has also often been credited to La Varenne.*

*Little is known about La Varenne's personal life, but there is no doubt that* Le Cuisinier françois *played a role in the development of classic cuisine as we know it today.*

detailed and precise instructions for such things as puff pastry, macaroons, and the little cakes made in small baking ovens – petits fours. The layout of the book differs so much from *Le Cuisinier françois* as to put in doubt La Varenne's authorship of it, but it established the importance of pastry-making, and set standards for future cook-books in its detail and precision.

However, *Le Cuisinier françois* was much more than just a recipe book – it was an orderly text-book structured for professional chefs. Beginning with bouillon and two basic stocks and building up on a modular system, La Varenne introduced the spirit of organisation which remains the classic hallmark of French cuisine. Rather than having a favourite sauce, he was the first French writer to record the addition of the classic thickening roux (fat and flour) to bouillon to make a velouté sauce, and from that base a multiplicity of sauces, old and new. Catering for all types of equipment, from iron pots with hot coals on their lids to the latest ovens built into the fireplace walls, he identified all those ingredients that a chef must always have to hand. In addition, a major part of his work was concerned with the protocol of eating, serving and the ceremony of an aristocratic table, supported by a professional chef with teams of cooks and servants to assist him.

During the next hundred years his book was reprinted repeatedly and joined by the works of many other chefs, especially those of Massailot – his *Nouvelle Instruction pour les confitures* of 1692 is credited with being the first alphabetic cook-book; Menon – whose *La Cuisinière bourgeoise* of 1746 became the bible of the restaurateur and the most reprinted French cook-book until modern times; and Marin, who sought to simplify the art of cooking through the logically planned catalogue of recipes and menus in his *Dons de Comus* of 1739. All of these books were aimed at the rich, and it was among the nobility and the new restaurants that French cooking developed. Aristocratic patronage, including that of Louis XV's hostesses, raised chefs to great social importance, and while dishes may have become simpler the number at each meal was excessive – a typical menu for twenty guests would list over one hundred dishes, served among elaborate silver and crystal. The female chef to Madame du Barry received a great honour from the king after a particularly successful meal – the Order of

*Artichokes grew in the garden at Versailles. In the centre, chickens being 'barded', covered with pork fat to keep them moist during roasting. Pastry-making was also perfected at this time.*

*Nicolas Fouquet was Superintendent of Finances to Louis XIV, and built the estate at Vaux-le-Vicomte with funds diverted from taxes. He was reputedly jailed after he had made the mistake of inviting the King to a lavish festival, thus allowing the Sovereign to see for himself the flamboyant lifestyle enjoyed by his employee – at his expense.*

the Holy Ghost, known from its blue sash as the Cordon bleu, a term correctly applied only to female chefs. However, few other women were to appear on the French culinary scene in the 18th and 19th centuries.

This was in complete contrast to England, where cookery books were often written by women and directed at the middle classes rather than the aristocracy. Outstanding were Hannah Glasse, whose *Art of Cookery Made Plain and Easy*, published in 1747, sought to 'improve the servants and save the ladies a great deal of trouble'; Sarah Phillips, who pleaded in 1758 that cooks should stop boiling the goodness out of greens; Eliza Smith, whose *The Compleat House-Wife* was the first cook-book to be printed in America; and Elizabeth Raffald, whose experience was not in doubt when she published *The Experienced English Housekeeper* in 1769, having managed a confectionery store, two inns, a domestic agency and a cooking school, borne sixteen daughters, as well as being housekeeper to a Mrs Warburton.

*Previous page:*
*Louis XIV at table. Princess*
*Palatine credits Louis XIV with*
*a robust appetite. She said, 'I*
*have often seen the King eat*
*four plates of soup of different*
*kinds, a whole pheasant, a*
*partridge, a large plate of salad,*
*two thick slices of ham, a dish*
*of mutton in a garlic-flavoured*
*sauce, a plateful of pastries and*
*then fruit and hard-boiled*
*eggs'. However, a gentleman-*
*in-waiting would always taste*
*each dish first, to ensure that it*
*had not been poisoned.*

A feature of English cook-books of this period, again in contrast to the French, was their relative simplicity. This was possible because of the very high quality of available ingredients – especially meat, produced from the newly introduced Dutch grasses – lucerne, trefoil, etc. This fact led Gervase Markham, a prolific cookery writer of the 17th century, to recommend that 'if the quality of the meat was high, simple presentation and plain seasoning was preferable'. In his *The English House-Wife*, he centred his teaching on three factors: food of high quality, attractive presentation, and variety. It was during the 17th and 18th centuries that roast beef became the national dish, and there was no longer any need to make use of disguising sauces.

Perhaps the most distinct change from medieval times was the growing popularity of vegetables. In 1605 a Guild of Gardeners, consisting of those who lived within six miles of London, was established, members of which grew heavy crops using London's nightly sewerage as manure! Vegetables were traditionally sold at the gates of St Paul's; by the mid-17th century Covent Garden was well established; and the Earl of Bradford became rich by levying a toll on the traders using Inigo Jones's Piazza. Bananas came from Bermuda in 1633, and pineapples were introduced in 1661 – during the 18th century in England they were reared in hot-beds called pineres. Rhubarb, although known in Tudor times, was not widely eaten until it began to be imported from Italy in the middle of the 17th century.

It was the diarist John Evelyn who raised vegetables and gardens to a higher plane during the 17th century. A

founder-member of the Royal Society, widely travelled, especially in France, he translated Bonnefons' *The French Gardener* and de la Quintinie's *The Compleat Gardener* (the latter writer was employed by Louis XIV), and was responsible for the revival of the ice-house. In 1679, after a dinner with Pepys, he attended a lecture at the Royal Society given by his friend Dr Dennis Pain on the 'Digester', the first real pressure cooker specifically designed as such.

From his garden at Sayes Court he was able to provide a mixed green salad every day of the year, and his *Acetaria: A Discourse of Sallets* (Salad Calendar), published in 1664, ran into ten editions. Greens and herbs were carefully chosen, as 'all should fall into their place like notes in music'. In a fashionable style he favoured huge pyramids of vegetables as a centrepiece for the table, and he included melons, heads of celery from France, artichokes from the Arabs in North Africa, to be eaten with pumpkin and potato bread sprinkled with broom buds substituting for capers, all followed by ice-cream introduced from France and first recorded by Evelyn in 1671. Evelyn's salad dressing was modern – three parts olive oil, one of vinegar, dry mustard and the whites of hard-boiled eggs. The use of flowers in dishes and decoration was a peculiarly English characteristic established at this time, but a more fundamental innovation was taking place in drinking habits.

Wars often prevented the importing of wine from France, and although Portuguese wine (douro), sack from southern Spain and Chianti from Italy acted as replacements, these were only for the rich. (The use of cork-bark stoppers became common in the late 17th century, making it possible to lay

down wines and thus avoid such potentially dry spells!) For the poor, spirits such as genever were distilled and imported from Holland; and home brewing was being replaced by the efforts of bigger commercial breweries. By 1700 half a million gallons of Dutch spirits were being imported each year. At the same time came the development of the coffee houses. Pasqua Rosee's Inn in St Michael's Alley, later the George and Vulture, is reputed to have been the first in London in 1652, and there were over 3,000 in London by the end of the century.

Thus while La Varenne was establishing the foundations of cuisine for the maître d'hôtel in France, in England cooking was becoming primarily domestic, turning to France for banquets and state occasions.

*A mound of choux pastry buns, filled with cream or fruit mousse then dipped in caramel and veiled in spun sugar, is known as a croque-en-bouche, and is still served traditionally in France as a wedding cake.*

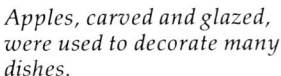

*Apples, carved and glazed, were used to decorate many dishes.*

*Roy Ackerman and
Raymond Blanc*

### The Food of the Sun King

During this time, the mantle of haute cuisine passed from Italy to France, and it seemed appropriate to invite a French chef, Raymond Blanc, to tell us about the earthy but romantic French cuisine which at least some people of this period enjoyed. Raymond Blanc opened Les Quat'Saisons in Oxford in 1977 and by 1982 had won two Michelin stars. Two years later he acquired a manor house just outside Oxford which became Le Manoir aux Quat'Saisons, and then he opened another restaurant in the city which was Le Petit Blanc. In 1988, Raymond publishes his first book *Recipes from Le Manoir aux Quat'Saisons*.

Louis XIV's reign saw a period of lavish eating which, with further refinement, proved to be a logical and worthy successor to Renaissance cuisine. The huge wealth and sumptuous lifestyle of the Sun King demanded of his cuisine a similar flamboyance. Dishes of game would be presented dressed with colourful plumage; foie gras carved to resemble small songbirds; and truffles might be used as a garnish for eggs or mousse of chicken. Crispy choux buns were filled with a fruit mousse, dipped in caramel and piled up to form the famous croque-en-bouche which was then coated with syrupy strands of spun sugar.

But flamboyance was not the whole story of the cuisine of this period; there was a measure of finesse too. Sauces became more subtle and varied, and the development of the roux as a thickening agent provided greater scope in creating individual flavours. Hitherto, sauces had been thickened by the addition of breadcrumbs or anything else that might be available. Now, for the first time, it was realised that if you add fat to flour, and cook it, the mixture will act very effectively as a thickening agent. A chef would mix a whole mass of roux and keep it for weeks on end, breaking bits off and throwing them into a sauce as necessary, rather than mix a roux as the base of each sauce and then add the liquid as we do today. Still, it was a start, and one that would be greatly improved under the ingenious eye of Carême in the 19th century.

With the emphasis in cooking now upon creating flavour (and not just a flavour sufficiently heavy to cover up the taste of putrid meat), all kinds of interesting taste combinations were produced: for example, pistachio nuts, wild mushrooms, asparagus and herbs were combined with veal forcemeat, to be placed inside a boned chicken and cooked in a sealed glass jar. At a stroke the first galantine of chicken was created and a new method of preservation achieved, for the sealed jar was even transportable by soldiers on the campaign trail. One of Louis' favourite recipes consisted of boning a turkey from his farm at Versailles, and stuffing it with a forcemeat containing wild mushrooms and raspberries. Our recipe for chicken breasts stuffed with oysters exlores similarly intriguing tastes. Louis was also obsessed with peas (see our recipe for peas cooked in the French style) and asparagus, both of which he enjoyed in soups, or as garnishes, or as vegetable accompaniment to meat dishes.

Pastry also became very popular. Puff pastry would be packed with sweet or savoury fillings, pies not dissimilar to today's pork pies would be made from all kinds of meat or game, and fish was also cooked inside a pastry crust, as with our sea trout in pastry with tomato sauce.

# Marinated Mackerel

Fresh foods simply cooked were a welcome change from the elaborately presented banquets of Louis' court. In this recipe, mackerel are lightly poached in an aromatic mixture of wine, herbs and paprika. They are equally good hot or cold, and can be served either as a first course or as a main dish.

## Ingredients

*4 very fresh mackerel fillets,*
*each weighing 8oz/225g*

*5fl oz/150ml olive oil*

*2 peeled and sliced cloves garlic*

*1 bay leaf*

*2 sprigs thyme*

*5fl oz/150ml dry white wine*

*2fl oz/60ml white wine vinegar*

*1 heaped tsp paprika*

*4 parsley stalks*

*chopped parsley for garnishing*

*salt and pepper*

## Method

Wash the fillets well in cold water and pat dry.

Heat the oil gently, add the sliced garlic and fry until golden.

Cool slightly, then add the bay leaf, thyme, wine, vinegar, paprika and parsley stalks, and season with salt and pepper.

Bring to the boil and simmer for 5 minutes.

Lay the fish in the pan, reduce the heat, cover and cook slowly for about 15 minutes.

Transfer the mackerel to a dish with all the liquid, and allow to cool completely in the refrigerator, occasionally spooning some of the liquid over the fish.

Serve cold, sprinkled with chopped parsley, and accompanied by crusty bread and perhaps a tomato salad.

## Notes

Fresh sardine or trout fillets can be prepared in the same way.

# Braised Salmon

Whereas today fish courses usually precede meat, game or poultry, during the 17th century it was customary to serve fish after the main courses, to remove the taste of meat from the palate. Larger fish or pieces of fish are excellent braised, enabling other flavours to be introduced to the flesh and a sauce to be created at the same time.

## *Ingredients*

*3oz/85g butter*

*1 small finely diced onion, 1 large finely diced carrot, 1 small finely diced leek and 2 finely diced sticks celery – total weight 8oz/225g*

*2lb/900g middle cut piece of salmon*

*10fl oz/300ml fish stock (see page 134)*

*4fl oz/120ml dry white wine*

*4fl oz/120ml double cream*

*1oz/30g flour*

*chopped chives for garnishing*

*salt and cayenne pepper*

## *Method*

Melt 2oz/60g of the butter in a saucepan, add the diced vegetables and stir for 2 minutes until they just begin to soften.

Transfer to an ovenproof casserole dish and allow to cool slightly, then season the salmon with salt and cayenne pepper and place on top of the vegetables.

Heat the fish stock and white wine in the pan used for frying the vegetables, then pour over the salmon.

Cover the fish with buttered greaseproof paper and cook in an oven preheated to 170°C/325°F/gas mark 3 for about 30 minutes, depending on the thickness of the fish.

Remove the casserole dish from the oven, transfer the salmon to a serving plate and keep warm.

Pour the cooking liquor and the vegetables into a saucepan, add the cream and bring to the boil.

Mix the flour with the remaining butter to make a smooth paste.

Take the sauce off the heat, and gradually whisk in small pieces of the butter and flour until the sauce is thick enough to coat the back of a spoon.

Season to taste with salt and cayenne pepper, then add the chopped chives.

Serve the salmon whole, handing the sauce separately; alternatively cut it into 4 portions and coat each piece with some of the sauce.

# Venison with Baby Turnips

Herds of deer provided sport and excellent food for the landowners, and a marinade of wine and herbs served to tenderise, flavour and preserve the meat. Small white turnips complement the richness of this delicious dish.

## *Ingredients*

*4oz/115g thinly sliced onion*

*4oz/115g thinly sliced carrot*

*1 crushed clove garlic*

*1 bay leaf*

*1 sprig thyme*

*3 parsley stalks*

*6 juniper berries*

*5fl oz/150ml red wine*

*2fl oz/60ml olive oil*

*2lb/900g venison cut into 1¼"/3cm dice (preferably from a shoulder or haunch of red deer)*

*2oz/60g lard or oil*

*2oz/60g flour*

*2oz/60g tomato purée*

*1½pt/800ml brown stock (see page 133)*

*1lb/450g small turnips*

*chopped parsley for garnishing*

*salt and pepper*

## *Method*

Mix the first 9 ingredients together, add the venison, cover and marinade overnight.

Heat the lard or oil in a frying pan, drain the venison, add to the pan and fry until evenly browned on all sides; then remove from the oil and transfer to a large saucepan.

Drain the vegetables from the marinade, fry until golden and add to the venison; dust the flour over the venison and vegetables, mix in carefully and heat gently.

Add the tomato purée and stir well, then add the stock gradually to prevent lumps from forming.

When all the liquid has been added, season with salt and pepper, cover with a lid and simmer gently, stirring occasionally, for about 75 minutes.

Peel and wash the turnips and cook in boiling salted water for about 20 minutes.

When the meat is cooked remove from the heat and, using a slotted spoon, transfer the venison pieces to a clean pan; strain the sauce over the meat, discarding the vegetables and herbs, add the cooked turnips and return to the heat.

Check the seasoning, adding more salt and pepper if required, and simmer until the meat and turnips are tender – the overall cooking time will depend on the cut of venison and for how long it has been hung, but should be between 1½-2 hours in total.

Sprinkle with chopped parsley and serve with a side salad or seasonal vegetables.

# Sea Trout in Pastry with Fresh Tomato Sauce

The following lavish presentation of sea trout baked in pastry is an excellent dish for a dinner party and can be prepared well in advance.

## Ingredients

*1 pink-fleshed trout of about 2lb/900g*

*1oz/30g butter*

*2oz/60g finely shredded carrots*

*2oz/60g finely shredded white of leek*

*2oz/60g finely shredded celery*

*2oz/60g finely sliced mushrooms*

*1 beaten egg yolk*

*1lb/450g puff pastry (frozen, or see page 136)*

*1 beaten egg for eggwash*

*1fl oz/30ml olive oil*

*1oz/30g finely chopped onions*

*1 crushed clove garlic*

*1lb/450g skinned, seeded and diced tomatoes*

*5fl oz/150ml water*

*1tsp chopped fresh basil*

*salt and pepper*

## Method

Ask the fishmonger to clean and fillet the trout, then remove any remaining bones.

Melt the butter in a frying pan, add the carrots, leeks, celery and mushrooms and cook gently, stirring frequently, so that they are just cooked but still crunchy.

Remove the pan from the heat, cool slightly, mix in the egg yolk then cool the mixture completely.

Take one of the trout fillets, skin side down, and cover with the vegetable mixture. Top with the second fillet, skin side up, so that the fish is re-formed.

Roll out the puff pastry to an even thickness of ⅛"/3mm and lay the fish gently on half of it. Damp the edges of the pastry, fold over to enclose the fish and press the edges together.

Trim the pastry to the shape of the fish, egg-wash, then mark on scales, gills and an eye using an icing nozzle or a small sharp knife.

Place in the refrigerator for 20 minutes, then bake in an oven preheated to 400°F/200°C/gas 6 for about 35 minutes, until the pastry is crisp and golden.

Meanwhile, make the sauce: heat the oil in a pan, add the onions and garlic, soften slightly, then add the tomatoes and water.

Cook for 15 minutes, season to taste, then liquidise and keep hot. Just before serving add the chopped basil.

Place the cooked sea trout on a serving dish and hand the sauce separately.

# Chicken Breasts stuffed with Oysters

At this time the custom of slipping well-seasoned forcemeat between the skin and breast of a bird became fashionable, and shellfish were often used in poultry stuffings. In this recipe, oysters complement the flavour of the chicken to produce an unusual dish for a special occasion.

## Ingredients

*4 breasts of chicken*

*12 oysters*

*10fl oz/300ml chicken stock (see page 133)*

*4fl oz/120ml dry white wine*

*15fl oz/450ml chicken velouté (see page 134 and substitute chicken stock for fish stock)*

*2 egg yolks*

*4fl oz/120ml double cream*

*lemon juice*

*salt and pepper*

## Method

Remove any skin from the chicken and leave only the wing bone at the broader end of the breast.

Take off the small fillet of meat lying beneath the breast.

With a sharp knife cut laterally into the length of the breast to create a pocket. Do not cut completely through the meat.

Open 8 of the oysters, reserving the liquid for the sauce, and put 2 oysters into each pocket of the chicken breasts.

Gently flatten the reserved fillets between 2 layers of moistened polythene, beating gently with the flat blade of a large kitchen knife, until quite thin.

Lay the flattened fillets over the openings in the breasts so as to seal in the oysters.

Reduce the heat and put in the chicken breasts, then cover and simmer very gently for about 15 minutes until firm to the touch.

Remove the breasts from the stock and keep warm.

Open the remaining 4 oysters, again reserving the liquid.

Take a little of the stock in which the chicken was cooked, and poach the 4 oysters in it for about 2 minutes.

Remove the oysters from the stock reserving the stock; replace the oysters on their deep shells ready for garnishing.

Add the liquid from the oysters and the chicken velouté to the pan containing the liquor in which the oysters were cooked.

Bring to the boil and cook for about 10 minutes, skimming if necessary.

Whisk the egg yolks and cream together, then gradually add the sauce to the egg and cream mixture a little at a time, whisking continuously.

Strain through a fine sieve back into a clean pan and heat very gently, seasoning with salt, pepper and lemon juice to taste. When ready the sauce will just coat the back of a spoon.

On no account must the sauce boil; if allowed to do so it will curdle and separate.

Put the chicken breasts back into the sauce to reheat for a few minutes.

Serve the chicken breasts immediately, coated with sauce and garnished with an oyster on its shell.

If you like raw oysters, simply open the last 4 oysters at serving time and use as a garnish.

Season the chicken stock and white wine, and bring to the boil in a shallow pan.

# Roast Rib of Beef with Béarnaise Sauce

The rib is perhaps the best roasting joint of beef, as it combines flavour with tenderness. A small, well-hung joint can be grilled; a larger joint should be roasted in the oven. There is a dispute as to the origins of béarnaise sauce. Some say that it originated in Béarn, others that it was first made in honour of King Henry IV of France, the great Béarnais. Whatever the case, the invention of the sauce was timely; and it is the perfect complement for roast beef.

## Ingredients

*2 fore-ribs of beef*

*a little olive oil*

*2oz/60g finely chopped shallots or onions*

*3 sprigs tarragon*

*4 sprigs parsley*

*3 sprigs chervil*

*8 crushed peppercorns*

*4fl oz/120ml white wine vinegar*

*8oz/225g butter*

*2 egg yolks*

*juice of ½ lemon*

*1 bunch watercress for garnishing*

*salt and pepper*

## Method

Ask the butcher to prepare the joint so that just the eye of the meat is left on the bone – use the trimmings for a casserole – then weigh the joint to calculate the cooking time: allow 15 minutes per 1lb/450g plus 15 minutes.

Season the beef with salt and pepper, brush with oil, and place in a hot roasting tin; cook in an oven preheated to 200°C/400°F/gas mark 6, reducing the temperature after 20 minutes to 180°C/350°F/gas mark 4.

Baste the meat occasionally during cooking.

Meanwhile for the sauce, put the shallots or onions in a shallow pan; chop the herb stalks and add them to the pan with the crushed peppercorns.

Add the vinegar, bring to the boil and simmer until almost all the liquid has evaporated, then add a tablespoonful of cold water.

Slowly melt the butter in a small saucepan without allowing it to become too hot, and finely chop the herb leaves.

When the shallot mixture has cooled slightly, place the pan in another, slightly larger pan of hot water, and add the egg yolks.

Whisk the mixture continuously until it begins to thicken, then remove from the heat.

Add the warm melted butter a little at a time, whisking continuously and ensuring that each addition is thoroughly incorporated before adding more – when all the butter has been incorporated, the sauce should be thick and smooth.

Pass the sauce through a fine sieve or, even better, fine muslin, to remove any solids.

Season to taste with salt and add a squeeze of lemon juice, then whisk in the herbs.

Keep the sauce warm, but do not allow to become too hot, as it will separate, nor too cold, as it will congeal.

When the beef is cooked, remove it from the oven, cover and rest in a warm place for 15 minutes to make carving easier.

Slice the beef, garnish with the watercress, and serve the sauce separately.

# French Style Peas

Peas became the most popular vegetable during Louis' reign, and this classic dish is a simple but delicious way of cooking them.

## Ingredients

*2lb/900g freshly shelled peas (or 1lb/450g frozen)*
*1 small shredded lettuce*
*12 peeled and washed button onions*
*2½oz/75g butter*
*1oz/30g caster sugar*
*10fl oz/300ml (approx) water*
*or white stock (see page 133)*
*½oz/15g flour*
*salt and pepper*

## Method

Put the peas into a saucepan with the lettuce, button onions, 2oz/60g of the butter and the sugar; barely cover with the stock or water, season with salt and pepper and bring to the boil.

Cover with a lid and simmer gently for about 30 minutes, until the peas and onions are tender.

Mix the remaining butter with the flour to form a smooth paste; add the paste gradually to the pan, stirring continuously, to thicken the sauce.

Adjust the seasoning to taste and serve immediately.

# Gâteau Pithiviers

This classic dish is a speciality of the town of Pithiviers some 50 miles (80 kilometres) to the south of Paris. Puff pastry is filled with rich almond frangipane and can be served with a fresh custard sauce.

*Above: Gâteau Pithiviers*
*Left: Roast Rib of Beef with Béarnaise Sauce*

## Ingredients

*20oz/550g puff pastry (see page 136 or use frozen)*

*raspberry jam*

*brandy or rum*

*8oz/225g frangipane (see page 136)*

*1 beaten egg for eggwash*

*icing sugar*

## Method

Roll out the puff pastry ⅛"/3mm thick and cut out 2 circles, one 8"/20cm and the other 8½"/21cm in diameter.

Put the smaller circle on to a moistened baking tray.

Spread a thin layer of raspberry jam on to the pastry, keeping it within ½"/1cm of the edge.

Mix the brandy or rum into the frangipane and spread it evenly on to the pastry, again keeping within ½"/1cm of the edge.

Brush the edge of the pastry well with eggwash, and place the larger circle of pastry on top of the frangipane.

Press down the edges and seal well together.

Brush the top with eggwash.

Using a very sharp knife draw arcs from the centre to the edge of the pastry, just cutting lightly into the pastry.

Allow to stand in a cool place for at least 30 minutes (to rest the pastry), then put into an oven preheated to 220°C/425°F/gas mark 7. Cook for about 30 minutes.

Remove from the oven and dredge the surface with icing sugar.

Return to the oven and continue cooking until the surface of the pastry is glazed.

This dish is best served hot, or warm.

# Apple or Quince Turnovers

In Louis' reign, pastry was used in many ways, and cooks experimented with puff pastry to create light sweetmeats such as these apple turnovers. The acidic quince appears in many recipes of the period, and when baked in puff pastry also makes a superb pudding. Although imported quince paste is ideal for this recipe, if you can get fresh quinces, make a purée of them by cooking them with sugar to yield the required quantity.

## Ingredients

*1lb/450g cooking apples*

*2oz/600g caster sugar*

*1oz/30g unsalted butter*

*juice of ½ lemon*

*[or 8oz/225g quince paste (see notes below)]*

*12oz/340g puff pastry (see page 136 or use frozen)*

*4oz/115g caster sugar for dipping*

*10fl oz/300ml fresh custard (see recipe on page 135)*

## Method

If using apples, peel, core and chop them, then put them into a saucepan with the sugar, the butter and the lemon juice.

Cover with a lid and cook slowly, stirring frequently, until reduced to a purée, then allow to cool completely.

Roll out the pastry to an even thickness of about ⅛"/3mm, and cut out 8 circles about 3"/8cm in diameter, either using a pastry cutter or by cutting around a cup or glass.

Gently roll each circle in one direction to form an

oval, then place a spoonful of the cold apple purée or quince paste in the centre of each oval.

Brush the edges of the pastry with cold water, fold half the pastry lengthwise over the filling to form a neat envelope and press the edges together to obtain a good seal.

Brush the tops of the envelopes with cold water then dip them evenly in caster sugar.

Put the puffs on a dampened baking tray; place the tray in an oven preheated to 200°C/400°F/gas mark 6 and bake for about 10 minutes, until well-risen and golden.

Serve hot with hot fresh custard sauce.

## Notes

Quince paste may be found in Spanish and Italian delicatessens. It is most often imported from Spain, and called dulce de membrillo. Fresh quinces may be used to make a sweet purée when they are available, which is in the autumn.

# Apricots Colbert

Colbert was a leading statesman and adviser to Louis XIV. He developed the French navy, improved road and canal networks and reformed taxes. It was probably owing to the latter achievement that some grateful chef devised this delicious pudding and dedicated it to him.

## Ingredients

*10fl oz/300ml milk*

*1½oz/45g short grain rice*

*1oz/30g caster sugar*

*2 drops vanilla essence*

*1 egg yolk*

*12 poached fresh apricots*
*(if not in season use 12 tinned ones)*

*plain flour*

*2 beaten eggs for coating*

*fresh breadcrumbs*

*8oz/225g apricot jam*

*4fl oz/120ml water*

*½oz/15g arrowroot*

*deep fat for frying*

## Method

Put the milk into a heavy saucepan, bring to the boil, add the rice and cook until the rice is soft and the mixture fairly thick – about 30 minutes.

Remove from the heat, add the sugar, vanilla essence and egg yolk and beat well.

Allow to cool completely.

If using fresh apricots remove the stones, keeping the fruit as intact as possible. Fill the cavities with the rice mixture.

If using canned apricot halves, dry them and sandwich two halves together with the rice mixture.

Coat the prepared apricots firstly in the flour, removing any excess, then in the beaten eggs. Make sure they are well coated with egg, then pass them through the breadcrumbs, again ensuring that they are completely coated.

Put the apricots on a tray and refrigerate until ready to cook.

Make the sauce by boiling the jam with the water, then straining through a fine sieve.

Dissolve the arrowroot in a little cold water then whisk into the sauce until adequately thick. Keep hot.

Heat the deep fat to a temperature of around 180°C/350°F, then put in the apricots.

Cook for a few minutes until golden, remove and drain on kitchen paper.

Serve immediately, handing the sauce separately.

*Apricots Colbert*

*Apple Turnovers*    (*recipe on page 86*)

# REGENCY DAYS
## (1800 – 1850)

The Regency was at the centre of a period of profound social change, where the certainties of the 18th century were destroyed by the French Revolution, and new wealth was placed in the hands of the new classes. An equally fundamental change was taking place in culinary matters: until the 19th century the upper classes had been primarily concerned with ingredients and how they should be cooked and displayed; but after the Revolution attention was turned to those who ate, namely the guests at the feast.

Carême, believed by some to be the greatest chef of all time, was the pivot between the centuries. He made his reputation

*Though engaged by the Prince de Talleyrand as a pastry cook, Carême wished to expand his knowledge of cooking, and learnt from Boucher who was in charge of the kitchen. Before long he had acquired skills superior to those of his master, and in 1815 he came to England to work for the Prince Regent.*

at a series of grand feasts held after Napoleon was defeated, especially one in 1814 for Louis XVIII, when 1,200 people sat down at twelve tables in the gallery of the Louvre. His speciality was creating architectural pieces whose design he had learned at the Cabinet des Gravures, where he had studied whilst working for Bailly, the most famous pâtissier of the day. Hundreds of designs for forts, windmills, ruined temples, etc., were included in his first two books, *Le Pâtissier royal* and *Le Pâtissier pittoresque*, both published in 1815. He learnt his trade as a cuisinier from Boucher, Talleyrand's chef, in whose kitchen he regularly worked as an 'extra'. He was the first great chef to specialise in pâtisserie rather than rôtisserie, and was brilliant in cold buffet work (the Italian 'credenza'), creating classic chaud-froid and aspic dishes. It was his great skill at display that made him the most sought-after chef in Europe, working in Moscow for Tsar Alexander, in Vienna for the British Ambassador, and in Paris for the Rothschilds, as well as in Brighton for the Prince Regent. However, his lasting

# CARÊME

*Turned out on to the streets of Paris by his father, who could no longer manage to feed his large family, Antonin Carême chanced to knock at the door of a cook-shop. Thus began at the age of ten the amazing career of one of the most influential figures that cookery has ever spawned. After serving an apprenticeship at the cook-shop, he began working at a restaurant, and then moved on to the Pâtisserie Bailly in rue Vivienne.*

*Carême showed exceptional skill, and by the time he was seventeen he was creating decorative pieces based on architectural works. He entered private service with M. de Lavalette and then with the legendary Prince de Talleyrand, whose table, he declared, was furnished with grandeur and wisdom. He next spent two years with the Prince Regent, but found the English fogs depressing and, despite tempting offers, returned to France.*

*Further travel saw Carême with Czar Alexander in St. Petersburg, at the British Embassy in Paris, at the Congress of Aix-la-Chapelle, and with the Baron de Rothschild.*

*He died before reaching fifty years of age, 'burnt out by the flame of his genius and the fuel of his ovens'.*

*His books provided exquisite detail on all aspects of cooking, and elevated cookery to an art form.*

reputation was based on his later books, culminating in *L'Art de la cuisine française au XIX siècle*, an exhaustive survey of classic French cooking, part of which was published post-humously. In 1822 he published *Le Maître d'hôtel français*, which described hundreds of menus he had served in great houses, and showed that he remained essentially a chef to a rich employer.

However, Carême was seldom happy in his work, and combined what Ellwanger accurately dubbed 'unctuous self-puffery' with immense dedication. He found employers, fellow-chefs and the staff who worked under him perpetually inadequate. In England, he criticised everything from the weather to the butchers' shops. Wheaton, in *Savouring the Past*, suggests an interesting reason for his unhappiness in England: 'English servants did not have the capacity for servility that could be expected of citizens of a despotically governed land like France.' Nevertheless, by sobriety, sacrifice and a profound sense of duty, he attempted to elevate his profession to an art, and in so doing provided the foundation for the development of haute cuisine in France during the 19th century.

In his native Paris, a different cuisine was being established. The supply of cheap food meant that the auberges (inns), with their fixed menus available at all times of the day, had made home cooking uncompetitive. The first restaurant was supposedly established in 1765 when a M Boulange added a dish of sheep's feet to his hot soups. He was sued by the ready-cooked-meat dealers, but won the right to sell a choice of food. However, as early as 1686 a Sicilian, M Procopio, had, as an alternative to the taverns, opened the first café which had become a literary and political meeting place, serving ice-cream as well as coffee. These were the beginnings of that great French habit of eating out. Probably the first real restaurant was Antoine Beauvillier's La Grande Taverne de Londres, opened in 1782 at 26 rue de Richelieu. Beauvillier, originally a friend and then a rival of Carême, provided the best of English cooking, and sought 'to combine an elegant dining room, smart waiters, and a choice of wine with superior cooking'. The restaurants drew their recipes from the cook-books of Massailot, Marin and Menon, who were attempting to turn

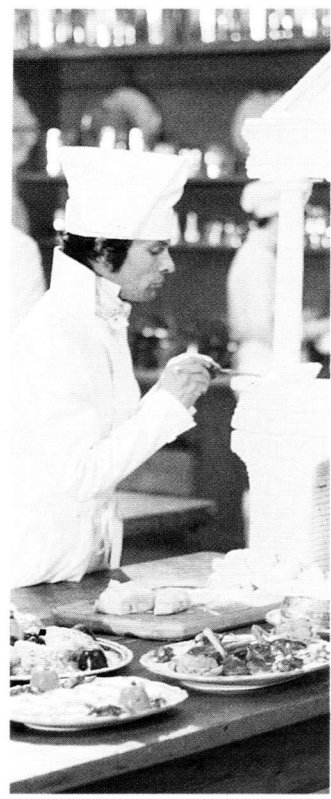

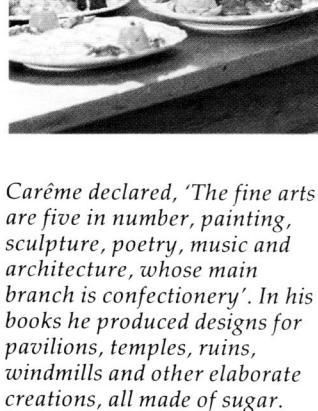

*Carême declared, 'The fine arts are five in number, painting, sculpture, poetry, music and architecture, whose main branch is confectionery'. In his books he produced designs for pavilions, temples, ruins, windmills and other elaborate creations, all made of sugar.*

away from huge displays, extravagant dishes and complex sauces towards the simpler dishes of rural France.

One of the most famous restaurants was Au Rocher de Cancale, which was shared by theatricals and a literary group that included Brillat-Savarin, Dumas and Grimod de la Reynière, who were to establish cuisine as an essential part of the French cultural scene. In fact, culinary matters in France during the early part of the 19th century fell into the hands of these literary greats. In *La Philosophie du goût* (*The Philosophy of Taste*), published in 1826, Brillat-Savarin coined his well-known aphorism: 'Animals feed, men eat; only men of intellect know how to eat'; and he advised that the 'right order of eating is from the most substantial to the lightest, and drinking from

*A selection of Carême's chaud-froid pieces: clockwise from top left: a whole poached turkey, a fish mousse, a roast saddle of mutton and a poached loin of pork.*

the mildest to the heaviest'. In *La Grande Dictionnaire de la cuisine* (*The Great Dictionary of Cooking*) Dumas included dishes ranging from snails to elephant's feet. He was himself a skilled cook, and one of the few gourmets welcomed into the kitchens of Parisian restaurants by chefs and given recipes of the dishes he had particularly enjoyed. Grimod de la Reynière came from a long line of gourmets but only turned his attention to eating after being spurned by a young actress (which probably accounts for his belief that women could never do anything because they ate only sweets and puddings). He is usually only remembered for his perverse feasts but was, in fact, probably one of the most famous food writers of his day. His *Manuel des Amphitryons* was an annual miscellany of food history and gossip, and much sought after for advice rather than recipes. Of servants he said, 'Let them steal a little, it was always thus.' He did much to establish sautéing, and believed that 'a well-made sauce will render even an elephant or a grandfather palatable'. His principal contribution was the journal *Almanach des gourmands ou calendrier nutritif*, in which, as its editor, he published criticisms made by gourmets selected to form a 'jurie dégustateur' of both the Paris restaurants and their suppliers. He did much to restore the quality of French cuisine.

England, too, had its bon vivants. Probably the best known was the Reverend Sidney Smith, who regularly visited the most famous French restaurants and dined with Talleyrand when Carême was working in his kitchens. Sidney Smith was convinced that digestion was the secret of life, the source of humour and friendliness, and that one could feed to achieve vice or virtue. This attitude – that eating was a means to an end rather than an end in itself – distinguished the English attitude from the French. It was epitomised in Dr Kitchiner's *The Cook's Oracle*, published in 1817, and later in his *The Art of Invigorating and Prolonging Life*, which attacked overladen tables, pompous food and too many wines, and aimed for plain cookery as a means of rendering food acceptable to the palate without heavy expense to the purse. He devised sauces which were the forerunners of bottled commercial sauces and ketchups – catsups, which, when boiled down to double strength, he claimed should be called dogsups. He also insisted that guests should be punctual, locking his door five minutes after the time of the invitation.

The French chefs who came to England when the French Revolution removed their employers, would have found a

tradition of domestic cook-books that sought to simplify rather than glorify. In *The Experienced English Housekeeper* Mrs Raffald's 'chiefest Care was to write in as plain a Style as possible so as to be understood by the weakest Capacity', and indeed any cook or housewife could understand her. Articles by Thomas Walker in the magazine *Original* bore a resemblance to the *Almanach* in teaching 'Content the stomach and the stomach will content you,' as well as how to dine, serve wine and manage dishes.

Alexis Soyer, chef at the Reform Club, was taken to the hearts of the English, adopting their traditions at the same time as becoming the epitome of all things French. His qualities were many – he was a humorist, a wit, an inventor, a humanist and an excellent chef. Persuaded to come to England by the riots against the Bourbon monarchy in 1830, he was caricatured as M Mirobalant by Thackeray, because he chose to play the eccentric Frenchman. He published sycophantic satires in addition to extremely successful cook-books, and was responsible for the triumph of the Reform Club kitchens, as well as for producing his Portable Magic Stove and his own relishes, pastes and demi-glaces. He had a modern approach to marketing: a week before launching his new Soyer Sauce he ensured that every newspaper publisher and magazine editor received a free bottle. He elected to go to Scutari, and did as much for the soldiers' kitchens in the Crimea as Florence Nightingale did for their hospitals. *The Modern Housewife*, which he published in 1849, appealed to the wealthy, but it was his *Shilling Cook-book for the People*, the first cook-book to achieve mass sales (over a quarter of a million) that proved his greatest triumph and inspired others to aim their cook-books at the mass market.

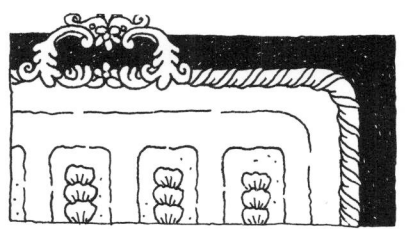

*The great kitchen of the Royal Pavilion was built in 1816 to a most practical design. There were cast-iron stoves, hot cupboards, steamers, sinks with hot and cold running water and a wonderful range of copper pots and pans, neatly stacked on dressers.*

As the century progressed, the traditions of the two countries changed subtly. In France a spate of family cook-books, many written by women, including Mlle Marguerite's *Le Cordon bleu* (1827), were published at a time when the standard of living rose and the division between books for professional chefs and those for the household, grew. One of the most popular was Audot's *La Cuisinière de la campagne et de la ville* (*The Country and City Cook*), which not only provided recipes for simple dishes not requiring expensive equipment or ingredients but also gave a list of modest restaurants throughout France where such fare could be found. After its

The Prince Regent once remarked to Carême that dinner on the previous evening had been superb but that such wonderful food would cause him to die of indigestion. 'Your Highness, my duty is to tempt your appetite, not to control it', replied Carême.

The Prince Regent was well known for organising formal dinners and gatherings where he entertained many old associates, among them Richard Sheridan, the Hon George Hanger, George 'Beau' Brummell and Mrs Fitzherbert.

initial publication in 1827 the book was continually revised and reprinted, and by 1890 was three times its original length. A second aspect of these domestic cookery books, which set them apart from those dealing with haute cuisine, was their preoccupation with leftovers. Audot had referred only to 'the best way to rescue meat with a bad taste', but Baron Brisse's *The Art of Using Leftovers* of 1864 proved so popular that it was followed by *More Ways of Using Leftovers* in 1868, and *Leftover Cooking* in 1869.

In England, although still primarily concerned with domestic cuisine, more and more of the middle classes began to dine outside the home, and the successful cook-books were those which sought to advise about household management as well as cuisine, assisting the housewife to persuade her husband to dine at home. This movement culminated in the enormously successful *Beeton's Book of Household Management*, edited by Isabella Beeton and published in 1855. Its huge sales were due to its appeal to women, and the book was regularly given to young brides. In addition to the recipes (which provided ingredients, quantities and preparation details as well as cost, the number served and the best season of the year for the dish), sections were included on etiquette, the natural history of animals and vegetables, and all that was necessary for managing a household, especially servants.

However, whilst the traditions of France and England differed, the objective in each country was to satisfy the diner, and by the last quarter of the 19th century there emerged public dinners, the gentlemen's clubs, and the new fashionable hotels. Three factors made this possible. In France, Carême had established the intellectual foundation of haute cuisine. In England, the wealthy classes were well versed in quality cooking at home and now wished to display themselves in public, both in London and on the Continent. Finally, 'service à la russe' replaced 'service à la française' – now dishes were served consecutively rather than simultaneously, and food could be eaten at its best with waste reduced to a minimum. It only remained for cooking to be raised to the highest level and for the belief, credited to de la Reynière, to be fulfilled that 'the host whose guest is obliged to ask for anything is a dishonoured man'.

### Food in Regency Days

Carême was, of course, French, but in his very precise, Swiss way, Anton Mosimann epitomises this great chef's philosophy, and like Carême, succeeds in making very complicated, detailed dishes while also running a very large and busy kitchen.

There was, too, a singlemindedness about Carême that is again characteristic of Anton Mosimann, who claims that at the age of six he already knew that he would become a chef. When only fifteen he was invited to become an apprentice at the Hotel Baeren in Twann, and for the next thirteen years he applied himself with characteristic dedication to forging a career which brought success and glittering awards. In 1975 he became first sous-chef at the Dorchester Hotel in London, and in 1976 – at twenty-nine, the youngest ever to hold the position – he became Maître Chef des Cuisines.

The importance of the development of kitchen equipment cannot be underestimated in the improvement of culinary standards and versatility during the Regency period. The first appliance for cooking by gas was made in 1824, for example, and by 1841 gas cookers had been installed by Alexis Soyer in London's Reform Club. The kitchens at the Brighton Pavilion were designed by John Nash and it was here that the celebrated Carême prepared many banquets during his brief stay in England. At one of these, a banquet for the Grand Duke Nicholas of Russia, he offered no fewer than thirty entrées, thirty-two side dishes and soufflés, and eight magnificent centrepieces made of pastry, spun sugar and marzipan.

Carême believed that cooking is as much an art form as any other, and his creations certainly did justice to this view. With his architectural masterpieces made out of pastillage (a mixture of sugar and gum), exquisite symmetrical dishes made from nougatine, and his chocolate extravaganazas topped, perhaps, with a swan made of pulled sugar, Carême described new limits of perfection in the elaborate and dramatic display of food.

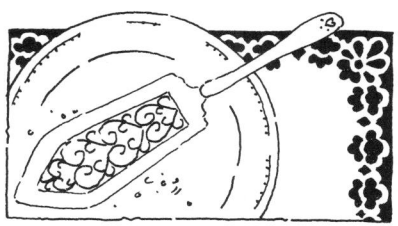

*Roy Ackerman and
Anton Mosimann*

Meat and poultry would be coated with a chaud-froid sauce, a mixture of velouté and aspic jelly which formed a base for further decoration. The intense colour of truffle would be used to form a chequerboard design and, nestling around the edge of the dish, would be tiny, colourful mounds of vegetables set in aspic.

But taste and subtly produced flavour were really at the core of Carême's art. Over 100 of his sauces were in fact based on just three basic recipes – for example, his basic brown sauce was derived from bacon, ham, chicken, veal, hare and partridge, but his skill lay in his ability to produce the precise flavour he desired from the complex workings of a large number of additional ingredients. Necessarily our recipes for the period are somewhat simpler than Carême's, though subtlety of flavour, as for example in the venison and salmon dishes, remains a very important feature.

# Escalopes of Salmon with Ginger

Delicate sauces were created to enhance rather than overpower the main ingredients of a dish. Subtle flavours were introduced, such as the interesting combination of fresh ginger and spring onions with salmon in the following recipe.

## *Ingredients*

*8 × 3oz/85g thin slices of fresh salmon*

*a little flour*

*4oz/115g butter*

*4 spring onions, sliced into thin rings*

*1½oz/45g finely chopped fresh ginger*

*2fl oz/60ml dry white wine*

*10fl oz/300ml fish stock (see page 134)*

*4fl oz/120ml double cream*

*1oz/30g butter and 1oz/30g flour mixed together to form a smooth paste, or beurre manié*

*salt and cayenne pepper*

## *Method*

Season the salmon with salt and cayenne pepper and coat with the flour, patting well to remove any excess.

Heat the butter gently in a frying pan, and when hot cook the salmon quickly for a couple of minutes on each side.

Avoid overcooking; remove from the pan and keep hot.

Put the spring onions and ginger into the same pan and stir with a wooden spoon for a couple of minutes.

Add the white wine and bring to the boil; add the fish stock, return to the boil, then simmer for 5 minutes.

Add the cream, reboil, then remove from the heat.

Whisk in the butter and flour mixture until the sauce has thickened slightly and the flour has cooked.

Season to taste with salt and cayenne pepper.

Serve the salmon slices immediately, on a pool of sauce.

# Broccoli Salad

Broccoli first appeared on menus during Regency times. This dish makes an excellent first course, or it could be served with plainly grilled or roast meats or poultry.

## *Ingredients*

*1lb/450g trimmed and washed fresh broccoli*

*2 slices white bread*

*a little cooking oil*

*1 sliced clove garlic*

*2fl oz/60ml lemon juice*

*5fl oz/150ml olive oil*

*1oz/30g very finely chopped onions*

*1 hard-boiled egg*

*salt and pepper*

## *Method*

Cook the broccoli in boiling salted water until tender but still firm – about 10 minutes – then refresh in cold water and drain well.

Cut the crusts from the bread and discard; cut the bread into dice about ¼"/5mm square.

Heat the cooking oil in a frying pan, fry the garlic until golden brown, then remove from the oil.

Fry the diced bread in the garlic-flavoured oil, turning continuously, until golden brown in colour, remove and drain well.

Make a dressing by beating the lemon juice with the olive oil, add the onions and season to taste with salt and pepper.

When ready to serve, assemble the salad at the last minute: place the broccoli in a serving dish and pour the dressing over.

Shell the hard-boiled egg and grate it over the broccoli; scatter with fried bread cubes and serve immediately.

# Monkfish Skewers with Hollandaise Sauce

Carême was chef to the Prince Regent, and used skewers in many of his creations to embellish the dishes. Here, the skewers act in a functional way to support the grilled monkfish and mushrooms.

## Ingredients

*1½lb/680g filleted monkfish*

*4oz/115g button mushrooms*

*2fl oz/60ml olive oil*

*juice of 1½ lemons*

*a little chopped parsley & dill*

*2 egg yolks*

*8oz/225g butter*

*salt and cayenne pepper*

## Method

Cut the monkfish into pieces about 1"/2cm square, then wash and dry the mushrooms.

Thread the fish and mushrooms alternately on to kebab skewers, then place the skewers in a shallow dish.

Mix the olive oil with the juice of 1 lemon, add the salt, cayenne pepper and chopped herbs, and pour this mixture over the fish and mushroom skewers.

Leave to marinade at room temperature for about an hour, turning occasionally.

Preheat the grill, put the skewers on a tray beneath it and cook for about 10 minutes, turning frequently and basting with the marinade.

For the sauce, melt the butter gradually without letting it become too hot.

Put the egg yolks in a basin with a few drops of cold water, stand the basin over hot water and whisk the yolks: they will begin to thicken after a few minutes.

Remove from the heat and gradually whisk in the melted butter, beating well after each addition, until the sauce is smooth and all the butter has been incorporated.

Season to taste with salt and cayenne pepper, and sharpen with the remaining lemon juice.

Serve the brochettes off the skewers, handing the sauce separately, accompanied perhaps by a green salad.

# Wild Duck with Chestnuts

Game featured heavily on menus of the Regency period. In this recipe the ducks are served in the modern manner, but are still combined with braised chestnuts and a rich wine sauce as they would have been in the early 19th century.

## Ingredients

*2 mallards*

*2fl oz/60ml brandy*

*4 sprigs parsley*

*4 sprigs thyme*

*2fl oz/60ml olive oil*

*4fl oz/120ml white wine*

*15floz/450ml jus lié (see page 135)*

*12oz/340g fresh chestnuts (or use whole tinned chestnuts)*

*a little stock and butter for poaching*

*a little chopped parsley*

*1oz/30g butter*

*2oz/60g finely chopped shallots or onions*

*salt and pepper*

## Method

Carefully remove the legs and breasts from the duck carcase and trim away any silvery sinews.

Sprinkle the meat with a few drops of brandy.

Place the parsley and thyme on a plate, and place the duck meat on top (the breast flesh side down). Pour over the olive oil.

Leave for about an hour at room temperature, to allow the meat to absorb the flavours of the herbs.

Meanwhile, chop up the carcase and fry the bones in a little oil in a saucepan to brown. Add the white wine and the jus lié, and simmer for about an hour.

Meanwhile, prepare the chestnuts. If using fresh chestnuts, make small slits in the skins, then plunge into hot oil for about 2 minutes.

Cool slightly, then peel – the outer shell and the inner brown skin will come away together.

Put the chestnuts into a small casserole, and half cover them with stock and a little butter.

Cover with greaseproof paper and cook in an oven preheated to 175°C/350°F/gas mark 4 for about 30 minutes.

Remove the nuts from the dish, boil down the cooking liquor to a syrup, then mix the nuts into the glaze with a little chopped parsley.

If using tinned chestnuts, which are very fragile, simply boil down the liquid from the tin with a little butter to a glaze, add a little chopped parsley, then add the nuts to the glaze, just as for the fresh ones, but handling very carefully.

To cook the duck, season the legs and breasts with salt and pepper, and put into a little hot oil in a frying pan. Cook the flesh side of the breasts first, then the skin side; turn the legs over to give a golden brown colour.

Put the joints on a roasting tray and place the tray in an oven preheated to 200°C/400°F/gas mark 6; roast the breasts for about 10 minutes (less if you like them very pink) and the legs for about 15 minutes.

Put the cooked breasts on to a warm plate to 'set' and keep warm whilst the legs finish cooking and you finish the sauce.

Melt the butter in a clean saucepan, add the finely chopped shallots or onions and herbs, and soften.

Add the brandy and the jus lié from the bones;

bring to the boil, skim and simmer for 10 minutes.

Strain and season to taste with salt and pepper.

To serve, skin the duck breasts and slice them thinly into fan shapes.

Place one sliced breast and one leg on each plate, pour some sauce over, and garnish with a few chestnuts.

# Potted Pheasant

Game pâtés and pies appeared frequently on menus of the Regency period. Apart from this being an excellent way of preparing pheasant, it is also a means of preserving the meat. It is delicious either as a first course, or as a main dish with salad.

## Ingredients

*1 dressed pheasant*

*8oz/225g pork fillet*

*1fl oz/30ml brandy*

*1 sprig fresh thyme*

*12 dried green peppercorns*

*8oz/225g butter*

*salt*

## Method

Remove the flesh from the pheasant carcass, reserving one whole breast intact.

Remove the sinews from the legs, and finely chop the leg meat, the meat from the other breast and the pork.

Cut the whole breast lengthwise into 4 equal slices, season, spinkle with a few drops of brandy and reserve.

Remove the leaves of thyme from the stalk, finely chop these and the peppercorns, and add them to the chopped meat, add the remainder of the brandy and season with salt.

Mix well and leave to stand for a few hours to allow the flavours to develop.

Meanwhile, clarify the butter: put the butter into a saucepan and melt it very gently, allowing the solids and the buttermilk to sink to the bottom of the pan; pour off and cool the clear butter from the surface.

Pour a little of the clarified butter into a terrine and thoroughly coat the sides and base.

Mix the remaining butter into the chopped meat mixture.

Place a third of the chopped meat in the terrine, lay 2 of the fillets on top, cover with another third of the meat, the remaining 2 fillets, and the final third of the chopped meat.

Level the top, and cover first with foil and then with a lid.

Put the terrine into a roasting tin containing sufficient hot water to come half-way up the sides of the terrine, then place the tin in the bottom of an oven preheated to 170°C/325°F/gas mark 3.

Cook for 60-90 minutes, then test to see whether the terrine is cooked: when it is ready, the liquid which will have come out of the meats during cooking will be totally clear – any trace of cloudiness indicates that the terrine is not fully cooked. Remove the terrine from the oven and from the water bath, allow to cool completely, then refrigerate.

To unmould, dip the terrine into hot water for a few seconds, then turn it out on to a serving dish. Serve accompanied by a cold Cumberland sauce.

# Chicken Sausages with Mushrooms

More refined kitchens and kitchen equipment initiated the advancement of cookery techniques. The food blenders of today have replaced the laborious and tedious use of mortar and pestle to reduce meat to a purée, but the result is the same. In this recipe, chicken is combined with cream to make a very light 'sausage' meat. This is then wrapped in pig's caul, which serves as a skin for the sausage. Such dishes might have been served as an entrée at one of the Prince Regent's dinners in the Brighton Pavilion.

## Ingredients

1lb/450g chicken meat, off the bone, completely free of skin, bone and sinew

1 egg white

10fl oz/300ml double cream

1 pig's caul

1oz/30g butter

2oz/60g finely chopped shallots or onions

2 sprigs chopped fresh tarragon

4fl oz/120ml dry white wine

15fl oz/450ml jus lié (see page 135)

8oz/225g button mushrooms

4oz/115g clarified butter

salt and ground white pepper

## Method

Make the filling using, ideally, a food processor. Chill the bowl and the blades well before commencing, ideally in a freezer.

Drop the meat, in small pieces, on to the revolving blades and process until a smooth purée is obtained.

Add the egg white, mix well, then slowly add the cream and process until a light, creamy, mousse-like consistency is obtained.

Season with salt and white pepper, and refrigerate.

Alternatively if no blender is available, mince the chicken meat very finely, then put into a large basin and place this in the refrigerator for 30 minutes.

Remove from the fridge. Beat in the egg white with a wooden spoon, then pass the mixture through a fine sieve. Refrigerate again.

Set the mixing bowl containing the mixture into an even larger bowl containing crushed ice, and gradually work in the cream, beating well between additions.

Season with salt and white pepper, and refrigerate.

Cut the caul into 8 pieces, each large enough to wrap around an eighth of the prepared mousseline.

Lay each piece on a board, place an eighth of the mixture in the centre, and wrap the caul completely around the mousseline, folding the ends in, to form an oval, sausage-like parcel. When you have made 8 sausages, place them in the refrigerator until you are ready to cook them.

To make the sauce, melt the butter in a saucepan, add the finely chopped shallots or onions, and the tarragon, and cook slowly to soften.

Add the white wine, boil to reduce slightly, then add the jus lié.

Simmer for 15 minutes, strain, and season to taste. Reserve and keep warm.

Wash and dry the button mushrooms, then cook in some of the clarified butter with a little salt and pepper. Drain and keep warm.

To cook the sausages, melt the remaining clarified butter in a frying pan. Put the sausages in, best side down first, and cook for about 4 minutes.

Turn, and cook the other side for about 4 minutes.

Remove the sausages from the pan, drain, and serve garnished with the mushrooms and coated with the sauce.

# Breaded Lamb Cutlets with Cumberland Sauce

In this recipe, the crisp coating of crumbs on the lamb gives a lovely texture and flavour, and Cumberland sauce is a perfect accompaniment to the cutlets. The same sauce is also an ideal accompaniment, when cold, to the potted pheasant recipe in this section.

## Ingredients

*8 lamb cutlets, flattened to about ½"/1cm thick*

*2oz/60g flour*

*2 beaten eggs*

*8oz/225g white breadcrumbs*

*1 orange*

*1 lemon*

*8oz/225g redcurrant jelly*

*¼tsp ground ginger*

*¼tsp dry mustard powder*

*5fl oz/150ml port*

*a little cooking oil*

*a little butter*

*salt and pepper*

## Method

Season the cutlets on both sides.

Put the flour, beaten eggs and breadcrumbs in 3 separate trays, and pass the cutlets through the trays in this sequence, shaking to remove any excess at each coating.

For the sauce, finely peel the orange and lemon, avoiding any pith, then cut the peel into very fine strips about ¹⁄₁₆"/1mm wide and squeeze the juice from the fruits.

Put the redcurrant jelly into a saucepan with the orange and lemon juices, ginger, mustard powder and port.

Heat gently to melt the jelly, bring to the boil, reduce the heat and simmer to reduce by half.

Meanwhile, drop the strips of rind into a little boiling water, boil for one minute then drain and add to the sauce.

When the sauce has reduced by half, remove from heat and keep warm until required.

Heat the oil and butter in a shallow frying pan and cook the cutlets for about 4 minutes on each side, until golden.

Remove from the pan, drain and serve, handing the hot sauce separately.

# Venison with Orange and Cinnamon Sauce

Game was used extensively in the classic cooking of the Regency period. Subtle sauces such as this combination of orange and cinnamon helped to create dishes which found favour in fine restaurants.

## *Ingredients*

*2lb/900g loin of venison*

*olive oil*

*2 oranges*

*1oz/30g caster sugar*

*4fl oz/120ml white wine*

*10fl oz/300ml jus lié (see page 135)*

*1tsp ground cinnamon*

*2oz/60g pine nuts*

*1tbsp orange curaçao*

*salt and pepper*

## *Method*

Ask the butcher to prepare the venison, using the meat from the saddle, trimmed, rolled in a thin slice of pork back fat and tied so that rosettes can be cut when required.

The fat keeps the somewhat dry meat moist during cooking, and providing the meat has been properly hung, it should not require marinading.

Cut the loin into 8 rosettes, brush lightly with olive oil and season with salt and pepper.

Grill or shallow fry for approximately 3 minutes each side, so that the meat will still be pink. The more it is cooked, the tougher it will become. Reserve the rosettes and keep warm.

Remove the zest from one of the oranges, taking care to avoid the pith, and cut into very fine strips.

Blanch the strips in boiling water for a minute, drain and cool.

Squeeze the juice from both oranges and remove any pips.

To make the sauce: put the caster sugar into a heavy-based saucepan, over heat.

After a few minutes the sugar will melt and caramelise as the temperature rises.

When the sugar is golden brown, carefully add all of the orange juice. Avoid splashes from the spray and steam produced by this vigorous boiling.

Add the white wine and boil rapidly until reduced by half.

Add the jus lié and the cinnamon and simmer for about 10 minutes.

Check the seasoning and adjust to taste.

Strain the sauce through a fine sieve, stir in the pine nuts, the strips of orange rind and the curaçao. Reheat gently.

Serve the rosettes of venison surrounded by a pool of sauce.

# Pears Stuffed with Marzipan

At this time, marzipan was a popular sweetmeat; and here it is combined with pears under a rich, creamy sauce.

## Ingredients

*10oz/300g caster sugar*

*1pt/500ml water*

*juice of 1 lemon*

*pinch ground cinnamon*

*4 firm pears (Williams or Conference)*

*10fl oz/300ml milk*

*few drops vanilla essence*

*1½oz/45g flour*

*3oz/85g caster sugar*

*2 egg yolks*

*4oz/115g marzipan*

*4fl oz/120ml whipping cream angelica (optional)*

## Method

For the syrup boil the 10oz/300g sugar, water, lemon juice and cinnamon for 5 minutes and keep on the boil.

Prepare the pears: peel them with a potato peeler and remove the cores from the bases with a ball cutter or a small sharp knife, keeping the fruit intact and the stalks on.

As each pear is prepared, put it into the boiling syrup, to prevent it from discolouring.

When all 4 pears are in the syrup, cover the pears with greaseproof paper and simmer very gently until tender – the cooking time will depend on the ripeness of the fruit, but should be between 15 and 40 minutes: they are ready when soft and almost translucent in appearance.

Cool the pears completely in the syrup.

For the pastry cream, heat the milk in a saucepan with the vanilla essence.

Whisk the flour, the remaining sugar and egg yolks to a smooth paste in a basin, pour over the hot milk, whisking all the time, then return the custard to the saucepan.

Bring to the boil, stirring continuously, cook for 2 minutes, then transfer to a clean basin; cover the custard with greaseproof paper to prevent a skin from forming on the sauce as it cools.

The dish may be prepared in advance up to this stage.

When the pears are cold drain well, fill the core cavities with marzipan, then place them upright on a serving dish.

Beat the cold pastry cream, whisk in the whipping cream until a thick coating consistency is obtained and cover each pear evenly with the sauce.

Cut leaf shapes from the angelica and use to decorate the stems.

Serve cold.

## Notes

Tinned pear halves may alternatively be used, but they must be very well drained and dried, then sandwiched together with marzipan to make whole pears.

# Plum Fritters

Fritters were a popular pudding in Regency times, and other fruit may be used in this recipe; apricots, apples and bananas are all good alternatives to the plums. The beer and whisked egg white provide an exceptionally light and crisp batter.

## Ingredients

*5oz/145g plain flour*

*pinch salt*

*1oz/30g butter*

*2½fl oz/75ml beer*

*3½fl oz/100ml tepid water*

*1tbsp brandy (optional)*

*1lb/450g fresh plums (or 1 × 1¼lb/500g tin)*

*4oz/115g caster sugar*

*1 egg white*

*cooking oil for deep frying*

## Method

Sift the flour and salt into a bowl.

Melt the butter and add to the flour, then add the beer, water and brandy (if using) and beat the mixture to a smooth paste.

If using fresh plums, cut them in half, remove the stones, sprinkle with a little caster sugar and leave for about 30 minutes.

If using tinned plums, drain well and remove the stones.

Preheat the oil to 180°/350°F or until a cube of bread browns in 30 seconds.

Beat the egg white stiffly, then carefully fold into the batter mixture.

Dip the plum halves one at a time into the batter, and place carefully in the hot oil.

Cook a few at a time, turning until they are an even golden colour.

Remove from the oil, drain well on kitchen paper and keep hot.

Sprinkle with the remaining caster sugar and serve immediately.

# LA BELLE ÉPOQUE

## (1890 – 1905)

The culinary feature characteristic of the Belle Époque was that people around the restaurant table became just as important as the food upon it. The diners were on display, service was all important, and now dishes were even named after the famous. The surroundings had to excel, especially the entrance to the dining room, and the lighting had to flatter, for the presence of ladies had become an essential feature of dining out. By the end of the century both England and France had arrived at the same culinary destination, but the routes they took were different.

In France the Belle Époque may be said to have begun on 14 July 1880, the date of the Storming of the Bastille, henceforth a national public holiday. The impact of the holiday was huge because it relieved France both of the sense of defeat by the Prussians ten years earlier, and of the fear that the monarchists might return to power. This triumph of the Left reunited France and gave birth to a period of social liberty and gaiety, best demonstrated by a group who called themselves Les Incohérents. They challenged uniformity, tradition and boredom throughout the cultural scene, and at their annual balls the can-can was first danced by the upper classes, 'loosening the morals of France and causing the decline of the family'.

*A seating plan would be listed on one of the menu pages, and was shown to guests before they entered the dining room. Each person knew in advance who one's neighbour would be. It was discourteous to dine next to a lady with whom one was not hitherto acquainted without delivering one's visiting card to her the following day.*

Restaurants were already well-established venues for the rich to meet, and dinner was a fine ceremony rather than a prelude to a show. Professionals were engaged to dance, and it was not expected that guests should let their food grow cold. Conversation was encouraged, and being heard, as well as being seen, was all important.

By the end of the century, of the many respected restaurants in Paris, Foyot's was one of the most famous. Named in 1848 after the chef to Louis-Philippe, it was frequented by senators from the nearby Palais de Luxembourg. A century earlier, Prince Joseph (later the Hapsburg Emperor Joseph II) had stayed in the house to keep an eye on his sister, Marie Antoinette.

Equally famous was the Tour d'Argent, where early in the 20th century, M Delair became known worldwide for his caneton pressé. Each duck was numbered when ordered and the tradition continued after Delair's death into the present century when, in 1930, the 100,000th duck was served. Delair

*Large kitchens were divided into sections, each with its own chef responsible for particular preparations. Here, the pastry chefs are working on bread, pastries and petits fours.*

named dishes after his guests: sole after the Duc de Mornay, tournedos after E. V. Lucas, escalope de ris de veau after James Gordon Bennett, and pêche Anatole France after the well-known author – he differed from Escoffier in honouring the male sex.

Other restaurants also developed their own notorieties: Voisins made siege menus a speciality. The Christmas menu in 1870 after ninety-nine days of siege included roast camel, stuffed donkey and cat with rat dressing. At L'Escargot Mme Leconte adjusted her menu prices in response to her success in backing winners. Laperouse was a honeycomb of tiny rooms, some with Boucher decorations, and contained a secret cubbyhole for two. The Café de Paris was the first luxury restaurant to encourage its customers to dance (in 1893). In 1872 a young couple opened a small café whose English and American customers suggested they include on the menu a plate of cheap oysters with a glass of Chablis – and the now legendary Pruniers were on their way to establishing their group of fish restaurants.

Meanwhile in England the Belle Époque arose out of a less dramatic development, social changes caused by the growth in material wealth of the middle-class industrialists – an affluence which they wished to display. The new railways could deliver people to London more quickly than ever before, but initially the taverns were not suitable for ladies, and the London clubs also rebuffed them. So those who did not maintain a house in town, where they could give elaborate (and often very boring) dinners, felt excluded from society and began looking for alternatives.

In the traditional pubs and taverns, food was very much secondary to drink. Then in 1829, the first gin palace, Thompson and Fearon's, opened at 94 Holborn Hill, dressing its waitresses as 'belle limonadières' in the Paris coffee-house style. At the other end of the scale were the small, elegant

# ESCOFFIER

*Whilst Carême had developed culinary art for the tables of the rich in their homes, Escoffier demonstrated his talent in the kitchens of restaurants and grand hotels.*

*When only twelve years old he began his career at his uncle's restaurant in Nice, and from there spent a few years at Le Petit Moulin in Paris. Following war service in Metz he returned to Paris and then went to Monte Carlo to work for César Ritz. This remarkable partnership was to change the restaurant scene in Europe when they opened firstly the Savoy hotel in 1890, the Ritz in Paris in 1896, then the Carlton Hotel in London in 1899.*

*Despite this incredibly busy schedule he managed to write* Le Guide culinaire *in which he assembled over 5,000 recipes. The book has become known as the chef's bible. He laid down guidelines for planning menus based on the Russian style of service which meant that dishes would be served consecutively rather than all together. This change also meant that he was able to reorganise a restaurant kitchen into different sections, each of which would prepare component parts of a dish, thus saving the time lost by repetitive work. Whilst* Le Guide culinaire *was based on haute cuisine, he also wrote a book for the domestic market called* Ma cuisine, *and this featured cuisine bourgeoise based on family cooking.*

*August Escoffier worked for sixty-two years before returning to Monte Carlo at the age of seventy-four. He died in 1935.*

hotels of the West End, originally developed by French refugees for officers on leave from the Napoleonic wars. Admittedly, 250 restaurants were listed in the *Guide nouveau* for the 1851 Exhibition, and Simpson's fish restaurant in Billingsgate merited a European reputation, but as late as 1860 it was still difficult to find places where ladies could dine, although the Ship at Greenwich was an exception. Not until restaurants like Gatti's and the Café Royal were established in 1863, along with Kettner's in 1867 and Paganini's in 1871, was this situation remedied. And even at the new Savoy Hotel, Lady de Grey – who had been partly responsible for its creation – initially felt it necessary to have a screen between her party and the public gaze.

The success of the high-class restaurant was not achieved overnight, but resulted from a number of developments during the 19th century. 'Service à la russe', which had long been used in English country houses and had made the intimate dinner possible, led to the adoption of the à la carte menu. Now each dish was individually priced and then cooked to order for each customer, thus concentrating interest on the quality of the dish. Attention to décor had already become one of the major features of the successful hotel business which flourished in Europe, catering for rich tourists. César Ritz, friend and employer of Escoffier, specialised in washable fabrics and painted walls, not least for hygiene and sanitation. More importantly, he made attending balls respectable in his European hotels, accustoming ladies of rank to dining in public, at the time unthinkable in London or Paris. Ritz's contribution to the Belle Époque in England was all important, and was first expressed fully at the Savoy.

Ritz created a restaurant dining room which was superior to the dining rooms in the homes of the wealthy, and where the idiosyncrasies of each guest were given consideration. He was the first to recognise that the future for restaurateurs lay with the Americans, and despite his view that 'they put food into their mouths in the same way as they tossed dirty clothes into a laundry bag', he was sensitive to their own customs, for instance that they required iced water to be placed on their tables, without having to ask for it.

It was the gentry, headed by Lady de Grey, who persuaded

*Novelty was not lacking during the Belle Epoque. Whilst on one occasion at Maxim's, Sarah Bernhardt's birthday cake revealed an attractive model, on another occasion a newspaper magnate had a naked young lady placed in the middle of the table during dinner!*

Ritz to develop hotels in London, particularly the Savoy. When it was established, the Prince of Wales brought Lillie Langtry, among others, and made it fashionable. Meanwhile, Lord Randolph Churchill changed the laws to allow restaurants to open on Sundays and to remain open after 11 o'clock at night. Strauss played Vienna waltzes to the diners as they ate sweets from the Viennese pastry chef.

While there were sufficient restaurants to tempt at least the male middle classes to dine out in London, the quality of the food was uneven, although whether it was any worse than in Paris is open to question. Monet complained of dishes concocted from stale cheese, and Daudet described a chicken at a meal with Zola as tasting of the 'scented flesh of an old tart marinaded in a bidet'. It was in raising the quality of the food that two remarkable chefs united the two countries' traditions.

Born in 1867, Rosa Ovenden was from the domestic tradition, beginning at the age of twelve as a maid-of-all-work for a shilling a week. However, inspired by the stories about

*Restaurants flourished in Paris. Apart from the legendary Maxim's there was Prunier's, Weber, Le Doyen and the Café de Paris. In addition to the restaurants there were some 2,000 cafés and brasseries.*

*Top right:*
*Poached eggs on a bed of diced chicken, coated with a light cream sauce and set in a hollowed-out brioche, glazed with aspic jelly and decorated with truffle.*

society hostesses (in particular Lady Randolph Churchill), which she read in newspapers that were given to her for lighting the fires, she decided to better herself by learning to cook. She secured a place – at twelve shillings and sixpence a week – in the kitchens of the exiled Comte de Paris at Sheen House in Mortlake, and learnt both the French language and French cuisine. Here she met the Prince of Wales and many others in high society, and also had the good fortune to be lent to the Duc d'Aumale in his French château at Chantilly, where her education in haute cuisine was completed. Returning to England, she became an agency cook and chef and friend to her idol, Lady Randolph Churchill. Their dinners became the most famous in London, and she was often lent to those who had to entertain the Prince of Wales as she understood his tastes so well. Finally, becoming Rosa Lewis after a marriage of convenience, she bought and made famous the Cavendish Hotel in Jermyn Street, and more recently achieved still wider fame as the television character, 'The Duchess of Duke Street'.

Auguste Escoffier came from the French restaurant tradition, but he was a remarkable character. Early in his career, he had developed a new system of running a professional kitchen, dividing the work into various 'parties' or sections, each dependent on the other: all pastry and dessert requirements in one, cold dishes in another, soups and vegetables in a third, roasts, grills and fries in a fourth and, under the assistant chef, the sauces. This system, still often used today in large kitchens, greatly speeded up the service.

However, Escoffier's contribution to cuisine was restricted neither to the kitchen (where he did everything he could to alleviate the debilitating conditions for the cooks, including providing cauldrons of barley water to quench their thirst), nor to describing 5,000 recipes in his *Guide culinaire*, published in 1902, which he intended to be a chef's 'tool' rather than just an interesting 'read'. His fame rests in establishing the principles of a well-planned meal, not the dishes which composed it. This required consideration of the occasion itself, knowledge of the guests who were to attend, the season of the year, and the hour when the meal would be served. While his *Guide culinaire* cannot be regarded as just another cook-book, it was his *Livre des menus*, published in 1912, which established the familiar shape of our menus today, and which had the greatest lasting impact. (In fact, his *Guide culinaire* is not easy to follow, as Prosper Montagne, later to write the *Larousse gastronomique*, was quick to point out; and as late as 1934, in *Ma cuisine*, a book for bourgeois cooks and one Escoffier intended for everyday use, he omitted to give temperatures, cooking times, numbers served and even some quantities.)

Except for his sweets, which he named after famous ladies, Escoffier's cuisine was not so much that of an innovator as an improver. His belief that sauces both represented the summit of haute cuisine, and created and maintained the universal superiority of French cuisine, was pure Carême, as was his definition of the three essentials of a sauce: a distinctive taste, a texture which was smooth and light without being runny, and a glossy appearance. He was certainly a romantic, as his book *Les Fleurs de cire* demonstrates, relating – often in verse – his passionate love of flowers, even artificial ones; and his flights of imagination are again evident in the introduction to

*Ma cuisine*, when he describes the body as a clock needing to be oiled and wound up from time to time by the skilled use of nature's raw materials. Nevertheless, his sincerity and simplicity won him many friends, and in 1920 Poincare came to England to award him the Légion d'honneur. The opportunity to celebrate this great honour came when he was made an Officer of the Legion at the Paris Autumn Salon of 1927, when cooking was acknowledged as a fine art equal to painting and sculpture. (He arranged that each of the top Parisian chefs should cater for the salon in turn.)

In the kitchens of both the Cavendish and the Savoy, traditional culinary foundations remained but were reduced to essentials: ornate garnishes were replaced by a few simply cooked vegetables; and ornamentation of dishes with skewers, truffles and so on was abandoned. Food, Escoffier believed, should look like food and be a perfect balance of a few superb ingredients. He held that there was only one principle which should govern the composition and cooking of a dish: that it should satisfy the sense of taste, a sentiment that had been present in English domestic cooking for 300 years. (The two chefs had another feature in common: both had especially strengthened high-heeled boots, Auguste's to raise him above the heat of his stove, and Rosa's to support her during the long hours she spent standing over hers.)

Not all restaurants of the Belle Époque were Savoys or Ritz Carltons, but it was always their clientele which made them successful rather than their cooking. The success of Maxim's was largely due to Maxim Cornichet's idea of employing a certain class of women, more or less attached to the restaurant, whose purpose was to attract male visitors. (This was before the restaurant was bought by an English company in 1900 and decorated in its Art Nouveau style.) Romano's on the Strand was noted for its poor food and high prices, but succeeded because it was the unofficial headquarters of the *Sporting Times, the Pink 'Un*, and was frequented by sporting gentlemen for whom tips were more important than taste. Conversely, the success of the Holborn restaurant lay in the fact that it had an entrance to the dining room which ladies could use without passing the public buffet.

In England the Belle Époque blended into the Edwardian era

*A swan carved from a single huge block of ice, such as the one in which Escoffier first served Peach Melba as a tribute to Dame Nellie Melba.*

when its main protagonist, the Prince of Wales, was crowned in 1902. But its whole way of life was ended by the Great War. Displays of wealth and superiority became offensive to a generally depressed society, especially as people assumed that anyone with money had probably made it out of the sufferings of soldiers. This was not the case in France, where differences between rich and poor were simply accepted.

Although the Belle Époque is associated primarily with London and Paris, it was an equally important but different period for the history of food in Italy, which in so many respects was the birthplace of European cuisine. After the Renaissance, Italy had fragmented and, although politically unified by Garibaldi in 1870, it remained a loose alliance of different states. Real unity came twenty years later when Pellegrino Artusi, following in the footsteps of Apicius, Martino and Scappi, published *La sienza in cucina e l'arte di mangiar bene* (*Science in the Kitchen and the Art of Eating Well*). The book brought together the three main regional cuisines: that of the Po valley (based on butter and lard); that of Tuscany (utilising olive oil); and the coastal cuisine, which had been influenced by Greeks, Arabs, Spaniards and the New World. In particular, Artusi included recipes for the potato, which transformed soups, and the tomato, which, when added to spaghetti or macaroni, was to create the national dish. Both vegetables had been neglected in Italy and it was Garibaldi who, when short of funds, fed his army on tomatoes. They proved so popular that when the soldiers returned to their homes all over Italy they took their love of tomatoes back with them. Thus the one outstanding national cuisine in Europe came to be re-established, and, unlike the French haute cuisine, remains available to both rich and poor throughout all European countries. The culinary wheel had come full circle: the chef no longer went to the noble master, rather the master went to the most fashionable chef. Ostentatious display and profusion had been replaced by simplicity, both of service and of taste, and the flavour of each ingredient was supreme. All the qualities of the English upper-class cuisine had now been appropriated by the French; and the oldest national cuisine, that of the Italians with its multiplicity of cheese dishes, had been re-established.

*Roy Ackerman and
Michel Bourdin*

*Fillet steaks with a Madeira
sauce, garnished with artichoke
hearts filled with onion purée,
and timbales of haricot bean
purée.*

## The Food of the Belle Époque

Carême had laid the foundations of classic cuisine – he was the first technical master, but Escoffier developed the art into what is, today, recognised as haute cuisine. Again, this was partly due to better facilities (better ovens to cook with and more up-to-date gadgetry) but also to the streamlining of systems and facilities required to make food service easier in restaurants, which were now becoming increasingly popular.

Amongst other things, haute cuisine is about subtlety and refinement in the cooking of traditional foods, and thanks to greatly improved communications chefs could now obtain the very highest quality produce and concentrate their skills on maximising the flavour of those ingredients in the preparation process.

Presentation was still of great importance, of course. Indeed it was during this period that cooking was officially recognised in France as one of the arts, and the great chefs began to mix socially with other artistes (particularly performing artistes) in society. Escoffier's dinner with Sarah Bernhardt would have been quite usual for a leading chef, and his naming of dishes after famous people (see the recipe for peach melba and the one for fillets of sole Sarah Bernhardt) was all part of the same éclat.

As Chef de Cuisine at London's Connaught Hotel, Michel Bourdin's credentials in haute cuisine are of course impeccable. His classical approach to cooking and presentation of food, and his knowledge of Escoffier, singled him out as the ideal companion on our journey to turn-of-the-century Maxim's de Paris. But in the recipes we have not sought to repeat Escoffier's own widely available recipes (although our basic recipes for velouté and jus lié are of course quintessentially Escoffier). Again, in a more practical vein, we have opted for a mixture of styles and even included some dishes that would have appeared at poorer tables, like pigeon pie.

# Fillets of Sole Sarah Bernhardt

Sarah Bernhardt was perhaps the best known actress of the Belle Epoque, and during this period it was fashionable for chefs to dedicate dishes to the famous. La Divine Sarah's name appears as a classic garnish for three dishes – a consommé, a fillet steak, and this simplified version of sole cooked with wine and herbs.

## Ingredients

*1oz/30g butter*

*8 fillets of lemon sole, each weighing 3oz/85g*

*1oz/30g finely chopped onions*

*5fl oz/150ml dry white wine*

*4oz/115g carrot, cut into thin strips*

*10fl oz/300ml fish velouté (see page 134)*

*1tsp chopped chervil*

*1tsp chopped tarragon*

*salt and pepper*

## Method

Grease an oven-proof dish with the butter.

Season the sole fillets and fold them in half.

Sprinkle the onions into the dish, lay the fish on top, pour over the wine, cover with greaseproof paper and cook in an oven preheated to 190°C/375°F/gas mark 5 for 10-15 minutes.

Meanwhile, cook the carrot strips in boiling salted water for a few minutes, keeping them crisp.

Remove the fish from the oven, drain the fillets and keep hot.

Add the cooking liquid from the fish to the fish velouté and bring to the boil.

Strain into a clean pan, add the carrot and herbs and adjust the seasoning to taste.

To serve, put 2 fillets on each plate, coat with the sauce and serve immediately.

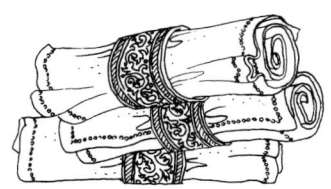

# Salade Tourangelle

This salad comes from Tours, the capital of the market garden of France. The combination of French beans, potatoes and flageolet beans provides an excellent first course or it can be served as an accompaniment to roast meats, poultry or game as an alternative to hot vegetables.

## *Ingredients*

*8oz/225g flageolet beans*

*1 small onion*

*1 small carrot*

*1 clove garlic*

*6oz/170g fine French beans*

*6oz/170g peeled potato, cut into batons*

*4fl oz/120ml French dressing (see page 134)*

*chopped parsley*

*salt and pepper*

## *Method*

Soak the flageolet beans in cold water overnight.

The next day, pour off the water, put the beans into a saucepan and cover with fresh cold water. Bring to the boil and skim.

Add the onion, carrot, garlic and a little salt and simmer until tender – usually about 45-60 minutes.

Top and tail the French beans, wash and cook quickly in plenty of boiling salted water.

Keep the beans slightly firm, and when done plunge into running cold water to preserve their bright green colour and arrest further cooking by residual heat.

Drain well, and cut into 2″/5cm lengths.

Cook the potatoes slowly for just a few minutes in boiling salted water, then drain well in a colander.

Whilst the potatoes are still warm, toss them gently in a little of the French dressing so that the flavour is absorbed.

When the flageolets are cooked remove them from the pan and drain well.

Toss also in a little of the dressing, and cool slightly.

Combine the potatoes and flageolets, but do not add the French beans until 10 minutes before serving, as the dressing would spoil their colour. (No harm would be done to the flavour, but the charm of the salad is in the contrasting colours of the vegetables.)

To serve: mix the French beans gently into the flageolet and potato salad, adding a little more dressing if needed, and sprinkling with chopped parsley.

# Deep-fried Mussels

In this recipe, good, fresh mussels in a saffron sauce are enclosed in pastry and deep-fried to become light, crisp and delicious. The mussels can be eaten as a first course at a dinner party, or served as part of a buffet. The same method can be employed to utilise left-over meat, poultry, game, fish or vegetables.

## *Ingredients*

1½lb/680g fresh mussels

1oz/30g finely chopped onions

1oz/30g finely chopped celery

4fl oz/120ml dry white wine

10fl oz/300ml fish stock

1oz/30g flour and 1oz/30g butter mixed together to form a smooth paste

1tsp finely chopped parsley

10oz/300g puff pastry (see page 136 or use frozen)

1pkt saffron powder

2fl oz/60ml double cream

fat or oil for deep-frying

parsley for garnishing

salt and pepper

## *Method*

Clean the mussels well in several changes of cold water, discarding any that are open or have broken shells, put into a saucepan with the onions, celery, wine and a little ground pepper (but no salt) and cover with a lid.

Cook quickly, shaking the pan occasionally, until the shells open; strain the mussels from the pan, reserving the cooking liquor, and discard any mussels that have not opened.

Allow to cool slightly, then remove the mussels from their shells, discarding any remaining beard.

Strain the mussel stock carefully to remove any grit, add the fish stock, reboil, then whisk in the flour and butter mixture to thicken the liquid.

Remove from the heat and strain.

Add the chopped parsley to the mussels, then pour over just enough of the sauce to coat the mussels, and allow to cool completely.

Roll out the puff pastry to and even thickness of ⅛"/3mm and cut out 16 circles measuring 2½"/6cm in diameter.

Place 2 or 3 of the coated mussels in the centre of 8 of the circles – avoid overfilling, as the mixture might boil out during cooking.

Brush the edges of the pastry with cold water, place the 8 remaining pastry circles on the filled circles, press the edges firmly together and refrigerate for about 1 hour before final cooking.

Add the saffron to the remaining sauce, bring slowly to the boil and simmer gently for 5 minutes.

Add the double cream, reboil, then pass the sauce through a fine strainer and keep warm.

Preheat the fat or oil to 180°C/350°F or until a cube of bread browns in 30 seconds, then deep fry the mussel parcels for about 4 minutes each side, turning them once.

Remove from the pan, drain on kitchen paper and serve, garnished with parsley, handing the sauce separately.

# Pigeon Pie

Whilst the rich and famous dined at Maxim's many poorer tables might have been graced by this delicious pigeon pie, a lovely lunch dish which combines the humble pigeon with smoked bacon and mushrooms.

## *Ingredients*

*4 pigeons*

*2oz/60g butter*

*8oz/225g thinly sliced smoked streaky bacon*

*6oz/170g sliced mushrooms*

*2oz/60g finely chopped onions*

*1 crushed clove garlic*

*1tsp chopped thyme leaves*

*1tbsp chopped parsley*

*5fl oz/150ml red wine*

*10fl oz/300ml (approx) brown stock (see page 133)*

*8oz/225g puff pastry (see page 136 or use frozen)*

*beaten egg for glazing*

*salt and pepper*

## *Method*

Cut each pigeon into 4 pieces, removing the legs first, then taking the meat from each side of the breast bone; discard all the skin.

Make a stock with the bones.

Melt the butter in a frying pan, season the pigeon pieces with salt and pepper, fry in the butter until brown on all sides, then remove and leave to cool.

Wrap each breast in bacon.

Fry the mushrooms, onions and garlic in the same butter until just soft.

Put the pigeon pieces in a pie dish in layers, alternating with the mushroom and onion mixture.

Sprinkle with thyme and parsley, season with salt and pepper, pour the wine over the birds, then add stock to come about half way up the dish.

Roll out the puff pastry until slightly larger than the dish, then cut from the edge a strip of pastry about ½"/1cm wide.

Wet the rim of the pie dish and press the strip of pastry on to it, moisten this strip, then lay the sheet of pastry over the whole dish.

Press the edges of the pastry well together, and trim to remove any excess.

Make a small hole in the centre of the pastry to allow steam to escape during cooking.

Brush the top of the pastry with beaten egg and bake in an oven preheated to 200°C/400°F/gas mark 6 for about 30 minutes.

Cover the pastry with aluminium foil to prevent burning, reduce the temperature to 170°C/325°F/gas mark 3 and bake for a further 90 minutes.

# Bakers' Potatoes

This dish used to be cooked in an old-fashioned baker's oven. The housewife would take the prepared dish to the bakery in the morning, often with a joint of meat set on top of the potatoes. The baker would then cook the dish slowly in his bread oven so that it would be ready for the housewife to serve at lunchtime.

## Ingredients

*1½lb/680g peeled and washed potatoes*

*6oz/170g peeled and thinly sliced onions*

*3oz/85g melted butter*

*15fl oz/450ml water or white stock (see page 133)*

## Method

Cut the potatoes into thin slices and reserve the best ones for the top of the dish.

Mix the sliced potatoes and onions together, season with salt and pepper, and place in a buttered oval earthenware dish.

Arrange the reserved potato slices neatly around the top of the dish, brush well with melted butter and two-thirds fill the dish with the white stock or water.

Place in an oven preheated to 200°C/400°F/gas mark 6 and bake for 20 minutes.

Remove the dish from the oven, gently press the potatoes down to flatten them and brush with more melted butter.

Reduce the oven temperature to 170°C/325°F/gas mark 3, return the dish to the oven and cook until the potatoes are soft and the top of the dish is golden brown.

Remove from the oven, brush with melted butter and serve immediately.

# Chicken with Mushrooms and Cream

Whilst this recipe uses chicken and mushrooms, guinea fowl or young pheasant could be substituted for the chicken; and oyster mushrooms or chanterelles could replace the button mushrooms.

## Ingredients

*1 chicken, weighing 2lb/900g, cut into 8*

*2oz/60g butter*

*1oz/30g flour*

*1pt/500ml chicken stock (see page 133)*

*4fl oz/120ml dry white wine*

*8oz/225g button mushrooms*

*2 egg yolks*

*5fl oz/150ml double cream*

*a little lemon juice*

*salt and pepper*

## Method

Season the chicken pieces with salt and pepper.

Heat the butter in a pan large enough to hold all the ingredients, add the chicken pieces and cook gently, turning frequently, so that they scarcely colour.

Sprinkle in the flour, mix thoroughly into the butter, and cook gently for a few minutes; add the stock and wine a little at a time, stirring continuously to obtain a smooth consistency.

When all the liquid has been incorporated, cover and simmer gently for about 30 minutes, then add the mushrooms and simmer for a further 20 minutes.

Remove the pan from the heat, and take the chicken and mushrooms from the sauce with a slotted spoon, then set aside and keep warm.

Beat the egg yolks with the cream in a large basin and pour in the sauce slowly, beating continuously until all the sauce has been incorporated.

Check the seasoning, sharpen if necessary with lemon juice, and add salt and pepper to taste.

Clean the cooking pan, return the chicken and mushrooms to it and add the sauce, pouring it through a fine sieve.

Reheat very gently, stirring continuously – on no account must the sauce boil; if allowed to do so it will separate.

Serve with pilaf rice or buttered pasta.

# Soufflé Pudding with Chestnuts

Soufflés tend to frighten most cooks, yet this recipe is quite tolerant and gives greater flexibility in handling and cooking than do soufflé recipes without flour. It is nonetheless very light and can form a spectacular finale to a lunch or dinner party. The mixture can be prepared and put into the moulds shortly before the guests arrive, and refrigerated for an hour or so prior to cooking.

## Ingredients

2oz/60g unsalted butter

2oz/60g caster sugar

2oz/60g plain flour

6fl oz/180ml milk

zest of 1 lemon

3 eggs, separated

12 chestnuts in syrup

1fl oz/30ml brandy

10fl oz/300ml fresh custard (see page 135)

## Method

Mix the butter, sugar and flour to a smooth paste in a basin.

Put the milk and lemon zest into a saucepan and heat slowly.

When the milk is about to boil, add the paste to the milk in the pan.

Stir with a wooden spoon until absorbed, then beat well over heat until thick (so that the flour cooks properly), about 3 minutes.

Remove from heat, put this base mixture into a basin and allow to cool.

Butter 4 dariole moulds and coat with caster sugar.

Whisk the egg whites until stiff but not granular in texture.

Beat the yolks into the base mixture, then add about a quarter of the whites, mixing carefully to slacken.

Carefully fold in the remainder of the whites. Do not beat as this would lose the aeration.

Fill the moulds with the soufflé mixture.

Stand the moulds in a tray of hot water and place the tray in an oven preheated to 185°C/375°F/gas mark 5.

Bake for about 15-20 minutes, until well-risen and firm to the touch.

Gently warm the chestnuts in their syrup, then strain.

Ease the soufflés gently from their moulds and top each with a warm chestnut, serving 2 more chestnuts alongside.

Add the brandy to the custard sauce.

Serve the soufflés in a pool of brandy custard sauce.

# Peach Melba

Escoffier created this simple pudding for Dame Nellie Melba, the Australian soprano. It was first served set in a giant swan, carved from ice.

## Ingredients

1½lb/680g caster sugar

1pt/500ml water

4 slightly under-ripe peaches

8oz/225g raspberries

juice of ½ lemon

4 scoops vanilla ice-cream

## Method

Put the sugar and water into a saucepan, bring to the boil and simmer for 5 minutes.

Wash the peaches, place in the boiling syrup, cover them with greaseproof paper and simmer gently until just cooked – the cooking time will depend on the ripeness of the fruit.

Cool the peaches completely in the syrup.

To make the sauce: put the raspberries, lemon juice and 2fl oz/60ml of the poaching syrup into a saucepan, bring to the boil over a low heat, then remove from the heat and allow to cool slightly.

Liquidise the raspberries, pass the sauce through a sieve and cool completely.

The dish may be prepared in advance up to this stage.

To serve, skin and stone the peaches, then cut in half.

Place a scoop of ice-cream in each of 4 pretty dishes, set half a peach on either side of the ice-cream, coat with the raspberry sauce and serve immediately.

## Notes

Strawberries could be used instead of raspberries in the sauce.

# Chilled Lemon Soufflé

Soufflés, both hot and cold, were a favourite pudding at this time, and provided cooks with the opportunity to show their expertise in preparing them. This creamy, light lemon soufflé is excellent for a party, and can be prepared well in advance.

## *Ingredients*

3 sheets leaf gelatine (or ½oz/15g powdered)

3 eggs, separated

grated rind and juice of 2 lemons

8oz/225g caster sugar

10fl oz/300ml double cream

2oz/60g chopped almonds for decoration

4fl oz/120ml whipped double cream for decoration

cherries and angelica for decoration

## *Method*

Tie a band of greaseproof paper around a soufflé dish measuring 6"/15cm in diameter to form a collar, standing about 2"/5cm above the rim.

If you do not have a soufflé dish, a pretty glass bowl is perfectly acceptable, but in this case do not use a paper collar.

If using leaf gelatine, soften for a few minutes in cold water; if using powdered gelatine, mix with a little cold water, then heat to dissolve.

Put the egg yolks, the lemon juice and rind and the sugar in a heat-proof basin over a pan of hot water and whisk together continuously until the mixture pales and thickens.

Remove from the heat and add the gelatine, whisking quickly to prevent stringing, then allow to cool completely, whisking occasionally.

In separate basins, whip the double cream until fairly thick and the egg whites until stiff but not granular.

Fold the whipped double cream into the lemon mixture, ensuring that it is thoroughly blended, then carefully fold in the egg whites.

Pour into the prepared soufflé dish or serving bowl, and refrigerate until set.

When ready to serve remove the soufflé from the refrigerator and take off the collar, decorate the exposed edge with chopped almonds, pipe whipped cream on top and decorate with cherries and angelica.

# Prune Tart with Brandy

This crisp sweet pastry with a creamy brandy and almond filling is at its best served warm and accompanied by thick cream.

## Ingredients

*8oz/225g dried prunes*

*8oz/225g sweet pastry (see page 136)*

*2oz/60g ground almonds*

*2 eggs*

*2oz/60g caster sugar*

*2fl oz/60ml double cream*

*2fl oz/60ml brandy*

*2 drops vanilla essence*

*1oz/30g melted unsalted butter*

## Method

Stone the prunes, and soak in warm water for an hour.

Line an 8"/20cm flan case with the sweet pastry and bake blind: line the pastry base with greased greaseproof paper, and cover with baking beans to prevent the pastry rising during cooking.

Bake in an oven preheated to 180°C/350°F/gas mark 4 for about 10 minutes, so that the pastry is 'set' but not completely cooked, then remove the beans and greaseproof paper.

Put the almonds, eggs, sugar, cream, brandy and vanilla essence into a bowl and beat well to mix thoroughly, then add the melted butter and mix again.

Drain and dry the prunes, place in the partly-baked pastry case then pour the almond mixture over and return the flan to the oven.

Bake for about 30 minutes, until the filling is set and the pastry is a light golden colour.

Serve warm.

## Notes

Dried apricots could be substituted for the prunes, if preferred.

# The Basics

## Brown Stock

### Ingredients

*5lb/2.25kg beef or veal bones, or some of each*

*8oz/225g onions*

*8oz/225g carrots*

*a little oil for frying*

*8pt/5ltr water*

*2oz/60g celery*

*3-4 sprigs parsley*

*1 sprig thyme*

*1 bay leaf*

### Method

Ask the butcher to saw or chop the bones into small pieces.

Put the bones into a roasting tin and place the tin in an oven preheated to 400°F/200°C/gas mark 6 for about 30 minutes, until well browned.

Cut the onion and carrot into 1"/2cm dice and fry in a little oil.

Put the onion, carrot and bones into a large saucepan and cover with the cold water.

Bring to the boil on top of the stove.

Remove any scum as it rises to the surface and add to the pan the celery and herbs tied together.

Simmer for at least 3 hours.

Strain, remove fat and use as required.

Makes 7pt/4ltr.

The stock will keep in the refrigerator for a couple of days, or can be frozen in small quantities.

## White Stock
## (Veal, Beef or Chicken)

### Ingredients

*5lb/2.3kg veal bones, beef bones or chicken carcasses and giblets*
*(use whichever flavour is required)*

*8oz/225g prepared carrots*

*4oz/115g prepared onions*

*2oz/60g prepared leeks*

*1oz/30g prepared celery*

*a few parsley stalks*

*1 sprig thyme*

*½ bay leaf*

*8pt/5ltr water*

*salt*

### Method

Ask the butcher to saw or chop the bones into small pieces.

Put the bones into a large saucepan, cover with the cold water & a pinch of salt, and bring slowly to the boil.

Carefully remove the scum as it rises to the surface.

Add the vegetables and herbs, and simmer gently for about 3 hours.

Strain and use as required. The stock will keep in the refrigerator for a couple of days, or can be frozen in small quantities.

Makes 7pt/4ltr.

# Fish Stock

## Ingredients

*4lb/1.80kg fish bones and trimmings*

*4oz/115g sliced onions*

*3-4 parsley stalks*

*juice of 1 lemon*

*6pt/3.5ltr water*

*6 peppercorns*

## Method

Place the bones, trimmings, onion and parsley stalks in a large saucepan.

Add the lemon juice and water and bring quickly to the boil.

Carefully remove any scum that rises to the surface.

Simmer for 15 minutes, add the peppercorns, then simmer for a further 10 minutes.

Do not add the peppercorns any earlier as this will cloud the stock.

Strain, reserve and use as required.

Makes 5pt/2.5ltr.

This simple and quickly-prepared stock can be used to make a fish sauce, or for poaching fish. Use only the bones of prime white fish such as sole, turbot, brill or whiting, avoiding those from oily fish such as salmon, herring or mackerel.

# Fish Velouté

## Ingredients

*3oz/85g butter*

*3oz/85g flour*

*3pt/1.5l fish stock (see page x)*

## Method

Melt the butter in a heavy saucepan and stir in the flour to make a smooth paste.

Cook very gently, stirring frequently until the roux is a light straw colour.

Add the fish stock a little at a time, beating well between each addition to prevent lumps from forming.

Simmer very gently for about an hour, stirring occasionally.

Strain and keep until required.

This quantity makes 2pt/1lt.

# French Dressing

There are perhaps as many variations on French dressing as there are French people, and we give here simply the basic ingredients, which may be varied at will.

## Ingredients

*2fl oz/60ml wine vinegar*

*8fl oz/240ml olive oil*

*salt*

*pepper*

## Method

Put all the ingredients in a bowl and whisk them together.

## Notes

The flavour may be varied by adding a little mustard; or it may be sweetened with a little sugar; or you can add chopped garlic, tarragon, basil or parsley.

Hazelnut, walnut or sesame oil may be substituted for part of the olive oil.

Corn oil or sunflower oil may be used instead of olive oil.

The permutations are endless, but it is a good idea to bear in mind the items to be dressed when choosing the flavours of the dressing ingredients.

This quantity makes 10fl oz/300ml.

# Jus Lié

## Ingredients

*4lb/1.8kg raw veal & chicken bones, chopped into small pieces*

*4oz/115g diced carrots*

*3oz/85g diced onions*

*2oz/60g tomato purée*

*6pt/3.5ltr cold water or white stock (see page 133)*

*1 small bay leaf*

*1 sprig thyme*

*3-4 parsley stalks*

*1½oz/45g arrowroot*

## Method

Cook the bones until golden brown in a roasting tray in an oven preheated to 180°C/350°F/gas mark 4, drain to remove excess fat and place in a large saucepan.

Fry the carrots and onions in the roasting tray until golden brown, drain and add to the bones with the tomato purée.

Add a little stock or water to the roasting tray to loosen any sediment left by the bones or vegetables; add this liquid to the saucepan, cover with water or stock and bring to the boil.

Remove any scum that rises to the surface, reduce the heat, add the herbs and simmer gently for 3 hours.

Strain the stock into a clean pan and measure – you should be left with about 3pt/2.25ltr.

Mix the arrowroot with a little cold water or stock to form a smooth paste, then add to the hot stock.

Reboil, stirring constantly, until it thickens; cook for 2 minutes, strain and use as required.

This sauce will keep in the refrigerator for up to 3 days, but if a larger quantity is made, only the amount needed immediately should be thickened and the rest frozen in small portions.

# Fresh Custard

## Ingredients

*1pt/500ml milk*

*4 egg yolks*

*2oz/60g caster sugar*

*few drops vanilla essence*

## Method

Put the milk into a saucepan and gradually bring to just below boiling point.

Beat the egg yolks, sugar and vanilla essence in a basin until light and creamy, then pour on the hot milk, whisking vigorously until it is fully incorporated.

Return the mixture to the saucepan and heat gently without boiling, stirring continuously until it reaches a coating consistency.

On no account must the mixture boil, or it will separate.

This custard will not be as thick as custard made with cornflour or custard powder.

Strain through a fine sieve and keep warm. Use as required. This quantity makes 1pt/500ml.

# Frangipane

## Ingredients

*4oz/115g unsalted butter*

*4oz/115g caster sugar*

*2 eggs*

*1oz/30g plain flour*

*4oz/115g ground almonds*

*few drops almond essence (optional)*

## Method

Put the softened butter into a bowl with the sugar, and beat together until light in colour and creamy in texture.

Beat the eggs, then add them to the sugar and butter mixture a little at a time, beating well between each addition.

Sieve the flour and the almonds together, then add to the mixture gradually, folding them in gently.

Add the almond essence if an intensified flavour is required.

Use immediately.

This quantity makes 1lb/450g.

# Puff Pastry

## Ingredients

*8oz/225g unsalted butter*

*8oz/225g strong white flour*

*pinch salt*

*3fl oz/90ml cold water*

*squeeze lemon juice*

## Method

Make sure the butter is of similar texture to the dough, ie, not too firm: if it is used straight from the refrigerator it will not spread evenly through the dough, thus spoiling the pastry.

Sift the flour and salt into a bowl, add the water and lemon juice and mix to a dough.

Knead until smooth and leave in a cool place for 30 minutes.

Cut a deep cross in the centre of the ball of dough and pull each point out from the centre.

Put the butter inside the dough and completely enclose it by folding the flaps back over it.

With a floured rolling pin, roll the pastry into a rectangle, the long side 3 times the length of the short side, keeping the edges parallel.

One-third of the way along the long side, fold one-third of the pastry back over itself, and fold the remaining third over this.

Wrap in greaseproof paper and leave in a cool place for at least 20 minutes.

Roll into a rectangle as before, fold as before, wrap and rest as before.

Repeat twice more (ie, 4 turnings and foldings in all), always allowing a 20-minute resting period.

The final resting time should be for one hour, after which it is ready for use.

This quantity makes 1lb/450g, but larger quantities can be made and frozen.

# Sweet Pastry

## Ingredients

*12oz/340g plain flour*

*pinch salt*

*8oz/225g butter*

*2oz/60g caster sugar*

*4oz/115g beaten whole eggs*

## Method

Sift the flour and salt into a basin.

Cut the butter into small pieces and rub into the flour until the mixture resembles fine breadcrumbs.

Dissolve the sugar in the beaten egg and add to the flour and butter mixture.

Gently work the pastry to a smooth dough, taking care not to handle it too much.

Allow the pastry to rest for at least 30 minutes before using.

This amount will line 2 flan rings of 8"/20cm in diameter.

The pastry will keep in the refrigerator for a few days, or can be frozen.

# BIBLIOGRAPHY

ARESTY, B.B., *The Delectable Past*
AUSTIN, T., *Two 15th Century Cookery Books*
BALSDON, J.P.V.D., *Life and Leisure in Ancient Rome*
BRIDGE, T., *The Golden Age of Cookery*
CHAMBERLAIN, E.R., *Everyday Life in Renaissance Time*
CLAIR, C., *Kitchen and Table*
DAVIS, *Cooking through the Centuries*
DEGHY, G., *Paradise on the Strand*
DRUMMOND, J.C., and WILBRAHAM, A., *The Englishman's Food*
EDWARDS, J., *The Roman Cookery of Apicius*
ELLWANGER, G.H., *Pleasures of the Table*
FURNIVAL, F.J., *Early English Meals and Manners*
FURNIVAL, F.J., *A Book of Precedence*
GRIGSON, J., *Food with the Famous*
HARCUM, C.G., *Roman Cooks*
HARTLEY, D., *Food in England*
HAZLITT, W.C., *Old Cookery Books and Ancient Cuisine*
JACKSON, S., *The Savoy*
KNOWLES, M.D., *Monastic and Religious Orders*
MARGETSON, S., *Victorian High Service*
MASSINGBIRD, *The London Ritz*
McGEE, H., *On Food and Cooking*
McLEISH, K., *Food and Drink*
OXFORD, A.W., *English Cookery Books to the year 1850*
PAGE, E.B. and KINGSFORD, W.P., *The Master Chefs*
PAOLI, U.E., *Rome, its Peoples, its Life and its Customs*
POWER, E., *Medieval People*
POWER, E., *The Goodman of Paris*
PRUNIER, A., *La Maison*
QUALE, E., *Old Cook-Books*
REARICK, C., *Pleasures of the Belle Epoque*
ROUND, J.H., *The Commune of London*
SAUL, K., *Scenes from Provincial Life*
SPILLER, B., *Victorian Public Houses*
STREET, J., *Where Paris Dines*
TANNAHILL, R., *Food in History*
WHEATON, B.K., *Savouring the Past*
WILLAN, A., *Great Cooks*
WILSON, A.C., *Food and Drink in Britain*
WRIGHT, T., *A History of Domestic Manners and Sentiments*

# INDEX BY RECIPE

# Internet

## Navigation and Exploration

Kathryn A. Marold

Gwynne Larsen

Metropolitan State College of Denver

EMCParadigm

| | |
|---|---|
| **Developmental Editor:** | Christine Hurney |
| **Editorial Assistant:** | Desiree Faulkner |
| **Copyeditor and Proofreader:** | Sharon O'Donnell |
| **Tester:** | Susan Capecchi |
| **Illustrator:** | Colin Hayes |
| **Cover Designer:** | C. Vern Johnson |
| **Text Designer:** | Leslie Anderson |
| **Desktop Production Specialist:** | Leslie Anderson |
| **Indexer:** | Terry Casey |

**Publishing Team:** George Provol, Publisher; Janice Johnson, Director of Product Development; Lori Landwer, Marketing Manager; Shelley Clubb, Electronic Design and Production Manager

**Photo Credits:** Cover image, Steve Rawlings/DigitalVision; page 7, Shaun Best/REUTERS/CORBIS; page 19, A/P Wide World Photo; page 29 (top and bottom), CORBIS; page 39, Peter A. Tunley/CORBIS; page 94 (left and right), EyeWire; page 95 (top and bottom), CORBIS

**Library of Congress Cataloging-in-Publication Data**

Marold, Kathryn, 1944-
      Internet navigation and exploration / Kathryn Marold, Gwynne Larsen.
            p. cm.
      Includes index.
      ISBN 0-7638-1312-5 (text)
   1. Browsers (computer programs) 2. Internet. I. Larsen, Gwynne. II. Title.
TK5105.882 .M37 2002
005.7'1376—dc21                                     2001033906

Care has been taken to verify the accuracy of information presented in this book. However, the author, editor, and publisher cannot accept any responsibility for Web, e-mail, newsgroup, or chat room subject matter or content, or for consequences from application of the information in this book, and make no warranty, expressed or implied, with respect to its content.

**Trademarks:** Some of the product names and company names included in this book have been used for identification purposes only and may be trademarks or registered trademarks of their respective manufacturers and sellers. The author, editor, and publisher disclaim any affiliation, association, or connection with, or sponsorship or endorsement by, such owners.

ISBN 0-7638-1312-5
Order Number 01531

© 2002 by Paradigm Publishing Inc.
      Published by EMCParadigm
      875 Montreal Way
      St. Paul, MN 55102
      (800) 535-6865
      E-mail: educate@emcp.com
      Web site: www.emcp.com

Printed in the United States of America
10  9  8  7  6  5  4  3

# Contents

## Chapter 1

## Chapter 2

## Chapter 3

# Chapter 4

## Communications: Getting Together through the Web      93

# Chapter 5

## E-commerce: The Fastest-Growing Aspect of the Web      129

# Chapter 6

## Creating Web Pages: Putting Your Mark on the Web      155

# Preface

*Internet Navigation and Exploration* is intended for anyone who wants to use a personal computer and the World Wide Web to interact with others and the world around them. Those who read this book will join the swelling ranks of individuals who use their microcomputers as their link to the Global Village. This text will demonstrate that the Internet—and its main component, the Web—have become the universal tool for communication and information.

The purpose of this book is to teach students to access and use the resources available on the Internet, using only the Web as the vehicle for access. Whether the reader's purpose simply is to surf the Web or communicate with a vast number of people in many different forums, this book should serve well as a general primer. Armed with the general concepts included here, students will discover a whole new world at their "electronic fingertips." Guided by screen images and tables of information within the text, students learn how to send and receive electronic mail, access the Web to obtain information, "chat" online with others, use Web search tools to help prepare papers, and experience a world of products and services available for purchase online.

You can complete this course using Internet Explorer (IE) or Netscape Navigator, regardless of their version. The examples in the book are based upon IE version 5.5 and Netscape Navigator version 4.7. In terms of the number of people who use each browser, IE is the most popular, with Netscape a distant second. Together, these two browser applications claim 90 percent of the Internet user market. Most Web developers design their pages with these two browsers in mind. Although the examples of browser elements in this course are limited to these two browsers, there are many different browsers available on the Internet. Some of them are proprietary—exclusive to individual Internet service providers (ISPs). Once you familiarize yourself with the elements of IE and Netscape, any other browser will be simple to master.

During the development of this textbook, the authors have cited numerous URLs for reference or instructional purposes. Please be aware that although all Web sites mentioned in the book have been thoroughly checked and screened for appropriateness and accuracy, it is the nature of the Internet to be continually in flux. Thus, it is possible that some of the URLs may have changed by the time students work with the material. The publisher, authors, and editor assume no responsibility for Web site changes that may have occurred after the book's publication. In certain situations, such as exercises requiring Web research, you can remedy the problem of broken links by conducting keyword searches to locate links of comparable value. We encourage all users to adopt an open attitude and a willingness to adjust as the Internet continues to evolve.

# Organization of This Text

*Internet Navigation and Exploration* is designed in a modular fashion so that it may be read either like a traditional text, sequentially chapter by chapter, or used as a reference. The Internet's dual role of connecting individuals and accessing information is stressed throughout.

The Quickstart Tutorials introducing *Internet Navigation and Exploration* allow students with limited Internet experience to browse the Web, conduct searches, and create a Web page using the Web Page Wizard in Word. This opportunity to get online and start finding and communicating information on the Web will help students get excited about this important resource.

The chapters are organized as follows.

➤ Chapter 1 distinguishes between the Internet and the Web. It identifies the hardware and software necessary to use the Internet and the World Wide Web and describes the basic Web elements such as hypertext, multimedia, URLs, and browsers.

➤ Chapter 2 explains the features and applications of the two major Web browsers—Internet Explorer and Netscape Navigator—and how to use them.

➤ Chapter 3 elaborates on the many ways to search for, access, and document information on the Web.

➤ Chapter 4 explains in detail how to use an e-mail software package, subscribe to mailing lists and newsgroups, and participate in instant messaging and chat rooms.

➤ Chapter 5 features e-commerce, the fastest-growing functionality of the Web, and its newly acquired dominance over the academic and research nature of the Internet of the past.

➤ Chapter 6 explains how to construct the basic building blocks of the Web—the HTML-coded Web page. It leads the student through construction and placement of a simple Web page on an Internet server.

Following the chapters are two appendixes. Appendix A provides basic hardware and software information. Appendix B provides the steps written for Microsoft Word 97 for the Try It Out exercises in Chapter 6. The comprehensive glossary lists all of the terms and definitions that were highlighted throughout the text.

## Special Features in the Text

➤ Sidebars with extension information and points of interest

➤ Tips and Tools features throughout the text

➤ Numerous Web links for exploration and further study

➤ Frequent Try It Out exercises to practice the skills

➤ Detailed summary of important items contained in each chapter

➤ Projects that require students to apply learned skills

➤ Review questions and exercises

➤ Teaching aids that include

- Interactive Web-based companion course
- EMC/Paradigm Web resource site for students and instructors at www.emcp.com/college_division/electronic_resource_center/

## Acknowledgments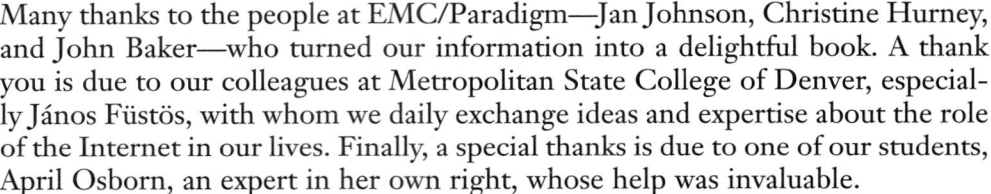

Many thanks to the people at EMC/Paradigm—Jan Johnson, Christine Hurney, and John Baker—who turned our information into a delightful book. A thank you is due to our colleagues at Metropolitan State College of Denver, especially János Füstös, with whom we daily exchange ideas and expertise about the role of the Internet in our lives. Finally, a special thanks is due to one of our students, April Osborn, an expert in her own right, whose help was invaluable.

Kathryn Marold
Gwynne Larsen

# Quickstart Tutorials

### Objectives

- ➤ Browse the Web using Web addresses.
- ➤ Conduct a simple Internet search using a search engine.
- ➤ Conduct an advanced Internet search.
- ➤ Create a Web page by using the Web Page Wizard in Word 2000.

# Tutorial 1

## BROWSING THE WEB USING WEB ADDRESSES

The Internet is a collection of computers around the world connected together through telephone lines, cables, satellites, and other telecommunications media. The World Wide Web, called the Web, is a part of the Internet that contains Web pages consisting of text, sounds, video, and graphics that link to other related Web pages. These links are called hyperlinks. Web pages are stored in a common language called HTML (Hypertext Markup Language) which can be viewed on any computer regardless of the operating system platform (Macintosh, Windows, UNIX, and so on).

To connect to the Internet and view Web pages, you will need the following resources.

1. A computer with a modem or a network connection to a server with Internet access.
2. Browser software, such as Internet Explorer or Netscape Navigator, that provides the interface for viewing Web pages.
3. An account with an Internet service provider (ISP) if you are using a computer that is not connected to a network server. An ISP sells Internet access usually by charging a monthly fee for a set time period. The ISP has the computers, network equipment, and modems to allow multiple users to connect at the same time.

In the steps that follow you will explore Web sites on the Internet using Web addresses and Microsoft's Internet Explorer version 5.5. If you are using another browser or a different version of Internet Explorer, you may need to alter these instructions slightly.

### Steps

1. Click the Launch Internet Explorer Browser button on the QuickLaunch toolbar, or click the Internet Explorer icon on the desktop. If there are no icons on your desktop, click the Start button, point to Programs, and then click Internet Explorer.

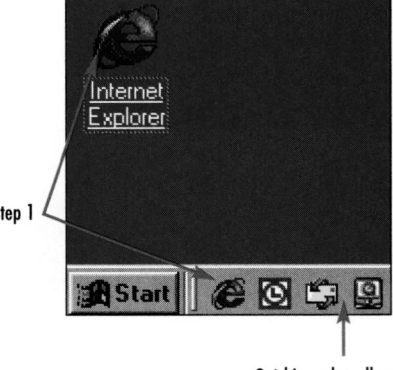

step 1

QuickLaunch toolbar

title bar ⟶
toolbar ⟶
address bar ⟶

status bar ⟶

scroll bar

**Microsoft Internet Explorer Window**

If you are completing this tutorial using your computer at home, you may need to enter your password and then click OK to connect through a dial-up connection to your ISP.

The Microsoft Internet Explorer window will appear with a Web page displayed in the window as shown in the screen capture above. (The Web page shown in your window may vary.)

2. Move the mouse pointer over the current entry in the Address text box, and then click the left mouse button.

Clicking the left mouse button selects the entire address and changes the white arrow pointer to an I-beam, which indicates you can key text and/or move the insertion point using the arrow keys on the keyboard.

3. Key (type) **www.usatoday.com**, and then press Enter.

The USA Today home page will appear in the window. Watch the status bar for messages displaying the status of loading the page. When the page has finished displaying all of its text, graphics, and other components, the status bar will display the word "Done."

step 3 ⟶

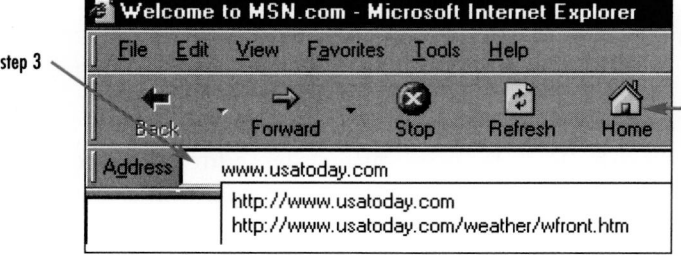

A feature called AutoComplete is invoked as soon as you begin keying an address. AutoComplete displays addresses visited by you in the past that match with the text as you key it. If one of the addresses offered is the correct address, click the mouse over it.

The entry in the Address text box is called a Uniform Resource Locator (URL). URLs are the addressing method used to identify Web pages. After pressing Enter, notice the browser automatically inserted *http://* in front of the address you typed: *http* stands for Hypertext Transfer Protocol, which is the communications standard used for transferring data within the Web.

4. Move the mouse pointer over the blue underlined headings displayed along the left side of the USA Today page.

Notice the pointer changes shape to a white hand with the index finger pointing upward when it is positioned over underlined text. When the pointer takes this shape, it means you can click the left mouse button to jump to a related Web page (called a *hyperlink*).

5. Click the left mouse button over *World*.

In a few seconds, the page with the top World news story is displayed.

6. Click the Back button [Back] on the toolbar to return to the previous page.
7. Click the Forward button [Forward] on the toolbar to redisplay the World page (the page viewed prior to clicking Back).

Notice the Back and Forward buttons on the toolbar contain down-pointing triangles. Click the down-pointing triangle, and then click a Web site name in the drop-down list to jump to a page previously viewed.

step 5 —————

Home
News
**Main Categories**
News briefs
Washington
Editorial/Opinion
States
World
**More News**
Health
Science
Politics
Offbeat news
Columnists
Lotteries
Talk Today
Money
Sports
Life
Tech
Weather

8. Click the mouse pointer over the entry in the Address text box, key **www.microsoft.com**, and then press Enter.
9. Click one of the hyperlinks on the Microsoft home page to jump to a topic that interests you. A hyperlink can be a word, button, or icon that serves as a door to other pages of information.
10. Continue exploring Web pages by keying URLs in the Address text box, and clicking hyperlinks, the Back button, and the Forward button on the toolbar.
11. When you have finished exploring the Web, click the Close button ⊠ in the upper right corner of the title bar to exit Microsoft Internet Explorer. If necessary, disconnect from your ISP.

If you want to browse the Web by *topic*, rather than addresses, click the Search button on the toolbar. Click in the Find a Web page containing text box, key the topic you are interested in, and then click the Search button beside the box.

### Web Links

**Popular online news sources to visit**
www.time.com
www.abc.go.com
www.cnn.com
www.msnbc.com

# Tutorial 2

## CONDUCTING A SIMPLE SEARCH

In the previous Internet tutorial, Web sites were explored by keying the Web address (URL) for a specific company. Another method used to find information is by entering a keyword or a phrase and then browsing through a series of Web pages that were found. Several search engines are available to assist users with locating Web sites by topic. A search engine is a company that uses specialized software to continually scan the Web to index and catalog the information that is published. These companies have created Web sites where the user begins a search by keying the word or phrase they would like to find information on. The search engine then lists the Web pages that contain the word or phrase as links, which are called *hits*. Some search engines maintain category indices where the user clicks through a series of categories and subcategories until they reach the desired list of Web pages.

In this tutorial, you will find information on the Web by entering keywords and then conduct another search by browsing through a list of categories.

### Steps

1. Start Internet Explorer. If necessary, connect to your ISP and enter your username and password.
2. Click the Search button on the Internet Explorer toolbar.

A Search Task Pane opens at the left side of the Internet Explorer window with categories displayed that can be searched and a text box to enter the keyword or phrase to find. The default category selected is Find a Web page. The default search engine that will be used on the computer you are using may vary.

3. Key **space station** in the Find a Web page containing text box and then click the Search button.

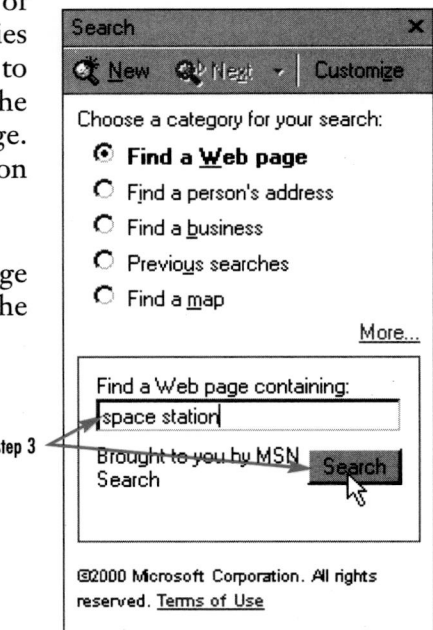

step 3

In a few seconds, a list of Web pages will be displayed as hyperlinks in the Search Task Pane. These pages are Web sites that the search engine has indexed to the text you specified.

4. Click the down-pointing triangle at the bottom of the vertical scroll bar to scroll down the Search Task Pane and view the search results.

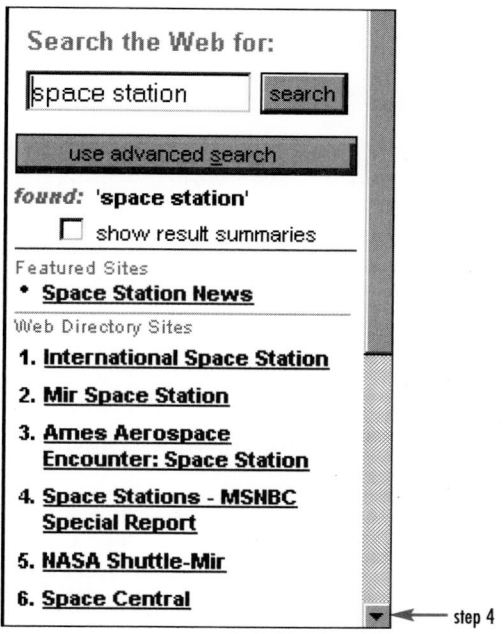

**Search the Web for:**

| space station | search |

use advanced search

*found:* 'space station'
☐ show result summaries

Featured Sites
• **Space Station News**

Web Directory Sites

1. **International Space Station**
2. **Mir Space Station**
3. **Ames Aerospace Encounter: Space Station**
4. **Space Stations - MSNBC Special Report**
5. **NASA Shuttle-Mir**
6. **Space Central**

◀— step 4

5. Click the *next>>* hyperlink at the bottom of the Search Task Pane to display the next 10 sites.
6. Click one of the links in the Search Task Pane to view the related Web page.

As you position the mouse pointer over a hyperlinked Web page, the name of the link changes color and the URL displays in the status bar.

7. Scroll down the Search Task Pane and then click another link to view another related Web page.

Another way to search for information is to use a search engine's category index. In the next steps, you will close the Search Task Pane, key the URL for a search engine, and then browse the category index.

8. Click the Search button on the Internet Explorer toolbar to close the Search Task Pane.

If you prefer to use the full screen for viewing Web pages, close the Search Task Pane and then go directly to the search engine's URL.

9.  Key **www.yahoo.com** in the Address text box and then press Enter.

Yahoo! is a popular search engine that maintains category indices and can also be used to search for a topic by keywords.

10.   Scroll down the Yahoo! Web page and then click *Science*.

11.   Scroll down the Yahoo! Science category page and then click *Space*.

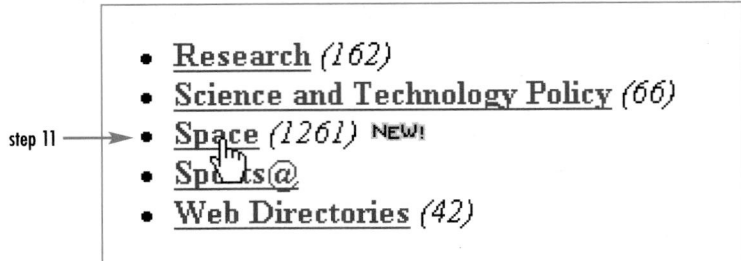

12.  Scroll down the Yahoo! Space category page and then click *Space Stations*.

13.  Click the *Skylab* link on the Space Stations category page.

14.  Click one of the links on the Skylab page and then view the Web page.

15.  Click the Back button on the Internet Explorer toolbar, click another link from the Skylab page, and then view the Web page.

16.  Close Internet Explorer. If necessary, disconnect from your ISP.

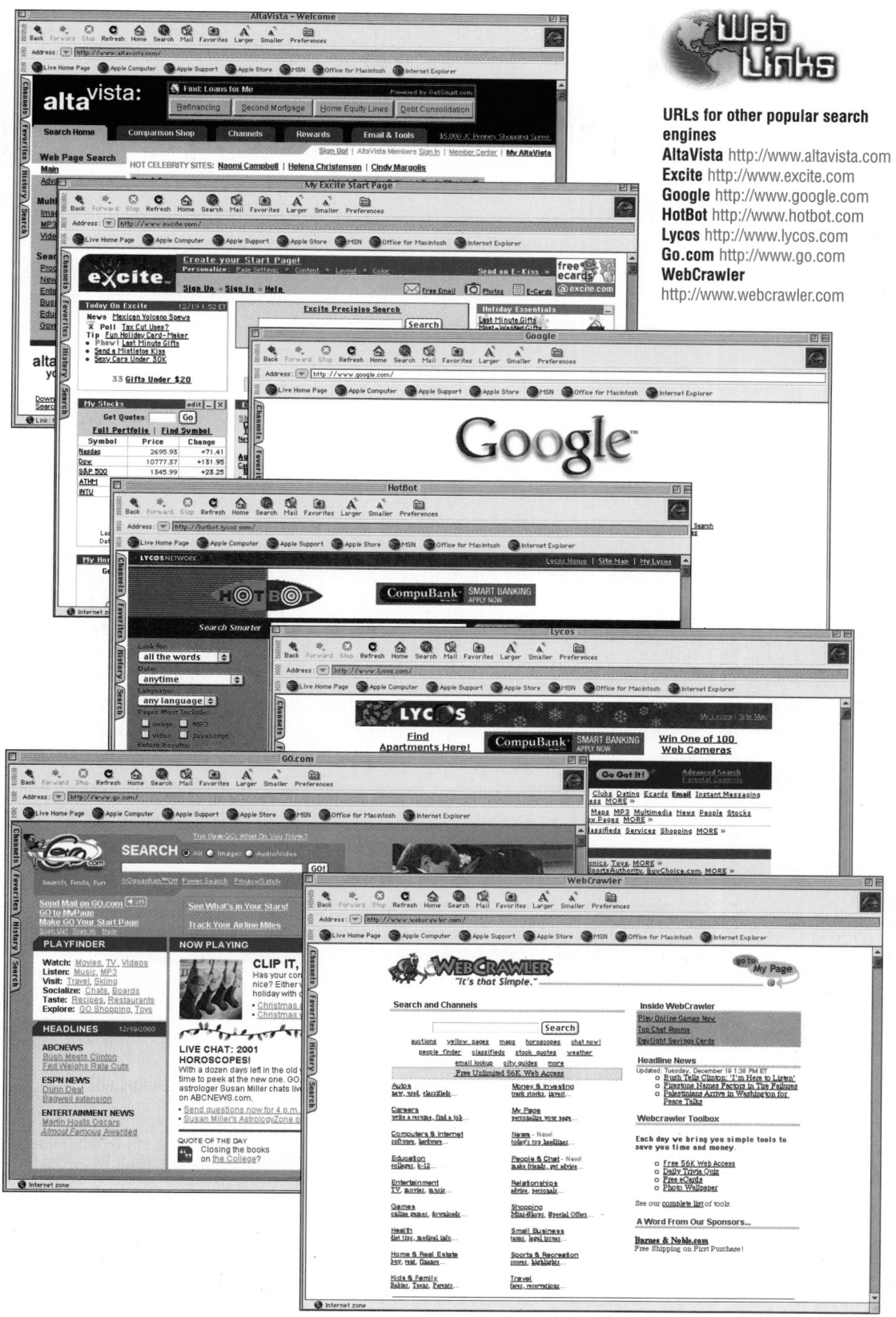

**URLs for other popular search engines**

**AltaVista** http://www.altavista.com
**Excite** http://www.excite.com
**Google** http://www.google.com
**HotBot** http://www.hotbot.com
**Lycos** http://www.lycos.com
**Go.com** http://www.go.com
**WebCrawler**
http://www.webcrawler.com

# Tutorial 3

## CONDUCTING AN ADVANCED SEARCH

The number of Web sites that an individual will see in a list as the result of a search request can be overwhelming. It is not uncommon to see thousands of hits result from searching using a few keywords. The challenge when searching for information on the Internet is to reduce the number of hits to the smallest possible number. Including a search operator with the keywords refines a search by limiting the sites that are displayed based on where or how the keywords are placed. Search operators vary between search engines, so it is best to view the Advanced Search Help for a search engine prior to using operators.

In this topic you will find information on the Web by reading Advanced Search Help and then entering keywords with search operators.

### Steps

1. Start Internet Explorer. If necessary, connect to your ISP and enter your username and password.

2. Key **www.lycos.com** in the Address text box and then press Enter.

Lycos, one of the oldest search engine companies, was developed in 1994 at Carnegie Mellon University. It is well known for its extensive categories, easy to use search page, and "Top 50" searches summarized and published each week.

3. Key **endangered species** in the Search for text box and then click Go Get It! or press Enter.

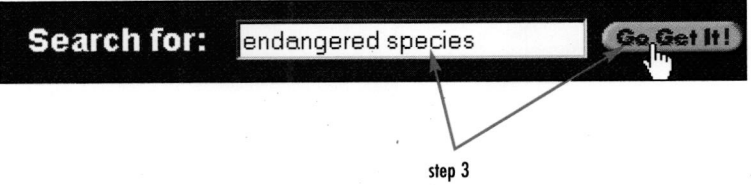

step 3

In a few seconds a list of popular Web pages based on user selection history are displayed, and then farther down the screen the total number of sites found from searching the entire Lycos catalog are listed.

4. Scroll down the Results for endangered species page and read the titles of the Web pages found.

In the next steps, you will refine the list to display only those pages that contain information about birds that are endangered.

5. Scroll to the top of the page and then click the Advanced Search button.

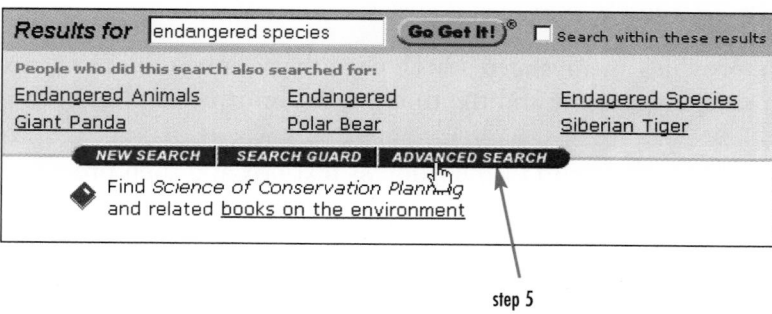

step 5

6. Click *Help*. Scroll down the Advanced Search Help page and then read the information in the Building a Search Expression section.

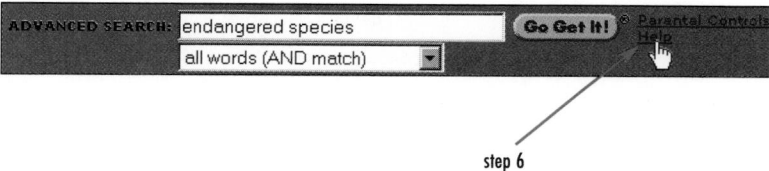

step 6

The information on Boolean operators is especially useful for narrowing search requests since these operators can be used in the primary search text box instead of using the Advanced Search page.

7. Click the Back button on the toolbar to return to the Advanced Search page.

8. Click in the Advanced Search text box after the text *endangered species,* press the spacebar, key **+ birds**, and then press Enter.

Key search + engines + review to find links to Web sites that review the popular search engines and provide helpful tips for effective searching.

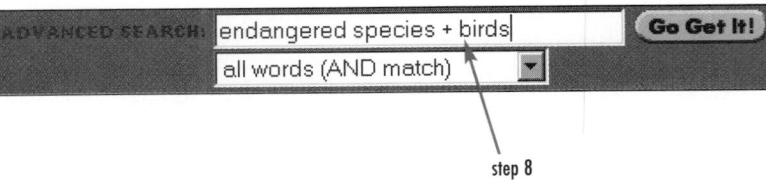

step 8

9. Scroll down the results page. Notice the Web pages found contain all three words: *endangered*, *species*, and *birds*.

Yahoo! provides an advanced search page that can be used to narrow a search based on search operators and the time period information has been published.

10. Key **www.yahoo.com** in the Address text box and then press Enter.

11. Click the *advanced search* link next to the Search text box.

12. Key **endangered species + birds** in the Search text box.

step 14

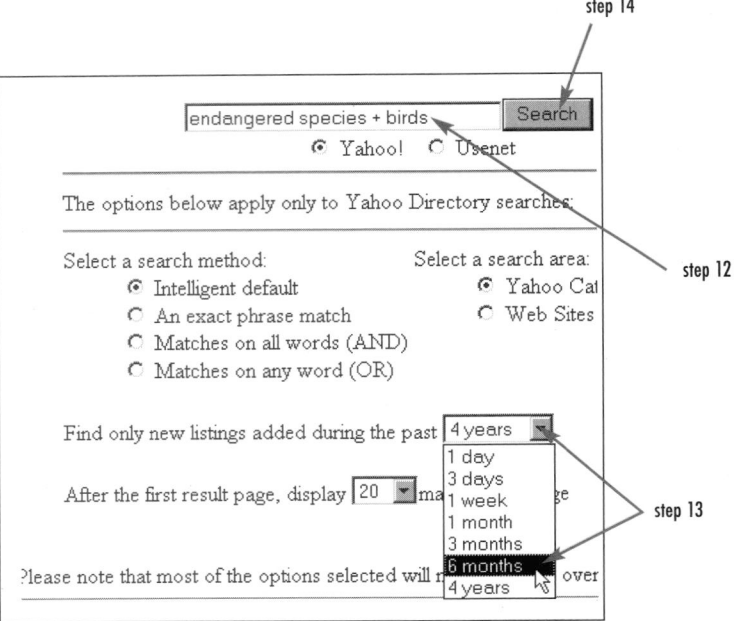

step 12

step 13

13. Click the down-pointing triangle next to Find only new listings added during the past [   ] and then click *6 months* in the drop-down list.

14. Click Search.

15. Scroll down the list of Web sites found.

16. Close Internet Explorer. If necessary, disconnect from your ISP.

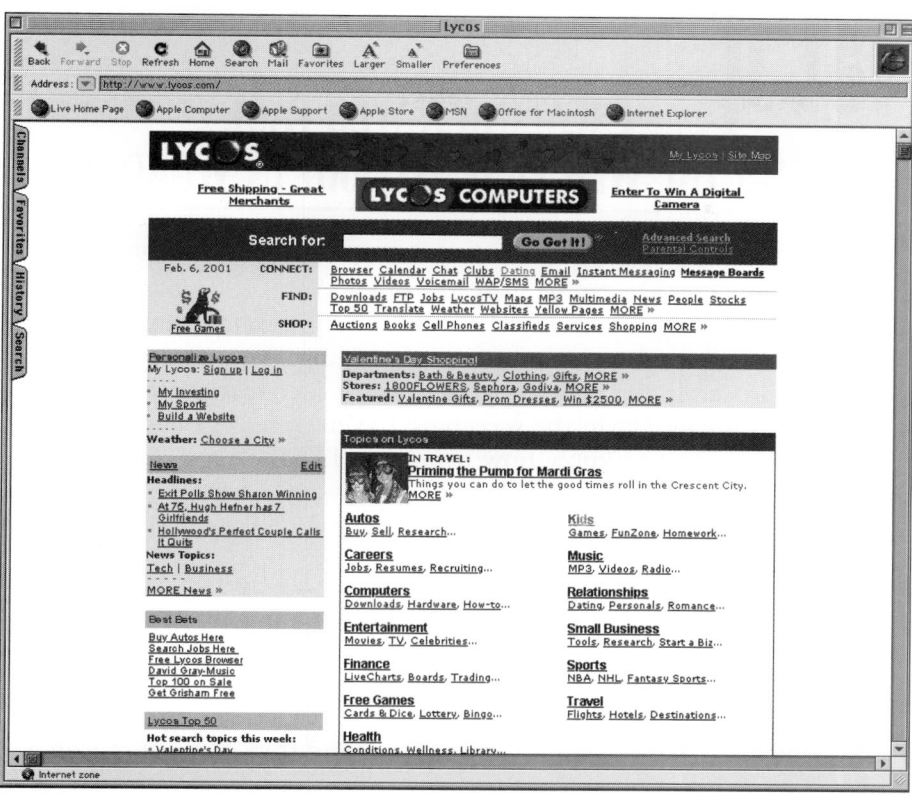

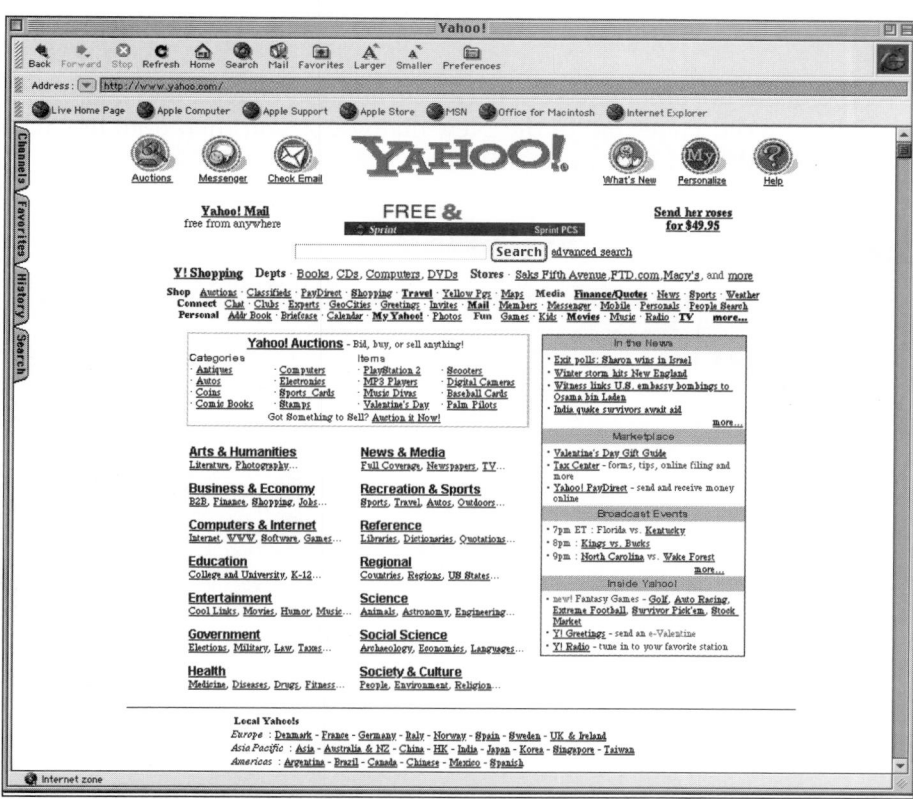

# Tutorial 4

## CREATING A WEB PAGE USING THE WEB PAGE WIZARD IN WORD 2000

Creating a document that can be viewed from a Web site involves storing it in hypertext markup language (HTML). Software programs such as Microsoft FrontPage are dedicated to creating and managing Web sites. Most software applications released in the past few years include a conversion feature that will save the current document in the screen as a Web page. Prior to these conversion utilities, users had to know how to insert HTML "tags" into documents. These tags were the codes that instructed browsers how to display the text. Microsoft Word 2000 includes Web Page wizards, Web Layout view, and several Web formatting options for creating Web pages.

In this topic, you will create a Web page in Microsoft Word using the Web Page wizard.

### Steps

1. Click the Start button, point to Programs, and then click Microsoft Word.

If necessary, check with your instructor if the steps to open Microsoft Word 2000 on the computer you are using are different than those in step 1.

2. At the blank document screen, click File and then click New.
3. Click the Web Pages tab in the New dialog box and then double-click the Web Page Wizard icon in the list box.

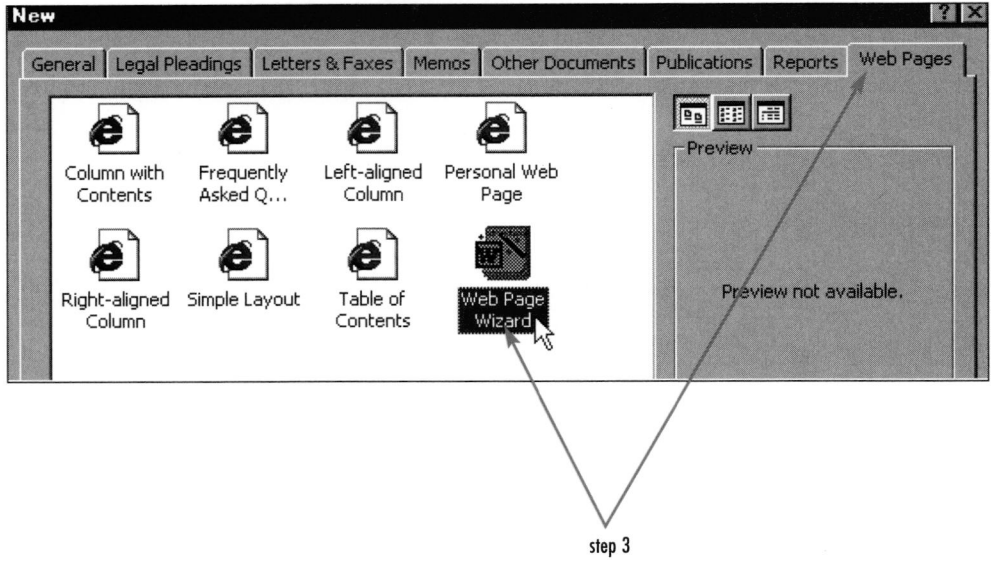

step 3

4. Click Next> at the first Web Page Wizard dialog box that describes what the wizard will do.

5. Key **Student Name** (substitute your first and last names for *Student Name*) in the Web site title text box, and then press Tab to move to the Web site location text box.

step 5 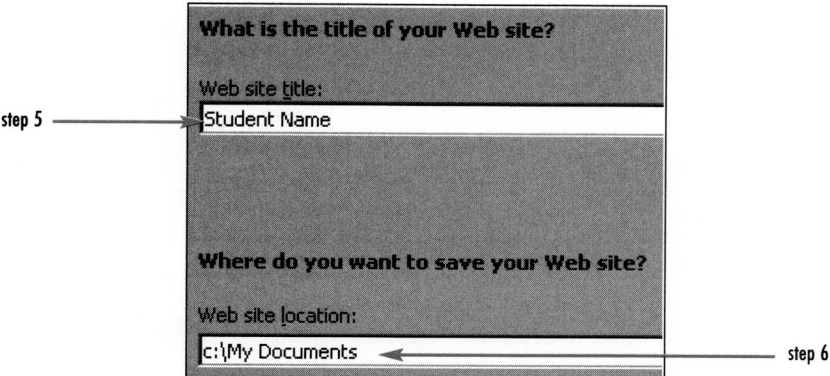 step 6

6. Key **C:\My Documents** or **A:\** in the Web site location text box and then click Next>. Check with your instructor to see where you should save the Web page if you are not sure.

7. Click Next> at the Navigation page in the Web Page Wizard.

When a Web site is created, the navigation links are usually displayed in a horizontal or vertical frame. Since your Web site is only one page, you do not need to be concerned with navigation links.

8. With *Blank Page 2* already selected in the Current pages in Web site list box in the Add Pages page of the Web Page Wizard, click Remove Page. Click *Personal Web Page*, click Remove Page, and then click Next>.

This will leave only one page, *Blank Page 1*, in the Current pages in Web site list box.

step 8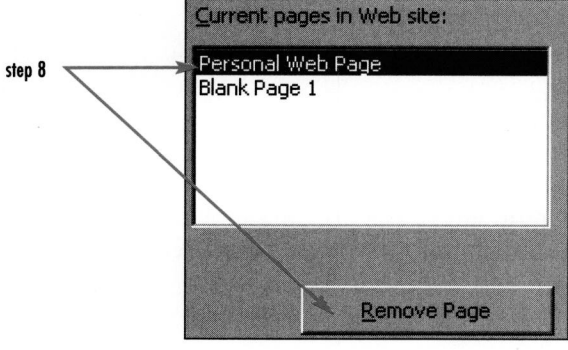

*Most ISPs include space on their Web server for clients to publish personal Web pages. If you want to publish to a Web server, check with your ISP for the correct address to key in the Web site location text box.*

9. Click Next> at the Organize Pages page in the Web Page Wizard.

If there were multiple pages that you were building for the Web site, you would use the Move Up and Move Down buttons with a Web page selected to move the page to the desired position in the Web site.

10. Click Browse Themes in the Visual Theme page of the Web Page Wizard.
11. Scroll up or down the Choose a Theme list box and then click *Clearday*. (If *Clearday* is unavailable, choose another theme.)

A preview of the colors, fonts, bullet style, and horizontal line style for the Clearday theme displays in the Sample of theme box. Microsoft Word includes several predefined themes that can be used to create Web pages with a professional appearance. Explore other themes in the dialog box by clicking the theme name and previewing it before continuing.

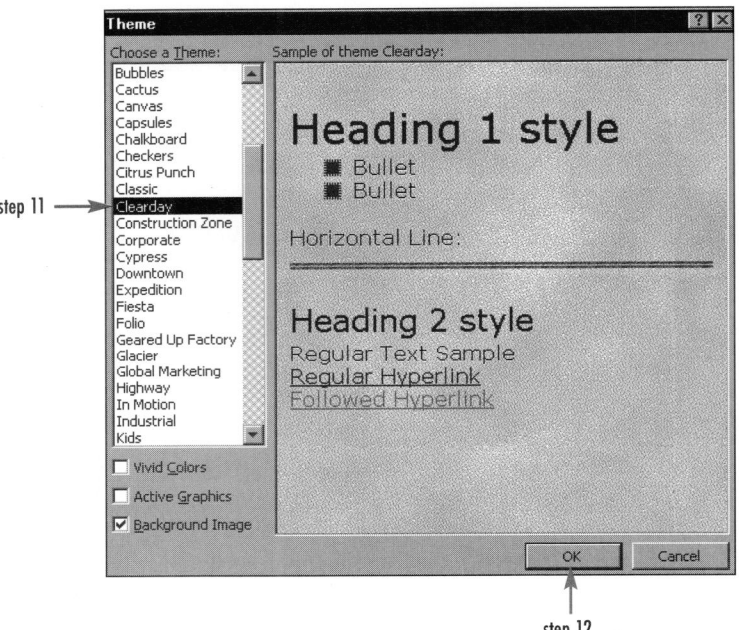

step 11

step 12

12. Click OK to accept the Clearday theme for the Web page, and then click Next> in the Visual Theme page of the Web Page Wizard.
13. Click Finish at the last page in the Web Page Wizard. Click No when the message appears that your Web site contains only one Web page and asks if you still want to include navigation features.

In a few seconds, a Web page will appear in the Clearday theme with the text *This Web Page is Blank Page 1* at the top left of the document. Microsoft Word is automatically switched to Web Layout view. At this point you would start keying the content for your Web page. Notice the title bar displays the document name *Blank Page 1.htm*.

14. Select the text *This Web Page is Blank Page 1* and then press Delete.
15. Key your first and last names and press Enter. Key your student identification number and press Enter. Key your e-mail address and then press Enter twice.
16. Experiment with formatting options such as styles, center, bold, font colors, or bullets by selecting text and then clicking buttons on the Formatting toolbar.

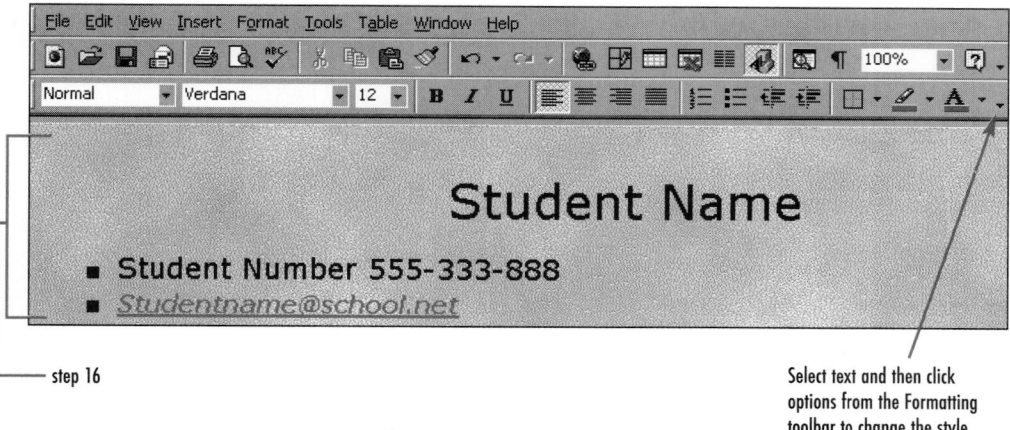

step 16

Select text and then click options from the Formatting toolbar to change the style, alignment, colors, or to add bullets.

Insert clip art in a Web page in the same manner you would a Word document. Click the Insert Clip Art button on the Drawing toolbar, or click Insert, point to Picture, and then click Clip Art.

17. Click the Save button on the toolbar, and then click File and Exit to close Microsoft Word.

# The Internet and the World Wide Web

## Going Online

# 1

## Objectives

➤ Describe the Internet and the Web and how they work.

➤ Identify elements of the World Wide Web (WWW) such as hypertext, hypermedia, URLs, and browsers.

➤ Identify the hardware and software necessary for Internet activity.

➤ Identify different types of Web connections.

➤ Describe the different kinds of services, content, and productivity aids on the Web.

# The Internet: A Daily Dose for Millions

The incorporation of the Internet into our daily routines in the last decade has been nothing short of phenomenal. The **Internet**, an infrastructure of networks connecting computers worldwide, was first established as a vehicle to share academic and government research, and has since become a commercial tool as well as an integral part of our daily lives. In more than one hundred and fifty countries, government agencies, private companies, universities, libraries, and individuals have access to the Internet. Today the Internet is so pervasive that virtually everyone has heard of it, millions use it daily, and most of those who do not, wish they did. More than one hundred million people regularly access the Internet to shop online, do research, find user groups, chat with other users, send e-mail, or just surf the Web. "Surfing the Web" is a popular term used to describe what people do when they log on to the Internet and view Web pages from around the world. Using the Internet is so popular that the number of users is increasing by about one million a month!

## The Internet and the Web: What Is the Difference?

The **World Wide Web**, also known as WWW or simply the Web, is by far the most widely used part of the Internet. Consequently, people use the terms Internet (the "Net") and Web interchangeably. There is, however, a difference. Strictly speaking, the Internet is a system of computers, storage devices, and connections, along with the software that allows people to use these connections (see Figure 1.1).

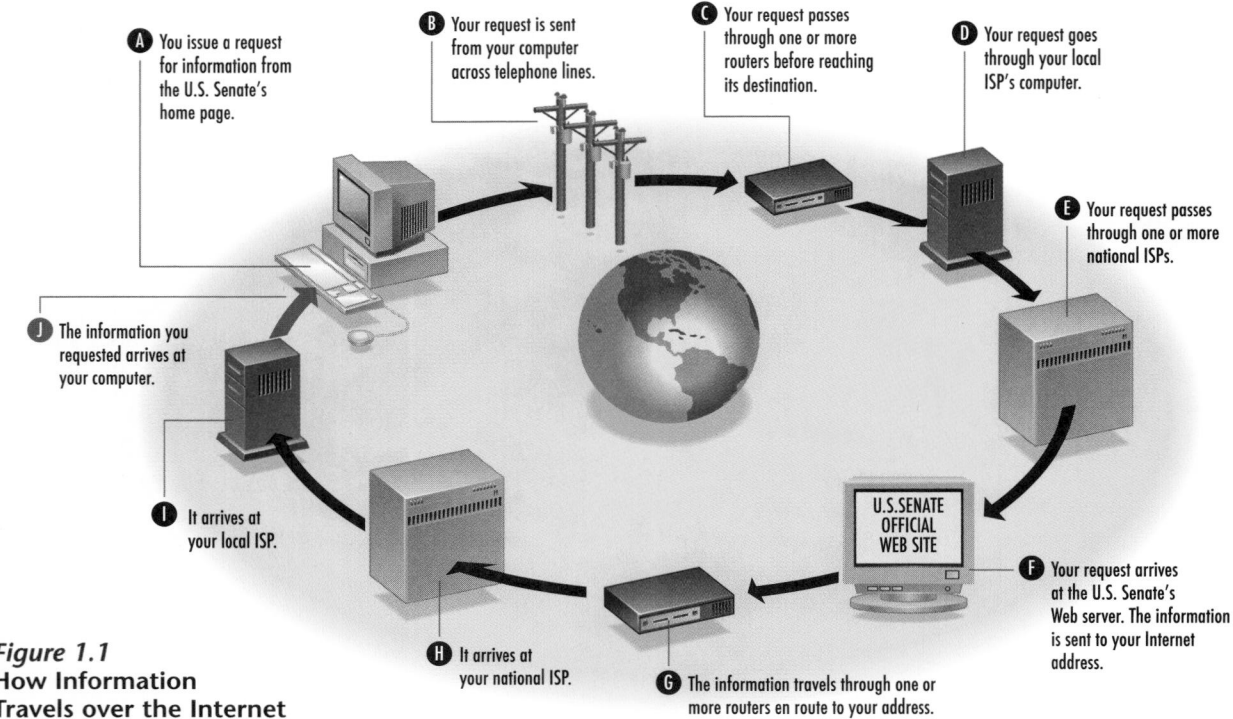

**Figure 1.1**
**How Information Travels over the Internet**

# Who Owns and Manages the Web?

The answer to "Who owns and manages the Web?" is "No one." The Web is in a state of true anarchy in the classical definition of the term—there is no supreme power controlling it. This is the way the Internet was designed, and this is the way the Web runs as well. There are policy-setting agencies and standards-setting agencies, but no real policing agencies. There are agencies that register domain names like ICANN (Internet Corporation for Assigned Names and Numbers), but there are no agencies that check Web content. There are controls to effectively filter Web sites from individual computers, but there is no agency to review and approve content placed on servers or to verify accuracy. There are Web Managers who manage sites, but they have no authority over the Web as an entire entity.

The Web exists in the blissful anarchy that its idealistic founders envisioned. The significance of this is that companies and individuals alike have the responsibility to protect themselves. The market will push the limits of what is and is not acceptable. Attempts are being made to exercise some control over the Internet but its very structure makes this difficult, if not impossible.

Because there is no authority policing the Web, it is up to us to decide how we use it and how we will behave. Therefore, a better answer to the question "Who owns and manages the Web?" might be "You do!"

The Web, in contrast, is the total collection of information available on that portion of the Internet that contains hyperlinked documents. The contents of the Web are organized by a collection of hyperlinks written in **Hypertext Markup Language (HTML)**—the primary coding system for Web pages—that point to various sites on the Internet where publicly available files are stored. By this means, documents on computers all over the world can be linked to one another.

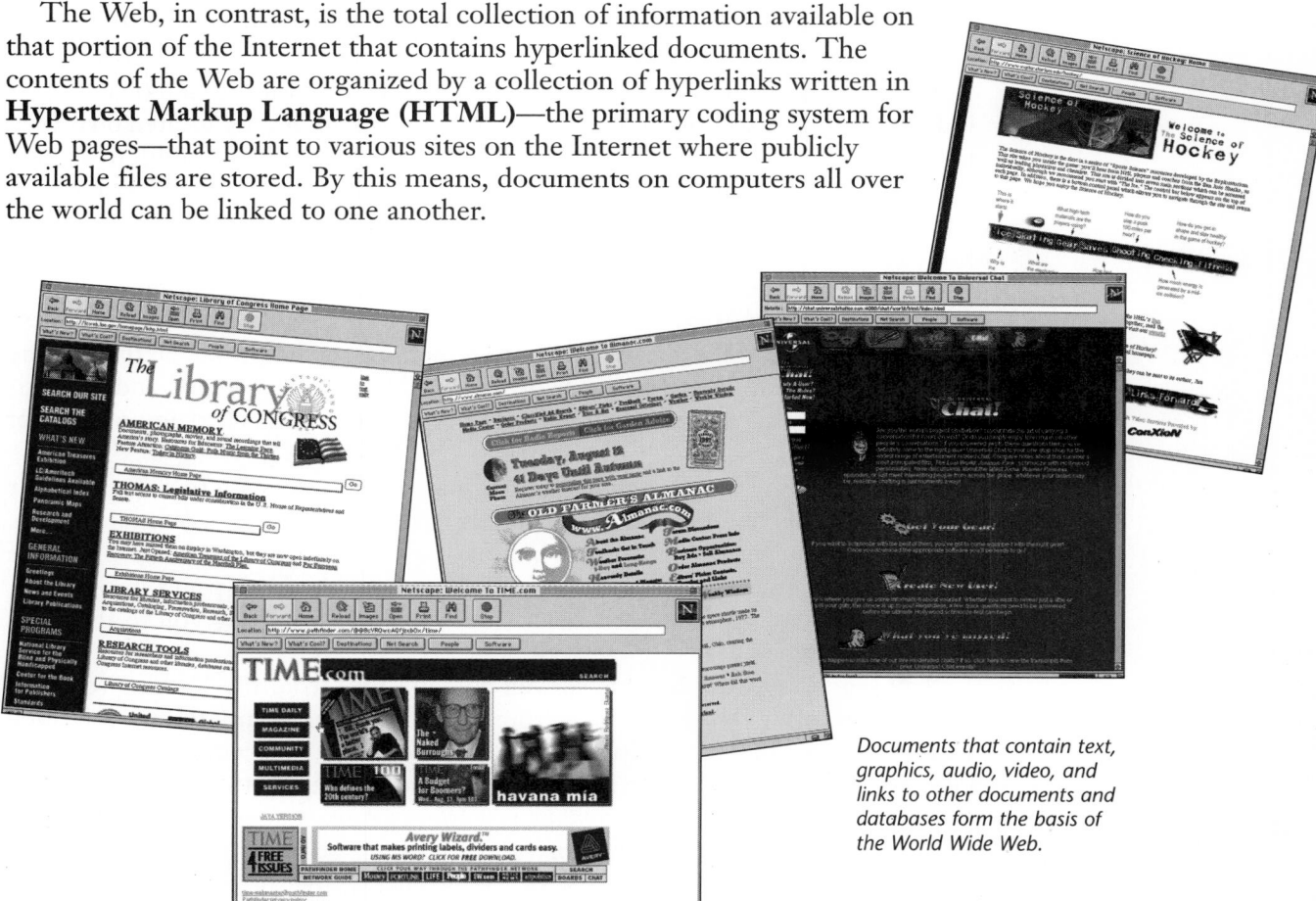

*Documents that contain text, graphics, audio, video, and links to other documents and databases form the basis of the World Wide Web.*

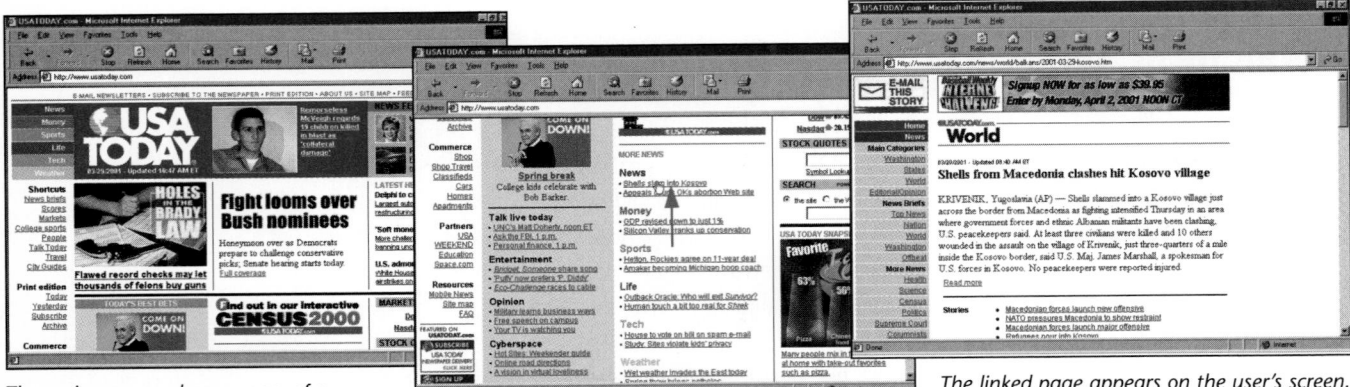

The main page, or home page, of a requested site appears on the user's monitor.

The user selects a link on the page.

The linked page appears on the user's screen.

Figure 1.2
How Hypertext Works

**Hyperlinks** are buttons, highlighted or underlined text (**hypertext**), or pictures that, when selected, send the user to a related, linked document. Hyperlinks can be made between text documents (hypertext), and objects (**hypermedia**). Hypertext is a **nonlinear** way of handling text. Words are linked, or associated with each other, not by their position in an article or by chronology or other order, but instead by a system of **pointers** (memory containers that store addresses, or locations, of other text or objects). These pointers are what allow you to move smoothly from one hot word, or hypertext selection, to another (see Figure 1.2).

Hypermedia carries the linking concept further by allowing one object to be linked to another, whether it is text or not. For instance, a song located on a Web page allows pointers from the first object, a sound file (.wav or .midi), to a video clip (.avi, .mov, or .mpg), and another pointer from the video scene to a graphic (.gif or .jpg) headline about the ballad. The effect is that all elements are linked together, or associated with each other, so that you can easily move back and forth from one element to another. It is not necessary to keep track of which medium you are in or how the objects are linked. Being able to bring all of these unrelated objects of different types together in one multimedia file on the Internet is the advantage of the World Wide Web. Unstructured and intrinsically different objects can all be related by hyperlinking them to any other spot on the Web.

If books had hypertext, the hypertext links would allow you to skip the index and the table of contents and jump directly to the subject you were interested in. That is what hypertext on the Web allows you to do; you can jump from one Web page to another without having to view all of the Web pages in between. Plus, unlike reading, hypertext has the advantage of returning you to the exact spot you started.

Any function of the Internet—even copying files from the Web to your PC (**downloading**) or copying files from your personal computer to the Web (**uploading**)—can be accomplished via the Web. The Internet is like a storage chest: the Web supplies its content; the browser is the key that allows access to those items in the chest. A **browser** is a Web **software** (computer program or coded stored instructions that drives computing sessions) program such as Microsoft Internet Explorer or Netscape Navigator that provides the graphical

## Understanding Web Page Elements

1. In Internet Explorer or Netscape Navigator, go to http://usatoday.com.
2. See how many of the following elements you can find on the home page: text, graphics, audio, movies, or animation.
3. Comment upon the visual appeal of the home page. What elements did you like? Why?
4. Were there elements that you disliked? Why? How would you redesign the page?

user interface (GUI) for the Web portion of the Internet. Instead of viewing a text-only screen, a browser allows you to view images (graphics) as well.

In addition to handling Web documents, the Internet also provides the physical basis for a number of other computer communications services, allowing people to send e-mail, access archives of files, and participate in discussion groups.

Today, the single most popular reason for purchasing a personal computer is to "go online" with the Internet. Ninety-five percent of new computer sales include hardware and software to connect to the Web. The closest parallel to a technology permeating a culture in such a way was the telephone a century ago. The Internet is such a powerful and pervasive communication tool that some governments, such as the People's Republic of China, have made attempts to control access.

# Personal Privacy Rights and Abuses

The Internet has been referred to as the "SnooperNet" because it makes it so easy to find personal information about individuals. It starts with **Internet service providers (ISPs)**—providers of access to the Web or the Internet in general—who examine users' hard drives to see what programs they are using. ISPs record how often you access a certain database, read a magazine online, order merchandise, engage in a chat session, or write an e-mail message. Even though 86 percent of Web users are concerned about the privacy of their personal information and 94 percent want privacy violators to be punished, the collection of personal information continues.

It is not just home PCs that are vulnerable to this kind of intrusion. Now that Web access is standard with office desktops, software applications that monitor an employee's Web activity have been developed. Employers take the position that the computers, the network, and the software are owned by the company. Employees are being paid for their time; therefore, they have the right to track the time employees spend on the Web and where they navigate. Court decisions have established that companies may monitor the e-mail of an employee as long as the company discloses the potential monitoring to the employees. Employee lawsuits in the last decade confirmed the right of employers to invade the privacy of employees by reading their e-mail correspondence. When a group of employees was polled, at least 10 percent knew someone who lost a job because of e-mail surveillance or Web activity on company time. Monitoring in the workplace is a reality and is unavoidable, even if it may be an invasion of privacy. Just as phone communications can be monitored by an employer, so can your Web activity.

Legislation to protect the security and privacy of online activity preceded the development of the Web in 1990. Online crime and privacy concerns existed in 1970 within the Internet community; there were just many fewer users then. And, of course, the business-to-consumer e-commerce did not exist then. Nevertheless, the legislation to protect online privacy and security dates from the mid-1970s and may not be adequate to protect you today.

The explosive growth of the Internet has caused concern that demand will outstrip the capacity of the infrastructure—namely, the **networks** (the system of linked computers that make up the Internet) and **servers** (the computers that host the information on the Internet). As a result, a new Internet2 standard is being designed and will be implemented within the decade. You can learn more about the Internet2 in the "History of the Internet" section of this chapter.

## Life on the Web

With its unlimited potential, the Web's growth has been rapid. After completing this course, you will find your own applications for using the Web. You will be Internet-savvy and Web-accomplished, joining the ranks of those who have incorporated the Internet into their everyday existence. There are so many ways of using the Web that it will take you years to explore all of the options. Some common uses for the Web are detailed in this section.

**E-mail**   E-mail is probably the most frequently used feature of the Internet. **E-mail** is electronic mail—the transmission of text messages asynchronously (time-delayed) between individuals. You can send messages to anyone in the world who has an Internet address virtually free, paying only the monthly service charge to your Internet service provider. Within minutes your message reaches its destination. You can also attach files and send images with your e-mail. In many cases it is a great advantage over playing "telephone tag" and is less costly than using long-distance telephone service. Today, an e-mail address on a business card is just as vital as a telephone number.

**Chat Sessions**   **Chat Sessions** allow people to key their message in the screen in real (synchronous) time and read what others have to say, again in real time. ISPs have dedicated chat sessions, with many different chat rooms, each featuring a different topic. Unlike e-mail, which is delayed, chat is immediate. It is group-oriented; the ideal number is 5 or 6, but chat rooms have been known to have 20 individuals online at the same time. America Online (AOL) has a feature called Instant Messenger that allows you to communicate with one member or a group of the ISP who are online at the same time. Other systems call this "talk" or "active e-mail."

## The Internet in China: Will It Crack the Great Wall?

The People's Republic of China has always counted on its ability to control information as a means of controlling its people. Yet the Chinese government's ability to censor information is rapidly being challenged by the exploding access to the Internet. The number of Chinese using the Internet quadrupled from 2.1 million in 1998 to almost 9 million one year later. With one billion users and counting, a virtual stampede toward Internet use is well under way.

How is the Chinese government trying to stem the free flow of information via the Web? It is doing it by imposing rigid regulations and blocking unauthorized sites. Chinese Internet sites are allowed to use only government-controlled news sources. What's more, Internet sites, chat rooms, e-mail messages, and newsgroups are forbidden from discussing anything that is not "government approved." The government has even gone so far as to block the Web sites of may top international news organizations, such as the BBC and the *New York Times*.

Nonetheless, the task of controlling the over 2,400 Internet sites that are now operating in China has become an almost insurmountable hurdle for the government. It simply can't keep up with blocking smaller news sites and other sources of information. As a result, in the same way that television played a role in bringing down the Berlin Wall, the technology of the Internet may start chipping away at the ability of the Great Wall to insulate China from the influence of the outside world.

**Source:** "Chinese Internet use explodes," *Windows User News*, August 2000.

**Usenets and LISTSERVs**   Both Usenets and LISTSERVs allow you to communicate with people on specific topics in which you have an interest. **Usenet** is a type of asynchronous group communication allowing users to read and post comments on specific topics on an electronic "bulletin board," accessed through a feature of your browser called a newsreader. With Usenets you can also join **forums** for specific subjects. Access to information is controlled within the forum. You must "log in" (give your login name and password) to read the information; it is not delivered individually to your e-mail box. Forums are organized around **threads**, or specific topics of discussion. They are treelike in structure, branching out in many directions from the original topic. In outline format, participants respond to each other's comments. Forums are not in real time, but may be reviewed or added to at any time. Table 1.1 provides a list of Usenet newsgroup categories.

# How the Web Changes Politics

Web-based marketing is a new force in political campaigns. Web-savvy campaign managers are marshalling the power of the Web to broadcast messages and to find potential donors and volunteers.

John McCain was one of the first politicians to make use of an interactive Web campaign on a national basis. Early in the campaign, he and his staff recognized the power of the Internet to cut costs and increase communication. McCain contracted with VirtualSprockets, a software company that provided the ability to create locally managed Web pages and e-mail lists from within the master Web site. In this way, the campaign was localized, delegating control to neighborhood levels.

When McCain needed signatures to get on the ballot, his staff created a form that could be downloaded from the Internet. They were able to obtain 17,000 electronic signatures with very little trouble. When news broke, information was immediately posted on the Web site.

Using e-mail, the McCain campaign was able to enlist e-volunteers. The volunteers would download lists of potential voters in their area and then place phone calls from their homes. This eliminated the need for costly centralized phone centers. In addition, campaign literature was designed to be downloaded from the Web. As the volunteers talked to voters on the phone,

www.mccain2000.com

they could e-mail a promotional piece, or they could print the piece and have it in the mail the next day. This saved the campaign thousands of dollars in printing and shipping costs.

The McCain campaign solicited donations through the Web site as well. Potential donors could make contributions using Visa or MasterCard. The convenience of using electronic cash brought in new funds: 40 percent of the donors were contributing for the first time to a political campaign. The campaign's creative use of the Web set the stage for future campaigns.

**Source:** *Net vs. Norman, Forbes ASAP, May 29, 2000.*

*Table 1.1* **Some Usenet Newsgroup Categories**

| Newsgroup Section | Designator Code | Subject Matter |
|---|---|---|
| alternative | .alt | general special interest; can be set up by anyone without making a special application to the Usenet oversight committee |
| business | .biz | business; may require payment of subscription charges |
| computer | .comp | computer science, programming, hardware, and software |
| miscellaneous | .misc | grab bag of topics |
| news | .news | Internet; Usenet issues and culture |
| recreation | .rec | holidays, television, sports, arts |
| science | .sci | scientific topics other than computers |
| social | .soc | relationships, politics, religion |
| talk | .talk | chat on wide-ranging topics |

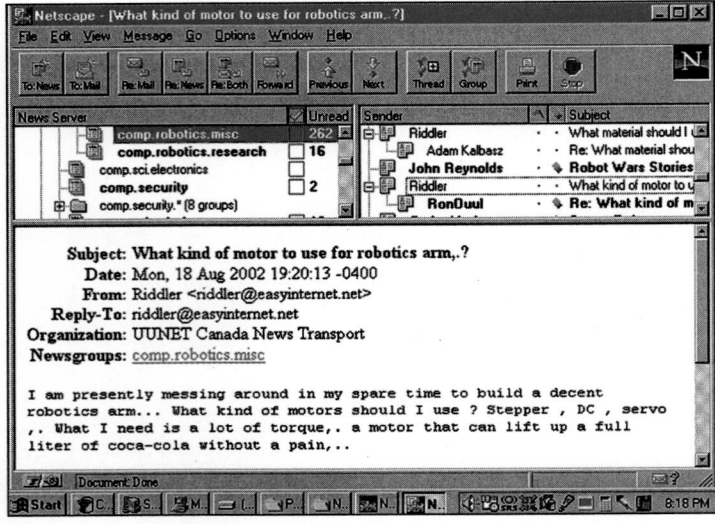

Usenets allow people to communicate by reading and posting comments on a bulletin board.

**LISTSERVs** differ from Usenets in that they deliver mail messages to your e-mail inbox, rather than through a newsreader—in a mass distribution to all of the members of a LISTSERV group. List subscribers periodically receive e-mail messages from other members pertaining to the list topic. For both Usenets and LISTSERVs there are literally thousands of different discussion topics (organized as forums or lists) available, and if you cannot find one to your liking you can create your own. LISTSERVs were a part of the Internet long before the Web was created, and continue to be one of its most popular features.

 **Using Forums**

1. Log on to the Internet forums site at http://forums.internet.com.
2. Find the search engine at the bottom of the page. In the text box, key **usenet**.
3. What did you find?
4. Try another computer-related topic that you are interested in. The forums are arranged around topics, and you can find people with similar interests. You may find answers to questions you have by looking at previous discussions.

**Greeting Cards**   You can send electronic greetings to someone by using greeting card services. The cards are customized from templates. You can make them as individual as you want, and even add music and animations. Recipients receive an e-mail that a greeting card is awaiting them, and they log on to a Web site to retrieve it. Blue Mountain and American Greeting Cards are the two most popular sites. Some sites offer free cards; others ask for payment for creating such cards or have other items for sale. Many people send electronic greeting cards for birthdays or other events. These cards are exceedingly popular.

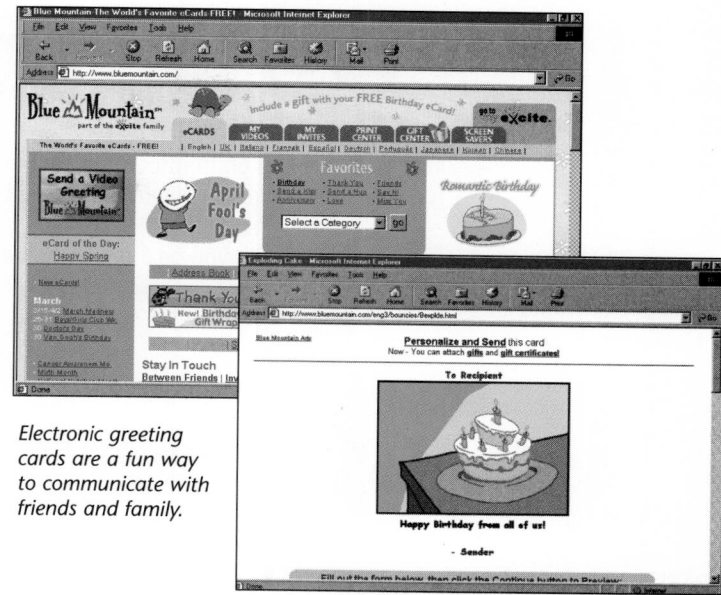

*Electronic greeting cards are a fun way to communicate with friends and family.*

## Sending a Greeting Card

1. Go to http://www.bluemountain.com.
2. Select the category **Coffee Break,** and then click Go.
3. Click on a card to select it. Follow the prompts to personalize the card.
4. Click to Preview, and then send the card.

**Blue Mountain**
http://www.bluemountain.com
**Amazon** http://cards.amazon.com
**American Greetings**
http://www.americangreetings.com

**Games**   Although computer games existed before the Web was created, they have multiplied since the Web brought graphical Internet computing to everyone. There are games that you play solo, but most involve a group, such as a chat or special interest forum group. Yahoo! and Excite have extensive categories of single- and multiple-user games. Gaming is one of the hottest areas of programming today. There are board games, card games, casino games, arcade games, and sports games. There are games for all ages, abilities, and interests. There are even groups who meet regularly on the Web to play, just as they might meet physically for weekly poker or bridge. Table 1.2 shows some of the categories of games on Yahoo.com and Excite.com.

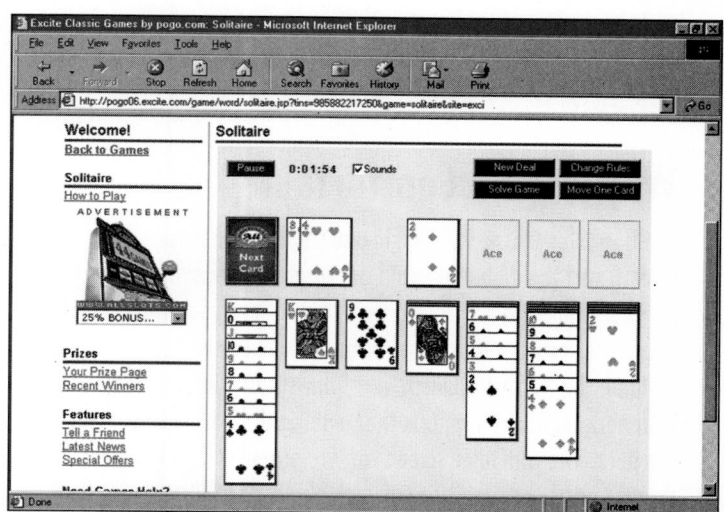

*Internet games are enjoyed by people of all ages and can be played individually or as a group.*

## Playing a Game

1. Log on to http://boulter.com/ttt.
2. Follow the instructions on the Tic-Tac-Toe page to set up your game, then click Let's Play!
3. Could you beat the computer?

 **Table 1.2** Web Games

| Excite.com | Yahoo.com |
|---|---|
| **word games** crosswords, Jumble, Sports Crossword, Word Search | **single player** Solitaire, Maze, Word games of Anagram, Crossword, Cryptogram, Word Search |
| **card games** Cribbage, Bridge, Euchre, Hearts, Spades | **card games** Blackjack, Bridge, Canasta, Cribbage, Euchre, Gin, Go Fish, Hearts, Pinochle, Sheepshead, Spades |
| **board games** Backgammon, Chess, Checkers | **board games** Backgammon, Checkers, Chess, Go, Reversi |
| **trivia Games** Pogini, 5 Alarm Trivia!, Triviatron, Pocket quiz | **tile games** Dominoes, MahJong |
| **arcade games** Poppit, Animal Ark, Doomsday, Tank Hunter, Tube Runner, Void, Overflow | **other games** Bingo, Yahoo! Towers, Word Racer |
| **casino games** Roulette, Video Poker, Keno, Bingo | **puzzles** Tic-Tac-Toe, Tile games, Trivia |

http://www.station.sony.com/jeopardy
http://zone.msn.com/cribbage/
http://zone.msn.com/bridge/

## Why Not Be Comfortable?

The Netsurfer Classic is an all-in-one solution for those who wish to surf the Web and avoid the carpal tunnel syndrome, stiff neck, and other assorted pains that often result from long hours spent seated in front of a computer. Designed in Finland, the Netsurfer Classic is a futuristic-looking armchair with neck and back supports that eliminate the need to tense the neck. The computer screen can be located at eye level, further reducing the possibility of neck strain. This ultimate in chairs is not for everyone, however; it is priced at $3,500!

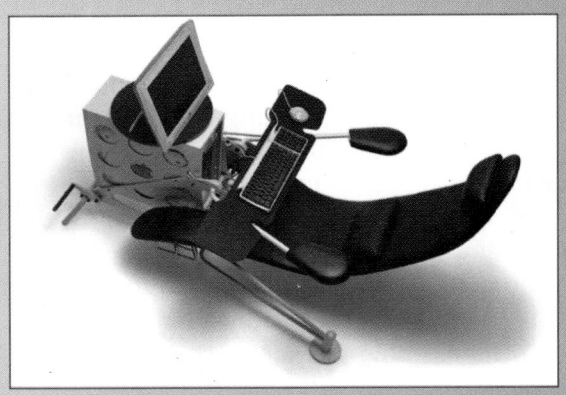

*Courtesy of SNOWCRASH, www.snowcrash.se*
*Photo by Urban Hedlund*

**Searching and Research** The Web has become one of the greatest research tools ever developed. A tremendous amount of information (not necessarily all correct) is available on the Web. You can look up your topic in a search on your ISP's **home page** (opening page of a Web site) or on another site and follow the leads. Searching is done by **keywords**, which form the basis of Web searches, and are found in the Web site's title and interior copy. Some of the more popular **search engines** (Internet software programs that look through databases on the Internet) are Yahoo!, HotBot, Google, Go, Lycos, and Northern Light.

The Internet is also a rich reference source. Students of all ages can use online dictionaries, reference libraries, and encyclopedias to find information. Just about everything you might

*With the amount of Web sites multiplying every day, the Web is a valuable source of information.*

want to look up in a thesaurus or a dictionary can now be found online. Most online libraries are associated with a particular institution or organization, and many major university libraries have an online reference or checkout option. Here is a list of just a few Web sites that will provide helpful reference information for you.

- **Merriam-Webster Dictionary Online** http://www.m-w.com
- **American Heritage Dictionary Online** http://www.bartleby.com/61/
- **Online Dictionary** http://www.dictionary.com/
- **Ruth H. Hooker Research Library** http://infoweb2.nrl.navy.mil/index.cfm
- **Encyclopedia Britannica** http://www.britannica.com/
- **Internet Reference Desk** http://www.refdesk.com/
- **Library of Congress home page** http://www.loc.gov/

**Search Engines**
**Yahoo!** http://www.yahoo.com
**Google** http://google.com
**Go** http://www.go.com
**Lycos** http://lycos.com
**Northern Light**
http://northernlight.com

## Searching

1. Go to http://www.google.com.
2. Key **roof shingles** and click the Google Search button.
3. If you were going to purchase a new roof for your house, which of these sites would be the most helpful?
4. How many of the sites in the first list do not appear to be appropriate for your search?
5. Do you find better links if you key **roof repair**?

## Using Online Dictionaries

1. Go to http://www.m-w.com.
2. In the dictionary window, key **lanky** and click Look it up.
3. In the thesaurus window, key **lanky** and click Look it up.
4. Compare the results of your two searches.
5. When would using an online dictionary or online thesaurus be helpful?

**News**   The Internet is a tremendous vehicle for the delivery of news. News-papers, magazines, television stations, and news organizations have all placed content online. On the Web you can read items "hot off the press," before they even reach the print media. You can customize your browser so that news head-lines appear on your screen every time you log on to the Web.

## Checking Today's News

1. Get a copy of your local newspaper and then visit that paper's Web site.
2. Compare how the newspaper is presented online versus in print.
3. How are headlines treated in the two formats?
4. Is the depth of coverage different in the two formats?
5. What is the cost comparison?
6. Which would you rather read, and why?

*Many newspapers and magazines, such as* The New York Times, *can be accessed via the Internet.*

*Sites such as Amazon.com provide an easy and convenient alternative to retail shopping.*

## Shopping at Auctions

1  Log on to www.ebay.com.
2  Look for something you like.
3  Did you find it?
4  Would you use eBay to buy or sell something?

**Amazon** http://www.amazon.com
**eBay** http://www.ebay.com

**E-commerce**   E-commerce is the fastest growing area of the Internet. Ordering merchandise on the Web is convenient; there is no tax added (at least as of this writing), and delivery charges are relatively low. One of the most popular e-commerce sites is Amazon.com, which began by selling books online and has now expanded its line to include a number of other products.

An Internet auction site called eBay has also become a popular place for people wanting to sell and buy items on the Internet. The eBay site is the Internet's answer to garage sales and flea markets. However, there are only limited safeguards in place to prevent bad trades, such as encouraging the use of an escrow service for higher value items. An escrow service allows for safer transactions by holding items or money until both parties are satisfied with the deal.

**Finance**   Today, many financial transactions are being done online—buying stocks, applying for a loan, making payments, paying bills, and even filing income taxes. Banks offer online bill payment and balance updates; the "virtual teller" is less expensive, and customers are happier with 24-hour banking. Finding and applying for credit and loan applications is easier, insurance quotes take minutes, and investment chat sessions are helpful for those with money to spend. If you have money to invest, you can use any one of dozens of online brokerage firms. Once you have registered with these firms and deposited money with them, you can begin your investment strategy and purchase financial instruments such as stocks and bonds with the click of a mouse.

In addition to conducting transactions, you can use the Web to find financial information. Only about 15 percent of Web users regularly access the Internet as a source of financial information. Of the individuals who access the Web for financial information, 41 percent do so to obtain information about ways to invest and save offline.

**Charles Schwab**
http://www.schwab.com
**E*TRADE** http://www.etrade.com
**Morgan Stanley Dean Witter**
http://www.msdw.com

# Do Your Taxes on the Web!

The latest figures show that over 1.5 million U.S. citizens file their federal income taxes online. The Internal Revenue Service (IRS) hopes to have two-thirds of the population filing federal income tax returns on the Internet by 2007. This might seem ambitious, given that only slightly more than half of American homes now have a personal computer. However, when you remember that there are 44 million e-commerce shoppers already, and that 95 percent of the new computer buyers purchase Internet access when they obtain their computers, this does not seem an unreasonable goal.

In 1989, legislation was passed that allowed taxes to be filed electronically. Now the IRS (and most state and city government sites) offers most of its forms and instructions online. You can view and print forms directly from the site, provided you have the Adobe Acrobat Reader, or order them just as you would in the mail. With the assistance of a third-party preparer, for a nominal fee you can figure and file your taxes right from the Web.

## Finding Financial Information

1. Go to the Bloomberg home page, http://www.Bloomberg.com.
2. Find the currency exchange rates for Asian countries.
3. What is the name of the currency in Thailand? in Hong Kong?
4. How many Hong Kong dollars are there to an American dollar?
5. Return to the Bloomberg home page.
6. Click the *Market Snapshot* link.
7. Check the Dow Jones performance for today. Is the market up or down from the prior trading day? By how many points?

**RealPlayer** http://www.realplayer.com
**Windows Media Player**
http://www.microsoft.com

**Virtual Broadcasting** It is possible to listen to the radio (virtual broadcasting) or view video over the Internet, provided your computer is equipped with the right software and speakers. The broadcasts originate on the Internet or are regular radio or TV stations that broadcast over the Internet using streaming audio and video. This gives you access to thousands of radio and video broadcast stations around the world. With this feature you can listen to radio broadcasts while you continue surfing. Two of the most popular software programs allowing you to do this are RealPlayer and Windows Media Player. Both programs can be downloaded for free over the Internet, although advanced versions are available for a purchase or subscription fee.

**Internet Telephony**    Traditionally, telephone calls have been carried over public switched telephone networks. It is now possible to route telephone calls over the Internet, avoiding any long-distance charges. This service is not yet perfected, and there are sometimes problems with transmission quality. To take advantage of this feature you must download and install an Internet telephony program. There are a number of programs available. Like Internet radio programs, many are available for free, with versions offering advanced features available at a price.

*Using an Internet telephony program, local and international calls can be placed right from a computer.*

**Distance Learning**    The Internet was developed as a vehicle to share academic research. That dedication to learning has continued and expanded with a proliferation of educational opportunities on the Web. These opportunities come in many varieties. There are the traditional degree-granting academic institutions represented on the Web. These sites have domain names that end with *.edu* for "education." Currently, more than 90 percent of American colleges offer online courses, and many offer complete degrees. Some fully accredited colleges and universities offer masters and doctorate degrees on the Web, and several hundred colleges and universities offer undergraduate courses online each academic year. It is estimated that there will be 2.2 million students taking at least one college course over the Internet by 2002.

There is an equally impressive industry arena that uses intranets and the Web for in-house Web-based training (WBT). An **intranet** is a network belonging to an organization, usually a corporation, accessible only by the organization's members, employees, or others with authorization.

There are also Web companies whose only business is Web education, such as JonesKnowledge e-education, WebCT, Blackboard, and E-college. There are e-learning portals that host others' Web courses, such as Click2Learn, and there are virtual universities, which are conglomerates of other institutions' courses. And of course, there are many independent information sites, some of them nonprofit and public service sites with *.org* domain names—for "organizational." There are various "edutainment" sites, which combine entertainment and learning—especially children's learning.

**Dialpad** http://www.dialpad.com
**Phonefree** http://www.phonefree.com
**Mediaring** http://www.mediaring.com
**Net2phone** http://www.net2phone.com

**US Distance Learning Association**
http://www.usdla.org/
**Peterson's searchable database**
http://www.petersons.com/dlearn
**Distance Learning on the net**
http://www.hoyle.com/distance.htm
**Yahoo distance learning links**
http://dir.yahoo.com/Education/
Distance_Learning/Colleges_and_
Universities/
http://dir.yahoo.com/Education/
Distance_Learning/Colleges_and_
Universities/Community_Colleges/
**The Distance Learning Resource
Network** http://www.dlrn.org

Some public school systems offer online opportunities to secure a GED (General Educational Development) or high school degree. Industry is also putting training courses on their intranets for their employees—in many cases replacing more expensive modes of training. WBT is replacing computer-based training (CBT) as the new standard.

## History of the Internet

Technically, the Internet began in 1957 when the launch of the *Sputnik* satellite by the Soviet Union set off alarms in Western governments. In 1958, fearing that the United States was losing its scientific superiority to the Soviets, President Dwight D. Eisenhower created the Advanced Research Projects Agency (ARPA) to fund and coordinate defense-related scientific research. In 1969, supercomputers at four sites—the University of California at Los Angeles (UCLA), the Stanford Research Institute, the University of California at Santa Barbara, and the University of Utah in Salt Lake City—were linked by telephone connections, and the ARPANET was born. The **ARPANET** was an experimental, wide-area computer network initiated by the U.S. government in the early 1960s. Its purpose was to allow government contractors to share expensive, scarce computing resources; it spanned the United States and was the precursor to the Internet.

The ARPANET was a product of the Cold War, and its structure reflected Cold War strategies. In particular, designers of the ARPANET were concerned that it be able to continue to function after a nuclear attack. Therefore, they gave the network a noncentralized, Web-like design to ensure that if one or several network computers or connections were destroyed, the remaining computers on the Net would still be able to communicate. They linked every computer to every other computer in the system in a modified peer-to-peer network (see Figure 1.3). The goal of ARPANET was to allow government contractors to share expensive, scarce computing resources. Those who had access to ARPANET could communicate with others involved in similar research.

A steadily increasing, eclectic mix of nonmilitary users began to transform the Net into an international communications vehicle for the academic world. The Net proved to be such a good means of linking government and academic institutions that it came to be under the arm of the National Science Foundation (NSF). In 1986, the NSF created NSFnet to connect scientific researchers in universities. NSFnet provided a high-speed communications backbone for the emerging Internet, and many more universities connected to the system. Table 1.3 shows a time line of key events in the history of the Internet.

PEER-TO-PEER NETWORK

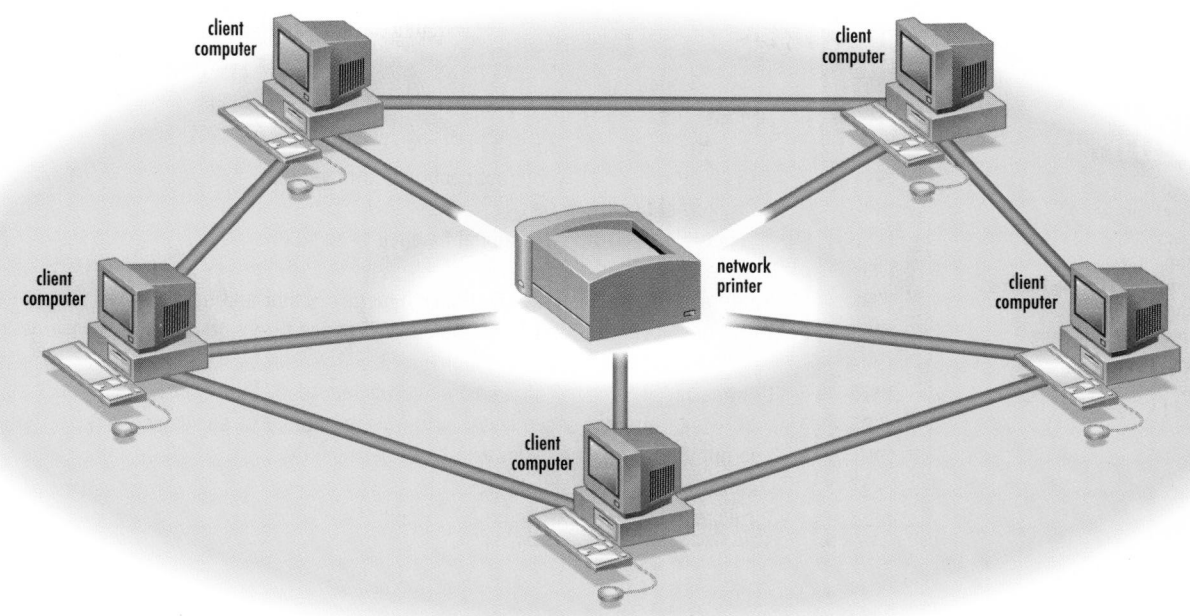

CLIENT-SERVER NETWORK

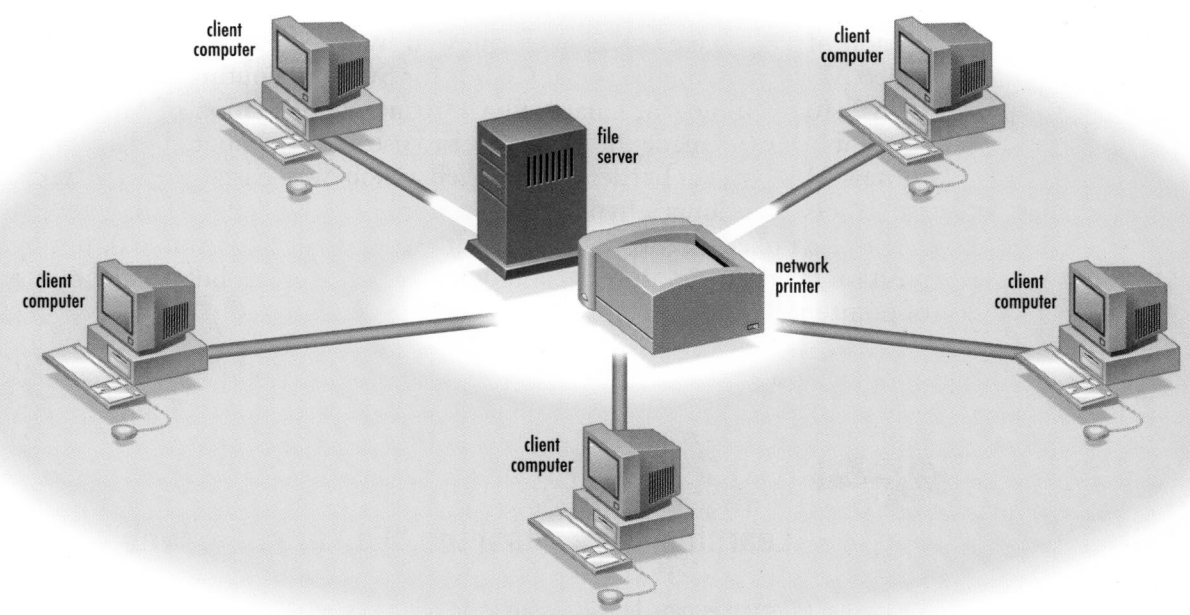

*Figure 1.3* **Peer-to-Peer and Client-Server Network Configurations**
*In a peer-to-peer network, the sites are connected individually to one another. In a client-server network, each site, known as a client, is connected to a single, central server, which makes it more vulnerable than a peer-to-peer network because an attack on the central server or on the main communications line may disable the entire network.*

**Table 1.3** Forty Years in the Life of the Internet

| | |
|---|---|
| **1957** | *Sputnik* launched |
| **1958** | ARPA founded |
| **1969** | ARPANET created |
| **1974** | Design of the Internet published |
| **1977** | The first three-network interconnection demonstrated |
| **1983** | The Internet begins |
| **1986** | NSFnet is created by the National Science Foundation |
| **1989** | Berners-Lee proposes Web |
| **1991** | Berners-Lee creates a point-and-click hypertext editor and the first Web server |
| **1993** | Only about 100 companies distributed Web pages throughout the Internet |
| **1994** | World Wide Web Consortium founded |
| **1994** | Control ceded to telecommunication companies |
| **1995** | Web-based/Internet-based instruction (synchronous and asynchronous) |
| **1997** | The number of Internet users climbs to between 60 and 80 million |
| **1997** | *.Com* becomes a household word |
| **1998** | Virtual campuses and learning communities proliferate |

**Visual maps of cyberspace**
http://www.geog.ucl.ac.uk/casa/martin/
atlas/atlas.html
**General information on the Internet and the Web**
http://www.historycentral.com
http://efl.org
http://www.arachnid.co.uk/award/
computer.html

The real breakthrough in exponential growth of the Internet came after the invention of the World Wide Web (WWW), also referred to as the W³, or simply "the Web." In 1989, Tim Berners-Lee proposed the creation of the Web.

Shortly thereafter, Berners-Lee wrote a graphical interface program for finding documents on the Web, the first Web browser. The browser allows the navigation of Web pages. This was followed by the creation of another browser, called Mosaic, by the National Center for Supercomputing Applications at the University of Illinois at Champaign-Urbana. The creation of Mosaic and subsequent browsers made the Web easier to use and contributed to a rapid growth in new Web users. Berners-Lee's Web vision was based on hypertext documents. As mentioned, hypertext is a nonlinear way of handling text so that words are linked and/or associated with each other (hyperlinked), not by their position in an article or by chronological or other order, but instead by a system of pointers.

**More about Tim Berners-Lee**
http://www.w3.org/People/Berners-Lee

## Learning More about the "Father of the Web"

1. Use a search engine to find information on the founder of the Web, Tim Berners-Lee.
2. Can you find a book written about Tim Berners-Lee?
3. Are there any publications written by Tim Berners-Lee?
4. In what year did he write the first Web browser-editor and server?
5. What is he doing now?

## Tim Berners-Lee and the Invention of the World Wide Web

Tim Berners-Lee, the "father of the World Wide Web," graduated from Queen's College, Oxford, in 1976. While working as an independent consultant for the *Centre Européen pour la Recherche Nucléaire* (**CERN**), he conceived of a program for storing information based on the associations between ideas. This program, which Berners-Lee called Enquire, later became the basis for the World Wide Web. In 1984, Berners-Lee began a fellowship at CERN, where he worked on computer systems for scientific data acquisition. In 1989, while a fellow at CERN, he proposed a global hypertext system, based on his Enquire program, to be known as the World Wide Web. This system would allow computer users around the world to exchange information using linked hypertext documents. Berners-Lee introduced a number of the key features of the Web today, including URLs, HTTP, and HTML.

- **Uniform Resource Locator (URL)** is a unique identifier that provides the global address of documents or other resources on the Web. Like fingerprints and snowflakes, there cannot be two identical URLs.
- **Hypertext Transfer Protocol (HTTP)** is the default Web protocol for Web page access.

- **Hypertext Markup Language (HTML)**, or "hypertext," allows you to link within documents to URLs located elsewhere in the document or in other documents on other servers.

Berners-Lee wrote the first World Wide Web server-and-client software, and created a WYSIWYG ("What You See Is What You Get") hypertext browser. The World Wide Web made its debut on the Internet in the summer of 1991. Since then, the Web has grown to become one of the primary modes of communication in the contemporary world. In 1994, Berners-Lee took a staff position at the Laboratory for Computer Science at the Massachusetts Institute of Technology, where he works as director of the W3 Consortium, an organization that sets standards and helps to bring coherence to global Web development.

## Requirements for Connecting to the Web

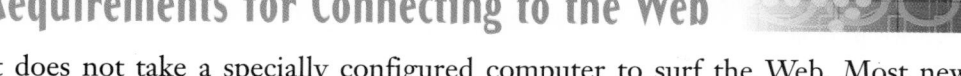

It does not take a specially configured computer to surf the Web. Most new computers will allow for Web access. However, there are some basic requirements. In order to connect to the Web, the computer must have the following:

- Hardware that includes the **Central Processing Unit (CPU), Random Access Memory (RAM),** storage, monitor, keyboard, mouse, modem, and printer
- Software with a TCP/IP protocol and other features to allow Internet access
- Web browser and an account with an ISP
- Public or private communications lines such as telephone lines, fiber optic, cable, or wireless

A **modem**, from *mo*dulator-*dem*odulator, is a special **hardware** (physical component of a computer) device that allows computer data to be sent in waveform (modulated) over phone lines, then demodulated back to digital form for reception by the target computer system.

**MPC3** (stands for Multimedia Personal Computer, level 3) standards are the bare-bones requirements that allow enough main memory and a powerful enough processor (CPU) to handle data coming in from Web pages. MPC3 machines have at least a 256-color video graphics adapter (VGA) display, a CD-ROM drive, and are capable of sound. A **CD-ROM** (Compact Disk-Read Only Memory) drive is a laser-generated compact disk with information already permanently written on it.

# Internet2

The infrastructure of today's Internet is fast becoming inadequate for current user Web needs and expectations. The proliferation of plug-ins, the need for greater access to more information, and the desire for high-speed connections are placing ever-increasing demands on the current system. The original Internet organization was perfect for the text-based Internet of the 1960s. Today the Web offers a multimedia environment, making available text, graphics, sound, animation, interactivity, and video, often at the same time. These additional features are taxing the current Internet system and leading to demands for a better and faster Internet. Internet2 promises an answer to this need.

Internet2, founded in 1996, is a consortium of 170 U.S. universities that are planning a new, improved Internet. Academicians are working with partners in industry, government, and other countries to respond to "the need of the hour." They will develop Internet2 with technology that will provide for powerful new applications. This system will allow high-performance multimedia applications to run quickly with a standard Internet user connection. Streaming technologies will be the new standard. Unfortunately, such an infrastructure will not be ready until well into the first decade of the twenty-first century.

The new Internet will also be more affordable, and will not require higher speed processors than are presently used. Authentication of and security for Web purchases will be standard, and multicasting will be possible for all connections. Most high-level network protocols, such as TCP/IP, provide only a unicast transmission service, meaning that network nodes can send to only one node at a time, or point-to-point. The drawback to this method is that if information needs to be sent to many different destinations it must be sent to each node, one after the other. With multicasting, a single node can send to many different nodes at the same time.

The Internet Engineering Task Force (IETF) oversees the development of the new Internet2 **protocol** (rules or software standards governing handling of data) to ensure that it will be of high performance and capable of any foreseeable needs. The industry-sponsored University Corporation for Advanced Internet Development (UCAID) manages the Internet2 consortium at the present.

The planned applications for a new Internet will enable collaboration among Web users and improve access to information and resources far beyond what is available on today's Internet. Digital libraries, virtual laboratories, tele-immersion, and warp speed will be standard elements of the system. **Tele-immersion** is the perceived immersion into computer-based virtual reality environment—the illusion of immersion into a distant environment. The equivalent of ten sets of encyclopedias will move over fiber optic lines in one second. Live feeds of medical MRIs (magnetic resonance imaging) in progress will be possible. Flicker-free, streaming video will be on home computer desktops. With streaming video, a video or audio file is "streamed," or downloaded in small increments, to the cache memory. It is buffered, or stored, until there is enough of it downloaded to start playing the file. While the file is being played, the next block is being downloaded, resulting in a constant stream of data.

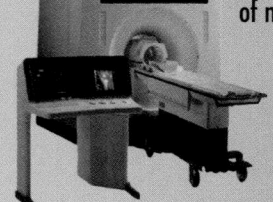

*Machines like this magnetic resonance imaging (MRI) system will be able to relay computerized images of the human body to doctors around the world quickly with Internet2 technology.*

The new protocol capable of doing all of this is named IPv6. More than 300 million dollars a year is allocated for Internet2 development, so that a new Internet standard will be available to users as quickly as possible.

**Table 1.4** **Typical Configuration for PC to Access the Web**

| Hardware | Configuration | Specifics |
|---|---|---|
| CPU | Pentium III | 300–800MHz |
| ram | 64MB to 128MB | the more the better |
| secondary storage | 1.2GB to 12GB hard drive | often multipartitioned into C, D, and E logical drives |
| monitor | super VGA; millions of colors | 17 inch or larger is better |
| keyboard/mouse | 101 keys, function keys | Web access keys, keypad |
| modem | analog, DSL, cable, satellite | analog for telephone access; other as service requires |
| printer | ink-jet or laser | 8–12ppm; color |

The more powerful the computer, and the more "bells and whistles" on it, the better the resulting display will be. However, this power does not ensure that your online experience will be any better. Connection and **bandwidth** (the capacity of the conduit to transmit and receive data) figure equally into the quality of your Internet experience. Some scaled-down versions of a personal computer are meant for a single purpose—accessing the Internet. For example, such a system might consist of a CPU monitor, keyboard, and mouse without a system unit. In addition, there are Web televisions that are Internet-enabled where you use the remote control as you would a keyboard and mouse.

Table 1.4 lists the typical configuration of a PC used to connect to the Web. Less-powerful components will still allow you to access the Web, but you may not be able to surf as quickly or save as much data on your computer. Also, what you see on the monitor or the quality of printed material may be different.

It is possible to use the Web without knowing everything about computers. Just as you can drive a car without knowing what is "under the hood," you can use the Internet without knowing the intricacies of its hardware, software, and network configurations. However, the more you know about the internal workings of your "Web machine," the easier it is to handle problems with memory management, downloading and decompressing files, and using resources on the Web. **Decompressing** means returning files that have been condensed to their original size and is usually done using special software for this purpose. The files are compressed to reduce their size, taking up less bandwidth and allowing them to travel more quickly along the Internet. The section that follows covers the specialized communications hardware and software that is specific to the Web.

## Hardware Needed for Web Access

A simple definition of a computer network is "two or more computers connected to each other by some means." Modems and network cards are the basis of network hardware. **Network cards** are a hardware peripheral that allows individual workstation computers to be networked.

Computers can be physically hard-wired by being connected to each other with cable, as in a **local area network (LAN)**, a computer network spanning a small area such as an office building. They can also be connected by public communication wires such as phone lines or wireless connections that use satellite transmission.

**Communications Hardware**   Communications hardware allows you to leave the single-user environment of the PC and enter into the client-server environment of the Internet. **Client-server** refers to a type of computer network relationship where a server stores, or hosts, material that is accessed by a connected computer (client) that in turn may also serve as a host for other connected clients. It can be a wired or wireless network connection. In a **wired** network connection, the nodes are connected by private or public physical lines, such as telephone or coaxial lines, or Ethernet cabling. A **wireless** connection is a network where the computers are not physically connected, but rely on infrared, radio, or satellite transmission. You can input data and send it (such as e-mail) and receive output (such as viewing a Web page) with the same connection hardware. You access more powerful and remote "servers" that store Web pages using your "client" PC which contains personalized information that can be read by the server.

The bandwidth, or capacity of the transmission media, varies enormously with each type of hardware. A LAN where computers are cabled together in one geographic location, as in a company intranet, has greater bandwidth and a more satisfactory delivery than a **wide area network (WAN)**, where a PC dials using a public telephone line with a modem that receives at 56Kbps (kilobits per second, a measure of transmission speed) or less (see Figure 1.4).

**Phone and Cable Modems**   There are several types of modems. Most personal computers sold today include an internal analog modem that is installed in one of the available slots on the main circuit board of the computer (see Figure 1.5). **Analog** signals are continuous waveforms similar to those of the human voice. This type of modem is referred to as a **phone modem**, which requires a software communications program, such as HyperTerminal, in order to "talk" to another modem. HyperTerminal will be covered in the section on software.

Phone modems use public telephone lines, and are conditioned to transmit to higher than 9600 **baud** (a unit measuring the capacity of a transmission line to change states) that is standard with **POTS** *(plain old telephone systems)* voice lines. Usually, modems transmit at 56Kbps (56,000 bytes per second), but there are some that still transmit at 28.8Kbps and slower. Your computer transmits and receives data according to the capabilities of its modem. A computer receiving data makes the necessary rate adjustments regardless of how fast that data was originally sent (see Figure 1.5).

There are several modems that are not phone modems. They are called modems for convenience; however, they work with digital signals as opposed to analog. **Integrated Services Digital Network (ISDN)** lines are digital lines for multimedia transmission. ISDN service can have one or two 64Kbps channels. With two channels present, you can use each separately—talk on the phone on

one and surf the Web on the other. Since the lines are digital, you do not need a phone modem to convert the signals to analog. You do, however, need an ISDN adapter connected to your computer. An ISDN connection is very reliable, but is not available to many individual computer users. The speed is only 256Kbps. Although ISDN has enjoyed a decade of being the faster access to the Internet using public-leased lines, it is rapidly being replaced by a newer technology—Digital Subscriber Lines.

**For ISDN** http://www.ralphb.net/isdn
**For DSL** http://www.rhythms.net
http://www.howstuffworks.com/dsl.htm

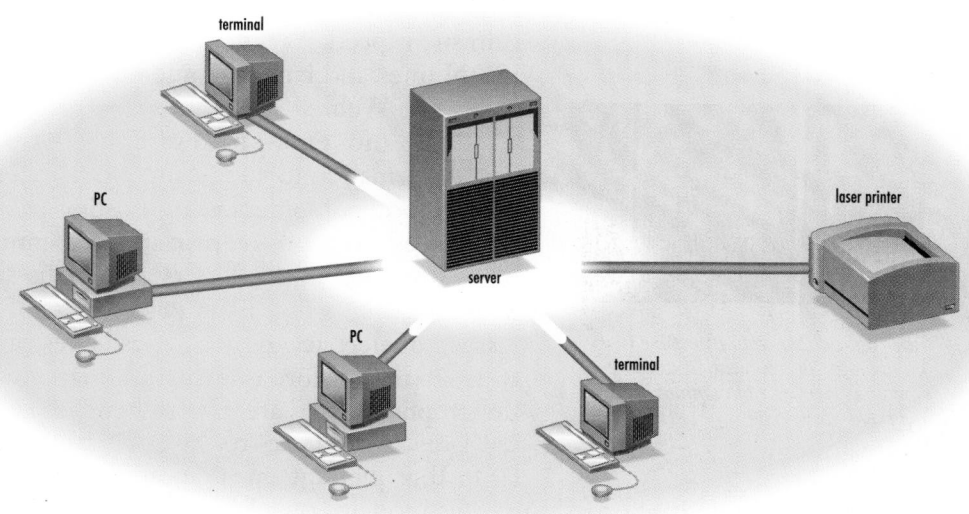

*Figure 1.4* **Local Area Network**
*Local area networks (LANs) are private networks that serve the needs of businesses or organizations with computers located in the same building or in nearby buildings.*

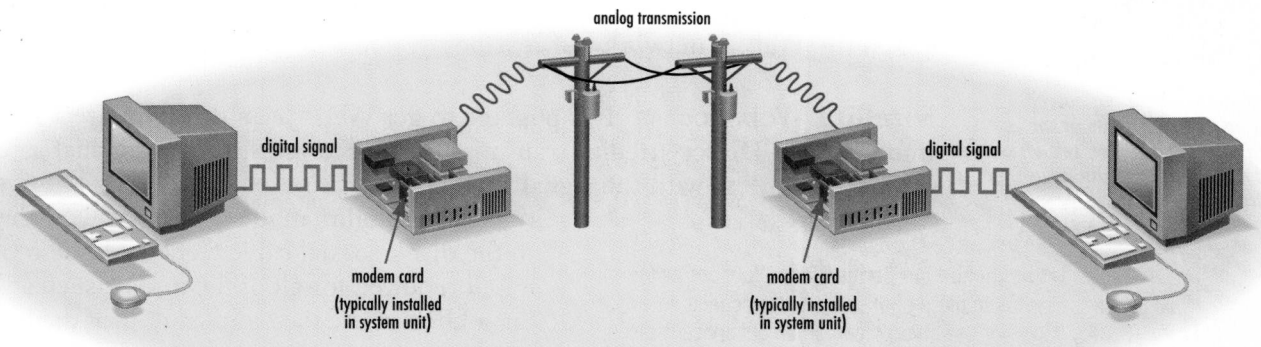

*Figure 1.5* **How a Modem Works**
*A modem modulates the digital signal from a computer, translating them into analog signals that travel along a conventional telephone line. On the other end of the connection, another modem demodulates the signals, translating them back into digital data.*

**Cable Modems** The contrast between uploading or downloading an audio or graphic file from a Web page with a new high-speed modem versus a standard, slow-speed modem is dramatic. For example, if you were using a slow-speed modem (2,400bps or less), it would probably take about 45 minutes to download a 24-bit graphic (a .bmp file). In contrast, a 28.8bps modem could do it in about 15 minutes; and a 56Kbps modem would take about five minutes. A **cable modem** or a DSL would download the file in one minute! That is the dramatic difference between cable or DSL and a POTS line.

Coaxial cable is used in cable television and VCR hookups and in computer networks.

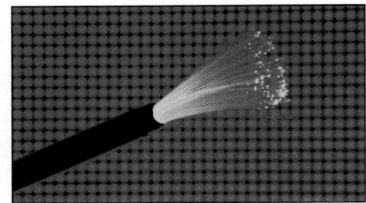

Fiber optic cables make possible high-bandwidth communication and are now the backbone of communication networks worldwide.

Three geosynchronous satellites making 24-hour orbits of the earth can provide telephone, tele-vision, and data communications to the entire world.

**Telephone Line Connections** Your computer needs to dial a phone number to connect to a location (a server) where Internet service is provided. This means that unless you have a specially conditioned line, you cannot talk on the telephone and access the Internet at the same time. This situation can be very inconvenient if you have only one telephone line and have not considered how busy that one line may now become! Some local telephone companies offer packages where your regular phone service can be combined with a second line dedicated to Internet connections.

**Digital Subscriber Lines (DSLs),** available through the local telephone company, increase bandwidth to allow voice and data to be transmitted simultaneously. That means you can access the Internet and receive a phone call at the same time. DSL allows the inherent bandwidth in plain telephone copper lines to be used more effectively. DSL can improve transmission up to 1.5Mbps (megabits per second). A DSL modem needs to be installed in the PC to gain such speed. As noted, DSLs are faster than ISDN lines and have become a popular way to access the Web.

**Cable modems**—hardware that allow digitized information to be transmitted from remote sites to local computers using existing television cable lines—use **fiber optic** lines to emulate a local area network. Fibers transmit signals through thin glass fibers as pulses of light instead of electrical pulses. These lines carry up to 1,000 times more information than unconditioned phone lines are able to handle. The network is also four to twenty times faster (150Mbps guaranteed) than an ISDN. A high-capacity television cable goes into cable modems on a PC. A small peripheral (an external device that attaches to the system unit) plugs into a network card that is in turn installed on the computer's system unit. After the card is attached to a serial port, the external cable modem is connected to **coaxial cable** (high-capacity fiber-based transmission cable for telecommunications) running to a cable service—most likely the same service that provides cable television transmission. The quality of a Web session is markedly faster and better with a cable modem than with a phone modem. However, if the cable network is down, you cannot access the Web; if network traffic is heavy, you will notice a slowdown.

**Satellite Web Access** It is possible to get Web access through direct satellite transmission. Direct satellite transmission is received by an individual satellite dish that is in line with the signal from the television company ISP. The system requires a satellite modem that connects the PC to the dish's coaxial cable feed. A phone modem is still required for all of the inputs, such as keying a URL in the location window of the browser. Satellite systems (DirecTV and DirecPC) are a popular option in rural areas where cable service or an ISDN is not available.

Most personal computer Web access and communication use can be accomplished with the minimal common carrier line leased from

*Table 1.5* **Internet Hardware Connection Options**

| Type | Performance | Availability |
|---|---|---|
| analog phone modem | 56Kbps downloading<br>33Kbps uploading | universal |
| ISDN line | 28Kbps uploading<br>128Kbps downloading | limited |
| cable modem | 1.5Mbps downloading<br>300Kbps uploading | spotty, mostly metro areas |
| DSL | 8Mbps downloading<br>1Mbps uploading | high in major metro areas |
| satellite | 400Kbps downloading<br>33Kbps uploading | high |

the local telephone company that transmits at 56Kbps. Of course, there are private communications lines and leased high-speed lines that businesses and schools use. Table 1.5 summarizes the types of Web hardware available, called $T_1$ and $T_3$ lines.

## Software Needed for Web Access

Along with the hardware, you need software programs for a Web connection. You need an operating system to handle memory, file, and resource management as well as all required operations for a successful computing session. You also need a communication program to handle the settings and connections for your modem hardware, a TCP/IP for transactions to and from the Internet, the proprietary software for your ISP, and a browser to view the Web graphically. Table 1.6 summarizes types of software and the application for each.

The Windows operating system (several versions exist, including NT, the network version of Windows) is a group of programs that perform basic functions of computing by interacting directly with the hardware. All operating systems allow a computer to perform standard operation tasks, such as preparing a

 *Table 1.6* **Software for Web Access**

| Software | Use |
|---|---|
| operating system | for memory management, file management, resource management, and session operations |
| communication | for modem settings and connections |
| TCP/IP | a suite of protocols for Internet transactions, usually included in the operating system |
| ISP utilities | to send and receive e-mail and files, use instant messaging, and so on |
| browser | to connect to the Internet to search for information, download files, and so forth |

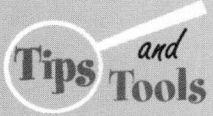

**Modem Setting** The Windows Control Panel lets you change settings for your modem. On the Start menu, if you click Settings and then Control Panel from your desktop, a window appears with a modem icon. If you double-click the left mouse button on that icon, the modem settings appear. If you have a modem already installed, its settings are shown. You can change the rate, the dialing properties (pulse or tone), and so forth, or leave the settings unchanged. This utility software is part of the operating system.

disk for use or deleting files. The operating system manages your computer session so that application programs do not interfere with each other.

Windows combines the **user interface**, or what you see on the screen, and the operating system into one program. You use Windows to copy and delete files from a diskette to a hard disk, manage folders or files, make backup files, install new ISP or browser software, or open the Control Panel and add new hardware.

**Communications Software** Communications software is general connection software that can be utilized with any client-server connection. **HyperTerminal** is the specific communications software included in the Windows and NT Accessories program group. Procomm, Bitcomm, and Crosstalk are alternate communications programs that include auto-dialers, file transfers, and other needed programs. However, HyperTerminal is the only communications software you need. Both HyperTerminal and the TCP/IP protocol are included with Windows. As mentioned, protocol is the set of rules or standards that regulate the way data is transmitted between two or more connected computers. The combination of these Internet "handshakes," as protocol has been referred to, ensures that whatever is transmitted on the Internet can be understood by all recipients.

The creation of the Web required establishing a computer standard for the transferring of information globally. This standard has two parts and is referred to as the TCP/IP (Transmission Control Protocol/Internet Protocol). This protocol became the universal standard that would soon be able to communicate with virtually all microcomputers in the world. TCP/IP is software for "packaging" the messages that travel over the Internet. To participate in Internet activities, you must be connected to a server that uses TCP/IP software.

The IP routes, or directs, messages correctly to a **domain address** (or **Internet address**). Each participant of TCP/IP has a unique 32-bit IP address, such as 144.440.35.6.

The TCP takes care of "packaging" messages—that is, ordering them so they can be transmitted and arrive in logical fashion. It breaks the message into pieces that can be managed by the protocol and numbers each piece so that it can be reordered upon receipt. In this way, whatever is shipped across this complex Web of networks can be delivered to the correct location. TCP even has a built-in checker, called a "checksum," that checks every time a message is delivered to verify the integrity of the data. If it fails the check, the message is retransmitted.

TCP/IP software is included in all microcomputer systems software today. There are other communications protocols as well. The **File Transfer Protocol (FTP)** that allows you to "get" and "put" files from remote computers into your computer via the Internet is available with the TCP/IP software, but **Real Time Streaming Protocol (RTSP)** software must be downloaded with a plug-in. A

**plug-in** is a helper application introduced to enhance the capability of the browsers to display Web pages. Plug-in RSTP is a set of software standards for transmission of live video and audio feeds via the Internet using caching (storing) and simultaneous playback.

**ISP and Browser Software**   An Internet service provider (ISP) acts as an interface for the Web and provides a connection to the Internet for a fee, generally on a monthly basis. ISPs can have their own proprietary browsers, such as America Online (AOL), that include mail server software and other add-on utilities. Other ISPs use public browsers, such as Netscape Navigator and Internet Explorer. Some ISPs, like America Online and The Microsoft Network, have additional features such as financial services, news, weather, popular movie reviews, and national and local events in your specific geographic area.

Most ISPs offer several different payment plans, and many offer unlimited usage for higher monthly fees. You pay for the access to their server and the quality of their software. There are ISPs free of a monetary charge, but you are assailed with advertising promotions contained in screen banners when you log on to that service. Most users opt to pay the subscription price instead, although you may find major ISPs also promoting products for sale.

ISP software is becoming more sophisticated and more extensive as companies vie for new Internet subscribers and fight to keep the subscribers they have. With so many providers vying for subscribers, users frequently cancel one and begin another—for better service, cheaper rates, more hours or mailboxes, and so forth. The intense competition for Internet subscribers is similar to the competition among cable TV services before the turn of the century. Table 1.7 shows

> **Tips and Tools**
>
> **ISP Software**  When you purchase a new computer, there may be several preinstalled ISP software programs. Click on the Windows utility, connect to the Internet, or go to Programs/Online Services to determine the ISPs preinstalled on your computer. ISPs often send out free CDs or disks in the mail, which you can easily install on most computers.

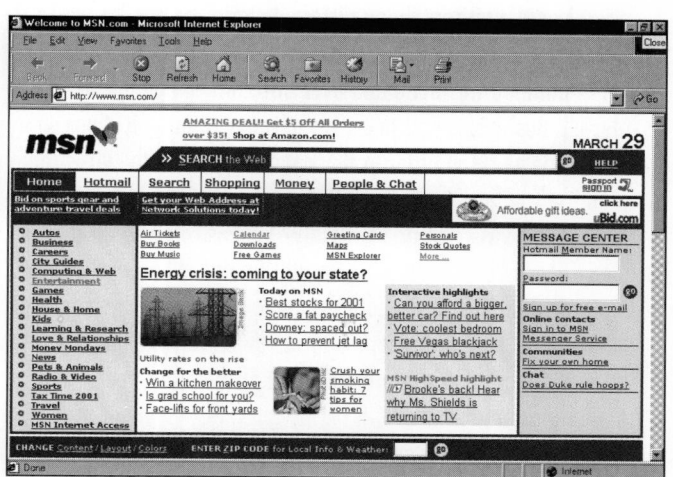

*Netscape Navigator and Internet Explorer are the most popular public browsers.*

**Tips and Tools**

**Your E-mail Address** Look at your e-mail address. Your e-mail address usually indicates the type of ISP that you subscribe to. For example, in the address johndoe@aol.com, *aol* indicates America Online (AOL) as the commercial ISP. The *.com* indicates that this is a commercial site. If your e-mail address ends with *.edu*, you are using an educational server. Since the Internet began as an academic resource, many universities established servers long before access to the Web became popular. A government server would be indicated by *.gov* and a military server by *.mil*. New domain names are under consideration to fulfill constantly increasing demand.

If you switch ISPs, your e-mail address will change. If you neglect to forward your new address to your e-mail contacts, and if one of your contacts fails to record the change in his or her personal address book, messages may be lost or misdirected. One way to prevent this is by using a Web page-based e-mail service such as Hotmail. Logging on to the Hotmail site allows you to select an e-mail name and password. You can then send and receive e-mail any time you log on to the Hotmail site. Because this service is independent of your ISP, you can switch providers without losing your Hotmail e-mail address.

It's always important to key all addresses just as they appear without any added spaces, letters, or punctuation. If you make an error, your e-mail may not go to anyone or may even go to the wrong person!

## The "I Love You" Virus

While the world passed into the new millennium without suffering the disastrous consequences many predicted for the Y2K bug, the year 2000 did bring one of the most disastrous computer viruses ever known. In a matter of days, some 45 million people reportedly received e-mail containing different strains of the "I Love You" virus. One research firm estimated that more than 2.6 billion dollars of damage was done and over 600,000 computers were infected. Businesses had to cut off network communications with the outside world in order to block the virus. Once the virus replicated itself in host systems, it destroyed information stored there. How did this virus spread so rapidly? Victims received an e-mail titled "I Love You," containing an attachment. When opened, the attachment automatically sent the same message to everyone on the Microsoft host computer's address book. Anyone detaching this file would therefore instantly infect all of the other people they regularly communicated with on the Internet. While not unique, this well-publicized incident served as a wake-up call for many. Any computer used to connect to the Internet should have antivirus software installed to detect viruses and prevent similar disasters.

**Table 1.7 Typical ISP Software Programs for Web Access**

| ISP | Connection Required |
|---|---|
| America Online (AOL) | phone modem |
| Prodigy | phone modem |
| EarthLink | phone modem |
| The Microsoft Network (MSN) | phone modem |
| MCI | phone modem |
| Qwest | phone modem |
| Sprint Internet | phone modem |
| GTE Internet | phone modem |
| AT&T Home | cable modem |
| DirecPC | satellite service |
| Web TV | phone modem |

some of the most popular ISPs. Note that the table spotlights commercial ISP services; there also are a number of well-used educational servers, government servers, and military servers.

**Firewalls and Virus Scanners** The virus threat and the fraudulent Internet activity that is inevitable once you open millions of systems to the public spurred the development of firewalls. **Viruses** are programs that search for and copy themselves to other programs. When these programs are executed the virus program is executed as well, thus spreading the "infection." The effects of a virus can range from harmless to catastrophic, depending on the nature of the virus. Firewalls help prevent these security breaches.

**Firewalls** are computer systems—hardware and software—that place an intervening fireproof layer between the outside user (source of the fire) and the vulnerable inside computer system. The firewall computer (usually a dedicated server) stands between the internal network and the Internet. Firewalls are established and maintained by ISP network administrators.

Common firewall activity includes monitoring and controlling FTP (File Transfer

Protocol, used for uploading and downloading programs) sessions and continuous monitoring of the server. Firewall software is available to protect home systems, but it is rarely necessary. On the other hand, antivirus software for home computers has become very popular because of the possible destruction viruses can cause. Antivirus programs conduct "search and destroy" missions for viruses that may have infected your computer. They identify virus programs and "clean" them by removing them from infected programs. Because new viruses are appearing every day, antivirus software must be constantly updated. This can be done through the Internet. If you should establish your own server to design Web pages and host Web sites, download files from the Internet, or if you have several people using the same computer, you need to research firewalls and virus scanners more thoroughly.

**Parental Control Software**  While there are many wonderful things on the Internet, there are also many things that are not suitable for children. Many parents worry that their children might visit Web sites with information or graphics they think inappropriate, or that their children might be victimized by unscrupulous individuals in chat rooms. Other parents worry about the amount of time their children spend surfing the Web, or that their child might download and use game programs that they don't approve of.

To assist parents in taking control of the Internet, enterprising companies have created software that allows parents to control their children's access to the Net in a number of ways. Parental control software programs can prevent access to sites, log sites visited, limit connection time, record keystrokes, prevent downloading, and allow parents to view sites accessed by their children. While some parents may feel that the use of parental control software is heavy-handed, many parents believe that it is justified given the potential harmful influences found on the Web.

## Cookies

**Cookies** are the small text files containing your user information that are downloaded to your computer when you first access some sites. The name originally comes from the UNIX mainframe world where tokens, or cookies, were issued when a host computer was accessed. Cookies customize your view of the Web, and may also reveal your online habits. Cookies record your preferences when you first access a Web site; then the site that originated the cookies stores the file on your hard drive, under the *C:\windows\Cookies* folder. The next time you access the same site, your computer configuration, display resolution, and other preferences are uploaded to present you with a customized view of the Web. However, each access your browser makes to a Web site leaves behind information about you, creating a trail across the Internet. Among the tidbits of data left along this trail are the name and Internet Protocol address of your computer, the brand of browser you are using, the operating system you are running, the URLs you access, the URL of the page you last viewed, how long you stayed on the site, and how often you log on to the site. Without cookies, it would be nearly impossible to follow your trail systematically to learn about your Web browsing habits. The tidbits stored in your *Cookies* folder can be accessed by the system operator on the server computer and by your ISP. They use the cookie data trail for marketing and demographic studies, and sometimes even sell the data to advertisers.

*Parents can choose from many different software programs to ensure their children's safety while surfing the Web.*

 # Summary

➤ The Internet was founded in 1969 as a network to share government and academic research and to communicate with participating individuals.

➤ The invention of browsers allowed users to move from the old text-based system to graphics and was the beginning of the World Wide Web.

➤ To access the Web, a user must have computer hardware and software to make the connection as well as the ability to manage the Internet session.

➤ Web documents are primarily written in HTML—Hypertext Markup Language—and are organized around home pages that are linked to other Web pages.

➤ For many, the Internet has become an integral part of daily life, allowing people to accomplish a variety of tasks that formerly would have taken a long time, were expensive, or might not even have been possible.

**analog** Signals that are continuous waveforms—such as the human voice. Converting an analog signal to a discrete binary signal requires digitizing the signal by recording samples of the waveform at a specific frequency, or speed, per second.

**ARPANET** An experimental, wide-area computer network initiated by the U.S. government in the early 1960s. Its purpose was to allow government contractors to share expensive, scarce computing resources. It spanned the United States, and was the precursor to the Internet.

**bandwidth** The capacity of the conduit to transmit and receive data; the number of bits that can be transmitted at one time over a specific medium.

**baud** Measurement of the capacity of a transmission line to change states.

**bps (bits per second)** Measurement of the speed at which data travels over a communication line.

**browser** A Web software program such as Microsoft Internet Explorer or Netscape Navigator that provides the interface for the Web portion of the Internet. The browser allows navigation of Web pages.

**cable modem** Hardware that allows digitized information to be transmitted from a remote site to a local computer, using existing television cable lines. Cable modems emulate a local area network and use fiber optic lines for transmission.

**CD-ROM drive** Computer hardware mass storage drive that uses a laser-generated compact disk with information already permanently written on it.

**Central Processing Unit (CPU)** The CPU is the brains of the computer, the hardware component in which all processing occurs.

**CERN** The *Centre Européen pour la Recherche Nucléaire* (European Laboratory for Particle Physics) where the World Wide Web was developed.

**chat sessions** Synchronous computer communication sessions where participants hold a conversation, typically by keying their messages which display in the screen in real time, and reading what other participants have to say. Voice-driven chat sessions are usually referred to as Net meetings.

**client-server** A type of computer network relationship where a server stores, or hosts, material that is accessed by a connected computer (client) that in turn may also serve as a host for other connected clients.

**coaxial cable** High-capacity fiber-based transmission cable for telecommunications.

**.com** The designation for Web-based commercial enterprises. Pronounced "dot com."

**cookie** A small text file containing user information that is downloaded to the user's computer when he or she first accesses some sites.

**decompressing** Returning files that have been condensed to their original size.

**Digital Subscriber Line (DSL)** Conditioned telephone line that adjusts transmission capability for much higher bits per second than originally possible, resulting in faster transmission.

**domain address** Each participant of TCP/IP has a unique 32-bit IP address, such as 144.440.35.6. The unique digital address of a domain server. Also called Internet address.

**download** To transfer files from an Internet or host source to the user's personal client computer.

**electronic mail (e-mail)** The computer transmission of text messages asynchronously between individuals.

**fiber optic** Transmission medium that uses thin glass fibers to transmit signals as pulses of light.

**File Transfer Protocol (FTP)** A software standard of transmitting data from one computer to another. FTP allows the user to "put" and "get" files to and from remote computers and save downloaded files to the user's computer.

**firewall** Computer systems—both hardware and software—that are used to put an intervening fireproof layer between the outside user and the vulnerable inside computer system.

**forum** A means of public asynchronous communication where individuals may read and post comments on various topics, organized by threads.

**hardware** The computer system's physical components.

**home page** The first of a series of pages for a specific address on a Web site.

**hyperlink** Nonlinear associated links to other URLs embedded within the source code; hot words or graphics. Hyperlinks are often referred to as "links."

**hypermedia** A system of relating by association, regardless of media type.

**HyperTerminal** One type of software program that allows modems to communicate with each other.

**hypertext** A nonlinear way of handling text so that words are linked and/or associated with each other, not by their position in an article or by chronological or other order, but instead by a system of pointers.

**Hypertext Markup Language (HTML)** The primary coding system for Web pages.

**Hypertext Transfer Protocol (HTTP)** The default Web protocol for Web page access.

**Integrated Services Digital Network (ISDN)** Special high-speed, high-capacity digital lines for multimedia transmission offered by telecommunication companies.

**Internet** An infrastructure of networks connecting many smaller networked computers in a global client-server environment. Also known as the Net.

**Internet service provider (ISP)** A provider of access to the Web or the Internet in general.

**intranet** A network based on TCP/IP protocols (an Internet) belonging to an organization, usually a corporation, accessible only by the organization's members, employees, or others with authorization.

**keywords** Words in a Web site that are included in the title and the metatags and in the text of some search engines. They form the basis of Web searches.

**link** See **hyperlink**

**LISTSERV** Type of Internet asynchronous group communication where postings are distributed to members via e-mail. LISTSERVs existed long before the Web.

**local area network (LAN)** A group of computers physically wired or connected to each other in order to share programs, data, and peripherals, and to allow communications within the group.

**modem** From *mo*dulator-*dem*odulator, computer hardware that has a special device that allows computer data to be sent in waveform over phone lines, then demodulated back to digital form for reception by the target computer system.

**MPC3** Stands for Multimedia Personal Computer, level 3 hardware and software standards. These are minimum requirements that allow enough main memory and a powerful enough processor (CPU)

to handle the data coming in from Web pages and hardware to hear sound files and view video files.

**network** Two or more computers connected to each other by some means.

**network cards** A hardware peripheral that allows computers to be networked.

**nonlinear** Words that are linked and/or associated with each other (hyperlinked), not by their position in an article or by chronological or other order, but instead by a system of pointers.

**operating system** System software necessary for a computing session; it manages the session and performs the primitive computing functions. The most common OS for microcomputers is Windows.

**phone modem** Internal analog modem installed in one of the available slots on the main circuit board of a computer.

**plug-in** Helper applications introduced to enhance the capability of the browsers to display Web pages.

**pointer** Variable that stores addresses, or locations, of other data to be linked.

**POTS** Plain old telephone system; voice lines that were originally designed to transmit at a maximum of 9600 baud rate.

**protocol** Set of rules or software standards governing handling of data.

**Random Access Memory (RAM)** A type of computer memory that can be accessed randomly. RAM is the most common type of memory found in computers and other devices, such as printers.

**Real Time Streaming Protocol (RSTP)** A set of software standards for transmission of live video and audio feeds via the Internet using caching and simultaneous playback.

**search engine** Internet software program that makes finding information on the Internet easier by using database queries to indexed material and returning a results list.

**server** Computer that hosts the information on the Internet.

**software** Computer programs or coded stored instructions that drive computing sessions.

**tele-immersion** The perceived immersion into computer-based virtual reality environment—the illusion of immersion into a distant environment.

**telnet** An Internet functionality that allows accessing a remote computer from within a computer logged on to another network, using the target computer's IP address.

**thread** Specific topics of discussion used on forums and Usenets. They are hierarchical, or treelike, in their structure. In outline format, participants respond to each other's comments.

**Transmission Control Protocol/Internet Protocol (TCP/IP)** A set of software standards that is required for Internet access; developed by V. Cerf and R. Kahn.

**Uniform Resource Locator (URL)** A unique identifier that provides the global address of documents or other resources on the Web. There cannot be two identical URLs.

**upload** To transfer files from a personal computer to a remote computer on a network, usually via FTP protocol.

**Usenet** Type of Internet asynchronous group communication where users may read and post comments on specific topics in a "bulletin board" fashion. Unlike LISTSERVs, Usenets do not use e-mail for transmission, but instead use newreaders.

**user interface** Computer software layer that allows users to interact with the underlying hardware and software. What the user sees in the screen; the place where the user and computer interact.

**virus** A program that searches for and copies itself to other programs. When these programs are executed the virus program is executed as well, thus spreading the "infection." The effects of a virus can range from harmless to catastrophic, depending on the nature of the virus.

**wide area network (WAN)** A network that spans a wide distance and connects two or more LANs (local area networks).

**wired** A computer network where nodes are connected by private or public physical lines, such as telephone or coaxial lines, or Ethernet cabling.

**wireless** A computer network where the connected computers are not physically connected, but rely on infrared, radio, or satellite transmission.

**World Wide Web** The total collection of information available on that portion of the Internet that contains hyperlinked documents. Also referred to as www, or the Web.

 # Navigating and Exploring the Web

## Working the Web

**Project 1**  In Internet Explorer or Netscape Navigator, go to www.cnn.com. Look for the underlined text. These are the hyperlinks. How many hyperlinks are listed? Do hyperlinks appear in more than one color? Select a link. Point and click on the link. You are now at a new page. Find the Home menu bar button on this page, and click. Are you back to your starting point?

**Project 2**  For this activity you will need a watch or a clock with a second hand. Go to each of the following Web sites:

- http://www.mos.org/home.html
- www.cdc.gov
- www.time.com/time/

Answer the questions for each site.
- How long did it take for the site to appear in the screen?
- Is there more text than graphics on the site?
- Did the graphics improve the site? In what way(s)?
- Does there seem to be a correlation between graphic elements and download time?
- Which would you prefer if you had to choose between faster download times and graphics?

**Project 3**  Go to www.ispinternet.com/compare.htm. Explore three ISP providers that are available to you (do not include free providers). List the three providers and compare their benefits.

## Are We Connecting?

**Exercise 1**

*Answer the following questions. Questions can be answered individually or assigned as small group discussion.*

1. Is the Internet the same as the World Wide Web? Which came first? How are they the same or different?
2. List the names of two ISPs. List the names of two search engines. What is the difference between the Internet, an Internet Service Provider (ISP), and a search engine?
3. What is the difference between a search engine and a browser? What is the name of the browser on the computer you use at school? at work? at home?

4. What is Hypertext Markup Language? What does it allow computers to do?

5. What is the difference between a computer network, an intranet, and the Internet? Which is the largest?

6. How would you describe an ideal Internet system? What would it allow you to do? Will the communications hardware be wireless? fiber optic? DSL? satellite? Will it be delivered on a PCN? a handheld device? a telephone? How much of the world will be online? What will search engines be like? Will the language of the Web be English?

7. What is communications software and why is it essential in order to access the Web?

## Exercise 2

*Match the acronym or term with the description.*

a. URL
b. Yahoo!
c. modem
d. AOL
e. HTML
f. Internet Explorer
g. ISDN
h. cable Modems
i. DirecTV
j. home page

1. a search engine
2. an Internet service provider
3. Uniform Resource Locator
4. Hypertext Markup Language
5. a browser
6. modulator–demodulator
7. a type of Web connection that uses fiber optic signals
8. digital lines that do not need modems to transmit data
9. first in a series at a Web site
10. satellite transmission service

## Exercise 3

*Compose a short answer for each of the following.*

1. What were the first two types of organizations to use the Internet?
2. What programming language is primarily used on the Web?
3. What would you use to help search for information on the Web?
4. What does the acronym URL stand for?
5. What is one of the most common ways of communicating on the Internet?
6. The Web was developed as a vast database of what type of documents?
7. When you go to an address on the Web, what is the first page called that appears at that address?

8. What is the name for the transmission capacity of the device that tranmits computer data?

9. What are the terms used for copying a file from the Web to your computer, and for copying a file from your computer to the Web?

10. An ISP typically provides a combination of hardware and software that protects its subscribers from security breaches and outside invasions. What is this system called?

11. Besides a computer, what four items would you absolutely need to connect to the Internet?

12. What optional items would prevent possible problems or improve your access?

13. When connecting for the first time to a specific ISP or to a forum, what would you have to enter on a form that would be unique to you?

# Navigation Tools
## The Keys to Access

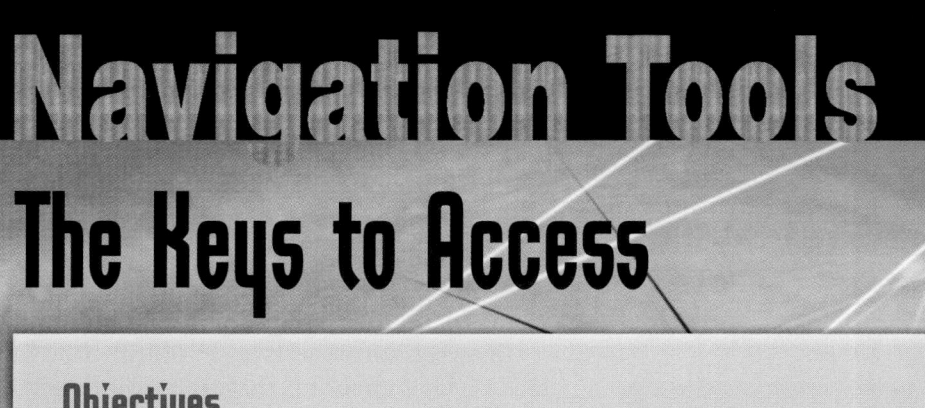

**2**

### Objectives

➤ Understand the features and applications of the two major Web browsers.

➤ Use URLs correctly.

➤ Navigate the Web using browser menus and toolbars.

➤ Recognize the standard parts of Web pages.

➤ Identify enhanced features of Web pages.

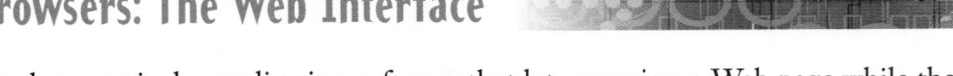

# Browsers: The Web Interface

The browser is the application software that lets you view a Web page while the underlying HTML coding is hidden from view. In fact, what you see when you look at a Web page is very much like what you see in open Windows application software such as Word or Excel. There are the same drop-down menus, the graphical toolbar(s) across the top, the horizontal and vertical scroll bars, and the same view of the document. The location—or the arrangement of items—is basically the same. This chapter provides guidance on using a browser and presents the basic elements of a Web page.

**Scroll Bars** Don't forget to use the horizontal and vertical scroll bars when viewing a Web page. These scroll bars work just like the scroll bars in a Windows operating system. If the scroll bars do not appear, all of the content of the Web page is in view.

Browser software is a graphical user interface (GUI), enabling the user to interact with on-screen objects and to navigate by pointing and clicking the mouse. Browsers allow you to jump from one hyperlink to another and move from one location to another with ease. You can perform all of the functions of the Internet with multimedia browsers. Besides the two dominant browsers, Microsoft Internet Explorer and Netscape Navigator, there are many public browsers (free for downloading) available throughout the Internet. The examples and exercises in this course utilize Internet Explorer and Netscape Navigator, although the skills used to complete that work are applicable with any browser.

Figures 2.1 and 2.2 show how a typical Web page looks in both IE and Navigator. Familiarize yourself with the *title bar*, the *menu bar*, and the other elements such as the *scroll bar* and the *status bar*. The status bar at the bottom of the page displays a *progress bar* that shows the connecting status or the download time remaining, which is helpful during long graphic downloads. In addition, when you roll the mouse over a hyperlink, the URL of the hyperlink displays in the status bar.

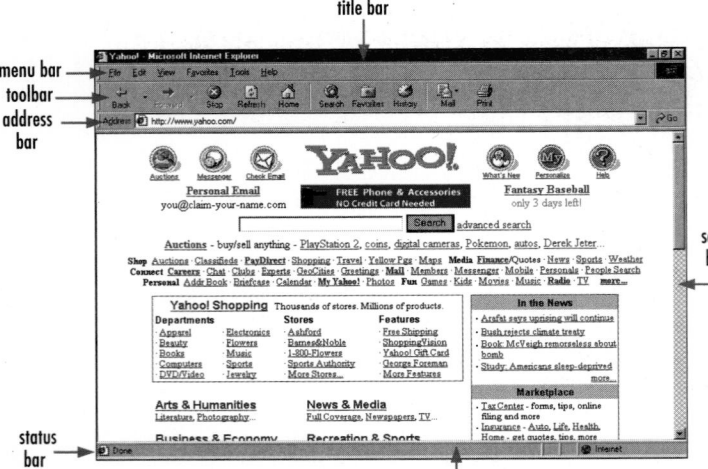

**Figure 2.1** **Typical View in Internet Explorer**

## Navigation Options

There are two ways to get from point A to point B (navigate) on the Web. You can point and click a hyperlink, or navigate to a specific location by keying the URL (Uniform

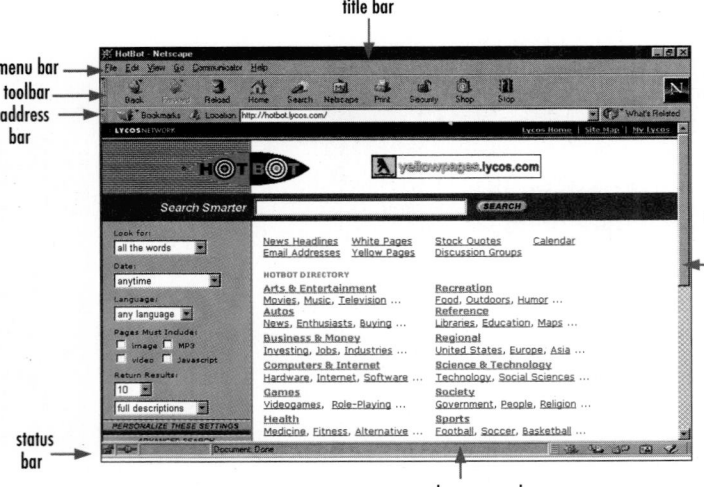

**Figure 2.2** **Typical View in Netscape Navigator**

Resource Locator) in the address bar. A home page, the first page or primary page of a series of pages at a specific Web site, usually links to other related pages within that specific directory. When users key the URL in the Address (IE) or Netsite (Navigator) text box of their Web browser, they are usually aware that they are changing location since the URL must be keyed correctly to connect to the location. (The **Address/Netsite** box drop-down list keeps a history of the sites visited during current and past Web sessions.) However, when users click a hyperlink, they might not realize that they may be exiting one server to view a page on a different server in a different domain.

For example, an airline's home page would most likely have links to its flight schedules, cost of tickets, and airports. Whenever the mouse cursor changes to a pointing hand (see Figure 2.3), there is a hyperlink to another Web page that has a different URL (address), and that page then may have subsequent links.

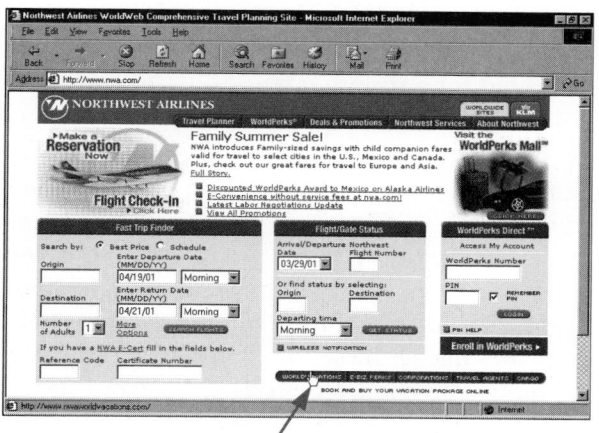

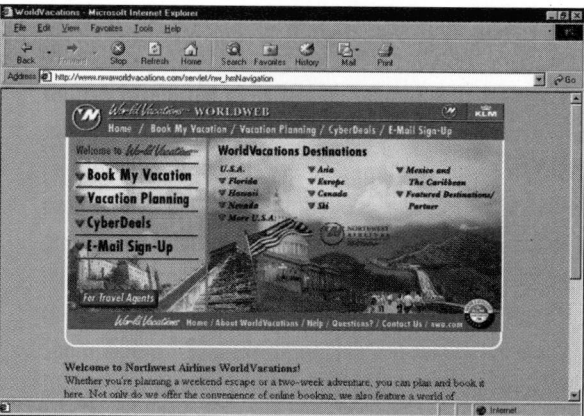

*Figure 2.3* **Pointing Hand**
*A pointing hand indicates a hyperlink is available to take you to another URL.*

**Selecting an ISP and Browser** When you purchase a new computer, it may contain several preinstalled Internet service provider (ISP) software programs. After choosing an ISP, choose a browser that works best for you and eliminate the others. Even if you think you may switch to another ISP or browser in the future, it is a good idea to discard the unused programs by moving them to the Recycle Bin on your computer. You can always download a different browser or version if you need one at a later time. You may have a computer with 11 gigabytes (GB) of hard drive space, but that drive space will quickly be consumed unless you regularly delete unnecessary programs and files.

# Battle of the Browsers

Netscape, founded by James H. Clark and Marc Andreesen in 1994, revolutionized the computer software market by giving away its popular Navigator software until it had acquired an overwhelming market share for this category of software. Microsoft successfully adopted the same strategy with Internet Explorer and eventually came to dominate the market. A federal court order to break up the Microsoft Corporation in the year 2000 stemmed from the battle to control the browser world. Microsoft was charged with intent to monopolize Internet delivery systems by bundling Internet Explorer browser software with all of its new Windows systems.

*Bill Gates, Microsoft founder and CEO*

## Finding a Flight

1. In Internet Explorer or Netscape Navigator, log on to http://www.nwa.com.
2. Search for a flight from Minneapolis to Chicago.
3. Did you leave the home page? *(Hint: Did the screen change?)*
4. How do you know if you have left a Web site and are on another Web site?

**For a virtual server**
www.earthlink.net
**To find a Web host** www.thelist.com
**For rating on servers**
www.cnet.com

In technical terms, Web sites are the directories on the servers where Web pages reside. Large organizations may have multiple servers that host (store) Internet material. Servers are computers designed to host and serve files to a network or the Web. Internet hosting, maintenance, and domain name assignment has become big business. When you key a URL, it appears that the Web pages reside at the physical location of the business, but in fact they may reside on a host server, where they are managed for a monthly fee.

**Home Pages and Home Sites** The opening page that you see after keying a URL is often named index.html or welcome.html. It is the main or home page for the particular site and serves as a Table of Contents. You can navigate to other directories and pages within the site from the home page, or you can key the specific name of the page you wish to see. Most well-constructed sites give you the option of hyperlinking from the home page to related pages, and may even give you internal navigation schemes inside the set of Web pages. Although some individual sites have a single home Web page, a reference to a Web site at http://www.mycompanyname.com is really a reference to a related set of pages, all hyperlinked at least to the home page.

You may set your computer to a default home page in your browser. Once this site is set, every time you start your browser, this home page will appear. If you hit the Home button, you will return to this site.

## Changing Your Default Home Page

1. Click Tools on the menu bar, and then click Internet Options from the drop-down menu, to display the Internet Options dialog box.
2. Click the General tab.
3. In the Home Page section, key the URL of the home page you want (such as http://www.msn.com), or click Use Current if the home page you want is open on the browser.
4. Click OK.
5. Close the browser and then open it again. You should see the home page you selected.

**Uniform Resource Locators (URLs)**   Each page on the Web has a Uniform Resource Locator (URL), an identifier that provides the global address of documents or other resources on the Web. A URL is the basis of Web browsing. Each URL is a unique identifier for a file on the Web, much like a social security number is a unique identifier for a person. URLs are composed of concatenated (separate elements attached together to form one unit) paths to file names of the source material. If you know the URL, you can key it and connect directly to a particular page on the Web. The URL is also referred to as the Web "address." As of this writing there are over 30 million registered URLs in the world. That figure is expected to double within two years.

URLs are an indispensable part of the Web; to navigate the Web, the URL must be entered in the Address (IE) or Netsite (Navigator) text box, stored as a Favorites (IE) or Bookmarks (Navigator) site, or hot-linked on a Web page.

The URL strings together the access paths to an object in standardized format and order—the access protocol, the Internet server, the domain name, the directory, and the file. A URL has several parts separated by a colon (:), slashes (/), and dots (.).

The part of the URL before the colon indicates the access protocol. Protocol refers to the rules or format for transmitting data between two devices. The most common Web protocol is Hypertext Transfer Protocol (HTTP). Other possible protocols include File Transfer Protocol (FTP), Hypertext Transfer Protocol, Secure (HTTPS), and Real Time Streaming Protocol (RTSP). These are shown in Table 2.1. An organization may have more than one type of server, such as a Web site providing information about the organization and an FTP site providing an archive of downloadable files. Web sites have www. after the protocol.

The text immediately following the protocol and *www.* in a URL is the ISP address or domain name. The **domain name** identifies the person, organization, server, or topic. The text following the second dot is the domain suffix. This text identifies the type of organization; for instance, *.com* identifies a business (i.e., http://www.bluemountainarts.com), *.gov* identifies a government site (i.e., http://www.census.gov), and *.edu* identifies a school Web site (i.e., http://www.oakland.edu). If the site is outside the United States, the domain name will have a country code. The URL http://www.abc.net.au tells you that the site is hosted in Australia.

 *Table 2.1*  **Protocols Used in URLs on the Internet**

| Protocol | Full Name | Function Associated with Protocol |
|---|---|---|
| FTP | File Transfer Protocol | download, upload files |
| Gopher | Gopher search databases | document retrieval |
| HTTP | Hypertext Transfer Protocol | links files across the Internet |
| HTTPS | Hypertext Transfer Protocol, Secure | for secure transactions |
| SMTP | Simple Mail Transport Protocol | e-mail |
| news | Usenet newsgroup | newsreader for newsgroup |
| RTSP | Real Time Streaming Protocol | streaming multimedia |

## Learning about Domain Names

InterNic is an online source for information about domain names.

1. Log on to http://internic.net.
2. Click *The InterNIC FAQ*.
3. What is a domain name? How do you register a domain name? How long does the registration last?
4. Go to www.icann.org.
5. Click *Frequently Asked Questions* or locate the hyperlink to find information on top-level domain names.
6. What are top-level domain names? Write a definition in your own words.
7. Go to www.networksolutions.org. Browse the site.
8. What can you find out about registering a domain name?

**Internet Network Information Center**
http://internic.net

Domain names that reflect the subject of the Web site, for example www.LandsEnd.com or www.foxsports.com, are sometimes called *vanity* domain names. They give the owner an advantage since they are intuitive and easy to remember, regardless of the server they reside upon.

You can register your desired Web site with its domain name, if no one has taken that name. There is a charge to register the name. However, if the name has already been registered, the owners may charge thousands of dollars for someone to buy use of that name, which they would then relinquish.

The proliferation of Web sites and the need to organize the sites has led to discussion about creating new domain suffixes. The current nomenclature is inadequate to capture all of the "flavors" of the Web. Some of the proposals have been *.shop* for shopping sites, *.arts* for art organizations, and *.news* for news sites. New suffixes would expand the list of possible names. On the other hand, they may create confusion for a site that spans many categories. For instance, what if an arts organization offered art news online? Would it be *.art* or *.news*? As of this writing the nomenclature has not been finalized. For an update, view the ICANN (Internet Corporation for Assigned Names and Numbers) Web site, www.icann.org. ICANN is an international organization that recommends rules for domain names. Tables 2.2 and 2.3 show common domain name suffixes. Table 2.4 shows domain suffixes that might be used soon.

## What's in a Name?

Domain names can be worth money, *lots* of money in some cases. A St. Paul, Minnesota, bookstore recently netted in the neighborhood of one million dollars by selling the rights to HungryMinds.com. The Hungry Mind bookstore has been doing business for almost 30 years, but an offer to buy the domain name from an Internet education portal was an offer the owner could not refuse, and he agreed to sell the rights and change the name of the bookstore.

In this case the owner of the bookstore had a legitimate business interest in establishing the HungryMinds.com domain name, and did not set out to profit by selling it. But there have been many incidents of people registering names of existing companies, products, and phrases in the hope that they can make money by selling it to a real business or person with that name. Called *cybersquatting*, this controversial tactic is coming under increasing fire from business and lawmakers, and recent court opinion has sided against the squatters.

## Understanding Domain Names

1. Go to www.icann.org.
2. Can you register a domain name on this site? Do you register directly through ICANN?
3. Go to one of ICANN's approved domain name registrars.
4. Make up a domain name using your first and last names and do a search to see if it is available.
5. Was it available?

**Table 2.2 Common Domain Name Suffixes for Institutions, Organizations, and People**

| Suffix | Category |
|---|---|
| .aero | the aerospace industry (since Nov. 2000) |
| .com | company or commercial institution (Ford, Intel) |
| .coop | cooperatives (since Nov. 2000) |
| .edu | educational institution (Cornell, Yale) |
| .gov | governmental site (NASA, IRS) |
| .info | unrestricted (since Nov. 2000) |
| .int | international treaty organization, Internet database (NATO) |
| .mil | military site (Department of Defense) |
| .museum | museums (since Nov. 2000) |
| .name | people's names (since Nov. 2000) |
| .net | administrative site for the Internet or ISPs |
| .org | nonprofit or private organization or society (Red Cross, Public Television) |
| .pro | professions (since Nov. 2000) |
| .biz | businesses (since Nov. 2000) |

**Table 2.3 Domain Suffixes Identifying Countries**

| Suffix | Category | Suffix | Category |
|---|---|---|---|
| .af | Afghanistan | .jp | Japan |
| .at | Austria | .kr | Republic of Korea |
| .au | Australia | .mx | Mexico |
| .be | Belgium | .nl | Netherlands |
| .br | Brazil | .no | Norway |
| .ca | Canada | .pl | Poland |
| .ch | Switzerland | .ru | Russia |
| .de | Germany | .se | Sweden |
| .dk | Denmark | .tw | Taiwan |
| .es | Spain | .uk | United Kingdom |
| .fi | Finland | .us | United States |
| .fr | France | .za | South Africa |
| .il | Israel | .zw | Zimbabwe |
| .it | Italy | | |

Complete list of country domain suffixes

http://virtualfamilybusiness.com/domain_suffixes_these_extensions.htm

**Table 2.4 Proposed New Domain Suffixes**

| Suffix | Category |
|---|---|
| .firm | general business |
| .store | online sales |
| .arts | culture and entertainment |
| .info | information services |
| .nom | personal name |
| .web | World Wide Web organizations |
| .rec | recreation/entertainment |

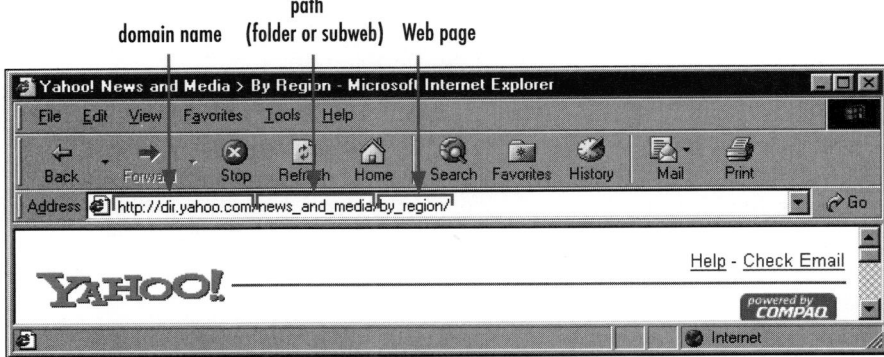

*Figure 2.4* **Tracing the Path Followed by a URL**

URLs are the pathways to the documents kept in servers around the world. The component parts of a URL are a set of instructions that lead right to the material you are looking for. For that reason, each URL is unique. For example, the regional listings for the News and Media directory on Yahoo! can be found at http://dir.yahoo.com/News_and_Media/By_Region/ (see Figure 2.4). The first part of the address, *http://*, indicates that the protocol used is *HTTP* (Hypertext Transfer Protocol). This protocol is used on the Web for HTML (Hypertext Markup Language) documents. The protocol links pages on the Web through hyperlinking. The http:// protocol is the default protocol, so in later versions of Internet Explorer and Netscape Navigator, you do not have to key the protocol when typing in a URL address. After the two slashes comes the host name, in this case *dir.yahoo.com*. This is the server location where all of the files are stored. The *.com* indicates that it is a commercial site (see Table 2.2). *News_and_Media* lead to the file by that name. The part of a URL leading to a file location is also known as a *pathway*. Finally, *By_Region* leads to a file where news and media items are sorted by region. Because many files may be linked together one after the other, URLs can be quite long.

**Hot Words**    When you scroll the mouse over underlined text within a Web page, you will notice the mouse cursor transforms into a pointing hand. This indicates a **hot word**, or hyperlink within the text. Click the mouse and you link directly to another location on the Web.

Hot words appear as underlined text, usually set off in a contrasting font color. What you won't see in the screen is the HTML coding. In this case a <A HREF> **tag**, or metatag, in the source code denotes a hyperlink. Hot words can be linked to areas on the same page, to a related page, or to a completely different location on the Web. Text with the URL appears on the status bar at the bottom of the browser screen as the mouse pointer stops on the hot word (see Figure 2.5). Hot words are not the only linking mechanism on the Web. Hypermedia works much the same way as hot words, but allows links between any elements including text, graphics, sound, and animation.

## Image Maps

**Image maps** are graphic equivalents of hypertext links; as a navigation option, image maps link by association to other Web locations by use of hot spots on a graphic that have the same <A HREF> tag as hypertext links; A graphic on the Web can link to other graphics, text, sound, movies, animation, and so forth. Creating and utilizing such links is true multimedia. You will see increasing use of image maps on Web pages. Most still have text user instructions, or have flashing areas or tooltips that advertise the hyperlink. A **tooltip** shows you the location of a hyperlink in an image map. A sample image map is shown in Figure 2.6.

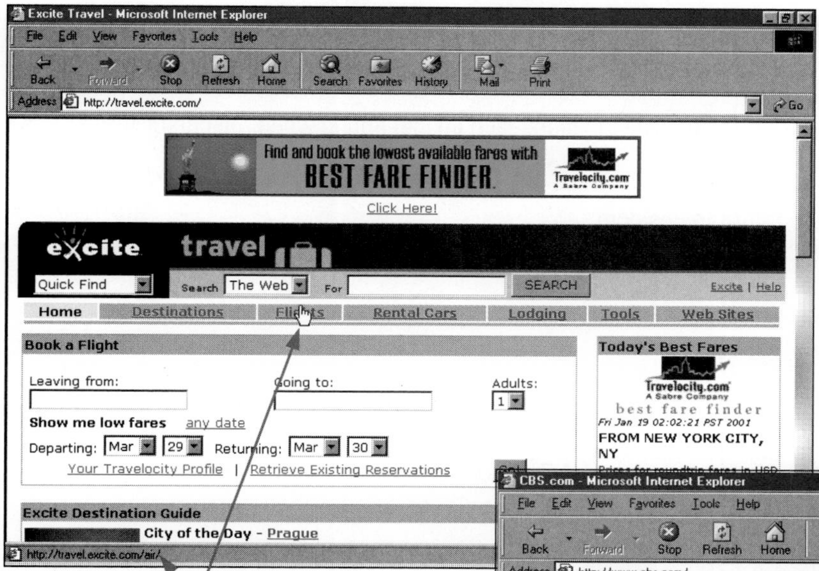

When the hand is positioned over a link, the location of the hyperlink displays on the status bar.

**Figure 2.5**
**Status Bar Showing Hypertext URL**

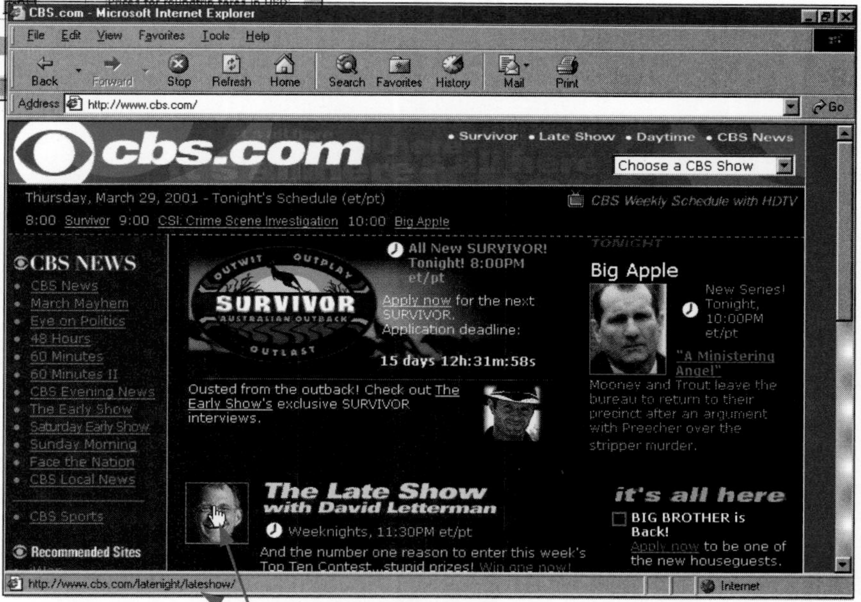

By positioning the hand on an image map, a tooltip appears on the status bar showing the location of the hyperlink.

**Figure 2.6**
**Hot Spot in an Image Map Made Visible by a Tooltip**

Just looking at an image does not reveal its "hot" nature, therefore users will miss it unless they roll the mouse over the image. Hypertext is underlined and appears in a contrasting color that indicates a hypertext link, but no such standard system exists for image maps. Until users become accustomed to image maps, they may need hints as to what is available. Use the mouse to browse broadly over the parts of a Web page to see if there are any links you have not noticed. Every hyperlink is an opportunity for interaction. The interactive environment of the Web increases with every new multimedia mode introduced.

## Investigating Hyperlinks

1. Go to www.cbs.com.
2. Roll the mouse over the page. Explore each image, noting when the cursor turns into a pointing hand.
3. Click one of the images.
4. Click Back to return to cbs.com.

## Toolbar Shortcuts

The most frequently used navigating functions are on the toolbar found on the browser software. You can customize your toolbar just as you can in other Windows applications. Figures 2.7 and 2.8 show the toolbar for IE and Navigator. These buttons allow you to navigate on the Web without using pull-down menus.

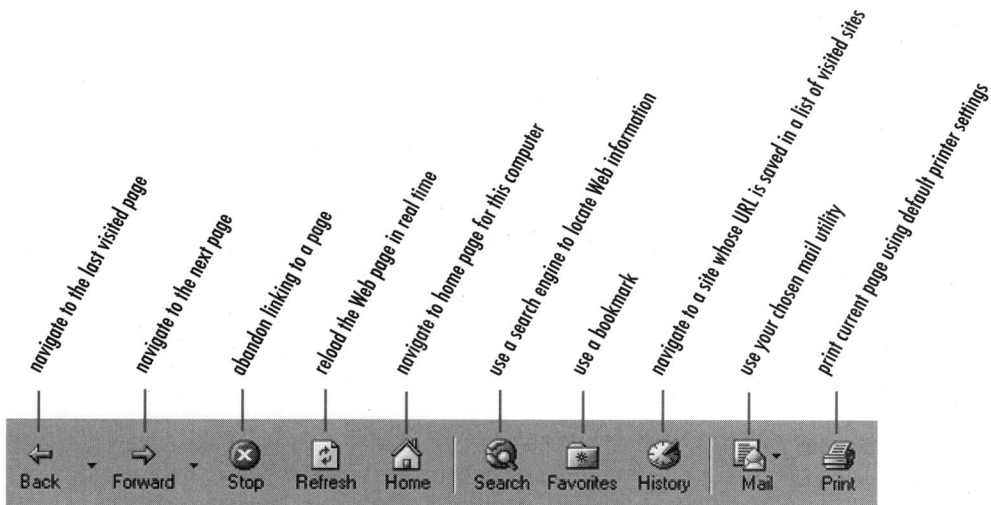

*Figure 2.7* Internet Explorer Toolbar

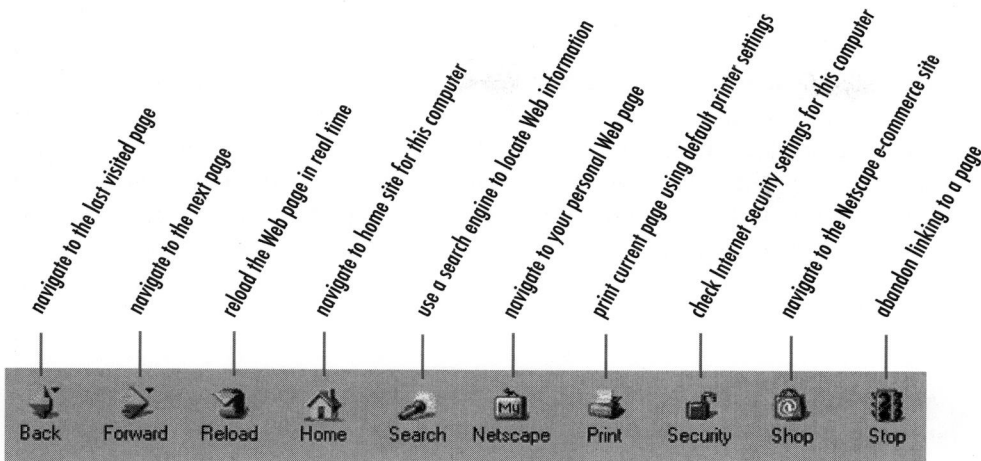

*Figure 2.8* **Netscape Navigator Toolbar**

The Stop button is of particular value. If you find the browser searching for a long time, downloading a memory-intensive page, or if you have a slow modem, you can click the Stop button and abort the link to that page. Along with the Back and Forward buttons, which let you move backward and forward among the pages you have already viewed, and the Home button, which takes you back to your starting place, the Stop button is one of the most frequently used buttons on the toolbar. Print and Search, which allow you to print and find information, are also very useful. So is the Mail button (IE) that lets you check your Internet mailbox, thus automatically launching your mail server. (E-mail is discussed in detail in chapter 4.) The Refresh (IE) or Reload (Navigator) button allows a Web page to be reloaded in real time.

**Navigation Buttons** Navigating through the maze of pages on the Web to reach the one you want is sometimes a daunting task. You may have advanced three or four pages before you realize you want to be back where you started. That is what the Back, Forward, and Home buttons and menus are for on the browser toolbar. They maintain a history of the pages visited during a session so that you can return to them. Clicking the Back button will show you your actions in reverse. After you have clicked Back, you can switch directions again by clicking Forward.

## Using Shortcut Buttons

1. Go to www.usatoday.com.
2. Find and click a link on the page.
3. As the page is loading, click the Stop button to stop the page from loading.
4. Click Refresh/Reload. Note the screen that appears.
5. Click Forward. Note the screen that appears.

Why are these buttons necessary? When you first access a Web page and add it to your Favorites (IE) or Bookmarks (Navigator) section, a copy of the page is cached (saved) in the *Internet Temporary Files* folder located on the hard drive. When you want to access that page again, you may click on it from Favorites or Bookmarks where it is stored. The quick display you then see may be the cached or the outdated page stored in the *Internet Temporary Files* folder on your hard drive and not the latest version. If you want to view the most current version of the page, click the Refresh/Reload button and the page will be updated. Using Favorites/Bookmarks is explained in more detail later in this chapter.

## Changing Icon Size

1. On the browser menu bar, click View, point to Toolbars, and then click customize to display the Customize Toolbar dialog box.
2. At the bottom of the screen in the Icon options text box, change the size of the icons. (You can select either Small icons or Large icons.)
3. Click Close.
4. To revert to the previous icon setting, repeat steps 1–4 and change back to the previous icon size.

Navigating to URLs may not occur in a logical pattern, and the URL itself may be difficult to remember. The nonlinear, associative way the Web is browsed does not establish a linear, logical path; browsing the Web is just that—grazing from one site to another at will. Favorites and Bookmarks store URLs and automatically guide you to frequently visited sites. However, when you are online and wish to review how you arrived at the current site, or revisit a page you have recently left, the history and address options can help. (The **history** function keeps a record of the pages visited during a Web session so that you can return to them by simply clicking on the stored URL.

The drop-down list in the Address/Netsite text box (shown in Figure 2.9) keeps a history of the sites visited. The Back button on the toolbar also has a similar drop-down list for the current session (Figure 2.10). The Address/Netsite function works somewhat like the trail of breadcrumbs left behind by Hansel and Gretel by allowing you to retrace your steps back to where you came from. Viewing these URLs will allow you to select the URL of any site you wish to revisit.

Using Internet Explorer, the History button allows you to see recently visited URLs. When the History button is clicked, the URLs appear in the left side of the screen.

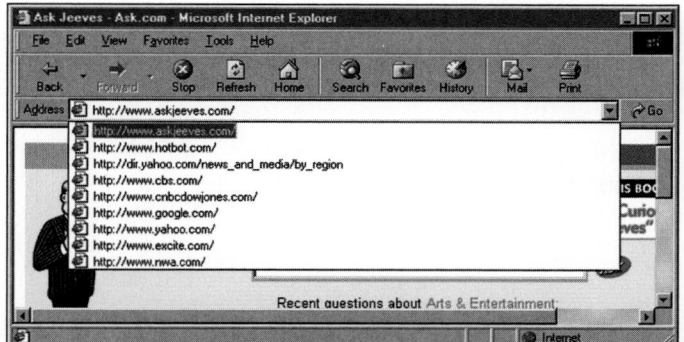

**Figure 2.9  Address/Netsite**
*This function allows you to review the sites you visited in your latest session.*

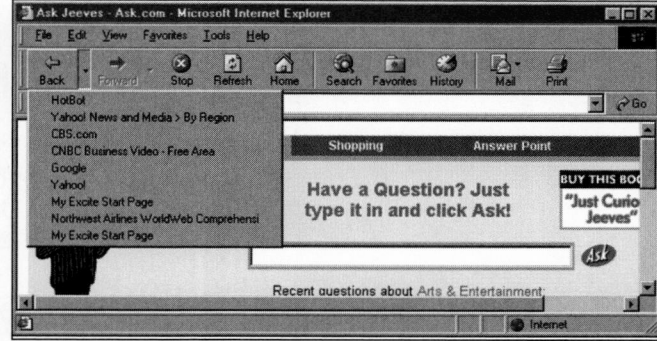

**Figure 2.10  Back Button**
*The Back button has a drop-down list similar to the Address/Netsite drop-down list.*

## Using the Back Button to Show History

1. Go to www.google.com.
2. Go to www.cnbcdowjones.com.
3. Now go to www.askjeeves.com.
4. Click Back, then click the down arrow to the right of the Back button, and a drop-down list of URLs appears. Find and select google.com by double-clicking on it.
5. Continue with the next Try It Out!

## Using Address/Netsite to Show History

1. Find the Address/Netsite text box on the browser.
2. Click the down arrow to the right of the text box and a drop-down list of URLs appears. Are the URLs the same as the URLs that displayed when you clicked the Back button?
3. Select a URL by double-clicking on it.

## Using the History Button to Show History

1. In Internet Explorer, click the History button.
2. Open one of the files by clicking on it.
3. Click on the desired URL.

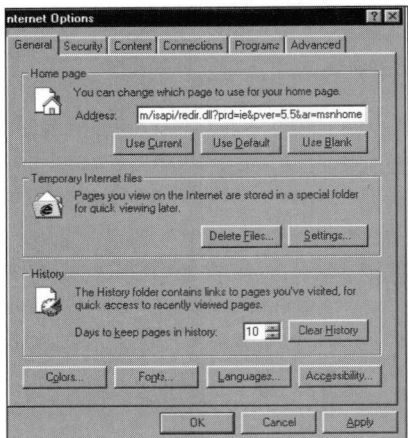

**Figure 2.11**
**Selecting Days to Keep Pages in History in Internet Explorer**

In Netscape Navigator, to see where you have navigated, click Communicator, Tools, and then History to see a window with Web page titles, URLs, the date you went there, how many times you accessed the site, and other useful information for the time period established in the Preferences option.

To select the number of days you want to store history data in IE, click Internet Options on the Tools drop-down menu and then click the General tab. In Navigator, select Preferences on the Edit drop-down menu and then key the number of days you wish to maintain the list. You can also clear the history or address list at any time by using these menus. Figure 2.11 shows the Internet Options dialog box in Internet Explorer with the General tab selected.

## Selecting the Number of Days to Store History

1. In Internet Explorer, click Tools from the menu bar, and then click Internet Options to display the Internet Options dialog box.
2. Make sure the General tab is selected.
3. In the Days to keep pages in history text box, key the desired number of days.
4. Click OK to close the dialog box.

Additional toolbars on the browser are usually located directly under the main toolbar. These have been automatically added to IE or Navigator by your ISP upon installation. From these toolbars you may be able to navigate to chat rooms, AOL Instant Messenger, Yellow Page listings, or specific search engines. The main toolbar is faster to use than the drop-down menus; however, both the menu bar and the main toolbar serve the same functions.

## Browser Functions and Web Page Management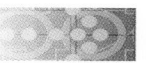

Internet Explorer and Netscape Navigator each come with a standard menu bar. The menu bars for both browsers are similar. The names of Favorites, Tools, and Communicator categories differ slightly, but their functions are almost identical. In fact, most browser menu bars show File, Edit, View, Favorites (or Bookmarks), Tools (or Communicator), and Help as standard menu choices.

Figures 2.12 and 2.13 show standard menu commands. Even if you have a different version, or an entirely different browser from what is shown, the menu bars and toolbars are similar. A quick review of the menu offerings gives you an idea of what is available with your particular system. As new elements of the Web are introduced throughout this course, the menu selections will be covered more thoroughly.

menu bar

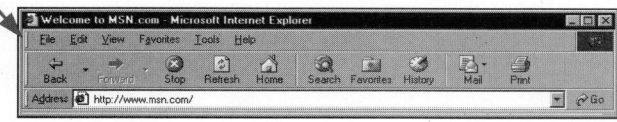

**Figure 2.12**
**Internet Explorer Menu Bar Commands**

menu bar

**Figure 2.13**
**Netscape Navigator Menu Bar Commands**

## From HyperCard to Hypertext

Bill Atkinson is the legendary programmer who created the first painting program for personal computers, MacPaint. His concept for the program, which helped popularize the first personal computer graphical user interface, was simple and clever. The user was presented with a white screen (a sketchpad) and a set of painting tools, including a paintbrush and a paint bucket. Selecting the paintbrush with the mouse cursor changed the cursor into a brush tip. When the brush tip was moved in the white screen with the mouse button depressed, it turned the pixels beneath from white to black. By this means, shapes were formed in the screen. Selecting the paint bucket enabled the user to fill an area with a predefined pattern.

Atkinson initiated a second software revolution by creating HyperCard, a program that enabled users to build customized programs, called stacks, without learning a complex programming language. To develop a program in HyperCard, the user would create a stack of cards, adding buttons, icons, text fields, and simple scripts in HyperTalk scripting language. The scripts caused the buttons, icons, and text fields to perform tasks such as moving to another card, making mathematical calculations, importing text, and animating graphics. Using HyperCard, nonprogrammers were able to create their own programs.

HyperCard was the program that introduced many personal computer users to the concept of hypertext—pages linked to one another in an associative way. HyperCard was ahead of its time because it gave ordinary computer users the ability to create their own programs. Today that trend continues, with nonprogrammers able to create Web pages using HTML tags. Atkinson was a visionary, a programmer whose work took software a quantum leap into the future.

Many menu commands contain *submenus*. The functions of these submenu commands will be described as they are introduced later in this chapter and throughout the course. The drop-down menu lists for Internet Explorer and Netscape Navigator are shown in Tables 2.5 and 2.6.

 **Table 2.5** Internet Explorer Version 5.5 Menu Commands

| Menu Command | Submenu Command | Description |
|---|---|---|
| File | New | begin a new message or Web page display, for multiple views |
| | Open | open a page on the Internet or open a file on the local computer |
| | Edit with Notepad | edit with Microsoft for Windows |
| | Save | save current Web page |
| | Save As | save current Web page |
| | Page Setup | change margins, customize the way the page prints |
| | Print | print current Web page or active frame |
| | Print Preview | view current Web page or active frame before printing |
| | Send | forward a page or link by e-mail, or define a shortcut for desktop |
| | Import and Export | import and export information from a Web page to other applications or a file on your computer |
| | Properties | lists the general properties of the Web page |
| | Work Offline | use browser to work locally, without connection to ISP |
| | Close | exit the browser |
| Edit | Cut | remove selected material on Web page |
| | Copy | duplicate selected material on Web page |
| | Paste | insert the material you have cut or copied |
| | Select All | select whole Web page (even part not in view) for duplication |
| | Find (on This Page) | search for text on current Web page |
| View | Toolbars | add or delete standard or specific toolbars to browser display |
| | Status Bar | add or delete the status bar on the browser display |
| | Explorer Bar | place selected command from toolbar in frame on browser display |
| | Go To | navigate to a specific saved URL and display it |
| | Stop | stop the Web page from loading |
| | Refresh | redisplay current page as it exists now on the server |
| | Text Size | change the browser display font size |
| | Encoding | to correctly display Web pages encoded in any language |
| | Source | displays the HTML or other scripting code for current page |
| | Full Screen | displays screen without any toolbars or other menus visible |
| Favorites | Add to Favorites | add a bookmark, a shortcut to a Web site |
| | Organize Favorites | reorder or arrange bookmark hierarchy |
| | Channels | links to preinstalled channels |
| | Links | provides preinstalled links to Hotmail, Microsoft.com, and others |
| | (Other items) | bookmarks specific to user computer, such as media and search engines |
| Tools | Mail and News | use your e-mail utility and read news |
| | Synchronize | set data on computer to data online (slows operation) |
| | Windows Update | connects to Microsoft Web site for program updates |
| | Show Related Links | shows URLs related to current topic |
| | Internet Options | set preferences for channels, properties, saving temporary files |
| Help | Contents and Index | topics covered in online documentation, hypertext-enabled |
| | Tour | guided tutorial of browser functions |
| | About Internet Explorer | lists version number and other information |

*Note: Depending upon the version of your browser, the menu commands may vary from this list.*

*Table 2.6* **Netscape Navigator Version 4.7 Menu Commands**

| Menu Command | Submenu Command | Description |
|---|---|---|
| File | New | begin a new message or Web page display, for multiple views |
| | Open Page | open a Web page, locally or online with Internet |
| | Save As | save current Web page |
| | Save Frame As | save just frame at cursor point |
| | Send Page | forward a page or link by e-mail, or define a shortcut for desktop |
| | Edit Page | edit page in Netscape Composer |
| | Upload File | send local file to FTP location currently connected to |
| | Offline | use browser to work locally, without connection to ISP |
| | Page Setup | change margins, customize the way the page prints |
| | Print Preview | view current Web page or active frame before printing |
| | Print | print current Web page or active frame |
| | Close | close the browser window |
| | Exit | exit the Internet |
| Edit | Cut | remove selected material on Web page |
| | Copy | duplicate selected material on Web Page |
| | Paste | place duplicated material at point of cursor |
| | Select All | select whole Web page (even part not in view) for duplication |
| | Find in Page | search for text on current Web page |
| | Search Internet | conduct search on the Internet |
| | Preferences | set Internet options for channels, properties, saving temporary files |
| View | Show | add or delete standard or specific toolbars to browser display |
| | Increase Font | increase font size on display |
| | Decrease Font | decrease font size on display |
| | Reload | redisplay current page as it exists now on DNS (Domain Name System) |
| | Refresh | redisplay current page |
| | Stop Page Loading | abandon navigation to hyperlinked page |
| | Page Source | display the HTML or other scripting code for current page |
| | Page Info | view information about the files that compose a page |
| | Character Set | change text display to language of choice |
| Go | Back | navigate to previous URL |
| | Forward | navigate to next saved URL |
| | Home | return to home page for this computer |
| Communicator | Composer | HTML editor to prepare Web page |
| | Bookmarks | add to bookmarks, reorder, and edit bookmarks |
| | Newsgroups | set Usenets, discussion groups |
| | Address Book | maintain your mail utilities |
| | Tools | set preferences for history, channels, properties, saving temporary files, set security |
| Help | Help Contents | topics covered in online documentation, hypertext-enabled; also contains an index |
| | About Plug-ins | lists the plug-ins already installed on this computer |

*Note: Depending upon the version of your browser, the menu commands may vary from this list.*

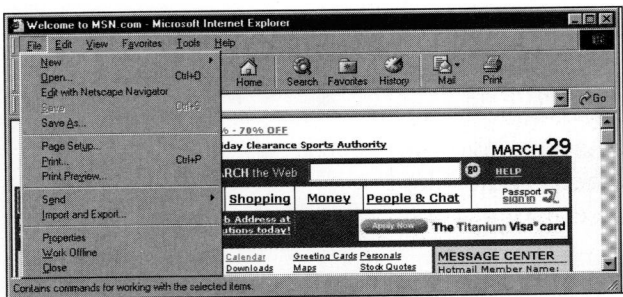

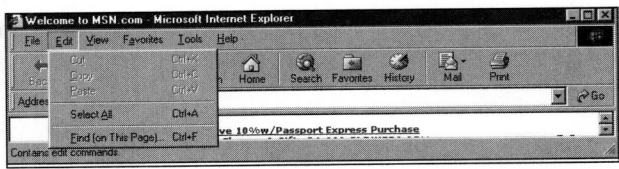

*Figure 2.14*
**Internet Explorer**
**File Drop-Down Menu**

*Figure 2.15*
**Internet Explorer**
**Edit Drop-Down Menu**

## File Management Functions

On the File menu (see Figure 2.14) you can work **offline** (use the browser while not connected to the Internet), open other Web pages, begin a new Web page, print the current page(s), upload (Send) files to a site you have access to, and save Web resources from other sites.

Within the Edit drop-down menu choices (see Figure 2.15) you can copy, cut, or paste from the Windows Clipboard, or select the entire Web page for duplication. Selecting Find (on This Page) allows you to search for words or phrases in the text.

### Finding Text

1. In Internet Explorer, go to www.cnn.com.
2. At the bottom of the displayed page, click on a news article of interest to you.
3. On the browser menu bar, click Edit and then click Find (on This Page) to display the Find dialog box.
4. In the Find what text box, key a word or phrase about a topic that interests you, such as **jobs** or **personal computers**. Click the Find Next button. *(Hint: If your word or phrase isn't found, try another.)*
5. Note what happens to the cursor.
6. Continue your search or click Back to return to the CNN home page.
7. Look for other items that interest you.

On the View menu (see Figure 2.16) you can stop the Web page from loading, redisplay (Refresh) the current page, change the size and type of fonts to see a page better (Text Size), view the HTML source codes for that Web page, and through the Explorer Bar menu you can search through the history of pages in a session.

The source code reveals the programming for the Web page. Most Web pages are constructed in HTML, although they could be composed in a word processing or spreadsheet application, and then exported to HTML. The HTML codes appear in angle brackets < >. You will learn simple HTML codes when you create a Web page in Chapter 6. Figure 2.17 shows the source code for www.juno.com, displayed in Windows Notepad.

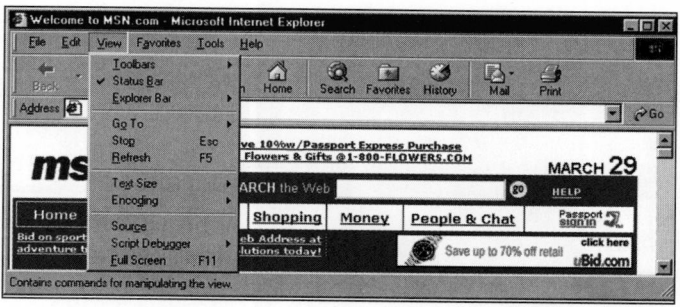

**Figure 2.16** Internet Explorer View Drop-Down Menu

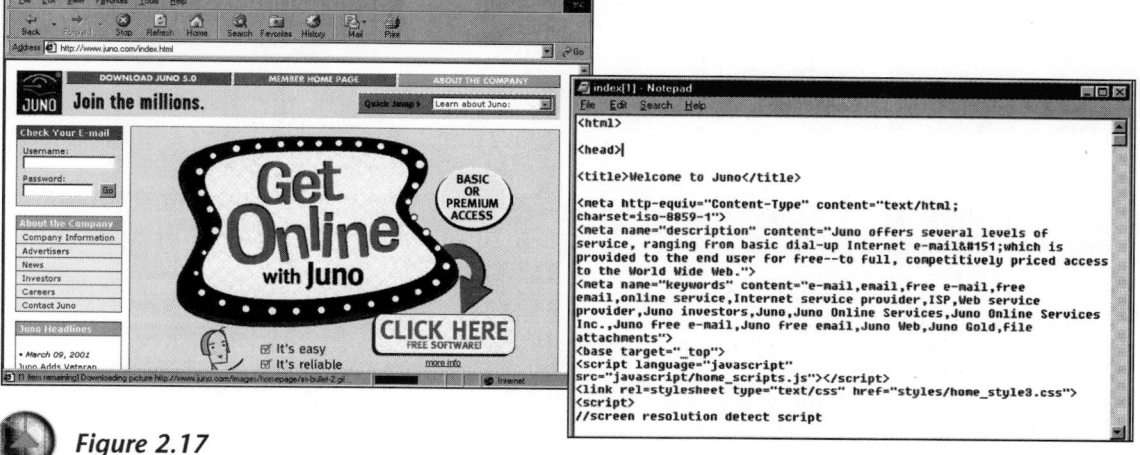

**Figure 2.17**
**Web Page Source Code Shown in Windows Notepad**

## Favorites and Bookmarks

As you navigate from one Web page to another, you may wish to return to pages or sites you have viewed previously. If you cannot remember where they are or how you found them in the first place, you may never be able to locate them again. You can prevent this problem from occurring by using the Favorites (Internet Explorer) or Bookmarks (Netscape Navigator) feature of your browser. Using these allows you to save a URL and categorize it by subject so that you can quickly and easily find it again. For example, if you have located the online newspaper for your hometown, you could create a favorites or bookmarks category called newspapers and store it there (see Figure 2.18). You can even rename the favorite or bookmark if the Web page title automatically displayed does not readily reflect its content.

The file that contains the URLs themselves is stored in the Internet directory on your computer's hard drive. You can add or delete as many favorites or bookmarks as you wish. Individual favorites collections are very important to savvy Web users. Few individuals bother to memorize long URLs; they simply click Favorites or Bookmarks when wanting to go to a particular Web page or site. For example, in IE you can renew and delete favorites by clicking Organize Favorites.

allows you to add sites to your Favorites list
allows you to create folders of favorites

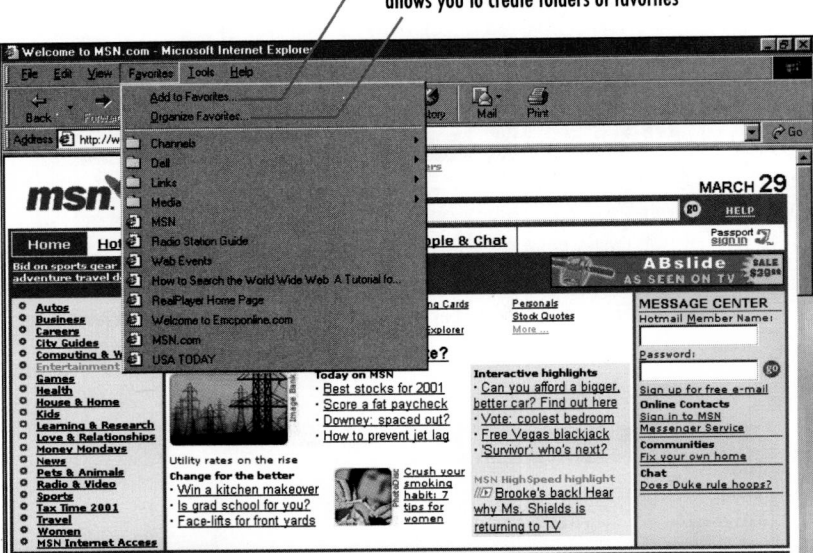

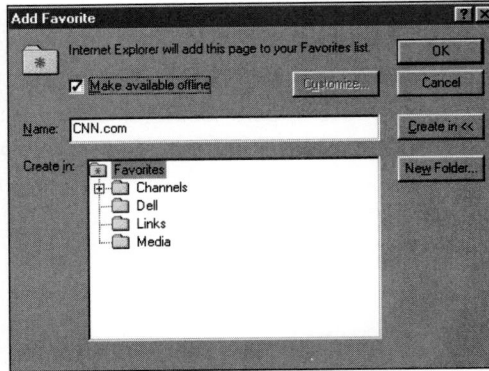

**Figure 2.19**
**Add Favorite Dialog Box**
*You can view Web pages offline by checking the Make available offline box in the Add Favorite dialog box.*

*Figure 2.18* **Favorites Drop-Down Menu**
*You can store your favorites in folders you create.*

### Adding a Favorite

1. In Internet Explorer, go to www.altavista.com.
2. On the browser menu bar, click Favorites and then click Add to Favorites to display the Add Favorite dialog box. If you wish to be able to view this favorite when you are not connected to the Internet, click in the Make available offline check box (see Figure 2.19).
3. Make sure AltaVista - Welcome displays in the Name text box and click OK.
4. Check your work: click Favorites, and then scroll down to find AltaVista.
5. Click Tools on the menu bar and then click Synchronize to display the Items to Synchronize dialog box.
6. If you checked the Make available offline box when you added your favorite, you should see it here. Then click Synchronize at the bottom of the screen to make sure you have the latest version of the favorite stored on your hard drive.

An additional option of the Favorites feature in Internet Explorer allows you to save favorites offline so that you can view them when you are not connected to the Internet. When you are online again, your offline pages can be refreshed to make sure they are up-to-date. This is called **synchronizing**. In previous versions of IE, the offline feature was known as channels or subscriptions.

## Creating a Personalized Favorites File Folder

1. Go to www.google.com.
2. On the browser menu bar, click Favorites and then click Add to Favorites to display the Add Favorite dialog box. Click the Create in button, then click the New Folder button to display the Create New Folder dialog box.
3. Click OK to close the dialog boxes.
4. Check your work: click Favorites, then click on your file folder. Find Google in the list.

## Organizing Favorites

1. On the browser menu bar, click Favorites and then click Organize Favorites to display the Organize Favorites dialog box.
2. Scroll down to find and select a site name you are interested in and click to select it.
3. Click the Move to Folder button. Select your personalized favorites folder, then click OK.
4. At the Organize Favorites dialog box, click Close.
5. Check your work: click Favorites, then select and click on your file folder. Find the site.

## Deleting or Renaming Your Favorites

1. On the browser menu bar, click Favorites and then click Organize Favorites to display the Organize Favorites dialog box.
2. Select the item to be removed or renamed.
3. To rename, click Rename and key the new name.
4. To remove, click Delete.
5. ClickClose to close the dialog box.

## Understanding Web Page Elements

1. Go to http://usatoday.com.
2. See how many of the following elements you can find on the home page: text, graphics, audio, movies, or animation.
3. Comment upon the visual appeal of the home page. What elements did you like? Why?
4. Were there elements that you disliked? Why? How would you redesign the page?

## Getting Help Organizing Your Favorites or Bookmarks

1. In Internet Explorer or Netscape Navigator, go to www.acqurl.com, www.alertbookmarks.com, or www.webroot.com. Browse the site.
2. Now go to www.backflip.com or www.itlist.com. These sites offer the software free.
3. Compare them with the sites above. Which site is your favorite? In your opinion, which site is the most useful?

## Tools and Help Functions

In Internet Explorer, within the Tools menu choices (see Figure 2.20), you can read your mail, create a new mail message, synchronize so that when you work offline your computer will synchronize the Web pages stored on your computer with the data on the network, send a page, and show related links. In addition, you can set your Internet options (see Figure 2.21).

The Help menu choices (see Figure 2.22) allow you to search the contents or a detailed index of the browser, find out what version you are using (About Internet Explorer), and locate other information customized to your browser.

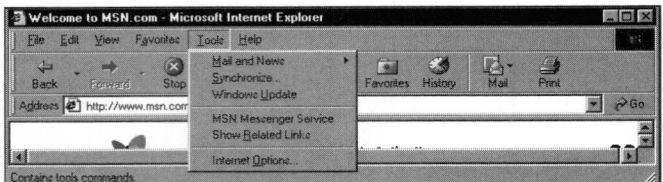

**Figure 2.20** Internet Explorer Tools Drop-Down Menu

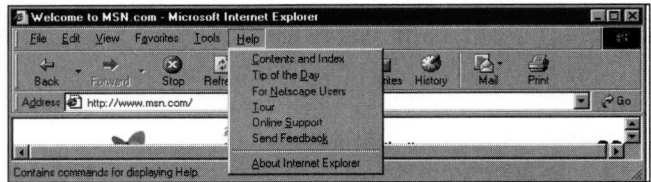

**Figure 2.22** Internet Explorer Help Drop-Down Menu

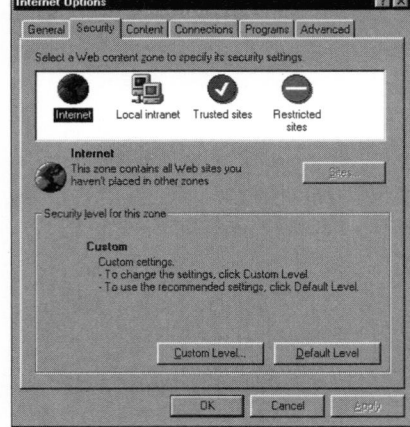

**Figure 2.21** Internet Options Dialog Box with Security Tab Selected

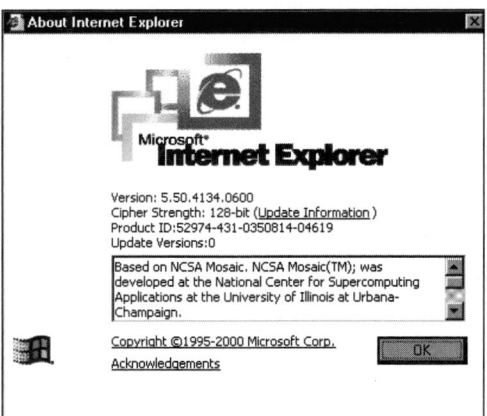

**Figure 2.23** About Internet Explorer Window

## Try IT OUT — Using Help

1. Click Help on the browser menu bar, then click About Internet Explorer from the drop-down menu.
2. View the information about the browser. Write down the version number of your browser and compare it with the version number listed in Figure 2.23.
3. Click OK to close the About Internet Explorer window.

# Frames and Web Page Enhancements

The great appeal of the World Wide Web is its graphical interface representing images and text together in the same environment. If text were enough, we might still be back in the pre-browser world of Internet Gopher with its cascading hypertext-only text menus. Gopher was a system for organizing and displaying files that was created at the University of Minnesota and named after the school mascot. Gopher sites are still available over the Web, but they pale beside the newer elements of the Internet.

When Web pages are split into separately functioning panes, or independent areas, they are called composite Web documents. When more than one Web page is being displayed at the same time in the same screen, each is in a frame. **Frames** are separate windows with their own horizontal and vertical scroll bars. You can explore the contents of one frame without disturbing the display in the adjoining frame, or you can synchronize the scrolling on all page frames. You can also navigate to other hyperlinked pages from within one of the frames. A Web page that contains multiple frames is shown in Figure 2.24.

Earlier versions of browsers did not support frames, and some proprietary browsers still do not. However, the demand for browsers to support composite Web documents is so great that the ability to do so is fast becoming a necessity. Such documents allow controlled disclosure of much more material without going outside the confines of the page. Their presence increases the comfort level of beginning users and gives advanced users more options. Web pages with frames are obviously more complicated to create, but they are becoming a Web standard.

Many frame pages are written with Java, a programming script that allows compatible browsers to read everything from moving banners to complicated maps and games within those frames. Java uses applications called applets which are downloaded and run by your

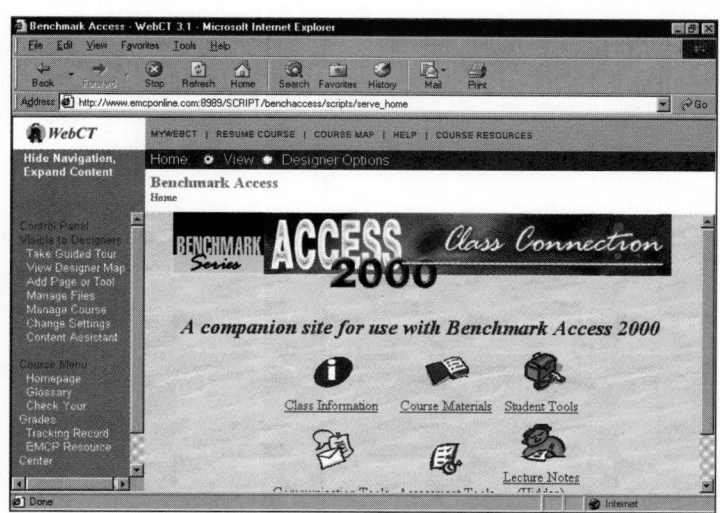

**Figure 2.24**
**Web Page with Multiple Frames**

computer, provided you have a Java-compatible browser like Internet Explorer or Netscape Navigator.

The instant that graphics became available on the Internet, the world wanted more—more graphics, more color, more animation, more interactivity, more everything! The Web's global environment was perfect as an all-encompassing, interactive arena of sights and sounds.

Plug-ins, or helper software applications, enhance the capability of the browser to display Web pages. Plug-ins update browsers with features that their internal programs currently lack. Without these applications you would not be able to view a video clip on a Web page, hear the latest recording of a popular vocalist, control interactive animations, or view the evening news.

Some plug-ins provide multimedia streaming technology. **Streaming** data transfer was developed because of the huge data transfer and processing requirements of multimedia elements, and the limited bandwidth of Internet connections. The video or audio file is "streamed," or downloaded in small increments, to the cache memory. It is buffered, or stored, until there is enough of it downloaded to start playing the file. When the buffer fills up, the video or sound begins to play. At the same time, the rest of the file continues to stream into the buffer. If the buffer should empty before it is replenished, the replay will pause until the buffer accumulates enough to resume playing. For this reason it is not recommended to stream files if you have a modem that transmits at less than 28.8Kbps. If you have a powerful enough processor (300MHz or more), using streaming technology is the only practical way to experience quality video or sound files on the Web.

Prior alternatives to streaming required downloading the entire file—often 12 to 20MB or more—to your hard drive, and playing the file after the entire file was stored. This was problematic. Unless there was a very fast connection to the Internet, the process took up to several hours or more. On slower speed connections to the Internet, a 1MB file can take an hour to download uncompressed if using a slow FTP!

Table 2.7 shows only a few common plug-ins. There are a huge variety of available plug-ins and multimedia systems delivered on the Web. If a Web page requires a certain plug-in and you do not have it on your computer, the page will not display correctly.

**Streaming Site**
http://www.webmedia.ie
**Virtual Reality Gallery**
http://www.3dgallery.com
**Creating Quality Web Sites**
http://www.glowingtoad.com/
toadflash/humanfactors.htm

 *Table 2.7* **Common Web Plug-Ins**

| Plug-In | Function |
| --- | --- |
| Shockwave, Flash, Splash | used with Macromedia's Director, DreamWeaver, and Authorware programs |
| Neuron | used with Toolbook programs |
| RealPlayer | used with Progressive Network's RealAudio and RealVideo resources |
| QuickTime | Apple's movie viewer (.mov files) |
| Java Classes | Java interpreters |
| ActiveX components | used with .ocx, .vbx files written in Visual Basic |
| Broadway | view movie clips in MPEG format |
| Coldfusion | tag utility to allow queries to a server database |
| Adobe Acrobat Reader | view .pdf files |

One plug-in in Table 2.7 that is required to view formatted document files that are not Web pages, but camera-ready word processing files, is Adobe® Acrobat Reader. It allows you to read PDF (Portable Document Format) files. Versions are updated frequently, which can present a problem: You must use the version of the plug-in that was used to develop the Web enhancement you wish to view. Not only do you have to go to the company Web site and download and install the plug-in on your computer, but you also have to install the correct version. Most Web sites that require plug-ins point you to the free download location right on the page that requires one. Some even have a test image, sound, animation, and so on for you to view before you download.

## Downloading Forms

1. Go to the Internal Revenue Service (IRS) site located at http://www.irs.gov/forms_pubs/.
2. Click the *Forms and Instructions* link.
3. Click the *freely available* link in the paragraph about Adobe Acrobat.
4. This takes you to the Adobe Acrobat site. Follow the instructions and install the latest versions on your computer. You do not need to purchase any of the enhanced version, unless you want to.
5. Once you have installed Acrobat on your computer, use the Back button on your browser to return to the IRS page that led you to Adobe.
6. Scroll down the page to find a list of tax forms. Select .pdf from the file format list if it is not already selected. (Click on the circle to fill it in.) Acrobat file extensions are indicated by *.pdf.*
7. Click the file or files you want to download. (You may select more than one file, but the more you select the longer this will take.)
8. The document(s) you requested will appear with the title(s) underlined on the results page.
9. To save the document(s) to your hard drive, click on the underlined portion of the document title(s) using the *right* mouse button.
10. Click Save Target As on the menu that appears in your screen.
11. Select the file you wish to save the document(s) in and click Save. You can also print the document by clicking Print, or view and print it later after opening documents in Internet Explorer. *(Note: You cannot write on or otherwise alter these forms, except for some special Acrobat forms that the IRS has created that allow data entry.)*

If you are advised that you need a plug-in to view a Web page, there will be a hyperlink to the site where you can obtain the plug-in free of charge. Point your browser to that page, and follow the download directions. You will have to save the compressed plug-in executable file to the C drive and exit any open applications and disconnect from the Web. Then you need to find the compressed plug-in file on the hard drive, and double-click on the plug-in executable file icon. The file will uncompress and install on your computer.

Reconnect to the Web and locate the site you wish to view. You have now customized your computer to view that page and any other pages that require this version of the plug-in.

Some Web users refuse to visit sites that require plug-ins. Because of the hassle of installing plug-ins, Web authors and users alike would rather not use them, but if it is a choice of not having a knockout Web site, or requiring plug-ins, they usually opt for the latter. Eventually, greater bandwidth, high-speed connections, and the new Internet2 standard discussed in chapter 1 will eliminate the need for plug-ins. In the next generation, the Web will be a true global multimedia environment. Until then, you probably will want to try downloading a few of these plug-in applications to increase your enjoyment in utilizing what is available on the Web.

 # Summary

➤ Browsers are the software that allow you to view the many individual pages that constitute the World Wide Web and access the hyperlinks.

➤ Microsoft's Internet Explorer (IE) and Netscape Navigator are the two primary browsers. All other browsers have similar menus and toolbars.

➤ Your Internet service provider (ISP) may have its own browser, and may also alter the menu items you see in IE or Navigator.

➤ The URL (Uniform Resource Locator) for a Web page is its address. It indicates the Internet protocol being used and locates a page (file) stored in a directory on a Web server or in a domain.

➤ Hot words or hyperlinks within a Web page connect you directly to another frame, area of a page, or other pages on the World Wide Web.

➤ Web pages are constructed with some variation of a markup language, usually HTML.

➤ You can navigate to other Web sites, put a favorite site in a bookmark or history file, and subscribe to Web services by using URLs.

➤ Hypermedia create similar links between different multimedia elements like graphics and sound.

➤ You can often save graphics and other resources stored on a host server once you have navigated to a Web page.

➤ Knowing the basic design and navigation of a Web page will make a significant difference in the quality of your Internet experience.

➤ Displaying certain Web pages may require smaller applications such as plug-ins that run locally on the user's computer or on the server where a page resides.

# Key Terms

**Address/Netsite**  In browser context, the drop-down list in the Address (IE) or Netsite (Navigator) text box that keeps a history of the sites visited during the current session and past sessions; a URL is an address.

**bookmark**  A copy of a Web page is cached in the *Internet Temporary Files* folder on the hard drive; it provides a quick way to navigate to a URL in a Web session.

**domain name**  A registered Web site name. This name is included in the unique URL following the *www.* part of the URL.

**frame**  Separately functioning panes, or independent areas in one screen with their own horizontal and vertical scroll bars. Navigation in one frame can be done without affecting the other frame(s) in the screen.

**history**  A record of the pages visited during a Web session so that you can return to them using Back, Forward, and History buttons.

**hot word**  A hypertext selection that allows you to jump directly to the subject on a Web page.

**image map**  Graphic equivalents of hypertext links; can be sections of a main image connecting to different anchors, or URLs.

**offline**  Working on interface programs, such as composing e-mail messages, when not logged on to the Internet.

**streaming**  A video or audio file is "streamed," or downloaded in small increments, to the cache memory. It is buffered, or stored, until there is enough of it downloaded to start playing the file. While file is being played, the next block is being downloaded, resulting in a constant stream of data.

**synchronizing**  An option of the Favorites feature (IE) that allows you to save Favorites offline. Then, when you go online these pages are automatically refreshed or updated.

**tags**  Tags are the building blocks of formatting and hyperlinking in Web pages. Tags are commands inserted in a document that specify how the document should be formatted, what graphics should display, or to what other location it should be linked. They form the basis of markup languages. Also called metatags.

**tooltips**  Text aids inside pop-up rectangles used to orient users or to explain or identify something on-screen.

 # Navigating and Exploring the Web

## Working the Web

**Project 1**   Use both Internet Explorer and Netscape Navigator to create your own Favorites/Bookmarks folder. Add several items to the folder. Use the Help menu in each browser to find information on copying Web page information into a document. Compare the results of the search. Comment on or discuss with a group which browser you prefer using, and why.

**Project 2**   What can domain names tell you about the entity (person, business, or organization) that owns the name? Go to each of the following sites:

- www.IBM.com
- www.Kelloggs.com
- www.ata.org
- www.lungusa.org
- www.healthmag.com
- www.mscd.edu

What is the name of each organization?
Was the organization's name captured in the URL?
Which URL was the easiest to remember?
Which URL told you the most about the organization?
Which URLs could you use in the future without using a search engine?

**Project 3**   Using the Lycos search engine, search for New York City maps. At the Lycos home page, to the right of Find, click Maps. Write down the URL of this page. Under Get a Map, in the City and State or Zip Code text box key **New York, NY**. Click Get Map. The map that appears is an image map. Click on the red + in the center of the map. (New York City is on Manhattan island; the red + should be at midpoint on the island, at about the position of Central Park.) Use the zoom and arrow keys to enlarge the map until you can see a large rectangular green area on the map that represents Central Park. Zoom until you can read the street names.

> What are the street names that form the border of Central Park?
> What two hospitals are within two blocks of Central Park?
> Do you think you could find your way to this place from the closest airport? Why, or why not?

Using a search engine, search for an image map. Click one of the links and explore the image.

**Project 4** Go to www.space.com or another site with images. Browse the site and select an image to save to the desktop. Write down the steps you used to save the picture to the hard drive. *(Hint: Remember to right-click on the image.)* Comment on your experience. What steps were easy to execute? What steps were not easy?

## Are We Connecting?

### Exercise 1

*Answer the following questions. Questions can be answered individually or assigned as small group discussion.*

1. Discuss the importance of a domain name. Make a list defining a "good" domain name versus a "bad" domain name.
2. Browse the Disney.com Web site. Does the site tell you whether the images are trademarked? Is there any wording on the site that may indicate you have permission to copy an image? Discuss the implications of saving an image from a site. In your opinion, when is it OK to save an image and when should you be cautious?
3. Select three news and media sites such as www.foxsports.com, www.nbci.com, www.cbs.com, www.businessweek.com, and www.usnews.com. Which sites did you like best? Can you identify what you liked about the sites? Discuss use of color, banners, headlines, images, text, and hyperlinks.
4. How many days does your computer store URL history? Check your Internet Preferences to find out. What are two advantages of storing addresses for more than five days? What are the disadvantages? How many sites do you typically visit in one day?

### Exercise 2

*Compose a short answer for each of the following.*

1. What lets you see a Web page, but hides the language coding?
2. What are the names of the two most popular World Wide Web browsers?
3. What is the acronym for a unique address for documents or pages on the Web?
4. Where in the screen can you check to see how long it's taking to download a file?
5. What features in Internet Explorer and Netscape Navigator let you save a connection you have made for future use?
6. Where can you find a list of sites you have visited before in the IE menu and in the Navigator menu?
7. What are the parts of a Web page called that function independently?
8. The link from one word to another, nonlinearly, is known as what?
9. What is the term for a picture or graphic that contains a link?

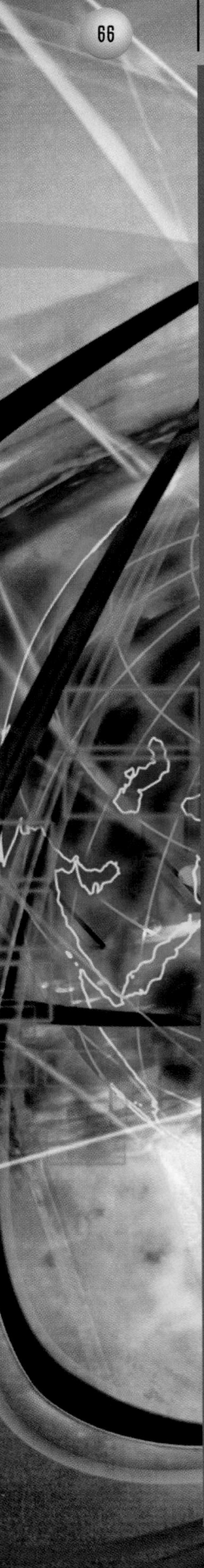

10. Name two popular commercial brand plug-ins.
11. What common language defines the structure and layout of a Web document?

**Exercise 3**

*Indicate whether each of the following statements is True or False. Rewrite the false statements to make them true.*

1. All browsers support all Web languages.
2. The most common Web language is HTML.
3. No two URLs can be exactly the same.
4. A home page is always a Table of Contents to a site.
5. Synchronizing delivers updated news to your computer.
6. All material on the Web is public domain and doesn't have copyrights.
7. A plug-in helps you view video and audio items on a Web page.

# Information Retrieval
## How to Find It, Verify It, and Document It

**3**

## Objectives

➤ Conduct Web search as to obtain information.

➤ Distinguish among search engines, directories, meta-search engines, and virtual libraries.

➤ Use Web search strategies to narrow a search for specific information.

➤ Save material from the Web to a file.

➤ Apply criteria to evaluate the validity and reliability of information found on the Web.

➤ Use effective documentation techniques.

# Searching the Web for Information

The Web is your key to the vast repository of information on the Internet. The answer to almost any question you might have is out there, somewhere in the vast electronic universe known as cyberspace. The trick is finding the information you are looking for. How do you find the needle (what you are looking for) in the haystack (the Internet)? Once you find it, how do you verify its accuracy and use it? In this information age, the overwhelming amount of available information is useful only if it is applicable to your needs, and only if you know how to access it.

There is so much information, it is easy to be overwhelmed by its sheer mass. But you need not worry: all Web users face these challenges. Once you have mastered the Web search techniques and strategies in this chapter you will be able to find almost any type of information you are searching for quickly and easily.

Search tools are just what the name implies, tools that you can use to search the Web. The two most popular types of tools are search engines and directories. Many people think search engines and directories are the same thing, but this is not the case. Search engines are databases or indexes of Internet URLs that are compiled automatically, whereas **directories** are compiled manually by human beings. One of the main advantages of a search engine is that it is more likely to have up-to-date information, whereas the advantage of a directory is that the information is organized in categories that may make finding what you are looking for a bit easier. Some search engines now help categorize information, so the distinction may not be as great as it once was. There are also search engines that search other search engines and directories for information called **meta-search engines**.

Retrieving information is only half the battle. There is a glut of information on the Internet—some trivial, some priceless. You may discover useful information for a report, but find that you cannot use it because it is undocumented. Learning to glean only the appropriate and most useful information from the Web is an art that takes time to master. Each type of search tool described offers different advantages and may be more suitable for some types of searches than others. This section explains the different types of search tools and offers short descriptions of some of the more popular examples. They are summarized in Table 3.1.

## Search Engines

A logical first step in many quests for information on the Internet often begins by using a search engine. A search engine is a **database** system, or collection of information, designed to index all types of Internet addresses including URLs, Usenet groups, FTP sites, and image locations. Search engines utilize special programs called **spiders** or **bots** (for robots). These programs crawl the Web (like a spider) to fetch Web pages and feed them to search engines for indexing. The process is mechanized and decisions are made without human intervention.

**For more information about bots:**
**The Web Robots FAQ**
http://info.webcrawler.com/mak/
projects/robots/faq.html#what
**BotSpot** http://www.botspot.com

*Table 3.1* **Categories of Web Search Tools**

| Search Engines | Directories | Meta-Search Engines | Virtual Libraries |
|---|---|---|---|
| **AltaVista**<br>*www.altavista.com*<br>**DirectHit**<br>*www.directhit.com*<br>**Excite**<br>*www.excite.com*<br>**Google**<br>*www.google.com*<br>**HotBot**<br>*www.hotbot.com*<br>**Go.com**<br>*www.go.com*<br>**Lycos**<br>*www.lycos.com*<br>**Northern Light**<br>*www.northernlight.com*<br>**WebCrawler**<br>*www.webcrawler.com* | **About**<br>*about.com*<br>**CNet**<br>*www.cnet.com*<br>**GTE Superpages**<br>*bigbook.com*<br>**Google**<br>*www.go.com*<br>**Go.com**<br>*www.go.com*<br>**Lycos**<br>*www.lycos.com*<br>**WebCrawler**<br>*www.webcrawler.com*<br>**Yahoo!**<br>*www.yahoo.com* | **Debriefing**<br>*www.debriefing.com*<br>**Dogpile**<br>*www.dogpile.com*<br>**Ask Jeeves**<br>*www.askjeeves.com*<br>**MetaCrawler**<br>*www.metacrawler.com*<br>**MetaFind**<br>*www.metafind.com*<br>**Monster Crawler**<br>*www.monstercrawler.com*<br>**Savvysearch**<br>*www.savvysearch.com* | **Argus Clearing House**<br>*www.clearinghouse.net*<br>**Internet Public Library**<br>*www.ipl.org*<br>**Internet Law Library**<br>*nsulaw.nova.edu/library*<br>**Library of Congress**<br>*lcweb.loc.gov/homepage/lchp.html*<br>**Library Spot**<br>*www.libraryspot.com*<br>**The On-line Books Page**<br>*digital.library.upenn.edu/books*<br>**The WWW Virtual Library**<br>*vlib.org* |
| **Purpose** | | | |
| Specialized, hard-to-find subjects | Subject by topic; subject catalogs; hierarchical organization—indexes | Directory of directories and search engines | Very narrow terms |
| **Maintained By** | | | |
| Spider or robot | Humans | Combination | Human experts |
| **When to Use** | | | |
| Hard-to-find material or new research | General search where you have little specific information | When you want to check the broadest number of sites; search several tools simultaneously | When you have very specific terms |

Search engines generally rank the results of a search by determining how closely the content of the material matches the search terms, allowing users to evaluate the likelihood that an item on a results list contains the information they are searching for. They do this by matching the search terms entered in the search engine with occurrences of those words in the Internet material reviewed by the search engine bots. These terms are known as keywords, because of their importance in conveying the essence of the information found on a Web page. Repeated matches mean a higher ranking. Keywords can be found scattered throughout the data contained on the page, or in invisible HTML **metatags** deliberately created to attract the attention of a search engine.

**The Keyword Popularity Contest**
If you operate a Web site, you can go to a ratings site and see how close to the top of a results list your site will be for a given keyword. The ratings sites continue checking what keywords are the most common and which Web sites appear at the top of a results list. Web site owners can then modify the content of their material to try to improve the chances of their site appearing on the first page of a results list. The majority of people using search engines rarely go beyond the first page of listed sites.

For daily ratings of search engines
http://www.webposition.com
http://www.topdog.com

**The *New York Times***
www.nytimes.com

Unlike ordinary HTML tags that provide page display information, metatags provide information about the content of the page including keywords, when the page was last updated, and the general topic of the page. When a new site goes online, it takes about three weeks before the site's metatag keywords are scanned by search engine spiders and bots. The automated process results in the site being included in an index and showing up as a link on a search engine.

Search engines can be categorized based on the scope of their search. Search engines that search the entire Internet, or at least a vast portion of it, are sometimes referred to as **external search engines**. Search engines that search only the contents of one Web site are known as **internal search engines**. You will frequently encounter internal search engines on the home pages of many commercial Web sites. Internal search engines allow you to perform a search on the contents of the Web site that are open to public view. Performing searches using internal search engines may shorten the time spent looking through a conventional search engine's results list, which means having less material to go through and making fewer decisions. For example, if you are looking for a news article, you can go directly to the *New York Times* site. The *New York Times* home page will have an index of articles for that particular issue, and a method for searching prior issues. Be warned that some Web sites allow you to search for free, but charge if you wish to view and save an item.

It is important to remember that search engines do not all employ the same search methods, and their features vary. As a result, on a particular search you may experience better results with one search engine than another. If at first you don't succeed, try another search engine! Some of the more popular search engines are described below, but feel free to do your own searching for the one that best fits your needs.

**AltaVista** AltaVista pioneered the first-ever multilingual search capability on the Internet and the first search technology to support Chinese, Japanese, and Korean languages. Presently, searches can be conducted in 25 languages. It is a large search engine with advanced features, currently searching over 130 million Web pages, with the number growing every day.

**Google** Google, like Yahoo! and Excite, is a former student project that ended up as a commercial site. The creators of Google, former Stanford Ph.D. candidates Larry Page and Sergey Brin, are undoubtedly very wealthy former students by now. One distinguishing feature of Google is that its rankings are partially based on how many pages link to a site and how important the pages are that reference it. Think of the links as votes in a popularity contest and the idea becomes clearer. The thinking behind this is that the more people "voting" for a site, the better it must be. Google lists only results that include the search terms, and these are shown in bold type contained in the snippets excerpted

## How do Search Engines list themselves?

Ever wonder how a search engine will list itself?
1. Using your favorite search engine, enter the search term "search engine."
2. See what site is listed first. Is it the home page for the search engine you are using?
3. Use three of the other popular search engines to perform the same search. Do any list a competitor first?

**AltaVista** http://www.altavista.com
**Google** http://www.google.com
**Northern Light**
http://www.northernlight.com
**HotBot** http://www.hotbot.com
**Lycos** http://www.lycos.com

from the page to aid in gauging the relevance of the results. Google claims to cover more than one billion URLs.

**Choosing a Search Engine** The search engine you get when you press the Search button on your browser may not always be the best one for you to use. The criteria used in picking these sites does not concern how good they are, but rather how much their owners have paid Microsoft or Netscape for the privilege of being linked to their browser's Search button. You will be better off if you save your favorite search engine URLs to the Favorites (IE) or Bookmarks (Navigator) list.

**Northern Light** Northern Light's modest goal is to "index and classify all human knowledge to a unified consistent standard and make it available to everyone in the world in a single integrated search." David Seuss, CEO of Northern Light, explains that the problem with the Web is that there is "too much data and not enough information." By information, Seuss means quality information. He aims to solve this by "focusing on finding high-quality, relevant results." Northern Light claims to offer full text searching of more than 150 million pages. Northern Light also categorizes documents that it indexes, which can make searching easier. One drawback is the cost: Northern Light charges a fee for some of its search services. This can be frustrating when a results list turns up something you want but requires a fee for you to view it.

**HotBot** HotBot, now owned by Lycos, displays only documents containing all of the words that users specify. Rankings are determined by word frequency, whether or not words occur in a title, whether or not words are in keyword metatags, and the length of a document. Short documents with frequent word repeats will be ranked higher than longer documents with the same frequency. This last technique means that attempts to "spoof" or "stack" the search engine by deliberately repeating keywords over and over in a document so that it is ranked near the top of a results list will fail, because the resulting document will be longer and therefore be ranked lower.

**Lycos** Lycos is a medium-sized search engine that searches more than 50 million Web pages as well as Gopher and FTP sites. It has some very sophisticated features for controlling proximity and sequencing of search terms. It searches for graphics or sound files as separate choices. One of the older search engines, Lycos suffers by ranking based on HTML tags, an outdated technique. A further drawback is that it searches only the first 200 or so characters on a page to create the page summary on the Lycos system.

## Comparing Search Engines

1. Go to www.altavista.com. Search for **bots**. Look at the information on the first results list and check out one or two of the most promising links. Print a copy of the first page of the results list when you are finished.
2. Go to www.lycos.com. Search for **bots**. Do the same exercise as you did for altavista.com.
3. Now compare the results of the two lists. Do the same Web pages show up on both lists? Do the links you followed offer the same quality of information? Is one search engine easier to use than the other? faster? Which one would you use again?

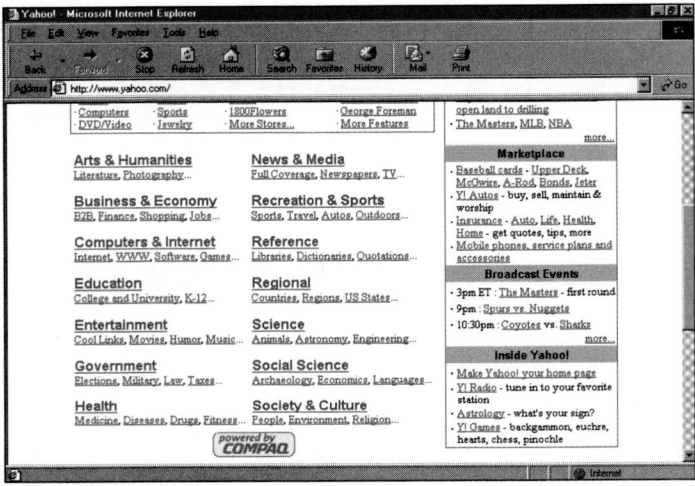

*Directories order information in a hierarchical fashion.*

## Directories

A directory is basically a manual entry (human-maintained) database system. Use a directory if you want to search deeper within a topic in a hierarchical fashion. Hierarchical in this sense refers to the ordering of information by descending levels of importance and relativity—similar to what a table of contents does for a good reference book, with its chapters, headings, and subheadings.

Since a search engine database is maintained by a robot, it will always be more current than directories that are maintained primarily by people and may be out of date. If you need very current material and you have a specific keyword that is definitely indexed, a search engine is what you want. When you do not know the exact words you are looking for and want to explore the subject more, a directory is a good place to start. For example, if you want information about a candidate currently running for office, you would probably want to put the name in a search engine to get the latest information. However, if you are looking for information about presidential candidates in general, a directory might be the best source. Directories assist your search by providing wide options in the results list. Directories can be browsed, whereas search engines are meant for direct linking. There are hundreds of directories; Table 3.1 includes some of the most popular ones.

**About** www.about.com

**About**   About, formerly the Mining Company, calls itself the "human Internet." What sets this directory apart from other search tools is the integration of its information database with people, called *guides*. Guides are experts in their fields, and their job is to scan the Web for the best sources of information on their topic. Currently there are over 700 guide sites, organized into 36 different channels. Each guide site shows a picture and biography of its guide.

**Yahoo!** One of the earliest directories to appear on the Web, Yahoo! is the precurser of all directories. Like Google, Yahoo! was the brainchild of two Ph.D. candidates, David Filo and Jerry Yang. While studying electrical engineering at Stanford, they developed Yahoo! to help catalog their diverse interests among all of the information on the Internet. On Yahoo! you will find information organized into categories, providing direction and simplifying your search process. If you are looking for several online newspapers, you do not need to enter each paper's name into a search engine; instead, you can enter Yahoo!'s directory of online newspapers that are categorized by state, by country, and so forth.

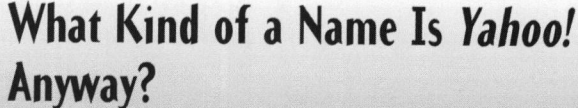

> ## What Kind of a Name Is *Yahoo!* Anyway?
>
> Some say the name *Yahoo!* is an acronym for "Yet Another Hierarchical Officious Oracle," but its founders, David Filo and Jerry Yang, insist they chose the name because they *are* yahoos. They like to give things obscure names. When they were still graduate students developing the directory, they named their personal computers after Sumo wrestlers!

## Meta-Search Engines

Meta-search engines combine the best of many tools: they search multiple search engines and directories, all from one location, and are maintained by a combination of spiders and humans. There is no need to open one search engine or directory after another. The results list will show information found on different search engines and directories, so it is an excellent way to learn about these search engines and directories and compare their effectiveness.

If you need to do a thorough search or need an extensive results list, a meta-search engine can be very useful. The results list will be ordered, the most likely sites appearing first, just as when using directories and search engines. In some meta-search engines you can specify several specific directories or search engines in your query—up to six at a time. One drawback of search engines is that it is not always possible to use some of the more advanced search tools. If you look at Table 3.1, you will see that some site names appear in more than one category; the distinction between conventional search engines and meta-search engines is not as great as it once was. Ask Jeeves and Dogpile are two popular examples of meta-search engines.

**Ask Jeeves**
http://www.askjeeves.com

**Ask Jeeves** Ask Jeeves, an intelligent Web search engine, is patterned after the author P. G. Wodehouses's classic English Butler, Jeeves, who knew just about everything and was able to interpret his master's needs before they were even spoken. Using Natural Programming Language (NPL) which mimics the way humans speak, Ask Jeeves allows users the ease of interacting on the Web the same way they do offline. Users pose questions in plain English and receive links to Web sites containing relevant information, services, and products. This feature of Ask Jeeves provides users the benefit of millions of previous searches. Growing smarter with each interaction, Ask Jeeves provides targeted, relevant responses to user queries. This simple, straightforward approach has made Ask Jeeves one of the most frequently visited sites on the Internet.

## Asking Jeeves a Question

1. Go to www.askjeeves.com. In the text box, key **What is a bot?** Click Ask.
2. What site shows up at the top of the results list?
3. Does this search compare with your search on Lycos and AltaVista?
4. Does Jeeves ask you further questions to help you refine your search?
5. How do the results compare with the results of your search using conventional search engines?

## DOGPILE

**Dogpile** www.dogpile.com
**Argus Clearing House**
http://www.clearinghouse.net
**Internet Public Library** www.ipl.org

**Dogpile**  Entering your keywords into Dogpile allows you to search dozens of search engines, directories, and other repositories of information on the Net all at the same time. Dogpile is unique among meta-search engines in that it displays results sorted by each search engine queried, rather than putting together results in one long list. This allows users to compare the different search engines, getting a feel for their strengths and weaknesses. If you love dogs, you will love Dogpile. Rather than hitting a Go button, you tell it to Fetch!

## Virtual Libraries

Another type of directory is called a **virtual library**. Virtual libraries contain collections of resources that experts have reviewed carefully and have organized topically, just like a brick-and-mortar library does. The compilers of virtual libraries do not just consider keywords when indexing sites, they actually read and analyze the content. So virtual libraries are the most dependable search tools; their drawback is that they are somewhat narrow in focus. If you have a subject that is specific, and perhaps more academic and research oriented, virtual libraries are helpful. Some virtual libraries charge a membership fee to pay for those experts to review the material. Virtual libraries rarely have the full text of the research article they list, but they will tell you how to locate it.

**Argus Clearing House**  Argus Clearing House is a virtual library dedicated to in-depth research that is peer reviewed. Academic environments and research institutions make heavy use of it. It specializes in three types of information: subject guides, reference works, and specialized databases.

**Internet Public Library**  The Internet Public Library (IPL) is a project of the University of Michigan School, created to provide library and information science students a way to learn more about their profession. This site is maintained by students and volunteers from around the world who assist in answering questions through IPL's Ask a Question feature. You will find the layout familiar; it is set up like your local library, with references, periodical and serial, newspapers, and online text pages.

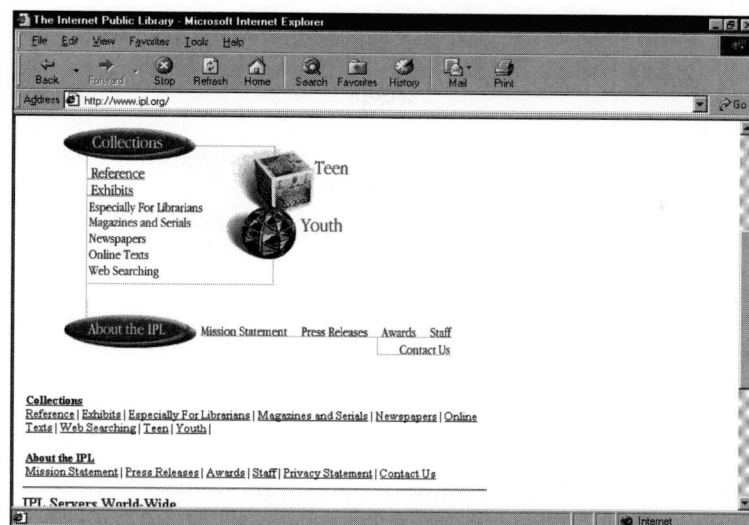

*The Internet Public Library is organized just like a regular library.*

# Employing Search Strategies

Now that you know about the various search tools available, you need to think about what strategy to use for finding what you want. A good search strategy can help you find the most direct route to what you are looking for. It will also help you avoid getting too much information. There is more than one way to find an item on the Internet, but many of these involve taking unnecessary detours that will slow you down.

To devise a search strategy, you need to define your search topic, choose the best keywords to find your search topic, choose the best search tools, and take advantage of the different search conventions.

## Defining Your Search

The first step in any search activity is determining exactly what it is you are looking for. Before you do any kind of search you should:

1. **Determine the objective.** What are you trying to do? Are you planning to apply for a job or to write a story about applying for a job? Your objective will help you narrow the focus of your search and determine what kinds of information about your search topic would be helpful.
2. **Define the topic.** Imagine your objective is to look for a job. It is more than likely you are not looking for just any kind of job, so you need to decide exactly what kind of work you are looking for, such as a forklift operator. You also need to define in what specific geographical area(s) you would be willing to work. There will be a lot of information on forklift operators on the Internet, much of which does not concern finding a job in that field. Since you are interested in finding out about job opportunities as a forklift operator, you would be interested in finding information on positions available for forklift operators in the state in which you want to work.

## Choosing Keywords

Once you have clarified exactly what kind of information you are looking for, then you can try to think of keywords that you would expect to find in the material you are seeking. When choosing keywords, it is useful to remember how a search tool works. When you begin a search, you key a keyword(s), and the search tool searches its database and returns a ranked list of sites that include your keyword(s). The search process is somewhat like a database or spreadsheet query, where the program searches data and returns information that matches criteria you have specified. A Web search may return an extensive results list with many hits that match your search term. Your goal is to get a helpful ranked results list that places the most meaningful and appropriate sites at the top of the list.

Bearing in mind the critical importance of keywords, take a look at what you wrote down when you defined your search topic. What keywords would you expect to find in any document related to what you are looking for? Keywords can be subject terms that reflect the topic of a single sentence, a passage, a page, or an entire Web site. Examples of subject keyword terms are "American writers," "maps," or "newspapers." Other keywords can be very specific, such as the name of a person, place, or thing— for example, "Hemingway," "Minnesota," or "*New York Times.*" You might decide to use either type of keyword alone or in combination, such as "maps Minnesota" or "American writers Hemingway."

If, after defining your search topic, you decide that you want to look for forklift operator jobs in Minnesota, try to visualize what the material you are seeking would look like. What would it say? An announcement for a job as a forklift operator in Minnesota would almost certainly contain the terms "forklift operator," "Minnesota," and "job," so key **jobs forklift operators Minnesota**. If the results list does not produce what you are looking for, try using synonymous keywords. For example, you might also try "positions available" or "work" in place of "jobs," or "drivers" instead of "operators." This is where creativity can help. If you still do not find what you need, try to think of any other terms that might be related to what you are looking for. Switching the order of the keywords can change the results as well, so you might try that if you are unsuccessful on your first few attempts. Remember that search engines generally consider the first word as the most important when ranking sites.

### Looking for a Job

1. Using your own keywords, try using a search engine to find out how many job listings you can find for forklift operators in Minnesota.
2. Try another search engine using the same keywords.
3. What terms produce the best results? Do the results lists from both search engines produce the same job listings?

## Limiting the Results List and Searching for Exact Words

You can limit the number of hits you produce in your results list. Hits are ranked, from the most likely valuable site to the least likely. If you want to speed up receiving the results list and do not want more than a few sources listed, limit the number of hits you get by adding more descriptive words.

1. Go to the search engine site www.altavista.com.
2. In the Search text box, key **dogs**. How many results are listed? The amount is staggering.
3. Return to the Search text box and key **schnauzers**. How many results are listed? The results are still overwhelming, but significantly less than for *dogs*.

**Have a question about business?**
www.bloomberg.com
www.cnnfn.com
www.hoovers.com
**Looking for a long-lost loved one, or trying to track down an address?**
http://people.yahoo.com
www.bigfoot.com
www.superpages.com
www.people.yahoo.com
www.whowhere.com

## Selecting the Best Search Tools

To conduct an effective search you need to use the right tools. If what you are looking for is easily categorized by subject, you will probably find the best results by using a directory. If what you are searching for is difficult to categorize, or very specialized in nature, you will probably find what you are looking for by using a search engine. If you are having trouble defining your search you might want to try a site like Ask Jeeves, which allows you to ask questions using Natural Programming Language (NPL), and assists you by asking questions in return to help you refine your search.

Do not forget to take advantage of the internal search features of many Web sites. Internal search engines and directories are usually found on commercial and government Web sites containing large amounts of information, often organized around a single subject. You will typically find these specialized sites during a search using a search engine. These sites can be a gold mine, and through their internal search tools you can find information that would not appear in the results list from a normal search engine or directory search. Web sites focusing on a topic or subject and with search tool features are too numerous to list, but you can find a site for almost any topic you can think of.

If you do not find what you are looking for right away, keep trying. Try different keywords, change the order of the keywords, change search engines or directories—just keep trying. The information is almost certainly out there somewhere on the Internet; it is up to you to find it. The more you use the skills you have just learned, the more adept you will become at finding what you want. You will soon be adding your own methods to your Internet search toolbox.

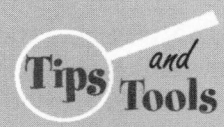

**Make Sure You Spell It Right!**
Everyone is in a rush these days, and when searching for information on the Internet, you may misspell a word in your haste to find what you want. Doing that will have a dramatic effect on your search, since the search tool you are using will be searching for the wrong term. The results list may find information from the Internet containing the same misspelling, if it is a common one, but it is more likely that it will fail to find anything related to what you want. If you cannot understand why you are not getting the results you expected, one of the first things you should do is use the Back button on your browser to make sure that your keywords are spelled correctly.

## Finding a Job

1. Imagine that you need a job. Use any search engine or directory to find some job or career sites where you could look for a job.
2. What search terms (keywords) do you find most effective in finding sites with job listings? Are you finding what you need on your first search?
3. Now look at three or more of the sites you found during your search. Are some easier to use than others? Are they helpful? Do you find any job listings for the type of work you are looking for?
4. Besides job listings, what other features do these sites offer?

**There's More than Text Out There!**
Because the Web is a multimedia environment, it is not limited to articles, books, and other text-based materials. You can search for audio, video, and other multimedia elements on the Web. For example, if you go to Excite.com or another search engine, you can choose multipurpose search options. If you click on the search audio or video hyperlinks, you can look for sound files or movies on your topic.

## Using Operators

In processing your search request, search engines and directories utilize rules to sort information known as **search conventions**. You can narrow your search and improve your chances of getting a meaningful results list by understanding search conventions and by using search operators. **Search operators** (sometimes referred to as qualifiers) are the symbols representing a specific action to be performed by the search engine or directory. The operators and conventions for searching are slightly different with each Web search tool, so using Help, Search Tips, and any local page hints and guides are recommended. Some of the operators and conventions are described that can boost the effectiveness of your search efforts.

**Boolean Operators** **Boolean operators** were named after George Boole, a mathematician. They are logical terms used to combine keywords, such as AND, NOT, NEAR, and OR. Depending on the search engine or directory, Boolean terms may be recognized by keying the Boolean operator, such as AND and NOT, a symbol such as "+" for AND or "-" for NOT, or they may be assumed, as is the case with AND. Most search engines assume the space before keywords as AND. Using the AND operator with keywords (if required by the search engine) will turn up any material in which all of the terms occur. This can be helpful but tends to produce a lot of results; you may have trouble finding what you need in a long results list.

If that is the case, using the NOT symbol (-) can be very helpful. Suppose that you want to find information on the style of music known as the blues. Entering **blues** might turn up a lot of documents related to the use of the word *blue* as a color. To avoid this, you can enter the search term as **blues - colors** or **blues NOT colors**, which should cut down on the number of hits relating to blues and color and increase those that concern blues as a style of music.

Using NEAR between two keywords (for example, **keyword NEAR keyword**) will turn up anything with those two words occurring within 10 words of each other. If you want to find out about concerts in New York, entering **concerts NEAR New York** will increase the odds that the appearance of the term *New York* in any document found will be related to *concert*. Without using NEAR, you will likely find many documents containing the terms *concert* and *New York*, but the two terms may come from different parts of the document and have no relationship to each other.

The Boolean operator OR can be used when keying several synonymous terms. Using OR means that the search tool will retrieve all documents containing either term. This is an advantage when you are looking for something that might be categorized under more than one subject. For instance, if you want to learn more about large bodies of water, enter the keywords **oceans OR seas**. This will produce hits that contain either of these terms. On the other hand, if you enter **oceans AND seas**, you will find hits containing both of those terms, but not material containing only one of the terms.

Knowing Boolean operators will be helpful, but many search engines and directories have now automated this function with their advanced search options. If you look at the Advanced Search page for Google shown in Figure 3.1, you will see that you need only enter keywords in the correct box rather than having to key Boolean operators. However, knowing Boolean operators can save you time because you won't need to open the Advanced Search page.

**Using Operators** When using operators, key the operator in all capital letters, not lowercase letters. Some search engines may accept the lowercase format, but the convention is uppercase.

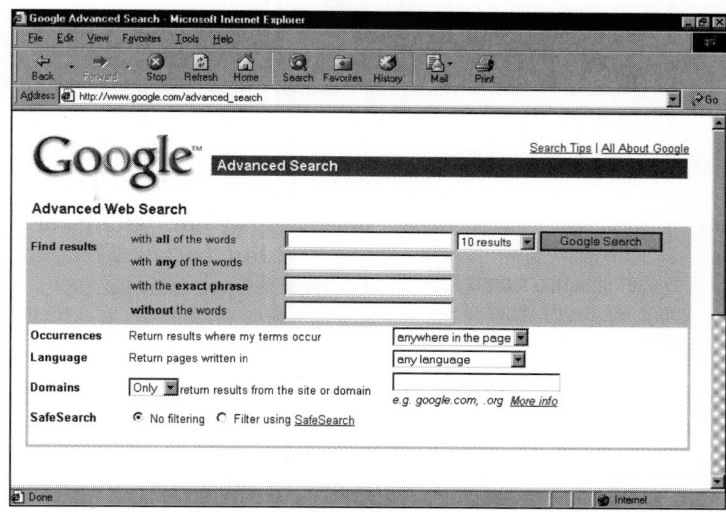

*Figure 3.1* **Google Advanced Search Page**

## Using Operators

1. Using the search engine of your choice, key **sail + boat** and look at the results list.
2. Using the same search engine, key **sail boat** or **sail, boat** and look at the results list.
3. Do you notice any differences in the results lists?
4. Now key **sail OR boat**. Do you notice anything different about the results list?

**Relational Operators**  The second type of operators that will assist your search efforts are known as **relational operators**, symbols describing the chronological (time-related) relationship between keywords and numbers. The most useful relationship operators are represented by:

| | |
|---|---|
| < | less than |
| > | greater than |
| <= | less than or equal to |
| >= | greater than or equal to |
| = | equal to |

**Tips** *and* **Tools**

**Relational Operators** When keying relational operators, include one space before and after the operator. For example, key **artists > 1990**, rather than **artists>1990**.

Suppose you want to find out more information on Jazz, but are not much interested in Jazz before 1980. You could enter **Jazz > 1980**, which will instruct the search engine or directory to look for any information on Jazz after the year 1980. The results will not be perfect, but you will find that your results list will mostly contain information on Jazz after the year 1980. You can even combine operators, just as you can in mathematical formulas. If you are interested only in a certain period in Jazz history, you could enter **Jazz > 1900 < 1930**, which will instruct the search engine or directory to look for information on Jazz containing dates between the years 1900 and 1930.

**Other Operators**  In addition to the relational operators, there are several special characters that will help define searches. For example, the wildcard operator is represented by the dollar sign ($) or asterisk (*). This operator allows you to find all words that begin with a root word or combination of letters that you specify. Entering **sail*** will find all keywords beginning with *sail* such as *sailors*, *sailcloth*, and so on. One example of how this feature can come in handy is when you do not care if a word is singular or plural. If you want to find information on skiing, you might also be interested in information containing the words *skiers*, *skis*, and *ski resorts*. Using the wildcard operator with *ski* (**ski***) will return hits with all of the ski-related words you are looking for.

The use of quotation marks around a phrase or combination of words instructs the search engine to look for this exact sequence of words. Keying **"George W. Bush"** will return a results list containing material with that exact sequence of words somewhere in the document. This can be helpful because you can often visualize a sequence of words that would almost certainly appear in the information you are looking for. If you do not place the keywords in quotation marks, the information retrieved will contain documents with your keywords in them, but they may be scattered around the document and meaningless in terms of what you want to find.

Whether or not you capitalize a keyword is usually important. Most search engines are case sensitive, meaning that they distinguish between words beginning with uppercase letters (capitals) and lowercase. If you are looking for information about the country Turkey, this would be very important. If you enter **turkey** in the search text box, you will find information dealing with the kind of turkeys you eat on Thanksgiving Day. But if you enter **Turkey**, you will find the results list contains mostly information concerning the country known as Turkey.

Using a period after a word or word stem will limit hits to information with that exact word or word stem. If you want to find material containing the word *news*, but not *newspaper*, keying **news.** will ensure that only material containing the keyword *news* will appear on the results list.

You also need to be familiar with the search conventions employed by search engines and directories. Do not include the articles and prepositions *a*, *an*, *the*, *in*, or *of* in your searches. Search engines index the full text of many files, but the articles are understood. So unless you are searching for an exact title, such as *The Declaration of Independence*, do not include these words. For example, in a search for the American Revolution you would key **American + Revolution**, without *the*. Table 3.2 summarizes the conventions and operators described above and can be used for reference.

 *Table 3.2* **Conventions and Operators for Web Searches**

| Operator or Convention | Purpose | Format | Example to Key |
|---|---|---|---|
| + <br> AND | include both terms; narrows the search | nothing (blank space) <br> + <br> AND | history Jazz <br> Jazz + history <br> Jazz AND history |
| - <br> NOT | exclude by term; narrows the search | - <br> NOT | blues - colors <br> blues NOT colors |
| , <br> OR | include either term; broadens the search | nothing (blank space) <br> , <br> OR | Jazz history <br> Jazz, history <br> Jazz OR history |
| NEAR | find keywords within 10 words of each other | keyword near keyword | blues NEAR city |
| > | greater than | > | blues > 1929 |
| < | less than | < | real estate < 100,000 |
| >= | greater than or equal to | >= | blues >= 1960 |
| <= | less than or equal to | <= | blues <= 1960 |
| = | equal to | = | assassinations = 1888 |
| $ * | truncate, cut off | word stem$, or word stem* | sail* (to find *sailing, sailors, sailboats*, etc.) |
| " " | search for exact phrase | "phrase" | "The Right Stuff" |
| . | avoid stems | word. | news. (to prevent *newspaper, newscast, newsletter*, etc.) |
| capitalization | distinguish between common and proper nouns | Use uppercase or lowercase initial | Turkey (for the country) turkey (for the bird) |
| articles | unnecessary unless looking for titles | Do not use *a, an, the, of, in*, etc. | The Agricultural Movement (wrong) Agricultural Movement (right) |

# Using Information from Web Searches

Once you have located information on the Web, how do you make use of it? Sometimes if it is a short definition, or a list of search sites, you can simply print the page. To print a Web page, from the menu bar click File and then Print. Be sure your cursor is in the frame you want to print since it will print the currently active frame.

Do not print everything you find on the Web! Be selective as you link to sites. Cull the material that is pertinent and that you will most likely use again. Try to limit the number of graphics on the pages you print as they take a lot of printer ink. Instead of printing entire Web sites, select relevant material for your topic and print that. To select material, highlight it with the mouse. To print the material, select File and then Print. In the Print dialog box click Selection, and then click OK. If you do not choose the Selection button, the entire page will print by default (see Figure 3.2).

Some sites allow you to download reports and published material. It is possible to save entire pages from Web sites for use in research. To do this simply click Save As on the browser menu bar, select the location you wish to save the file in, and then click Save. If a Web page contains a lot of graphic images or is very large, saving it takes a considerable amount of time and disk space. It is better to save specific paragraphs and certain graphics.

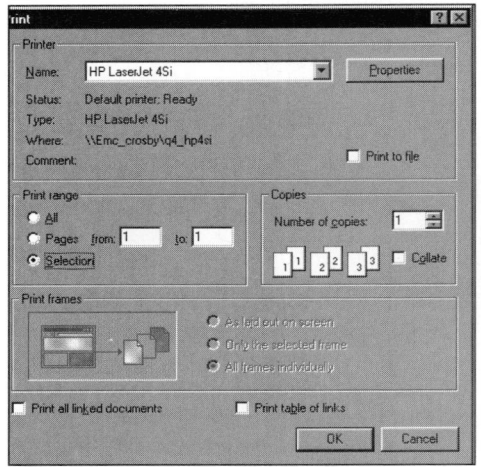

*Figure 3.2* Internet Explorer Print Dialog Box

## Copying Text from a Web Site to a Word File

1. Using the search engine of your choice, find a Web site and article you are interested in.
2. Using the mouse, highlight any text you wish to save.
3. Right-click the mouse button and then click Copy from the shortcut menu that appears.
4. In Word, click File and then New on the menu bar. With the General tab selected, click on Blank Document and then click OK.
5. On the new document page, place the cursor at the top and right-click the mouse button to display the shortcut menu. Click Paste.
6. The text you copied will appear in your new document. You can format it just like you would any Word document. When you are finished, name the file and save it.

## Saving an Image from a Web Site to a Word File

1. On the Web Site of your choice, place the cursor on any image you wish to save and then right-click the mouse button to display the Shortcut menu.
2. Click Save Picture As to display the Save Picture dialog box.
3. Select the drive and file you wish to save the image in, and then click Save.

If you want to retrieve the material you have just saved, you can do that by using software appropriate to the file format. For example, if you saved an entire Web page, you will need to retrieve it by opening it through the Web browser. If you open a Web file in Word it will appear as meaningless text. Images must be opened using image software, such as Microsoft Photo Editor or Adobe Photoshop. Text documents must be opened using a text editor such as Word or Notepad.

If you want to save several sections of material from different Web pages to one file using IE, Navigator, or most other browsers, you can use the copy and paste method.

You can add as many different sections of material as desired to that one document. Don't forget to save after each inclusion. You then have a master file of research, just as you might gather in a library.

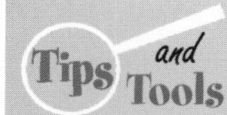

**The "Right" Way to Work**
You can make tasks easier by clicking the right button on the mouse. This will often open a menu with the same functions that can be found on the menu bar or toolbars. For example, here is how you would save an image from a Web page by right-clicking the mouse.

1. Move the cursor over the image and select it by clicking the right mouse button.
2. From the shortcut menu that appears, choose Save Picture As (IE) or Save Image As (Navigator) to display the Save As dialog box.
3. Select the location where you wish to place the image, and then click Save.

## Copying and Pasting Using the Taskbar

1. On the Web site of your choice, find an article you are interested in.
2. In Word, open a new file. Use the taskbar to switch between this file and the Web files containing material you wish to copy.
3. Locate the desired material on the Web site and highlight it using the mouse button.
4. Right-click the mouse button and select Copy on the shortcut menu that appears.
5. Use the taskbar to switch to the Word file you created.
6. Position the cursor on the page, right-click the mouse button, and then select Paste from the shortcut menu. You can continue to move back and forth between documents, cutting and pasting. When you are finished, name the new file you created and save it.

**idrive** www.idrive.com

Since saved text and graphics take up a lot of storage space on your hard drive or on a floppy disk, you may want to go to a Web site that allows temporary storage. If you link to www.idrive.com, you can register for free disk space on the server. You can save anything you obtained on the Web to this location. Netdrive.com is another such location where you can register for a "virtual" hard drive. You *must* register to get an account on idrive's or netdrive's server. Retrieving your information is easy—just log on to the site, enter your password, and follow the instructions for retrieving the material.

To incorporate material successfully from the Internet into documents you want to create, you need to understand how the software works. The first time you try it may be frustrating, but once you become accustomed to "electronic composing," you will see how valuable it is and how much time and work it saves. Browsing through instruction manuals, taking advantage of Help keys, asking friends for assistance, and lots of practice will rapidly improve your skill level.

## Verifying Web Information

The old saying, "Don't believe everything you read in the papers!," should be updated to, "Don't believe everything you read on the Internet!" Much of the information obtained online is undoubtedly valid, but you should exercise caution.

There are many fine electronic journals and renowned magazines offered online, and responsible researchers abound on the Internet. However, the Internet and all of its venues are open forums; anyone with access to a computer and some basic skills can post information on the Internet. Inaccurate material may reside next to very pure data. It is possible to find information with no solid research behind its assumptions and with no empirical data to support its conclusions. Worse yet, it is possible for someone to falsify data, which has happened in the print world as well. With Web research, however, the responsibility is on you to question what you are reading and to make sure it can be verified.

How do you know if online material is valid and reliable? The material on the Internet is not rated or ranked, nor are there standard publishing houses for materials within certain fields. There are, however, some general guidelines to follow in evaluating Web sites. Ask yourself these questions:

- What do I know about the site? What type of organization produced it? How current is the information? (The domain name may provide a clue as to how credible the site is. For example, sites with the domain name of *.edu* or *.gov* should be reliable. You will see the names of widely recognized Web sites recurring in directories and virtual libraries. Most sites list the date the site was last updated at the bottom of the Web page.)

- What do I know about the author? Is he or she a credible source, or are biases and commercial interests a determining factor? Does the author reference or cite or link to other sites? (To help answer those questions, you can search the Web to find background information on the author. The more frequently the author's name reappears in various sites, the more credible he or she is likely to be.)

- Does the information seem credible based on other sources you have researched? (If the material seems questionable and inconsistent with previous sources, you will want to find corroborating documents in other sites that support the various points of view.)

These are only basic guidelines, alerting you to exercise caution. The most important advice is to do your research with a critical eye. As your online experience increases, you will also become an experienced researcher.

## Avoiding Plagiarism

While it is true that no one person or entity owns and manages the Web, the content on an individual Web page can be owned. This ownership implies adherence to the same copyright standards that pertain to the spoken and printed word. Copyright standards are not easily enforced and are being challenged. Misrepresenting material as your own is never acceptable. The safest way to avoid being accused of **plagiarism**—taking someone else's ideas and passing them off as your own—is to document any material that you use, even if you quote only one line.

## Documenting Sources

When writing a report, you should include a list of references for any material you used in your report, whether it's a direct quotation or a paraphrase (restating someone else's ideas in your own words). There are standard guides for listing these references. The three most popular style manuals are the *APA Publication Manual*, the *MLA Style Guide*, and the *Chicago Manual of Style*. These guides cover written materials primarily, but they also contain sections on citing electronic media sources, which includes anything found on the Web or the Internet.

You can take advantage of your improved Internet skills by using one of the online citation services available on the Web. An example is The Right Cite (http://www.bluewillowpages.com/rightcite/), described on its home page as "a nonprofit Web site offered as a service to researchers."

When you log on to The Right Cite home page, you will see a dialog box in the left side of your screen (see Figure 3.3). You can select one of two citation styles, APA or MLA. All you

## Those Annoying Banners

All search tools have banners on their home pages. Even though some sites have trade banners where no money is exchanged, most banners are paid advertisements—a marketing device. The use of Web search tools is free to you, but their existence is financed by sponsors. Web search tools sell parts of their pages to sponsors. The sponsor pays the search tool to place its banner on the search tool's page. The banners are meant to attract your attention and entice you to click on a hot-linked graphic which immediately links you to the sponsor's site. If you click on a hyperlinked Web banner on the Yahoo! home page, however, the link is not necessarily endorsed by Yahoo!, it is simply one of its clients. Banners are becoming more numerous and frequently display multimedia characteristics. Many people feel they are a distraction, and they can lengthen the time it takes for a page to appear. Most users quickly train their eyes to ignore the flashing, scrolling, colorful "hot spots" on the search tool page. Banners, like billboards of the past, have become a way of life on the information highway.

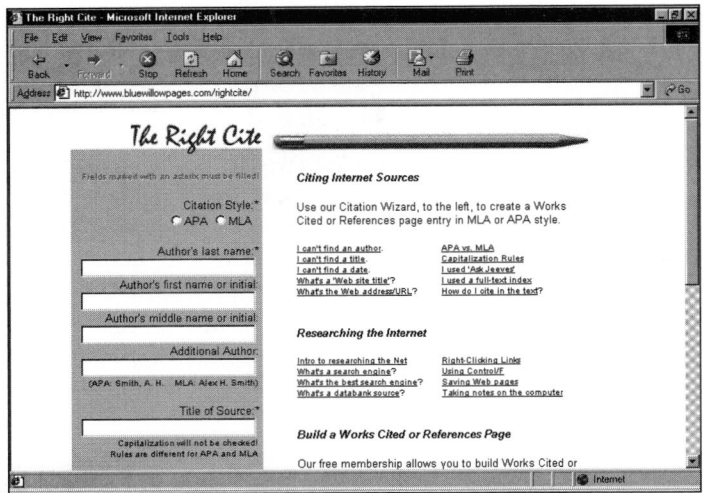

***Figure 3.3* The Right Cite Home Page**

*This site will format source information in either APA or MLA style.*

need to do is enter the appropriate information from the Web page contents you wish to cite, and click the Make Entry! button in the lower left side of the box. Presto! You have a perfect citation. If you are not sure what to do, or are missing some information, there are hyperlinks at the top of the page that will guide you.

Let's create a citation for an article found on the *CNNfn* Web site. The title of the article is "Sellers Swamp Wall St." and the dateline is February 9, 2001. The author is listed as Catherine Tymkiw. Finally, the URL for this page is http://cnnfn.cnn.com/2001/02/09/markets/markets_newyork/. This news report was accessed on the *CNNfn* Web site on February 10, 2001.

All of this information can be copied by highlighting the portions of the *CNNfn* Web page containing the information you want, right-clicking the mouse button, and selecting Copy at the shortcut menu. You can then paste it into the appropriate text boxes on The Right Source home page. You can do the same with the URL by clicking the cursor in the browser's Address (IE) or Netsite (Navigator) text box, and scrolling over the URL until it is highlighted. Then right-click the mouse, select Copy, and paste it in The Right Cite text box.

You can then copy and paste the citation into a document you have created. Note that in both the APA and MLA citation styles, the date the Web site was accessed is contained in parentheses.

APA citation:

Tymkiw, Catherine. "Sellers Swamp Wall St." CNNfn.
    http://cnnfn.cnn.com/2001/02/09/markets/markets_newyork/
    (2001, February 10).

MLA citation:

Tymkiw, Catherine. "Sellers Swamp Wall St." CNNfn. 9 Feb. 2001.
    http://cnnfn.cnn.com/2001/02/09/markets/markets_newyork/
    (10 Feb. 2001).

When you are ready to create another entry, just click on Create a New Entry. An additional feature of this innovative site is the ability to create your own Works Cited page, which allows you to store multiple entries for later use.

There is no absolute standard for Web citations as of this writing. If your instructor prefers a different format, by all means use it. Generally, any consistent citation format is acceptable—provided the URL and date of access are included. If certain details are unknown, it is acceptable that they not be included. However, the date you accessed the Web page, the title of the page, and the URL always must be included. References are alphabetized by author last name at the end of the report on a separate page titled "Works Cited." If a citation does not include an author name, arrange the entry alphabetically by the title of the page, then by the URL. Footnotes, on the other hand, are cited as they occur in the paper, at the bottom of the corresponding pages. If you use a mixture of print resources and Web resources, list them together alphabetically on the Works Cited page.

## Who Owns the Copyright?

Legal battles over the future of copyright protection on the Web are being fought as this textbook goes to press. One of the battles is over the availability of MP3 files—near-CD-quality, compressed music files "traded" over the Web through sites like Napster.com, founded by Shawn Fanning. The MP3 technology that allows music file sharing claims 25 million users. Napster calls itself the "File Sharing Community." Napster technology allows multidirectional use of the Web and is very innovative. You install the Napster software on your computer and agree to share MP3 files with other Napster members. The Napster site maintains a master song list and search engine. When a member requests a song, Napster searches and finds members who have the music files on their computers, and provides the Internet Provider address of their machines so that the member can access the music on their hard drives. The site inherently violates privacy by keeping a record of the IP address for each machine. Napster members do not seem to mind, however.

The resulting MP3 files are about 3MB in size, one-sixteenth the size of a CD single's file. These files are freely traded over the Web and are played on computers everywhere. Playing an MP3 file is a legal activity; the copying process is technically illegal, however, since the files can be easily saved to personal CD-Rs and played anywhere. Users argue that the files are not being distributed illegally, they are simply being played on others' computers, like a jam session where friends listen to each other's legally purchased music.

For some, it is the ultimate music matching service; others object to the lack of royalties to the artists who originally recorded the songs. The recording industry and some musicians have launched a defensive effort. Threatened with copyright infringement lawsuits, more than two hundred colleges and universities have pro-hibited students from downloading Napster software.

On February 12, 2001, the 9th U.S. Circuit Court of Appeals ruled that the company must stop allowing people to swap copyrighted music. The court did say that the company could survive if it is able to patrol misuse, something Napster's lawyers say is impossible. Napster plans to start charging for music later in the year, but still has not lined up any deals with major recording companies. It is also unclear whether or not Napster's fans will be interested in paying for something that was once free of charge.

**Sources:** "Deal Settles Suit Against MP3.com," by Amy Harmon, *New York Times*, November 15, 2000; "Why More Schools Are Expelling Napster," *Business Week*, October 9, 2000; and "Napster Looks to the Future," by Ron Harris, Associated Press Writer, Tuesday, Feb. 13, 2001, 12:26 a.m. EST.

 # Summary

➤ You can find almost any topic on the Web if you know some basic search tools and rules.

➤ The Web is a primary source of information for all areas of research.

➤ There are formal search tools such as search engines, directories, meta-search engines, and virtual libraries.

➤ Tools match the terms you key (keywords) with what they have indexed from their Web pages.

➤ You can also search for audio, video, and other multimedia elements on the Web by using search engines and directories.

➤ By combining keywords and using operators, you can narrow your search and generate a better results list.

➤ You can print a Web page easily by clicking File and then Print on the browser menu bar.

➤ Copying and pasting material to a file requires careful file management, but a superior report can be produced by using Web resources.

➤ Verifying the accuracy of source materials is the Internet user's responsibility and requires using caution.

➤ Citing sources properly is critical to using the Web as a research tool.

**banner** Web graphic used for advertising purposes, hyperlinked to a product.

**Boolean operators** Search operators (qualifiers) such as AND, NOT, NEAR, and OR that are used in advanced searches.

**bot (robot)** See **spider**

**database** An organized arrangement of data that can be retrieved by field or record; a self-describing collection of integrated records.

**directory (index)** A manual entry (human-maintained) database system; use if you want to search deeper within a topic in a hierarchical fashion.

**external search engine** A search engine that searches the entire Internet, or at least a portion of it.

**internal search engine** A search engine that searches only for material contained in its home site.

**meta-search engine** Search engine that searches multiple directories and multiple search engines, all from one location. Maintained by both humans and spiders or robots.

**metatag** HTML deliberately created to attract the attention of a search engine.

**plagiarism** Taking someone else's ideas and passing them off as your own.

**relational operators** Symbols describing the chronological (time-related) relationship between keywords and numbers.

**search conventions** Rules to sort information, utilized by search engines and directories. For example, one rule is do not include articles and prepositions in a search.

**search operators** Boolean operators (AND, NOT, NEAR, OR) and relational operators (+, -, >, <, =>, <=) and others used to further qualify a search.

**spider** Software tools for sifting through written material on the Web to scan Web content and update the search engine's index automatically. See also **bot**

**virtual library** In Web context, specialty collection maintained by human experts in an area.

 Navigating and Exploring the Web

## Working the Web

**Project 1**   Go to www.yahoo.com. Key **weather** in the search text box. Click on Search. How many Inside Yahoo! Matches are listed? How many total Yahoo! Category Matches are listed?  Go to www.dogpile.com. Key **weather** in the Fetch text box. Click Fetch. How many responses are listed for Search Engine: GoTo.com? Scroll down the screen. How many responses are listed for Search Engine: LookSmart? Scroll down the screen again until you come to Dogpile's Top Barks. How many documents are listed for Search Engine: Dogpile's Top Barks?

**Project 2**   Suppose you have to write a paper about five of the greatest American artists who painted still-life pictures. List the steps you take to find material on the Internet. (Write the search statement[s] you would use.)

**Project 3**   You want to find the titles of all of the movies Harrison Ford has starred in. List three search tools you might use. List five of his latest films.

**Project 4**   Using one of the map sites, print out the map and directions to get from your house to your favorite fast-food restaurant.

**Project 5**   Look for information about PC videoconferencing (try Webopedia at www.pcwebopaedia.com). Then search for two systems (hardware and software) to consider adding to your computer system.

## Are We Connecting?

### Exercise 1

*Answer the following questions. Questions can be answered individually or assigned as small group discussion.*

1. What is the first step in looking for information on the Web?
2. What is the difference between an internal search and an external search?
3. What is the purpose or function of a banner?
4. Describe the function of a directory, and give two examples of directories.
5. Describe the function of a search engine, and give two examples of search engines.
6. Describe the function of a meta-search engine, and give two examples of meta-search engines.
7. What are the relational operators used in a search statement?

8. What are Boolean operators? Give some examples.
9. What is plagiarism?
10. What can you do to verify information found on the Web?

## Exercise 2

*Match the Web search tool with the description. Tools can be used more than once.*

a. search engines
b. directories
c. meta-search engines
d. virtual libraries

1. survey a broad number of sites
2. survey specialized or difficult topics
3. survey subject catalogs and indexes
4. HotBot and Goggle are examples
5. MetaFind and Ask Jeeves are examples
6. DirectHit and Lycos are examples
7. The On-line Books Page and Library of Congress are examples
8. maintained by human experts

## Exercise 3

*Match the Web search operator with the description.*

a. " "
b. NEAR
c. >=
d. $*
e. NOT
f. .

1. matches exact phrase
2. do not include stems
3. truncate, cut off
4. exclude by term listed
5. greater than or equal to
6. finds keywords within 10 words

# Communications
## Getting Together through the Web

# 4

## Objectives

➤ Distinguish between time-delayed (asynchronous) and real-time (synchronous) communication on the Web.

➤ Describe the basic types of mail server protocols and their functions.

➤ Define the components of an e-mail address.

➤ Customize Outlook Express by changing settings.

➤ Compose, read, send, and delete e-mail messages.

➤ Write e-mail messages using netiquette.

➤ Add and delete addresses in the Address Book and create groups.

➤ Read, respond to, and forward e-mail attachments.

➤ Create and manage mail folders.

➤ Subscribe and unsubscribe to automatic mailing lists and newsgroups.

➤ Participate in instant messaging and chat rooms.

The Internet's purpose is the same today as it was at its inception: to communicate and to share information with others. With all of the marvels of the multimedia environment we experience, and all of the organization and the hyperlinking of documents that the Web allows, sending messages is still the Internet's most frequently used function. Communicating with each other—free of the constraints of time, space, and "hard copy"—has brought us to the Global Village that the visionary Marshall McLuhan prophesized in the 1950s. For those with access to the Internet, the ability to communicate instantly and inexpensively with others has made the world a smaller place.

Computer networks and the **asynchronous** (time-delayed) and **synchronous** (real-time) communication we experience via the Internet take off from where telephone communication began. While e-mail is the most popular method for communicating on the Internet, there are numerous other means of communication across the Internet. This chapter covers them all, but because e-mail is the most frequently used, it is covered in more depth.

## What Is E-mail?

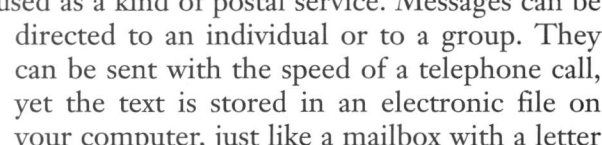

E-mail, or electronic mail, combines telephone and postal technology. It refers to a class of text messages transmitted and distributed through any computerized system where the computer is used as a kind of postal service. Messages can be

directed to an individual or to a group. They can be sent with the speed of a telephone call, yet the text is stored in an electronic file on your computer, just like a mailbox with a letter awaiting retrieval by the recipient.

Because e-mail is asynchronous, the delivery of messages is not instantaneous. There is a time delay, if only for a few minutes. Messages are stored in your **mailbox**, where the mail is indexed, awaiting retrieval. Because it is asynchronous, recipients do not need to be present when an e-mail is received. If they are logged on when an e-mail message arrives, they can reply right away. Unopened messages remain in the recipient's mailboxes to be read at a future time. E-mail eliminates the telephone tag that real-time interaction often requires, freeing users from the bounds of time and space. Participants can key messages on the computer at any time of the day or night and respond to computer messages in the same way.

Compared to the other types of Internet communication, e-mail has a rich and relatively long history. As soon as computers were linked together, whether by LANs (local area networks) or by WANs (wide area networks), individuals started relaying messages back and forth when they could not meet face to face.

Passing text messages back and forth while online predates microcomputers and the Internet. Before personal computers appeared on desktops, individuals using "dumb terminals" were able to connect to powerful host computers to relay messages back and forth from remote terminals. These computers had display units and keyboards, but no processing hardware. With the growth of messaging, **mail servers**, dedicated hardware and software for e-mail services within a network, were established. This setup reserved an area of the **host computer** (a mainframe or minicomputer) where individual accounts could be stored, and messages could be delivered to those accounts, stored in directories or folders. The mail server managed the incoming and outgoing e-mail messages, routing, storing and deleting them as requested.

With the introduction of the Internet, mail servers could pass messages outside of the corporate network to Internet Protocol (IP) addresses elsewhere. E-mail was soon used as much within the Internet world as was the transfer of research files. Today, e-mail is so popular that you can buy a handheld computer similar to a Palm Pilot but used solely for accessing e-mail, or you can order e-mail service, along with voice mail, from your telephone company. Dedicated low-cost Internet e-mail devices, called **mailstations,** allow you to send Internet e-mail without using a conventional computer.

## E-mail Systems and Servers

To use e-mail, you do not need to know all of the intricacies of software and hardware operations. You do need to know the interface and what is available to you as the user, however. A software **interface** is the computer software layer that allows users to interact with the underlying hardware and software. Regardless of the Internet Service Provider (ISP), Microsoft Outlook and Microsoft Outlook Express are the most-used e-mail software programs. Outlook is part of the Microsoft Office suite of programs, and Outlook Express is part of Internet Explorer which is included in Windows 98. The Netscape Navigator mail program is called Netscape Messenger. All of these programs are very similar in layout and

## The Global Village

Marshall McLuhan (1911–1980) was an influential professor who became famous for his study of communications. He rose to public prominence in the 1960s, and was famous for his clever pronouncements on media trends. Although he did not live to see the era of the personal computer and the Internet, his forecast that electronic media would someday create a "Global Village" seems closer than ever to coming true through the Web.

**Tips** *and* **Tools**

**Free E-mail Services** You can acquire a free e-mail address from any of the free e-mail services on the Web. For example, Microsoft's hotmail.com has free e-mail boxes, even if you do not use the Microsoft Network for your ISP. To sign up for Hotmail, key **www.hotmail.com** in your URL address text box and follow the prompts. There is a disadvantage to using a free mailbox, however; banner advertisements pop up and must be closed every time you open your e-mail account.

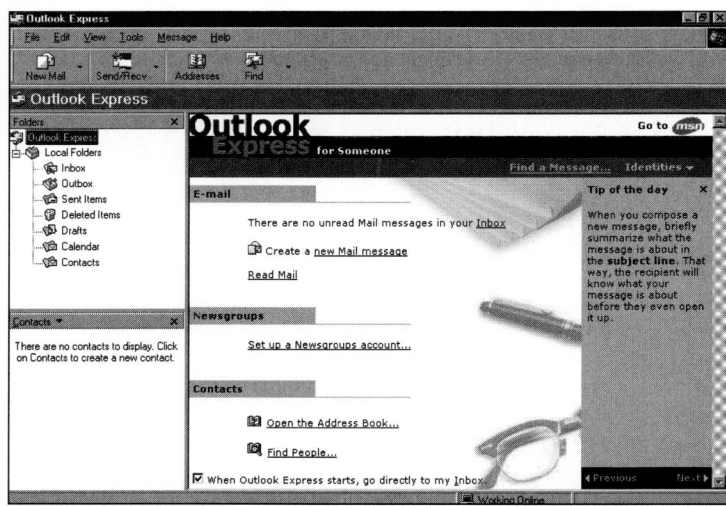

*Outlook Express is the e-mail program that comes with Internet Explorer.*

**Hotmail** http://www.hotmail.com
**Juno** http://www.juno.com

function. The exercises in this chapter are based on Microsoft Outlook Express.

You are not required to use the e-mail program that comes with your computer's software or your browser. As you become more experienced, you may encounter programs with features you prefer. You can obtain and install software for these other programs and use them in place of your existing mail program if you wish.

A mail server is required before you can send and receive mail. You do not have to worry about purchasing one because mail server service comes as part of any ISP Internet package. There are two popular mail protocols used to handle outgoing mail that you are likely to encounter when setting up your mail account: **Post Office Protocol (POP)** and **Internet Message Access Protocol (IMAP).** Both have advantages and disadvantages that you should know about. Many ISPs offer a choice of both types of protocols, allowing you to select the one you want.

The main advantage of POP servers is that they download all of the mail to your computer when you access the mail, and then delete it from the ISP's server. This makes it easier for you to work offline, and you can keep all of your Internet messages on your computer. Provided you access your mail periodically, using POP means that the disk space you use on the ISP's server is kept to a minimum. This is helpful because most ISPs have **quotas** for how much of their server disk space you can use. Every Internet account has quotas—for Web pages, for personal workspace, and for e-mail storage. Some ISPs are more generous than others, but all have limits. If you exceed your e-mail storage quota, messages intended for you will be returned to the senders with the notations "Returned: user's mailbox is full."

POP servers have a drawback if you access your mail from different computers. Because the servers erase your mail after you access it, you may not be able to find it if you have already accessed it from another computer. Unless your computers are linked in a network, you will have to go back to the other computer to access any messages that are stored there (see Figure 4.1).

IMAP servers differ from POP servers in that they download only the "headers" or subject portion of your e-mail messages to your computer. When you select the message, then it is loaded onto your computer. This allows you to receive your messages more quickly than with POP service. You can also be selective about which messages you wish to keep on your computer, retrieving only those you wish to read from the IMAP server. Your mail remains on the server, even after you download it. When you delete a message on your mail program, it is then deleted from the IMAP server as well. You need to be careful when using IMAP that you do not exceed the quota allowed by your ISP. Since your mail always remains on the server unless you delete it, you can check your mail using different computers.

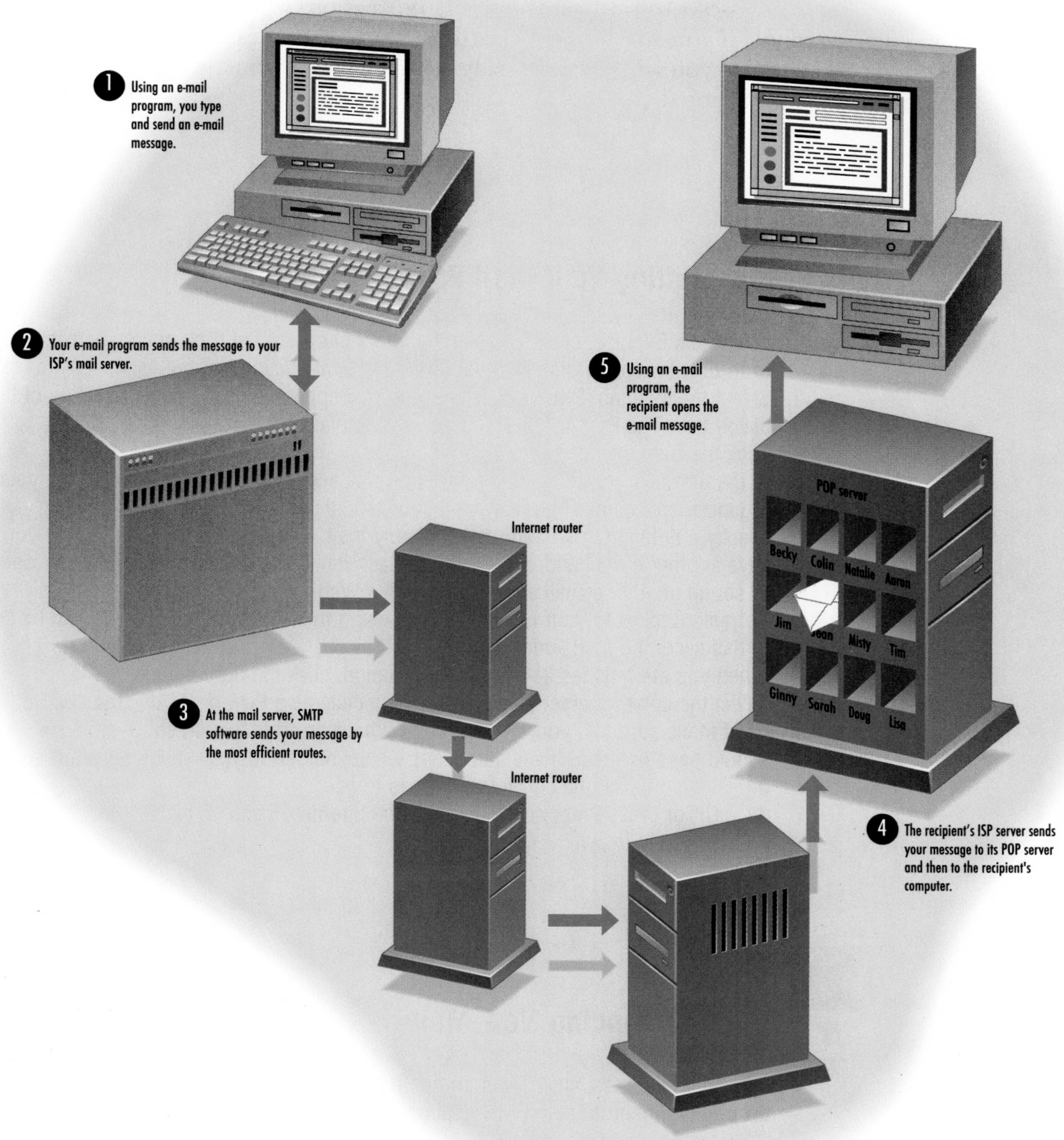

**1** Using an e-mail program, you type and send an e-mail message.

**2** Your e-mail program sends the message to your ISP's mail server.

**5** Using an e-mail program, the recipient opens the e-mail message.

Internet router

POP server

Becky  Colin  Natalie  Aaron

Jim  Jean  Misty  Tim

Ginny  Sarah  Doug  Lisa

**3** At the mail server, SMTP software sends your message by the most efficient routes.

Internet router

**4** The recipient's ISP server sends your message to its POP server and then to the recipient's computer.

*Figure 4.1* **Electronic Mail POP Servers**
Most electronic mail systems use a computer designated as a mail server that receives incoming e-mail messages. The messages are then sent to, and stored on, the ISP's POP server, from which the recipient can retrieve the messages.

The information package you receive from your ISP should include information about the mail server protocols the ISP supports, along with the mail server addresses. You will need this information when setting up your e-mail account. If you are using a Wizard program that takes you through the step-by-step setup, you will then be ready to input the information into the right boxes when prompted.

## Setting Your Mail Preferences

1. In Outlook Express, click Tools on the menu bar and then click Accounts from the drop-down menu to display the Internet Accounts dialog box.
2. Select the Mail tab. Double-click the icon that appears in the Account section of the dialog box. The Properties dialog box will appear.
3. Click the General tab.
4. In the first text box, key a name for your mail account. Also enter your name, your organization's name (optional), and your e-mail address. If you'd like, you can specify a different e-mail address for reply mail. Before doing this, make sure you have another e-mail address. If not, contact your ISP about obtaining another one, or set up another e-mail account through a Web-based e-mail service such as Hotmail. Replies to your e-mail sent out using the first e-mail address would be sent to this second e-mail address.
5. When you are finished keying the information, click the Servers tab.
6. Select the correct server protocol. It will usually be a POP or IMAP protocol, but you must make sure that your ISP supports whatever protocol you choose. Your ISP should have provided these addresses when you set up your account. If not, contact the ISP to find out the correct addresses to use.
7. Click OK or press Enter and then close the Internet Accounts dialog box.

## Announcing New Mail

1. In Outlook Express, click Tools on the menu bar and then select Options from the drop-down menu to display the Options dialog box.
2. Click the General tab.
3. Make sure that the Play sound when new messages arrive check box is checked. If not, click on it to make a check mark appear.
4. Click Apply and then click OK or press Enter.

# E-mail Software Features

All e-mail programs have basic features in common: mail editors, address books, and message delivery systems. These basic features allow a message to be composed and sent and messages to be received. There is variation within the features. For example, not all e-mail programs allow you to format text within a message.

**Mail Editors**   **Mail editors** are simplified word processing programs that allow you to type and edit an e-mail message. You can compose e-mail messages offline (when you are not logged on to the Internet) using the specific e-mail software loaded on the computer, and then dial in to the ISP to send the messages when you are ready. If you have only one phone line, you may wish to work offline and then connect to send the messages to avoid tying up the phone line. Working offline also allows you to do it anywhere your computer is located. You do not need to be connected to the Internet until you wish to send the messages. However, if phone-line access is not a problem, then you can compose messages while online.

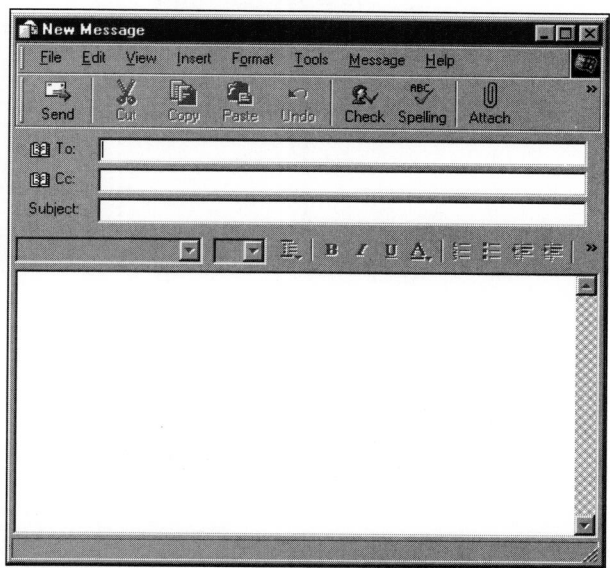

*A mail editor allows you to compose e-mail quickly and easily.*

**E-mail Addresses**   Since each ISP provides mail with a unique address, it is possible to have a separate e-mail address for every ISP you access. You may have a work address, a school address, and one or more home addresses depending on the number of Internet servers used. With multiple addresses, you may not remember to check all mailboxes consistently and may lose the opportunity to read and respond to messages in a timely manner. You may want to limit how many mailboxes you have and tell people which address you prefer them to use so you don't miss acknowledging important messages.

Your Internet address is crucial; it is how others contact you. Your ISP will assign you an Internet e-mail address when you subscribe. You are usually allowed to create the part of your address before the "at" symbol (@) using a combination of letters and numbers. Popular names go quickly, so if you want to be known as john@domainname.com there will almost certainly be hundreds of other people named John before you who wanted that name. Because of this, the ISP might suggest that you use John978@domainname.com, meaning that there are 977 people named John before you who had the same idea!

Your address is not the same as your Web page location, but it usually is similar. The @ symbol is the universal e-mail symbol of the Internet. If you see @ in any address, it is an e-mail address; if you see *www.*, it refers to a Web page location.

# Using E-mail Software

If you purchased a new computer, or recently added the Internet Explorer Web browser or the Office 2000 software application, Outlook Express or the full Outlook program was installed with it. The Outlook Express opening window looks like all other Windows programs, with a pull-down menu bar and a standard toolbar as shown in Figure 4.2. The frames show the folders that were discussed above, the address book, the individual messages in the selected folder, and a preview pane that shows the text.

To use Outlook Express as your mail editor for the first time, you may have to define it as your default mail package. On a new computer, you can go through the "Start Your Mail" process by clicking on the icon found on your desktop, or you can select Outlook Express from the Start menu on your computer by clicking Programs and then Outlook Express. You will be guided through a series of steps that define Outlook Express as your default mail client for the ISP you have chosen. If you already have an ISP, you can still select Outlook Express as your default mail editor. Many ISP programs will guide you through this process.

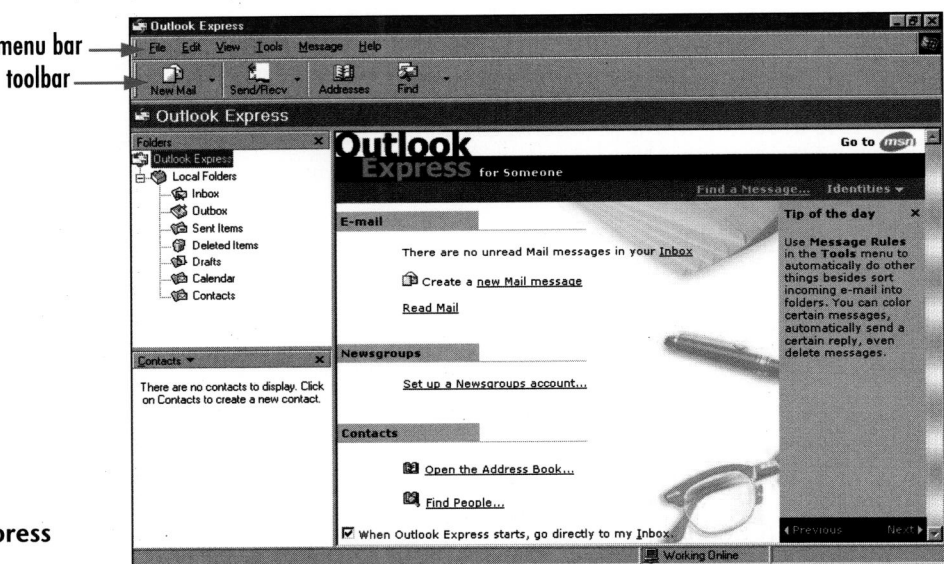

menu bar
toolbar

**Figure 4.2** **Outlook Express Menu Bar and Toolbar**

## Selecting Outlook Express as Your Default Mail Program

1. In Internet Explorer, select Tools on the menu bar and then click Internet Options to display the Internet Options dialog box.
2. Click the Programs tab.
3. In the E-mail text box, click the down-pointing arrow to select Outlook Express.
4. Click OK or press Enter.
5. If you have not yet configured your mail, click the Mail button on the IE toolbar. Click Read Mail and follow the prompts.

# E-mail Content

E-mail began as "work related" communication, and for the most part, it retains that flavor. The best e-mail messages are carefully composed and to the point. Messages need not be long, cleverly written letters. However, because e-mail is frequently composed on the spur of the moment, it often contains spelling and grammatical errors, although most mail editors provide spell checkers. It is considered bad taste to compose poorly written, long, or complex e-mail messages.

Although many people regard e-mail messages as temporary documents, there is nothing temporary about an e-mail message. Once a message is written and sent, it is saved electronically, often printed out in hard-copy form, forwarded to another Internet address, and may become available to many others besides the original author and recipient. Once an e-mail message is sent, it should be considered permanent. This is because a copy of it is likely to exist somewhere in cyberspace. Since Internet servers are regularly backed up on other servers, e-mail can often be more easily traced than a lost letter or a threatening phone call. Careers have been altered and lawsuits lost over archived (stored) e-mail messages.

Remember that your e-mail message can be passed on to others with a single click of the mouse. It's best to avoid writing a message that you would be embarrassed to have others read.

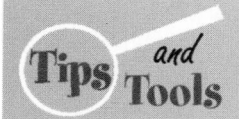

**To Send or Not to Send** To help you avoid any problems, a piece of advice that used to be given to letter writers is just as relevant for people composing e-mail messages today. If you write something in anger or when you are feeling overly emotional, it is best to wait a day before mailing it. More often than not, after "cooling off," most people decide it was not a good idea to send the letter and discard it. In the same way, you can compose and save an e-mail message and wait a day before sending it.

## Parts of an E-mail Message

E-mail messages are organized like office memos. They are not meant to be formal documents; their layout is very functional. A printout of a typical e-mail message in Outlook Express is shown in Figure 4.3.

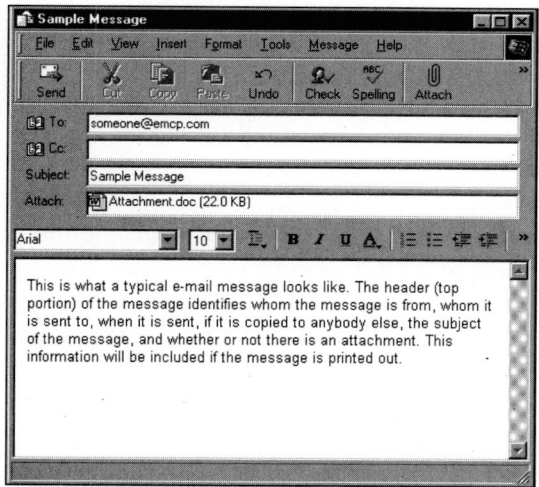

*Figure 4.3* **Typical E-mail with Attachment in Outlook Express**

## Just between You and Me . . .

A lawyer at a renowned British law firm found out the hard way that you can never tell where an e-mail message might end up. A girlfriend had sent him an e-mail containing some intimate comments. He forwarded the note to several workmates with the comment, "Now that's a nice compliment from a lass, isn't it?" His friends passed the note along to their friends, and within several days it was estimated that the note had been passed on to over thirteen million people around the world! The story eventually made the news, embarrassing both the lawyer and his girlfriend. To make matters worse, the lawyer was given a temporary suspension by the firm as a result.

**Using Blind Carbon Copy** The people you copy your messages to (Cc) will be able to see the names of all the other recipients. If you want to copy someone confidentially, you can use the blind carbon copy feature (Bcc). To send a blind carbon copy, in the New Message dialog box click the To text box. Compose your message in the blank text box below and then click the Bcc button under Message recipients.

When you compose a message, the mail program automatically enters the date. You must fill in the To, Cc, and Subject text boxes. You can send a message to as many addresses as you'd like or cc (carbon copy) as many recipients as necessary. You don't need to key a subject line in the Subject text box for the system to work, but including a subject is often preferred by recipients.

## Composing and Sending a Message

1. In Outlook Express, click File, point to New, and then select Mail Message to display the New Message dialog box.
2. In the To text box, key the address of the recipient. (Remember to key it accurately, with no extra spaces, letters, or dots.)
3. In the Cc text box, key the e-mail address of a friend or classmate, or you can send a copy to yourself if you prefer.
4. In the Subject text box, key a short description of the message. For example, **This is an e-mail assignment**.
5. In the blank text box below, key the message. For example, key *Hi!* **This is an assignment for my Internet computer class. Please send a message back to me so I know that you received it. Thanks.**
6. Key your name at the bottom of the message.
7. Click Tools on the New Message dialog box toolbar and select Spelling at the drop-down menu. This feature will spell check your message.
8. When the spelling check is finished, click OK or press Enter.
9. To mail your message, click the Send button on the toolbar.

**Spam-blocking software**
www.zdnet.com/downloads (search under "spam")
**Suespammers**
http://www.suespammers.org

Many of the same formatting commands in word processing, such as bold, italic, underline, formatting numbers and bullets, paragraph indentations, and alignment, are available when writing e-mail. Unlike older text editors, new editors often add significant formatting options. Other options for your e-mail are to copy, cut and paste, attach a file, undo, and check spelling. The copy, cut and paste, undo, and spelling check functions work the same way as they do in Word or other word processing programs.

The priority setting will let your recipient know when your message is of high priority (see Figure 4.4), normal priority, or low priority. This is a polite thing to do when sending messages to someone who might receive hundreds of messages in a day. The recipient can then know which messages to read first, and which messages can be read after all of the more important ones have been dealt with.

**Check Your Spelling** You can check your spelling and grammar in Outlook Express and Outlook just as you do in Word or other word processing programs. Once you have finished composing your message, click Spelling on the menu bar to make sure that your spelling and grammar are correct.

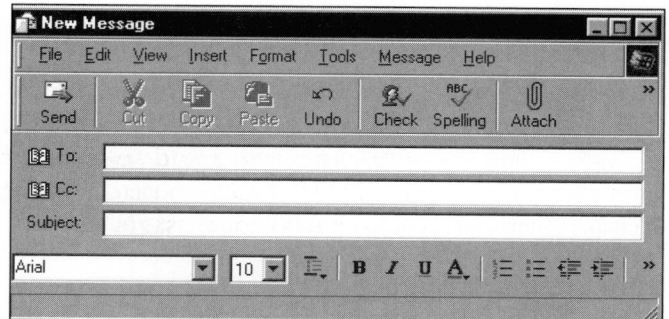

You can copy, cut and paste, undo, and check spelling just like you would with your word processing program.

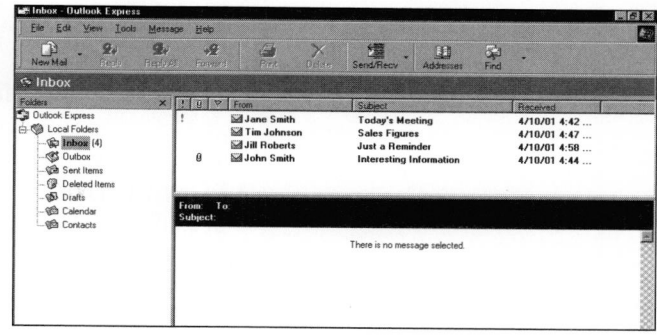

**Figure 4.4**

*A red exclamation point next to a message indicates a priority message.*

# E-mail Netiquette

**Netiquette** is a new word created by combining **net**work and e**tiquette** (rules for good behavior). The ability to compose and send messages in seconds or minutes leads more than a few people to abandon many of the traditional rules of courteous letter writing. As a result, many users unintentionally write messages that recipients consider rude. There is no single form of netiquette, but there is general agreement on many points. You should be aware of these rules before you start firing off e-mail letters around the world. Some of the most important rules are described later in this chapter; others you will learn as you venture out onto the Internet.

## SPAM

Unsolicited e-mail that arrives in your inbox from unknown sources is referred to as **spam**. Spamming is the practice of sending the same unsolicited messages to all users on an automatic mailing list, a newsgroup, a proprietary e-mail list, or even to members of the same ISP. The term *spam* has been around the Internet for many years. Some suggest that the term came from a song in one of the skits produced by the comic group Monty Python with the repeated refrain, "Spam, Spam, Spam." Spam is an unpleasant reality of using e-mail. Just as you receive junk mail in your postal mailboxes, spam may be deposited in your e-mail box as well. While Web pages with advertising banners and links to commercial sites are accepted as part of the commercial nature of the Web, receiving unsolicited e-mail in your personal mailbox is not.

Aside from some chastisement of those who misuse the Web by those who do not, other more stringent measures have not been taken due to the strong support of constitutional rights governing access and use of the Internet. Your Internet address, like everything else on the Web, is public information. Noteworthy exceptions to the wide legal parameters of Internet use include recent occurrences of viruses being attached to e-mail messages. Sending viruses is considered criminal behavior and can be prosecuted.

Do not reply to spam e-mail, or you will probably get more. Some users set up two different screen names: one for sending and receiving public information, and one for communicating with people they know. ISPs often have filtering techniques for e-mail from known spammers, but unfortunately the problem may get worse before it gets better.

## Copying and Pasting Text into an E-mail Message

1. In Internet Explorer, open an existing Word or Notepad document or create a new one. To open an existing document, click File on the menu bar and then click Open. At the Open dialog box, key the file name in the Open text box, or click the Browse button to find the file you want. To create a new document, go to Word, click File on the menu bar, click New, and then click OK or press Enter to create a Blank Document.
2. With the document open, use the mouse to select and highlight the text you wish to copy. If you wish to copy all of the text, click Edit from the menu bar and then click Select All.
3. Right-click the mouse button and then click Copy at the shortcut menu, or click Edit on the menu bar and then click Copy.
4. Now go to Outlook Express and click the New Mail button on the toolbar to compose an e-mail if you do not already have a message open.
5. Place the cursor in the blank text box, right-click the mouse button, and then click Paste on the shortcut menu. You can also click Edit from the menu bar and then click Paste. The text selection that you copied from the document is in your new message.

## Blocking Incoming Mail

1. In Outlook Express, click Tools on the menu bar, point to Message Rules, and then click Block Senders List from the side menu that appears.
2. In the Message Rules dialog box, click the Mail Rules tab and then click New.
3. In the New Mail Rule dialog box you can select your conditions for blocking incoming mail, such as blocking mail from certain senders or with specific subject headers, mail with attachments, and so on, and specify what to do with these messages (delete, move to a special folder, etc.). Click in the desired boxes to insert check marks. In the third text box, you will be prompted to key the e-mail address or words that you wish to have blocked. Fill in the appropriate information in the dialog box that shows in the screen.
4. Click Add and then click OK to close the dialog box. Click OK to close the New Mail Rule dialog box, and click OK again to close the Message Rules dialog box. The rule(s) you created will filter and block incoming messages as stipulated.
5. For a shortcut, skip steps 1 and 2 and begin by clicking an e-mail address in a folder, clicking Message on the menu bar, and then clicking Create Rule From Message from the drop-down menu. Proceed with step 3 to select and activate your conditions for blocking mail messages.
6. Another shortcut to blocking mail from a sender is to click the e-mail address in any folder, click Message on the menu bar, and then click Block Sender from the drop-down menu. All mail from that sender will be forwarded to the *Deleted Items* folder.
7. You can block messages from newsgroups in the same way as you do for mail. In the Message Rules dialog box, select the News Rules tab instead of Mail Rules. The selection method is the same as for Mail Rules.

**Capital Letters**  One very important netiquette rule, and one most frequently violated by those new to the Internet, is keying capital letters. By convention, keying words or phrases in capital letters is considered shouting. Once you understand this, you too will find yourself annoyed when you receive messages in uppercase. Besides communicating an angry tone, words set in all capital letters are harder to read than lowercase letters. For these reasons, it is best to avoid using an all-capital style.

**Flaming**  The anonymity of e-mail communication has led many to behave in ways they never would behave in face-to-face communication. Rude, insulting comments are known as flames, and the activity of writing such comments is called **flaming**. Inevitably you will receive messages from people that will provoke you, but it is best to avoid the temptation of responding in kind. Doing so will usually provoke a flame war, with increasingly strong messages being passed back and forth like a tennis ball. Take the high road and just ignore flames. There is no rule saying you have to respond to every message you receive. Flaming can be intentional; resist the temptation to join the "game."

**Emotional Cues**  The basic medium of e-mail communication is one of the causes of many flame wars. Because you cannot see or hear the person you are communicating with, you miss many of the visual and auditory cues to emotion that we take for granted in face-to-face or even telephone communication. The only clue to the emotional intent of the writer is the written word. You cannot see gestures, hear tone of voice, or see facial expressions. This can easily lead to misunderstandings. The ease with which people can compose and send an e-mail message compounds this problem. It is not unusual for people to receive replies that they interpret as curt or even hostile, yet the intent of the writer was nothing like that. Being aware of this should lead you to think about what you write, and to make sure that you are not writing in a way that could be easily misinterpreted. In the same vein, you should give people the benefit of the doubt, unless you are certain they are intentionally being rude or hostile.

To overcome these problems, some creative people have employed symbols and letters to communicate the emotion they wish to convey. Some take the form of **emoticons**, which are combinations of keyboard symbols expressing emotion. Perhaps the easiest to interpret is the smiley, created by keying a colon, a hyphen, and

## Hot Headed?
## Eudora E-mail Cools You Down

The newest version of Eudora, a popular e-mail program, adds Moodwatch, a "flame" checker that enhances current spell checkers. Moodwatch rates words by their potential to raise blood pressure. When the checker finds a match in the e-mail message, a chili pepper icon appears in the screen. A one chili pepper rating indicates that the e-mail should be sent with caution, and a three chili pepper rating indicates that the e-mail is almost guaranteed to raise the recipient's blood pressure.

Eudora maker Qualcomm worked with language experts and flame room newsgroups to develop the nearly three million entries in the flame dictionary. Some entries are words, others are phrases such as "you presume too much," "what part don't you understand?," or "I was shocked to hear." The program picks up phrases that accuse, blame, or incite anger.

Qualcomm says that the program cannot prevent flaming messages; it can only alert the user to the problem, and the user has the choice of changing the e-mail or ignoring the warning. Perhaps a warning will be enough to prevent hastily written messages from being impulsively sent into cyberspace.

**Source:** "Subject: You're an Idiot," by Adam Pasick, Foxnews.com/vtech/100400/email.sml, October 4, 2000.

*Table 4.1* **Common Emoticons**

| Button | Function |
|---|---|
| :-) | smiling, happy |
| :) | smiling, happy |
| ;-) | wink |
| :-D | Ha ha! |
| :-O | shocked |
| :-I | indifference |
| \|-O | snoring or yawning |
| \|-I | asleep |
| :-Z | sleeping |
| :-/ | skeptical |
| :-( | frowning |
| :( | frowning |
| :-> | sarcastic |
| >:-( | angry |
| :-* | sorry |
| }:-) | devilish, mischievous |
| [:-) | wearing a headset |
| (-: | left-handed e-mailer |
| %-) | spent too much time in front of the computer |
| &:-) | bad hair day |
| *:o) | just clowning around |
| :*) | clowning around, option two |
| <:-) | stupid suggestion |

a closing parenthesis—:-). These emoticons are used to make it clear that the writer's intent was friendly and not hostile or mean. Common emoticons are listed in Table 4.1. In addition, some people use combinations of letters to indicate emotion or mood. One of the most common of these is LOL, which represents "laughing out loud."

It is still important to ensure that what you write will be perceived the way you intended. If you are not careful, and you write something that might be misconstrued, even using an emoticon might not help.

**Subject Headers**   When writing an e-mail message, it is good netiquette to include a subject header—a line describing the basic theme of the message you are sending. Many people sort through dozens or hundreds of e-mail messages a day. By providing a subject, you can give the reader an idea of what your message is about and let him or her know whether or not it requires an urgent response. It also assists people who wish to file their e-mail correspondence by subject. If the person you are e-mailing uses IMAP protocol, his or her computer will download only headers (the portion of the message indicating its origin, date sent, subject, etc.). Since the recipient will have no idea what the message is about, he or she may choose not to download the message at all.

If you are using the Reply button, make sure to change the subject if the subject of your message has changed from the previous one. It is annoying and confusing to receive a message with a subject header completely different from the actual subject or content of the message.

Another thing to remember when using the Reply feature is to edit the content of the material from the original message. If you fail to do this, the message will become longer and longer as it is passed back and forth, taking up more bandwidth and rapidly filling up disk space.

## The Address Book

The **Address Book** is a simple, personalized database of names and e-mail addresses usually stored in alphabetical order. Addresses in the Address Book can be automatically inserted in the To text box when you compose a new message. Most e-mail systems can deliver a message individually or to many people at the same time. You can send a message to more than one person at the same time by keying or selecting multiple names in the To text box, or in the Cc (carbon copy) text box when composing your message.

Address books provide a shortcut by allowing you to store frequently used e-mail addresses. Most e-mail systems allow you to click the To button and enter directly into the Address Book feature. Once in Address Book, you click on a name to enter the address. With Outlook Express and many other mail editors, if you have a name stored in Address Book, keying the name will automatically enter the corresponding e-mail address into the Address text box.

### Just Like Being There

A new generation of software programs will soon allow your "image" to read your message to the recipient, with all of the visual and auditory effectiveness of face-to-face communication. LifeFX Inc. and Kodak have announced plans for such a program to be available by the end of 2001. LifeFX already has a free program with a generic "face" to read e-mails, and it is proving to be a very popular download. Microsoft, Apple, and a number of smaller companies are working on similar programs. But, don't throw away your emoticons just yet! In this first-generation software, emoticons are still necessary to cue the facial reader to the emotion the message writer wishes to convey.

**Source:** "Company Plans to Take E-motion Past the :) Stage," Justin Pope, AP, *International Herald Tribune*, Asia Ed., February 15, 2001, p. 13.

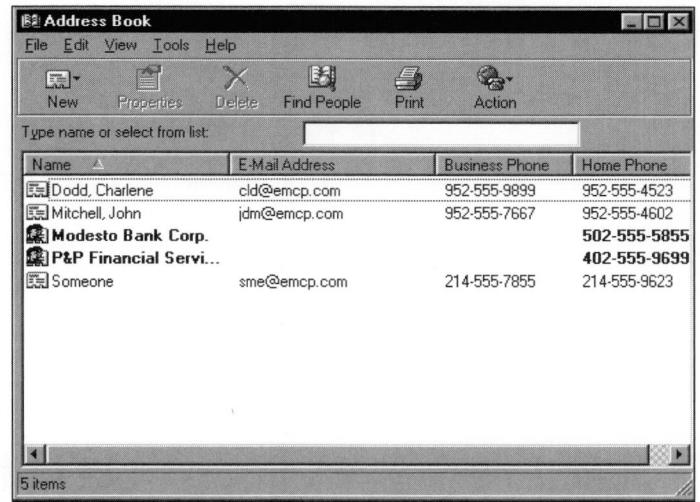

*Typical address book in Outlook Express with entries for individuals and groups.*

If you send messages regularly to the same groups of people, you can save a lot of time by creating a group mailing list. E-mail software lets you manage the Address Book by adding, changing, and deleting entries when necessary.

The Address Book needs to be kept current to remain useful, just like a regular address book. Doing a quick visual check of addresses on incoming e-mail and replacing outdated entries in the Address Book will help keep entries up to date.

## Entering New Names and Addresses

1. In Outlook Express, click the Addresses button on the toolbar to open the Address Book dialog box.
2. Click File and then New Contact.
3. The Properties dialog box opens with the Name tab showing. Key a first name, last name, title, and nickname in the appropriate text boxes. Key the E-mail address.
4. Click Add. The address appears in the window below the E-mail Addresses text box.
5. You can click on the other tabs to add information about the home, business, and personal life of the entry. Click OK to close the Properties dialog box, then close the Address Book dialog box.
6. Address Book entries can be edited or corrected. Click the Addresses button to open the Address Book dialog box. Double-click on the entry you wish to modify; the Properties dialog box for that entry appears. Click on the Name tab and edit the information in any text box. You can also edit information on any of the other tabs (except the Summary tab). Click OK or press Enter when you are finished.

## Creating Groups

1. In Outlook Express, click the Addresses button on the toolbar.
2. In the Address Book dialog box, click the New button on the toolbar, and then click New Group from the drop-down menu.
3. With the Group tab selected, key a name for your group in the Group Name text box.
4. If you wish to add e-mail addresses that are already in Address Book, click Select Members.
5. In the Select Group Member dialog box, click the addresses you wish to add to the group. Then click the Select button to add them to the Members list. Click OK or press Enter when you are finished.
6. If you wish to add an address that is not already in Address Book, click New Contact (instead of Select Members).
7. Fill in the information text boxes for the new contact and then click Add or OK.
8. When you are finished adding all of the names for the group, click OK and close all of the dialog boxes.
9. The Address Book will create a group mail address with a group icon. When you compose an e-mail message and address it using this group address, copies will be sent to everyone in the group.

## Sending an E-mail Using the Address Book

1. In Outlook Express, click the New Mail button on the toolbar to display the New Message dialog box.
2. Click the To button to the left of the To text box and the Select Recipients dialog box opens.
3. In the Name section, double-click the name to whom you wish to send the message. Click OK.
4. If you wish to send carbon copies, click the Cc button to the left of the Cc text box and the Select Recipients dialog box opens. Repeat step 3.
5. If you wish to include a subject line, key the word or phrase in the Subject text box. Compose your message in the blank text box below, and then click the Send button on the toolbar to send your message.

## Adding Names from the Address Book

*To automatically add a name to the Address Book from an incoming e-mail message:*
1. In Outlook Express, click the *Inbox* folder at the left side of the screen. Select one of the messages currently in your Inbox.
2. Right-click the mouse button, and click Add Sender to Address Book on the shortcut menu.
3. You have added the e-mail address to the Address Book.

*To manually enter an address in the Address Book:*
1. Click the Addresses button on the browser toolbar.
2. To add an address, click the New button and then click New Contact.
3. Fill out the information text boxes and then click OK or press Enter.

## Deleting Names from the Address Book

1. In Outlook Express, click the Addresses button on the toolbar.
2. Click on an address to highlight it.
3. Click the Delete buttonon the toolbar to delete the entry.

### Adding an Automatic Signature to Outgoing E-mails

1. In Outlook Express, click Tools on the menu bar and then click Options from the drop-down menu to display the Options dialog box.
2. Select the Signatures tab.
3. Click the New button at the right side of the dialog box.
4. Make sure the Add signatures to all outgoing messages check box has a check mark. If not, click in it to add a check mark. You can also select whether or not you want your signature added to messages you send using the Reply and Forward features.
5. In the Edit Signature section, click the Text button.
6. In the text box to the right of the Text button, key the signature you wish to appear in your outgoing e-mails. This might be a closing word or phrase ("Sincerely," "With Regards," and so forth) followed by your name, your e-mail address, and perhaps even a witty saying or wise words you wish to share. You are free to add whatever you wish, but remember that this will be added at the bottom of every e-mail message you send out.
7. When you are finished, click Apply and then click OK or press Enter.

## Responding to and Forwarding E-mail

*A user can respond to an e-mail by clicking the Reply button.*

When you receive an e-mail, you can respond by merely clicking the Reply button. Proceed as if you were composing a message, and click Send when finished. Remember to add that person's address to the Address Book if you need to keep it; the message eventually may be deleted from your server or your computer.

When you use the Reply feature, the body of the message will still appear and you can begin writing in the space above it. If the message is a long one, you can delete it or save only the portions you need to refer to. You can also insert text inside the message to respond to items point by point. If the mail editor allows it, you can bold or color these responses so that the recipient can easily distinguish your responses from what he or she wrote. You can also change the default setting on your computer so that the body of the original message is not included in the reply.

### Changing the Default Setting For Message Reply

1. In Outlook Express, click Tools from the menu bar and then click Options from the drop-down menu to display the Options dialog box.
2. Select the Send tab.
3. Click on the check mark in the Include message in reply check box to delete the check mark.
4. Click Apply and then click OK.

If you erase the entire message, make sure you refer to what it is you are responding to. Otherwise, the recipient may have no idea what your new message is about.

## Responding to a Message

1. In Outlook Express, open the *Inbox* folder by clicking on it. Locate the e-mail message called Attachment Exercise. Click on it to open the message.
2. Click the Reply button on the toolbar. The sender's address will appear in the Send to line. In the text box, key **I am learning how to reply to a message**.
3. Click Send.

*A user can pass on an e-mail message to other users by clicking the Forward button.*

Be careful about forwarding letters or material other people have sent you. You should always request permission before doing this. E-mail makes forwarding messages as easy as clicking a button, but the person whose message you forwarded might not be happy with this action. If there is any doubt, ask.

Forwarding a message from your mailbox to another Internet address is a common practice. Passing on an e-mail without comment is both convenient and expedient in some cases. You should never forward a private message without the composer's knowledge. Although everyone knows that e-mail is public, forwarding messages can be a sensitive issue if it concerns material that the sender intended only for your eyes.

**Chain Letters** You will almost certainly receive chain letters from time to time. These are annoying, and you will not make any friends by passing them on. In fact, passing them on violates the rules of many ISPs. Ignore the dire warnings or get-rich-quick schemes they advertise, and toss them into your recycle bin without opening them. Nobody has ever died from failing to pass on a chain letter!

## Forwarding a Message

1. In Outlook Express, open the *Inbox* folder by clicking on it. Locate the e-mail message called Attachment Exercise. Click to open the message.
2. Click the Forward button on the toolbar. The screen will show the cursor blinking in the To text box.
3. In the To box, key the address to which you want to forward the message. For this example, key the address of another student in your class. As a shortcut, click on the To button to open the Address Book, and then click on the person's name. Click To, and his or her address will appear in the To text box.
4. Click Send. A copy of the original message is sent to that person, with both the name of the composer and your Internet address as the forwarder.

*Clicking on the paperclip icon allows a user to send an attachment with an e-mail.*

## Attachments

If you are sending large attachments (generally over 50Kb), it is a good idea to ask the recipient if it is all right to do so. Not everyone has a high-speed connection, and your recipient might find that he or she cannot download and view the mail because the attachment is slowing things down. One solution for large documents is to compress the files using a compression program.

It is also a good idea to avoid placing too many attachments in one message. If you must send several attachments, try sending them in separate messages. In the first message, advise the recipient of what you will be sending in subsequent messages. In the subject header, append the subject with a number (Photos 1, Photos 2, and so on.) to indicate the message is part of a series. If you do not do this, your recipient might see the same subject header, think you inadvertently sent the same message more than once, and delete it without reading it.

The Attachment feature allows you to attach many types of files—from text to graphics to sound or video. The recipient can open the file if he or she has the software to read it, or can detach the file and store it on his or her computer. Attachments are very easy to append to a message, and easy for the recipient to view. In the past, attachments were a fairly complex process, and older mail servers could not handle anything but pure text attachments. Now you can receive digital photos with an e-mail letter.

Sometimes files are too large to send as attachments; graphic and multimedia files can be huge compared to text files. In this case, you have two options: you can break up a file into multiple files, or you can compress it for sending. For text files, breaking them into smaller files is easy; for graphic and multimedia files, this is not practical. You will need to compress the files using a compression software program such as WinZip. WinZip can be downloaded and used free of charge. However, your recipient must also have the WinZip utility software or other compression program so he or she can unzip, or uncompress, your attachments before viewing them. The compressed file will have a *.zip* extension when you attach it.

An exception occurs when you send and receive multiple or large files within the same ISP membership; the files may be compressed and uncompressed automatically by the ISP software.

If you receive unsolicited e-mail, do not read it or open any attachments. One of the most popular ways for a virus to infect your computer is for it to hitch a ride with an attachment. In general, it is a bad idea to open attachments that you are not expecting; even someone you know could unwittingly send you a virus. Aways review the subject line of an e-mail message before opening it. Be especially leery of subject lines that try to lure you into opening messages from unknown senders. It is possible to scan e-mails and attachments before opening them by using a virus scanner. You can download an attachment without opening it by double-clicking on the attachment in the attachment header. Click Save it to disk in the Open Attachment Warning dialog box that appears (Figure 4.5), and then select the file you wish to store it in. Make sure to remember where you placed it so you can use your virus software to check out the file before opening it.

**Download WinZip (winzip80.exe)**
http://www.winzip.com

If you want to take a chance and view an attached file right away, just double-click on it, choose Open it from the Open Attachment Warning dialog box that appears, and the program will open in the appropriate proprietary software program.

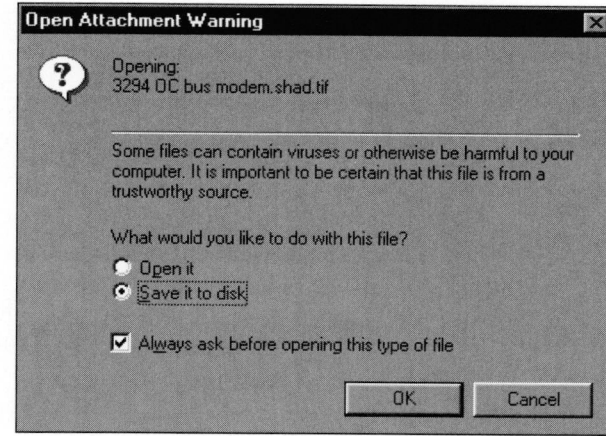

 **Figure 4.5 Open Attachment Warning Dialog Box**
*It is a good idea to save attachments to a disk for virus scanning.*

## Adding an Attachment

1. In Microsoft Word, on the menu bar click File and then New. Click OK to accept the Blank Document.
2. Compose a message that you can send as an attachment. For example, key **This is a sample Word document that I am going to send as an attachment**.
3. Save your message by clicking File and then Save As. Name the file Attachment to Send. Click Save, and then exit Word.
4. Open Outlook Express. On the menu bar, click File, point to New, and then click Mail Message to display the New Message dialog box.
5. In the To text box, key your e-mail address. (You will send the attachment to yourself.)
6. In the Subject text box, key **Attachment Exercise**.
7. In the blank text box below, key **I am practicing by sending an attachment to myself**.
8. On the menu bar, click Insert and then File Attachment. In both programs, the folders on your hard drive will be displayed. Using Windows techniques, browse through available drives, folders, and files to find the correct file—in this case, Attachment to Send. When the file is displayed, click Attach.
9. Click Send to send your e-mail with an attachment.

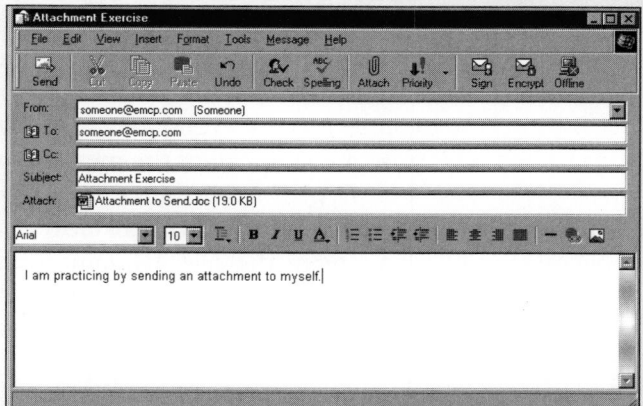

## Opening an Attachment

1. In Outlook Express, open the *Inbox* folder by clicking on it. Locate the e-mail message called Attachment Exercise. (This is the e-mail you sent to yourself in the Adding an Attachment exercise.) Click to open the message.
2. Double-click on the attachment in the attachment heading (see Figure 4.6).
3. Click on the file to open it. An Open Attachment Warning dialog box will open. Normally, it is good practice to save to a disk, but in this case you know who sent the attachment and what it contains, so it is safe to open the file. Click Open this and then click OK.
4. The message will open in Word. Close the message and return to Outlook Express.

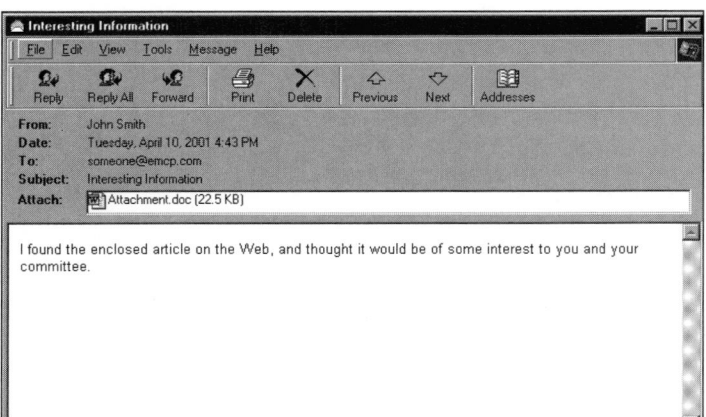

**Figure 4.6 An E-mail Message with an Attachment**
*Double-click on the attachment heading to view the attachment.*

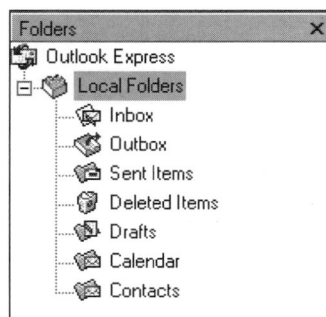

**Figure 4.7 Folder Options in Outlook Express**
*You can organize your mail using folders in Outlook Express.*

## Creating and Managing Mail Folders

Just as you needed to learn the "housekeeping" tasks of managing folders and files on your PC's hard drive, when you use e-mail, you need to manage your mail messages as well, organizing them into logical folders, editing, sorting, and deleting them as needed. Notice the folder icons at the left side of the screen in Figure 4.7 labeled *Inbox*, *Outbox*, *Sent Items*, *Deleted Items*, and *Drafts*. These are the basic mail folders. Your e-mail program may have additional folders as well.

The *Inbox* folder is where you will find mail that has been sent to your e-mail address. The *Outbox* folder contains any messages that you may have composed offline and wish to send later. (You can compose a number of messages offline and then send them all at once when you connect to the Web.) The *Sent Items* folder contains a copy of all of the messages you have sent. The *Deleted Items* folder contains any messages you have deleted. You can clear out deleted messages from the *Deleted Items* folder by clicking Edit on the menu bar, and then clicking Empty Deleted Items folder. The *Drafts* folder contains unfinished messages that you can return to and edit later. Because of the nature of e-mail, the *Drafts* folder is the least used folder in all e-mail systems. In Outlook Express, you can move messages from one folder to another, create new folders, delete unneeded ones, and generally perform the same housekeeping you do with files on your hard drive.

**Sorting Messages** You can change the way that messages are sorted in the various folders by clicking on the headers (From, Subject, Received, and so on). Doing this will sort messages alphabetically by sender or subject, chronologically by date, or by priority.

## Creating a New Folder

1. In Outlook Express, on the menu bar click File, point to New, and then select Folder from the drop-down menu to display the Create Folder dialog box.
2. Make sure that the *Inbox* folder is shaded (selected) and then key **Class Assignments** as the name of the folder. Click OK or press Enter.
3. The *Class Assignments* folder will appear under the *Inbox* folder in the main screen.

## Organizing Messages in Folders

1. In Outlook Express, right-click on a message in any of the existing folders.
2. At the shortcut menu that appears, click Move to Folder to display the Move dialog box.
3. Click Local Folder and then select the folder to which you wish to move the message. Click OK or press Enter. You can also create a new folder for the message by clicking on the New Folder button. Close the Move dialog box.
4. To delete or rename a folder, right-click on the name of the folder and then click Delete or Rename from the shortcut menu.

## Other Asynchronous Systems

E-mail is not the only asynchronous (time-delayed) system you are likely to encounter on the Internet. Automatic Mailing Lists and Newsgroups are two popular features that allow users with similar interests to share their ideas and learn about topics they find interesting.

## Automatic Mailing Lists

Another popular method of communicating using e-mail is through an **automatic mailing list.** An automatic mailing list is an online discussion group based on specific topics or common interests. Early in Internet history, groups of individuals with similar research interests formed e-mail lists to share each other's comments on a specific topic. The comments took the form of e-mail messages distributed to every e-mail address on the list. There are several popular automatic mailing list server programs, the most popular of which are LISTSERV and Majordomo. LISTSERV is a commercial system, whereas Majordomo is **freeware,** software available free of charge. An official catalog of LISTSERVs maintained by L-Soft International (www.lsoft.com) includes over 44,500 public lists.

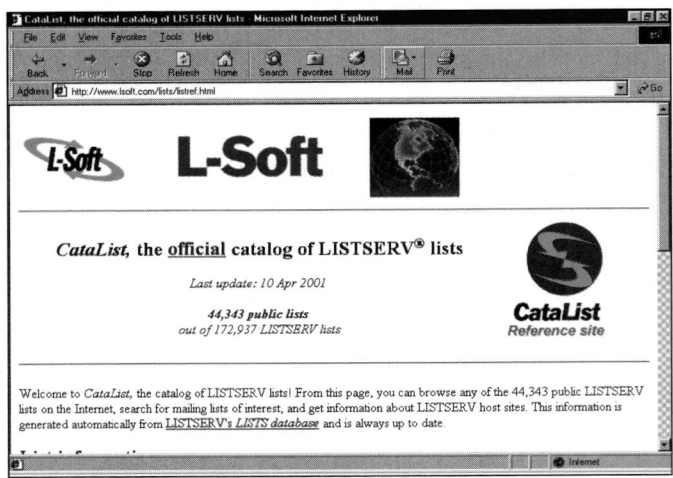

L-Soft CataList is a search engine for LISTSERVs worldwide.

Since automatic mailing lists are a form of e-mail, they share many of the same characteristics. The members of an automatic mailing list receive all contributions, and each can respond if he or she wishes. These groups are often very large with members from all over the globe. The largest automatic mailing list has more than 275,000 members! Lists exist in different languages, but English is dominant. Some lists are moderated; the messages are screened before they are forwarded to all members.

What distinguishes automatic mailing lists is that members must subscribe to join the group e-mail, and unsubscribe to end their involvement. A robot, or automated server system, adds members, forwards the messages, and deletes members when they unsubscribe. Most lists are extremely active. They are used to share opinions and experiences, ask and answer questions, and post information about certain topics. They continue to be one of the most popular forms of group communication on the Internet. One person can send a message about a specific topic that will reach thousands of people. Unlike chat, which is another form of group communication that has enjoyed great growth since Web chat rooms were introduced, automatic mailing lists are asynchronous. You do not have to log on to the Web at a certain time to enjoy automatic mailing lists.

Two Internet addresses are given for every automatic mailing list—one where members join the group and one to send messages to the entire list. Be careful not to get them mixed up! The term used to join is "subscribe." Because the e-mail sent to a list is received and processed by a robot, make certain your e-mail address and the information you submit are sent to the correct address. Also, remember to keep your acknowledgment message after you join an automatic mailing list. The number of messages you receive can be overwhelming, and you may wish to unsubscribe. The acknowledgment message tells you how.

## Joining an Automatic Mailing List

1. In Internet Explorer, go to the L-Soft International site, www.lsoft.com. Click on CataList at the left side of the screen.
2. Scroll down to List information and click on the _Search for a mailing list of interest_ hyperlink.
3. In the Look for text box, key **sports, hockey**. Click Start the search!
4. Click on ABCSPORTSINFO@listserv.aol.com. Scroll down the page until you come to the To Subscribe section.
5. Double-click on listserv@listserv.aol.com. An e-mail message screen will pop up, preaddressed to listserv@listserv.aol.com. Leave the Subject text box blank, and tab down to the blank text box. Key **subscribe ABCSportsinfo**.
6. Click Send. A message box may appear telling you that there is no subject. Click OK to send anyway.
7. An e-mail acknowledgment will be sent welcoming you and stating the group address to which you can send e-mail messages. Keep this acknowledgment, since it tells you how to unsubscribe.
8. Close the window and return to Outlook Express.

## Leaving an Automatic Mailing List

1. In Outlook Express, click File, point to New, and then click Mail Message to display the New Message dialog box.
2. In the To text box, key the automatic mailing list address. For this example, key **listserv@listserv.aol.com**. Just as was done when subscribing, leave the Subject text box blank. In the blank text box below, key **unsubscribe**. Immediately after the word _unsubscribe_ key the name of list. In this case you would key **unsubscribe ABCSportsinfo**.
3. Click Send.

Once you have subscribed to an automatic mailing list, you will receive all e-mails sent to the list. Lists allow you to immediately participate and send messages. Or you may choose to be a **lurker**—a silent participant who reads all, but chooses not to actively participate in the discussion. In fact, before you join in a discussion, it may be a good idea to lurk, and view the messages for a period of time, before you post a message. You may find that the question you wanted to ask has already been answered, or that the list topics are not exactly what you were looking for.

A disadvantage of automatic mailing lists is that there is no control over messaging. Mailboxes can fill up rapidly, especially if a user does not log in for a number of days. Another disadvantage is that the messages must be managed. If they are not put into special folders, content will spread all over, and you may be spending a lot of time reviewing and searching for specific content. If files are not organized, the user may have to read or print out every mail message he or she receives to find the needed message.

## Newsgroups

**Newsgroups** (sometimes known as Usenets or forums) are e-mail discussion groups that are a more formal method of communicating on the Web. Like automatic mailing lists, they are dedicated to certain topics. These groups are more like the typical bulletin board services of old, in that all messages are posted to the group, and members log in, read the posted messages, and respond or not as they choose. Users can select a topic or subject from various lists. The organization of newsgroups is treelike, similar to an outline. Within each topic, there will be subtopics, known as threads, or strands. Many newsgroups are completely uncontrolled, but some are managed.

One of the major advantages of newsgroups is that the user controls the reading. There is nothing posted to mailboxes; the discussion is stored elsewhere on servers. They are also asynchronous, so the user chooses when and how often to access the newsgroup. The responsibility of "keeping up" with what is being discussed rests upon the user. You can introduce a new thread at any time, but it is wise to read through what has already been said, lest you violate netiquette and ramble on about something that was covered two weeks ago!

Newsgroups are organized for you, so you do not have the maintenance of organizing messages into folders, deleting extraneous ones, and so forth. But this also means that you must go back and search through the many threads to reread content. The hierarchical structure and a local search utility will help with searching for content. You also have the option to print the material when you first read it. But unlike e-mail, where the messages are terse, newsgroup comments tend to be much longer, sometimes to the point of rambling.

**Table 4.2  Newsgroup Hierarchies**

| Designator Code | Subject Matter |
|---|---|
| news. | announcements about Usenet itself |
| comp. | computer science and technology |
| sci. | other academic topics (including humanities) |
| soc. | cultural interest groups |
| rec. | hobbies and sports |
| talk. | wide-range discussions |
| misc. | topics that do not fit into another category |
| alt. | trial newsgroups and "alternative" topics |

Forum structure in a newsgroup within Google.

Remember, messages are not verified, so users can post almost anything; you have the responsibility of determining what is or isn't true.

Newsgroups have descriptive names such as rec.music.reviews and are arranged in hierarchies or classifications as shown in Table 4.2. Hierarchies can assist you when browsing through long lists of newgroups by providing you with some idea of where to find topics that interest you.

Internet Newsgroups require a **newsreader**, a software application that allows the user to read articles that are posted by thread, or topic. Outlook Express and Netscape Messenger contain newsreaders. Before you can read newsgroups, you need to make sure that you have specified your ISP's news account address.

## Setting Up Your News Account

1. In Outlook Express, click Tools on the menu bar and then click Accounts to display the Internet Accounts dialog box.
2. Select the News tab.
3. Click Add, and then click News from the side menu that appears.
4. An Internet Connection Wizard appears that will guide you through the steps necessary to enter your ISP's news account address.

## Reading Newsgroups

1. In Internet Explorer, click the Mail button on the toolbar.
2. Click Read News from the drop-down menu to display the Newsgroups dialog box.

## Subscribing and Unsubscribing to Newsgroups

1. Click the Newsgroups button in the newsreader.
2. If this is the first time the newsreader function has been used, you will be asked if you wish to download available newsgroups. You can also check a box to download descriptions of each newsgroup at the same time. This is a good idea, as it is not always easy to determine the subject of a newsgroup from its name. Downloading will take several minutes since there are many newsgroups available.
3. You can subscribe to a newsgroup by clicking on the newsgroup to highlight it, and then clicking the Subscribe button.
4. You can easily unsubscribe to a newsgroup by clicking and highlighting it on the subscription list, right-clicking the mouse button, and then clicking Unsubscribe at the shortcut menu.

# Synchronous Communications

There are several types of synchronous, or real-time, communication on the Web. They include chat, instant messaging, and telephony. The most popular form, chat, had its beginnings long before the Web was developed. Internet Relay Chat (IRC) was one of the first types of chat on the Internet and it still exists. Users would log in with a nickname and join the online discussion. Browsers were not as developed as they are now, however, and users had to know the "language."

Since its awkward beginnings, synchronous communication has evolved into almost seamless conversation on the Web. Each advancement in delivery speed and quality propels synchronous communication further into the limelight. Despite the synchronous means of communication via the Web, they are still a telepresence—an illusion of physical presence made possible by telecommunications technology.

## Chat

**Chat** is an electronic mode of information exchange, similar to real-life conversation, and is short for **Internet Relay Chat (IRC)**. Originally text-based, some IRC services now are capable of voice transmission. Chat rooms are topic-based, similar to automatic mailing lists. Since users are online, they can receive responses to messages almost as soon as those messages are transmitted. This feature, similar to a conference call, allows multiple users to simultaneously converse via networked systems. Whoever can type the fastest gets to "speak" the most, since only one participant can transmit at a time!

The distinction between chat and e-mail is that the "messaging" text cannot be saved in chat and eventually scrolls off the screen. There are some systems that hold comments in a History frame, where you can review several back screens for a period of time while still online. Unlike automated mailing lists and newsgroups, once the chat session ends, the comments disappear into cyberspace forever. However, some chat services allow saving to a log. You can also see the chat identities of the users in the room, and if you wish you can correspond privately with them as well. Web chat rooms have become so sophisticated that with some ISPs, you can choose your own **avatar**, or **agent**—a graphical image representing you with sound and animation properties—and place it around a table in a virtual cafe setting for a graphical Web chat session.

All of the dominant ISPs have a chat option displayed prominently on their toolbars, or you can use the chat services offered on many Web sites such as Yahoo!, Excite, and so on. Chat rooms are typically organized by subject, age, area of the globe, and other categories.

Most chat sessions are similar to what is shown in Figure 4.8. Some have **whiteboards**, which allow participants to make drawings or key URLs that all members can link to without leaving the chat session. Whiteboards allow participants to discuss mathematical formulas, exchange information, draw pictures, display graphics and photos, and so forth.

## Participating in a Chat Room

1. In Internet Explorer, go to the Yahoo! home page (www.yahoo.com).
2. At the top of the home page you will see a list of features. Click Chat.
3. You will need an ID and password to participate in a chat room. If you are a new user, you must first click "Sign Up For Yahoo! Chat!" and fill in the information requested. After all registration is complete, click Submit This form and then Continue to Yahoo! Chat! In the future, when you go to the chat link, you will need to enter your name and password.
4. In the middle of the Yahoo! Chat! page you will see a Favorite Rooms section. It will be empty because you have not chosen any favorites yet. Click Edit, and choose the rooms that interest you. When you are done, click Finished.
5. A list of the rooms you selected in the Favorite Rooms section will appear on the Yahoo! Chat! page. Click on the room you wish to enter.
6. Once you are in the chat room, there are instructions on how to proceed as well as a help feature. With Yahoo! Chat! you can chat using text and voice if your computer is appropriately equipped.

Web chat sessions are extraordinarily popular. They represent a move to real-time interaction in a graphical environment that was simply not possible before the Web. The anonymity and the virtual proximity of individuals makes chat exciting. The conversation can be public (messages are displayed to all in the chat room at the time) or private (messages are for designated participants). There can be single or multiple conversations going on in the same chat room. For a beginning Web user, such an experience may be intimidating because once a comment is keyed, it immediately appears in the screen for the whole group to read. Nevertheless, in surveying new Web users, chat is one of the first things—after e-mail—that users try; the younger the user, the more likely he or she will try out chat before other Web activities. Be forewarned about Web chat sessions: they take a large amount of system resources and work better with faster connections. A user with 64MB of RAM and a 28.8Kbps connection probably will not have a satisfactory experience. Messages and responses would appear too slowly on the screen to keep up with the conversation.

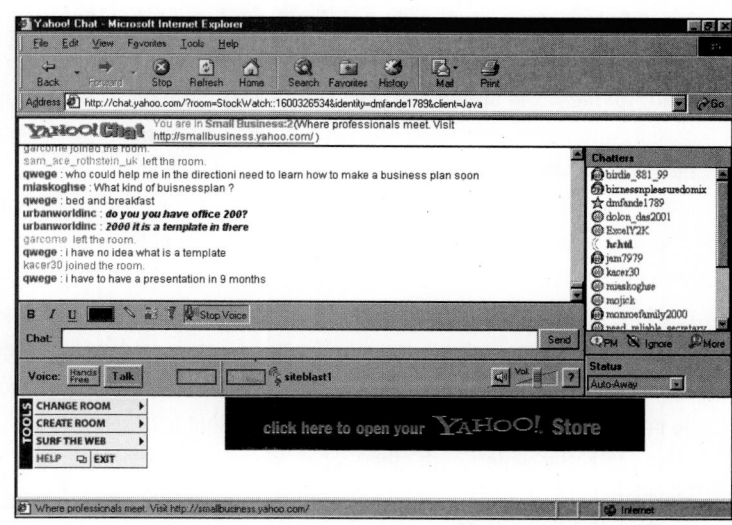

**Figure 4.8**
**IRC Chat Session in Yahoo! Chat!**

**Tips and Tools**

**Beware of Private Chats** Once you join a public chat room, someone might invite you to a private room where just the two of you can speak. Be cautious about doing so or giving out personal information that would allow someone to learn where you live, work, or attend school. Unfortunately, even though such rooms are used appropriately, they are also a haven for people to lure others into unwanted discussions.

AOL and other ISPs suggest that you create a chat screen name just for chat—one that tells about an interest or your personality. In addition to giving you a chance to build an online identity, a chat screen name can shield your privacy. Many people prefer to use their primary screen name only to communicate with people they already know, and use their chat screen name when they are in rooms with new users. If you prefer to use your primary screen name to chat, you can do that, too.

## Instant Messengers

Instant messenger (IM) services allow you to communicate in real-time (synchronously) with other users who are logged on to the Internet at the same time you are. When you set up an instant messaging program you create a list of people you might wish to communicate with using the instant messaging service. When you are using your e-mail editor, an instant messaging box is usually visible that lets you know if any of the people on your list are online. If one is online, you can send a message letting him or her know that you wish to initiate a dialog. He or she can choose to respond or ignore the message.

## David versus Goliath

Avner Ronen can count on his experience from five years in the Israeli Defense Forces to keep him cool and steady in his battle with America Online. In January of 2000, Avner founded Odigo, which specializes in instant-messaging technology. With his wife Maskit, who was his computer instructor in the military and is now one of Odigo's software engineers, Avner has opened an American office in New York's Silicon Alley.

Instant messaging allows communication to pop up in the computer screen without any files being opened, permitting real-time conversations among users. With innumerable personal and business applications, instant messaging is now used by almost 200 million people. Odigo's vision is for all IM users to be able to communicate freely, in the same way that telephone users can easily contact each other, regardless of their service providers.

AOL, which controls 90 percent of the instant message market, clearly does not share that vision. It immediately blocked

Yahoo! and Microsoft Network when they tried linking up with AOL's IM network. Within five months of its start-up, Odigo broke through the AOL wall, starting a battle that has gone on for months. Odigo was cut off in 24 hours, but its software engineers had it back running within 48 hours. So far, Odigo has been blocked by AOL 18 times. The length in time between each skirmish is getting longer, and each time Odigo has been successful in reestablishing contact.

Odigo is now growing by 10,000 users a day. Odigo's business plan is to earn most of its revenues from licensing its technologies. It already has 84 firms in 28 countries as clients. Avner feels validated by the fact that Odigo recently logged its millionth user.

**Source:** "Immigrants with an I.P.O.," by Marshall Sella. *New York Times Magazine,* pp. 86-88, September 17, 2000.

Communicating via instant messenger is very similar in appearance to a chat room, with lines of conversation appearing on the screen one after another until they eventual disappear from view. One drawback, however, is that there are a number of systems, not all of which are compatible. The most notorious example is AOL, which pioneered instant messaging. AOL deliberately blocks other instant messaging systems from its system. This means that AOL subscribers cannot use their instant messenger system to contact people using other ISPs, and vice versa. Since AOL has a large share of the market as an ISP provider, many people who would like to communicate using instant messaging cannot, unless they switch ISPs. Efforts are under way to try to persuade AOL to open up its system, but to date it has not budged.

## Internet Telephony

When the Internet changed from a research-dominant environment to a commercial one, it was only a matter of time before telephony was introduced. **Telephony** allows you to use the Web as you would a telephone—with full audio capability and in **full duplex mode**, meaning two individuals can speak at the same time, in real-time. Until recently, the Internet was a text-based environment.

Now full audio in real-time makes Web communication identical to telephone technology. Long-distance telephone calls can be made by using a Web site to dial a phone number anywhere in the world. What's more, it is free—except for the monthly ISP charge and software and service charges. Many Internet telephony services provide free or trial downloads of their basic service packages; you pay only if you want more advanced features. Although some services require hardware installation, many require only the download of special Internet telephony software. To get started, you need a computer with speakers and a microphone, or you can use a plug-in telephone headset. Internet telephony programs can be downloaded over the Internet and installed in minutes. With Internet telephony, sizable phone charges with long-distance carriers may soon be a thing of the past.

**Web Links**

**Dialpad** http://www.dialpad.com
**Mediaring** http://www.mediaring.com
**Phonefree** http://www.phonefree.com

**IT OUT**

### Finding Out about Telephony Hardware and Software Requirements

1. In Internet Explorer, go to http://www.mediaring.com.
2. Browse the site. What are the hardware and software requirements needed to use the mediating program?

 # Summary

➤ The Web makes asynchronous and synchronous communication via the Internet easy and user-friendly.

➤ The most common asynchronous, or time-delayed, form of communication is e-mail.

➤ All Web connections offer e-mail, and some ISPs offer multiple e-mail boxes, or accounts.

➤ The most commonly used mail server protocols for outgoing mail are POP and IMAP.

➤ Your Internet e-mail address is your screen name (user name), combined with the @ symbol and the name of your domain.

➤ E-mail messages can be sent to single or multiple Internet addresses. They can contain file attachments of all types.

➤ Web communication presents many of the same benefits—and the same potential for misuse—that all forms of communication offer.

➤ Learning the rules of netiquette will enhance your experience of communicating on the Web.

➤ The Address Book feature allows you to keep a simple database of Internet addresses you frequently use.

➤ All mail systems have quotas, so management of your *Inbox, Outbox, Sent Items, Deleted Items* and *Drafts,* folders is important.

➤ Automatic mailing lists are group e-mail distribution systems. Newsgroups are a type of asynchronous bulletin board system.

➤ Chat, instant messenger, and telephony are types of synchronous, or real-time, Web communication with individuals who are logged on to a common system.

➤ Internet phone conversations—telephony—offers the closest Web approximations to face-to-face communication.

**Address Book** A simple, personalized database of names and e-mail addresses usually stored in alphabetical order. Typically part of a mail editor.

**agent** See **avatar**

**asynchronous** Refers to communications where there is a time delay between the sending and receiving of a message that prevents simultaneous (synchronous or real-time) dialog.

**automatic mailing list** Type of Internet asynchronous group communication where postings are distributed to members via e-mail. Automatic mailing lists existed long before the Web.

**avatar** A graphical image representing the user with sound and animation properties. In some new programs, the avatar reads the e-mail to the recipient. Also called an agent.

**chat** See **Internet Relay Chat (IRC)**

**emoticons** Keyboard symbols used to express emotion or mood in text correspondence. Examples include :) for smiling, happy, and :-O for shocked.

**flaming** To engage in rude or insulting behavior in an e-mail message.

**freeware** Copyrighted software available free of charge. Freeware can often be downloaded from sites on the Internet.

**full duplex mode** A type of audio capability, meaning two individuals can speak at the same time, in real-time.

**host computer** A mainframe or minicomputer that stores individual e-mail accounts.

**instant messenger** A service that allows users to communicate in real-time with other users who are logged on to the Internet at the same time.

**Internet Message Access Protocol (IMAP)** A popular mail protocol in which mail remains on the ISP's server until the user deletes it.

**Internet Relay Chat (IRC)** A real-time (synchronous) way of communicating with text on the Internet. It predates the establishment of the Web.

**interface** Computer software that allows users to interact with the underlying computer hardware and software.

**lurker** A silent participant in an automatic mailing list or chat room who reads all, but chooses not to actively participate in the discussion.

**mailbox** The area where mail is indexed in a mail editing program.

**mail editors** Simplified word processing programs that allow the user to key and edit an e-mail message.

**mail servers** A type of computer with software dedicated to storing and routing e-mail.

**mailstations** Dedicated low-cost Internet e-mail devices that allow the sending and receiving of e-mail without using a conventional computer.

**netiquette** Short for **net**work et**iquette**. Rules for good behavior when communicating by e-mail.

**newsgroup** E-mail discussion group, also know as Usenet.

**newsreader** A software application that allows the user to read newsgroup articles that are posted by thread, or topic.

**Post Office Protocol (POP)** A popular mail protocol in which mail is downloaded to the computer and then deleted on the ISP's server.

**quota** The amount of server disk space an ISP allows the user to access for Web pages, for personal workspace, and for e-mail storage.

**spam** Unsolicited e-mail sent in bulk.

**synchronous** Communications where the time delay between the sending and receiving of a message is so short that two-way or real-time dialog (conversations) can be held.

**telephony** The use of the Web for telephone conversations.

**whiteboard** A display area in a chat room participants can use without leaving the chat session to input other than text of conversation.

 **Navigating and Exploring the Web**

## Working the Web

**Project 1** Create a group address using the e-mail addresses of your classmates, friends, or family. Next, create a signature that you would like to appear in your e-mails. Write a message to the members of the group, and copy the message to yourself. Was your signature in the message? Check with your friends to see if they received the message.

**Project 2** Use the Block Sender feature to block any messages with the phrase *Blocked Mail Test* in the body of the message, and direct these messages to your *Deleted Mail* folder. Next, compose an e-mail with the words *Blocked Mail Test* in the message and send it to yourself. Now check your *Deleted Mail* folder. If the message is not there, repeat the steps you used to block the message to see what you might have done wrong. Once you have found the message, delete it permanently from the folder.

**Project 3** Create a new folder to hold mail from one of your friends. Now use the Mail Rules feature to direct messages from this friend to this new folder. Ask your friend to send you an e-mail message. Did it arrive in the folder you specified?

**Project 4** Participate in a newsgroup for two weeks and comment on your experience. Did the newsgroup meet your expectations? Was it worth the effort of setting it up and participating in it?

**Project 5** Look through the list of newsgroups on your newsreader for any groups related to hiking. Using a search engine, search for the terms *hiking* and *newsgroups*. Did the results list turn up any newsgroups that were not on your newsreaders list? Which method was easier—using a search engine or subscribing to a newsgroup?

**Project 6** Go to any search engine and key the terms **newsgroup + student**. How many listings did you find? Can you tell anything about the newsgroups from the names? Are there any from a university in your state?

**Project 7** Join an automatic mailing list for one week, then report on your participation. How many messages did you receive? What was the average length of the messages? Did you send any messages? What did you like or dislike about the experience?

# Are We Connecting?

## Exercise 1

*Answer the following questions. Questions can be answered individually or assigned as small group discussion*

1. What is the difference between synchronous and asynchronous communication on the Internet? Which do you prefer? Why?
2. Describe three methods of synchronous communication. List them in order of your preference, with #1 being your favorite. Explain why you prefer one method over another, and describe a scenario in which one of these methods would be useful to you as a student.
3. Describe three methods of asynchronous communication. List them in order of your preference, with #1 being your favorite. Explain why you prefer one method over another, and describe a scenario in which one of these methods would be useful to you as a student.
4. Of the methods you have mentioned in questions 2 and 3, which do you think is the fastest growing? Why? Which of the methods is most used by students? Do you think this is likely to change in the next decade? Why?
5. What is the difference between flaming and spamming? Describe any online experiences that you or a classmate have had with flaming or spamming. How did you/he or she deal with the situation? What advice would you give to someone who is being flamed? Spammed?

## Exercise 2

*Match the term with the description.*

a. asynchronous
b. synchronous
c. automatic mailing list
d. mail server
e. WinZip
f. chat
g. avatar, or agent
h. emoticons
i. flaming
j. spamming

1. compression software
2. manages incoming and outgoing mail
3. sending unwanted messages
4. time delayed
5. keyboard symbols expressing mood
6. graphical image of user
7. real-time
8. exchanging abusive comments
9. real-time online conversation
10. time-delayed online discussion on a subject

## Exercise 3

*Write the words that each letter in the acronym represents and explain what the term means.*

1. LAN          _____ _____ _____
2. IRC           _____ _____ _____
3. POP          _____ _____ _____
4. Cc            _____ _____
5. IMAP        _____ _____ _____ _____
6. WAN         _____ _____ _____
7. Bcc           _____ _____ _____

# E-commerce
## The Fastest-Growing Aspect of the Web

**5**

## Objectives

➤ Define e-commerce and its applications.

➤ Describe the standard elements of an e-commerce site.

➤ Be aware of the BBB Code of Online Business Practices.

➤ Describe the security elements of an e-commerce site.

➤ Define digital cash and its variations.

➤ Understand different transaction security features.

➤ Describe the advantages and disadvantages of buying online.

➤ Be familiar with some of the basic e-commerce services available on the Web.

## E-commerce and the Web

With the invention of the Web, the business world immediately recognized that it could be used to advertise, market, and sell products and services around the world. What began as an academic and government arena exploded into one of the largest commercial environments in the world. According to Forrester Research, global e-commerce will skyrocket from the current $57 billion to $6.8 trillion worldwide by 2004. In North America alone, online retail sales surpassed $33 billion in 1999.

**E-commerce**, in the most general sense, is the electronic exchange of goods or services. E-commerce did not begin with the Web; it existed long before the Internet. Before the Web, e-commerce systems were mainly limited to **electronic data interchange (EDI)** systems where distributors, vendors, and consumers were networked to complete transactions using computers instead of traditional methods. Bookkeeping was electronic, often employing **electronic funds transfer (EFT)** from buyer to seller. What is generally referred to as e-commerce today is really Web commerce, because the Web is the interface and the "place" of this business. This chapter will use the term *e-commerce* for Web commerce at all levels.

Unlike some other Web functions, it is hard to avoid e-commerce; it is everywhere. The business world has been an engine of change for the Web, demanding better multimedia—sound, animation, and video. It constantly redefines what makes a good or a bad Web page, and what "user-friendly" really means. The attractive, professionally designed Web pages that are so common today did not exist five years ago. They were considered unnecessary by noncommercial Web sites. E-commerce has changed and improved the Web, and it would be difficult to find anyone who seriously wants to go back to the text-based Internet prior to the introduction of the Web in 1992.

Some online businesses or **e-tailers** (Internet retailers, from **e**lectronic re**tailers**), like Amazon.com (one of the first and still the most popular e-commerce sites), exist only on the Web. However, many e-commerce sites also have a physical location and sell things through retail sales or catalogs. Their Web e-commerce site supplements their traditional business. Whatever the background, the number of Web shoppers is expected to grow rapidly. E-commerce is big business!

## Standard Elements of a Web E-commerce Site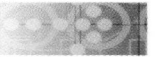

Standard elements, such as those listed in Table 5.1, are the basic features found in almost all e-commerce sites. These elements can be considered the necessities to attract customers and obtain their confidence. Buyers become accustomed to certain elements such as the shopping basket; if these are missing, they may find the shopping experience confusing or difficult. If any of the security elements are missing (these will be covered later in the chapter), potential customers may shy away, fearful of the security of their personal information.

*Table 5.1* **Standard Elements of an E-commerce Site**

| | |
|---|---|
| home page | The starting page for the company. |
| content or site map page(s) | Provides general information about the company. May contain a mission statement, testimonials, business plan, and links to a site map. |
| Help feature | A how-to-shop tutorial for new users. |
| shopping basket | A graphical shopping basket or cart where items are added one at a time. |
| product catalog | A listing of items for sale. It may include thumbnail product photos hyperlinked to larger graphics. The shopping cart icon often appears next to each catalog item. ToolTip prompts may appear near the catalog item. |
| search text box | An internal search engine that allows site visitors to search for a catalog item by name or description. |
| security and privacy statement | May list information about firewalls, security measures, and encryption. This should be required on all e-commerce sites. |
| order form | Standard order form hyperlinked to the catalog items selected for purchase. It is an accumulating summary, much like a written order form. It may include icons to change the order, delete or add an item, or cancel the order. It may also include shipping charges. |
| user profile and password | A form that collects data about the shopper and which must be filled out to complete the purchase. It includes name, address, phone number, e-mail address, and other pertinent information. The profile is used by marketers to analyze consumer purchases. |
| credit card authorization | A form to key credit card information. It may include a digital signature capability. There are several secure transaction encryption methods to ensure that the credit card number is not read by others during data transmission. |
| submit order and order confirmation | An order confirmation process that reviews items ordered, the user profile, and credit card information. After everything is confirmed and the order is placed, a confirmation message appears in the screen or is delivered by e-mail. |
| ethical or business practices policies | Describes the good business practices or ethical policy that a site promises to uphold. |
| contact information | A method for consumers to contact the company, asking for help, advice, order tracking, problem resolution, sometimes allowing them to comment on the Web site or its products. |
| return policy | This is the least standard item of an e-commerce site. Many options exist, from credits on future orders to product replacement. |

## Home Page

An e-commerce home page, like any home page, will be the first impression a visitor has of the site. Just as in personal relations, a first impression is important. If customers are not impressed, they may never go beyond the home page. For that reason it is particularly important that the home page is attractive and contains elements that will interest visitors and entice them to continue exploring the site. Individual preferences vary, so there are no fixed rules as to what makes a good e-commerce home page. However, there are some basic considerations that should be followed.

# The Rise and Fall of Amazon.com

Amazon.com, the online retailer that began by selling books online, has transformed itself into a Web entry point **(portal)**, now marketing such diverse products as toys, videos and music, electronics hardware, and electronics software. During the heady years of the e-commerce boom Amazon came to symbolize the industry. Regardless of the fact that it had never made a profit and would not predict when it would, Amazon shares continued to soar. It was touted as the e-commerce model, and there were many imitators.

The company that once could do no wrong has now fallen on hard times, and many are questioning whether or not it will survive. Its share prices are down more than 90 percent from their high. Security analysts have sent letters to Amazon asking for assurances that it will not go bankrupt, and Amazon's founder, Jeff Bezos, is under investigation by the Securities and Exchange Commission (SEC). The SEC is examining whether or not Bezos sold shares after receiving negative insider information. As Bezos recently put it, he has gone from being the "Internet poster boy" to the "Internet piñata."

It may be that reality has finally caught up with Amazon and other e-commerce companies. Expectations were so high for these front-runners that many people lost sight of reality. One economist lamented that people looked at him like he was an idiot when he questioned whether or not Amazon was worth the money people were paying for its shares.

By early 2001 the e-commerce "bubble" appeared to have burst. In March, the Nasdaq technology exchange had lost more than 62 percent of its value within the space of one year. Whether or not Amazon will be its largest and most visible casualty of the e-commerce fallout is still an open question. There is no question that e-commerce is here to stay, but the rules of the game appear to have changed.

**Sources:** "SEC said to be investigating Amazon head," Friday, 9 March 2001, UPI.
"Amazon Asked To Provide More Info," Allison Linn, AP Business Writer, Friday, 16 March 2001.
"With Bull Market Under Siege, Some Worry About Its Legacy," Floyd Norris, *New York Times*, Saturday, 17 March 2001.
"Bezos talks down his own stock," Tuesday, 13 March 2001, UPI.

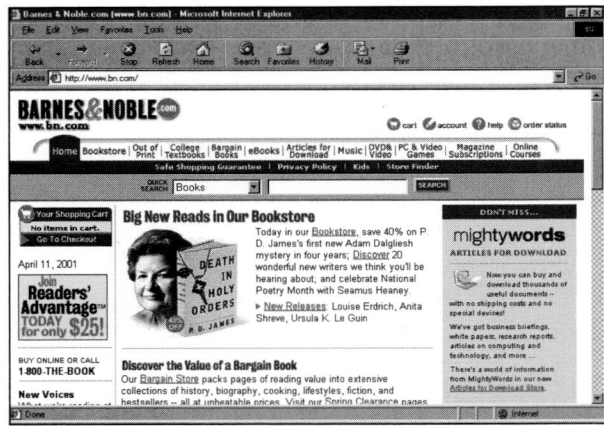

*The look of an e-commerce home page may hook or turn away potential customers.*

Avoid cluttering the page with too many banners—for specials, sales, new items, and related items on other sites. Web sites can make money hosting Web banners, so many sites will agree to host banners from other sites if they feel they do not compete with their own site. Too many banners will annoy customers and send them away quickly.

A home page should be easy to read. Some Web page designers use small fonts, forgetting that viewers may be viewing their pages on small or poor quality monitors. Some color combinations can also make type difficult to read.

Another common error is using too many graphics. Graphics may make the page slow to load. This is perhaps one of the most important things for any e-commerce site to avoid. If their pages are slow to load, customers will soon lose patience and go on to look at other sites.

Web page designers and e-commerce sites should bear in mind that customers may have Internet connections that are less than high speed, and it is a good idea for them to test their designs using the slower connections that many members of the target audience are likely to be using.

## Comparing E-commerce Home Pages

1. In Internet Explorer, visit the home pages of four online retailers: Macy's (http://www.macys.com), Nordstrom (http://www.nordstrom.com), Sears (http://www.sears.com), and Marshall Field's (http://www.marshallfields.com/).
2. Compare these home pages. What features did you like or dislike about them? Which one is easiest to use, and why? If you had to choose from among these sites to make a purchase, which one would you choose, and why?

## Contents or Site Map Page

Just as any good nonfiction book requires a contents page, so too does a good e-commerce site. A contents page, sometimes known as a site map, lets customers know the layout of the "store" so that they can quickly and easily find whatever they are looking for. Not knowing how to find something on an e-commerce site is as frustrating as going to a department store and not being able to find staff to help. A good contents page will clearly describe the site and the locations of the various elements that customers may be looking for.

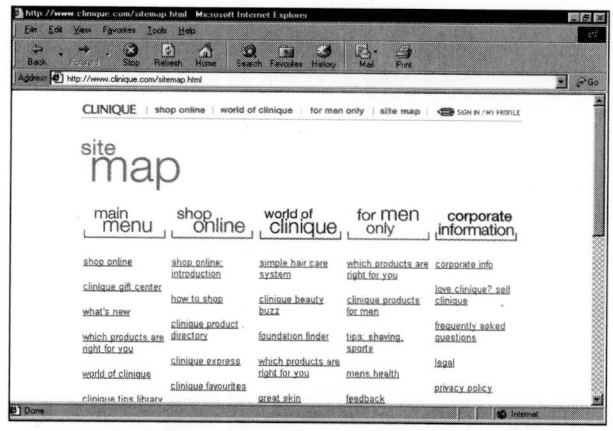

A site map makes online shopping more efficient.

## Reviewing Contents or Site Maps

1. In Internet Explorer, revisit the home pages of the four online retailers: Macy's (http://www.macys.com), Nordstrom (http://www.nordstrom.com), Sears (http://www.sears.com), and Marshall Field's (http://www.marshallfields.com/).
2. Do the home pages all have a contents or site map page? Did you have trouble finding them? Do they all have the same basic layout, or are they different? Did you find one style easier to use than another? If so, why?

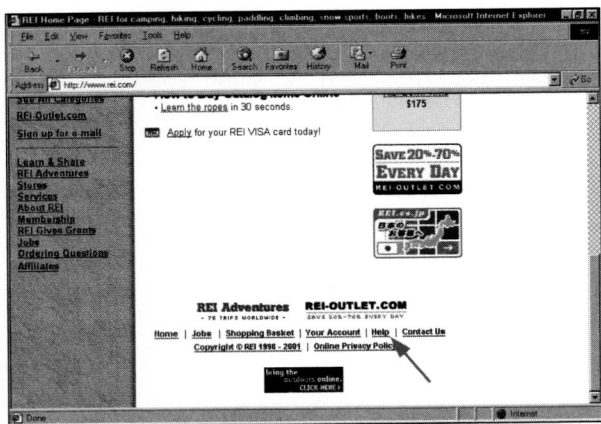

*The Help feature acts as an on-line sales associate.*

# Help Feature

As the saying goes, "When all else fails, read the instructions!" Despite the best efforts of e-commerce Web page designers, customers may still be confused and need to seek help. This is why it is essential for any e-commerce site to have a Help feature.

The kind of service the Help feature provides is very important. A lot of thinking and planning should be behind it. A good e-commerce team will spend a lot of time testing their site before rolling it out to the public, and the feedback they receive from people using the site should be incorporated into the Help contents. This is an ongoing development, and customer feedback should be encouraged as part of a continual improvement process. This feedback can be used to make improvements to the content of the site and to assess any recurring customer questions that should be addressed in the Help section of the site.

# Shopping Basket

The shopping basket, once a novelty, has become a necessity for any e-commerce site appealing to the public. The concept is easy to understand and familiar to anybody who has ever shopped in a grocery store. Customers are prompted to add any product they wish to purchase to their shopping basket (called a shopping bag or cart on some sites). Once they are finished shopping, they can press a Checkout button and the cost of all of the items in their shopping basket will be totaled and shipping costs calculated. This helps to ease the fears of those new to shopping on the Internet, and thus makes the shopping experience a pleasant one. The instructions accompanying the shopping basket need to be clear so that customers easily understand what to do in case they change their minds or what they must do when they are ready to make a purchase.

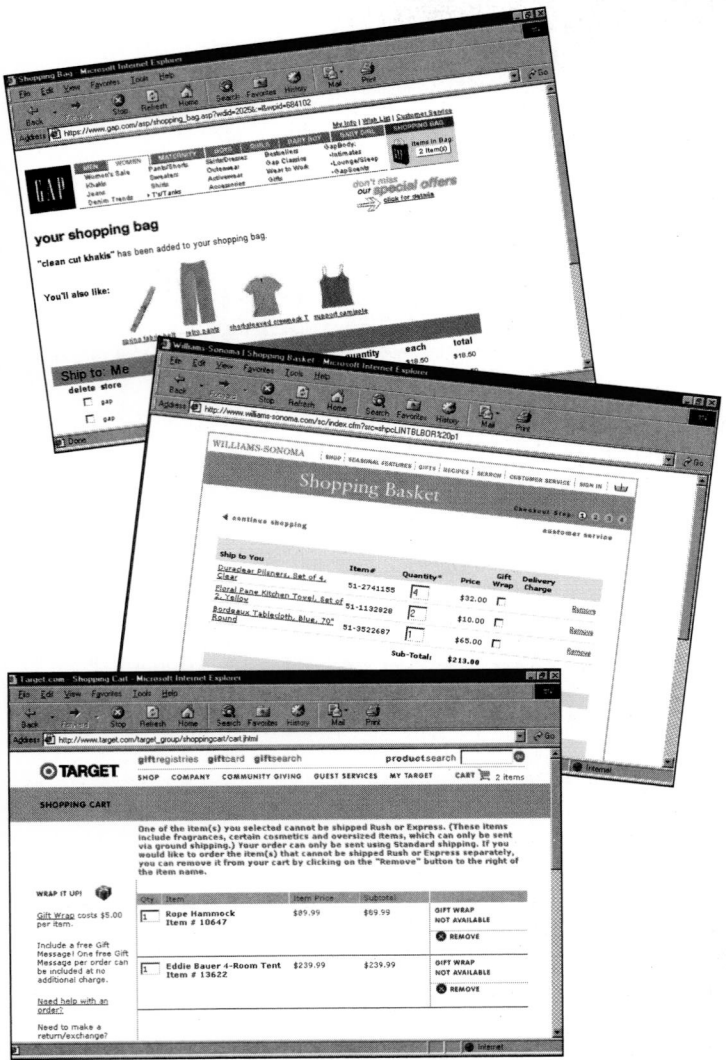

*The shopping basket feature assists the customer in collecting merchandise.*

## Product Catalog

After the home page, the actual catalog or contents of the "store" is probably the most important element on an e-commerce site. Just as in a brick-and-mortar retail facility, appearance is important. E-commerce sites need to accommodate customers who cannot see, hear, or touch the actual product. E-commerce sites need to provide attractive and accurate images of the product, accompanied by interesting copy describing the product and reasons why the customer should buy it. Just listing the product is usually not enough. Good advertising copy can persuade customers to purchase things they may not have been looking for when they first entered the site.

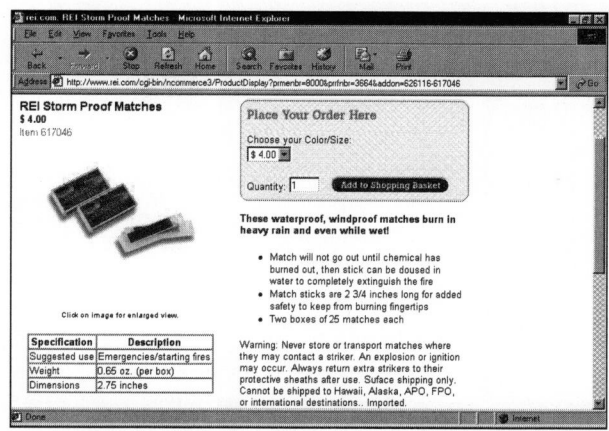

*A useful product catalog provides accurate and inviting descriptions of the items for sale.*

## Search Text Box

Most visitors to Web sites find search text boxes useful, and e-commerce sites are no exception. By using a search text box, customers may be able to find what they are looking for even faster than they could by looking at a contents page or by using the Help feature. Web page designers should pay careful attention to assessing the kinds of items that should be indexed by the search engine, and continue to improve the index by responding to customer feedback they receive about the site.

*A search text box helps a customer quickly locate a desired product.*

## Truly Global Web Site Design

Culture shapes the way we think and act—and shop. To ensure global reach, it is not enough for an e-commerce site to merely translate its site into different languages. Sites aimed at different societies must take into account differences in social norms. A Swedish e-business consulting firm discovered this recently after it had designed a retail catalog for a customer featuring the standard Send to Basket icon next to each catalog item. When the site was tested, the consultants found that while it was readily accepted by British and Swedish customers, French and German consumers found the Send to Basket icon next to each item annoying. The consultants investigated and discovered that German and French consumers like to be left alone when shopping, while British and Swedish customers don't mind store staff asking them if they need help or making suggestions. Taking these differences into account, the consultants redesigned the site aimed at Germany and France and replaced the multiple Send to Basket icons with a single icon at the top of each catalog page.

**Source:** Adapted from "Global Web-site Design: It's All in the Translation," Steven Levingston, *International Herald Tribune*, March 22, 2001, p. 17.

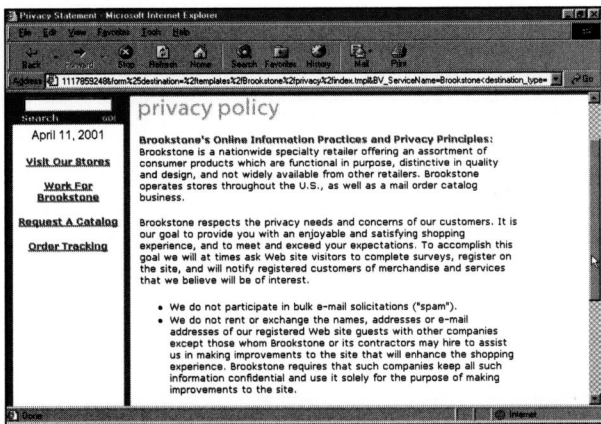

The Brookstone.com privacy statement informs customers about Brookstone's policies on sharing customer information.

## Security and Privacy Statement

Businesses want customers to feel secure purchasing items on the Web. One method they use to increase the comfort level of their customers is to provide security and buyer privacy statements. These vary from very basic disclaimers to complex statements listing transaction caveats (warnings) in detail. Most sites provide general business information, but many do not list contract-related information such as refund policies, cancellation terms, and warranty information. For example, only 26 percent of e-commerce sites provide refund policy information. If an e-commerce site does not have a security statement it may not be safe to buy from that site, especially if you are paying with a credit card. *All* information you give for an online transaction should be private, for use by the company only, and made secure by some method.

## Comparing E-commerce Sites

1. In Internet Explorer, go to two different e-commerce sites, find their security statements, and print them out.
2. Compare the two statements. Are they the same? If not, how do they differ? Would you trust one more than the other? Why?

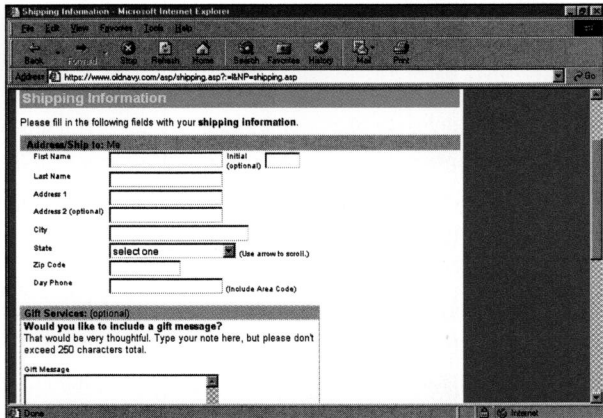

An online order form gives the customer the opportunity to fill out information required to complete a transaction as well as optional information. The order form should clearly differentiate between these two types of requests.

## Order Form

If an order form is confusing or difficult to understand, an e-commerce site can lose customers who are otherwise ready to make a purchase. A lot of time and effort should be spent ensuring that this portion of the buying experience goes as smoothly as possible. For the customers, by the time they reach the order form, the fun is over. They want to make their purchases and are eager for them to be delivered. They are not interested in order forms that remind them of filing an income tax return. Items that are mandatory or optional should be clearly indicated. Few things are more irritating than receiving a message that the form you have just spent time completing is missing an item.

## User Profile and Password

E-commerce organizations, like any retailer, want to know as much about their customers as possible. There are a number of ways that this can be accomplished, and some of them are controversial, such as the use of cookies to obtain information about customers. Cookies are small text files sent by the e-commerce Web site to customize your view of the Web. In addition to accomplishing that task they may also reveal your online habits by recording your preferences. E-tailers can then use this information to better market their products to you, or they may sell this information to other companies.

Another way that an e-commerce site can gather information about its customers is by requiring a user profile and a password. This usually requires filling out a personal profile asking the potential customer to describe personal characteristics (sex, age group, etc.) and preferences (hobbies, lifestyle, etc.). While some customers may be more than willing to provide information, others may feel this is a violation of their privacy, or just a waste of their time. Even willing customers will probably balk if the profile information process is long or tedious.

Personal profile information allows companies to track demographic information on their e-sales, verify customers' credit card information, and trace customer records. In addition, personal profiles allow customers who log on a second time to go directly to purchasing. If the e-commerce site shares personal information (never credit card information) with other sites, they must inform the customer in their privacy statement.

**Codewallet**
http://www.developerone.com
**MediaWallet**
http://www.applian.com/mediawallet

**Unsubscribing to an E-commerce Site Newsletter** E-commerce sites will often ask if you wish to sign up for a free newsletter that will periodically be sent to your mailbox. This is a nice feature for those interested in being advised of sales and learning about new product offerings, but if the customer loses interest, newsletters can be annoying. The sign-up page for most newsletters contains instructions for subscribing and unsubscribing. If you fail to note the URL for this page, however, you may have difficulty finding it again when you want to unsubscribe. It is therefore a good idea to print out and store a copy of any newsletter subscription form; it will save a lot of time and trouble when you wish to unsubscribe.

## Virtual Wallets

Most consumers find it tiresome having to enter their address, credit card, and other personal information into a customer profile or order form. Some experts have estimated that up to 27 percent of online customers abandon purchases midway through the order process as a result. To avoid this, many Web sites now offer what are known as **virtual wallets**, sometimes referred to as e-wallets.

A virtual wallet operates in a fashion similar to its physical counterpart kept in a pocket or purse by holding identification and credit card information. Once you fill out your personal profile and provide identification and credit card details, sites like Amazon.com remember them and let you order with the click of a button on your next order. This solves the problem of constantly filling out profile forms and ordering information on individual sites, but it still means that a customer has to do this every time he or she uses a new e-commerce site. To get around that, some virtual wallets can be stored on the customer's computer. Once the customer's digital wallet is programmed and installed, it can be used to make purchases on any site that recognizes the wallet.

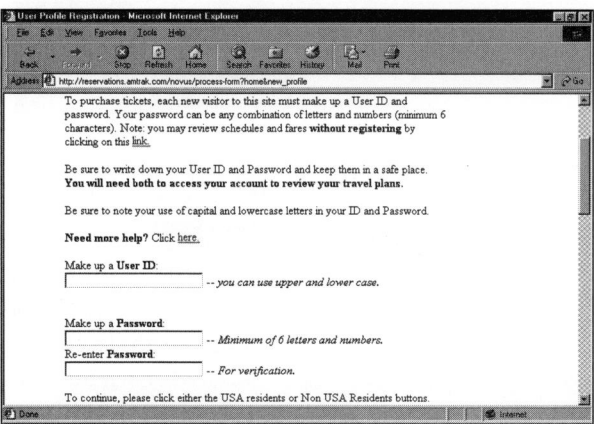

The Amtrak New User page asks for personal profile information and has the user provide an ID and password.

*A credit card authorization dialog box is used to check a customer's credit record and allows the use of credit at a site.*

**Web Links**

Federal Trade Commission, Privacy Online: A Report to Congress
http://www.ftc.gov/reports/privacy3

## Credit Card Authorization

Most e-commerce transactions are made using credit cards, and almost all e-commerce sites have a credit card authorization section where customers can provide their credit card details. When the credit card authorization or order form is submitted, a customer's creditworthiness can be automatically checked in a matter of seconds or minutes.

One of the biggest obstacles that e-commerce has had to overcome is customer fear that their credit card information may be stolen or shared without their knowledge. Although this fear is in most cases unwarranted, e-commerce companies were forced to come up with methods to deal with secure transactions to put customers at ease. Currently, there are several popular security technologies used to safeguard e-commerce credit card transactions. Most e-commerce sites clearly explain the technology they have in place to protect customer transactions. If they do not, or if you have doubts, do not provide your credit card details. It is safer to shop elsewhere. Transaction security measures are described in more detail in the "Security Elements of an E-commerce Site" section of this chapter.

## Submit Order and Order Confirmation

The sole reason for an e-commerce site's existence is to sell by attracting orders, so it is difficult to imagine one without a submit-order element. However, the need for order confirmation may be less obvious. It is quite easy to make mistakes when filling out any form, and it is human nature that these mistakes are sometimes realized the moment it is too late to do anything about them. Order confirmation

## Internet Crime and Fraud

The minute anything is online, it is vulnerable. Wherever there is a shared environment—whether an intranet or the Internet—there is potential for security leaks and invasion of privacy.

Computer crime is more prevalent than ever, and it is spreading around the globe. A 1998 study by the Computer Security Institute showed that 64 percent of the companies polled suffered information system security breaches. The number continues to grow as the Internet and e-commerce becomes more popular and more people have access to it. Computer crime fascinates many individuals; computer criminals are sometimes even admired for their ingenuity. Best-selling books and films are based upon high tech-crimes.

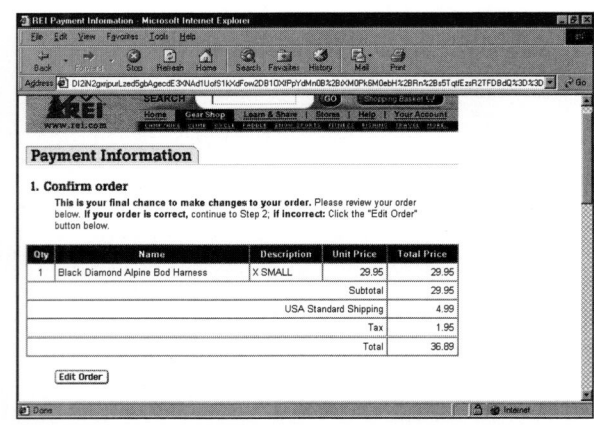

*An order confirmation page allows customers to review their order and provides them with one last chance to change their mind about making a purchase.*

gives customers one last chance to review and verify that the order information they have entered is correct. Because the order confirmation usually appears as a completed document rather than as a series of boxes, it is easier for customers to read it and make sure that it is correct. Order confirmation is one more feature that reassures customers and prevents mistakes and bad feelings on both sides of a transaction.

## Ethical or Good Business Practice Policies

Reputable e-commerce sites subscribe to standard business practices. Most companies understand that one way to ensure a loyal customer base is to follow ethical business practices. Some companies rely on their own policies to reassure their customers. This can work if the company has been long-established and historically enjoys a good reputation. One such company that fits this description is Eddie Bauer, which calls its business policies "Our Creed and Guarantee." However, some companies will look to organizations to help define and guarantee their pledges to following standard ethical practices.

The Better Business Bureau (BBB) has established a reliability program called BBB*OnLine*. Participants in this program must agree to follow the BBB Code of Online Business Practices (see Table 5.2). Participants must agree to work with the BBB to settle any disputes arising with customers. The program is voluntary, but the BBB invites consumers to report violations. Companies complying with the BBB*OnLine* requirements can display the BBB*OnLine* seal. A database of BBB*OnLine* companies is maintained for use by consumers.

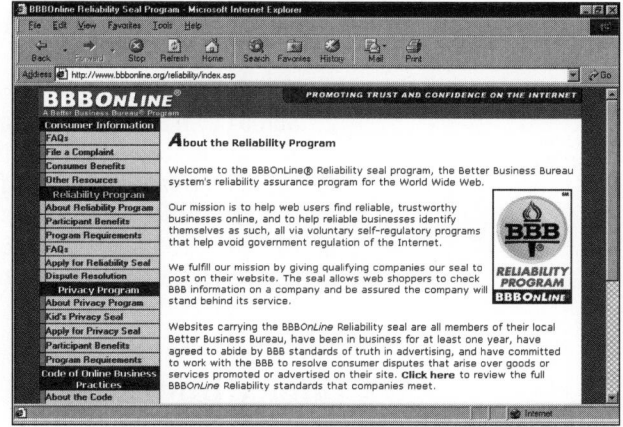

The Better Business Bureau allows companies following the requirements of its reliability program to display the BBBOnLine seal on their Web site.

 *Table 5.2* **The BBBOnLine® Code of Online Business Practices**

| Principle I: Truthful and Accurate Communications | Principle IV: Customer Satisfaction |
|---|---|
| Online advertisers should not engage in deceptive or misleading practices with regard to any aspect of electronic commerce, including advertising, marketing, or in their use of technology. | Online merchants should seek to ensure their customers are satisfied by honoring their representations, answering questions, and resolving customer complaints and disputes in a timely and responsive manner. |
| **Principle II: Disclosure** | |
| Online merchants should disclose to their customers and prospective customers information about the business, the goods or services available for purchase online, and the transaction itself. | **Principle V: Protecting Children** |
| | If online advertisers target children under the age of 13, they should take special care to protect them by recognizing children's developing cognitive abilities. |
| **Principle III: Information Practices and Security** | |
| Online advertisers should adopt information practices that treat customers' personal information with care. They should post and adhere to a privacy policy based on fair information principles, take appropriate measures to provide adequate security, and respect customers' preferences regarding unsolicited email. | **Source:** Better Business Bureau, http://www.bbbonline.org/code/CodeEnglish.doc |

**BBB*OnLine*** http://www.bbbon-line.org
**TRUSTe** http://www.truste.com

Another organization dealing with business practices on the Web is TRUSTe. TRUSTe awards seals to sites, indicating their adherence to following the TRUSTe e-commerce guidelines. Unlike the Good Housekeeping Seal of Approval, members pay licensing fees to TRUSTe and pledge to follow its e-commerce guidelines. More than 2,000 sites are members of TRUSTe and most are reliable. However, there is no regulating agency to enforce the TRUSTe e-commerce guidelines that a site professes to adhere to. In 2000, a seller of children's toys, Toysmart.com, collapsed and then tried to sell its customer names, addresses, shopping preferences, and children's birthdays. This attempt was aborted because as a TRUSTe member, Toysmart.com had pledged never to sell customer information to a third party.

### Checking Business Practices

1. In Internet Explorer, go to www.truste.com.
2. Scroll down and find the Search for Seal Program Participants button at the right side of the screen. Click on it.
3. Scroll down and find the listing for American Greetings and click on the hyperlink.
4. On the American Greetings site, find the TRUSTe logo and click on it.
5. Find the Click to Verify TRUSTe logo at the left side of the screen and click on it to reach the TRUSTe license validation page.

## Contact Information

Despite an e-commerce site's best efforts, there will be times when a customer feels the need to contact the company directly with a question. Questions can be minimized by improving the layout of the e-commerce site, making sure that the Help feature addresses potential questions, and that the contents page is clear, easy to understand, and covers the entire site. Clicking the Contact Us (or a similar) link usually opens up an e-mail message form pre-addressed to the e-commerce site. All the customer has to do is fill out the form and press the Send button. Some sites offer a toll-free phone number to deal with customer complaints.

If an e-commerce company wants its customers to enjoy the best shopping experience, it will make sure that messages or calls arriving from the Contact Us link are answered as quickly as possible. Computer users as a whole tend to expect things to happen in minutes, if not seconds, so if they must wait days for a reply they will be unhappy. It is likely, too, that many of the customers using the Contact Us feature will be unhappy or frustrated that they could not find the answer they were looking for on the Web site—another incentive for companies to address questions quickly.

Feedback from Contact Us queries should be combined with feedback from customer comment or feedback data to improve the Web site. Unfortunately, as a group e-commerce sites have not performed well in following up on customer complaints. Mature e-commerce sites get from 1,000 to 5,000 e-mails a week. Sometimes a product doesn't get delivered on time, or the order is lost. Many times this is the fault of the distributor or the third-party hosting service that the e-tailer has contracted to do their order processing. Nevertheless, follow-up is not always as it should be and this is an area that needs to be addressed for many e-commerce sites.

## Return Policy

Most customers have come to expect very liberal return policies from the regular brick-and-mortar stores they patronize. While many e-commerce sites have similar return policies,

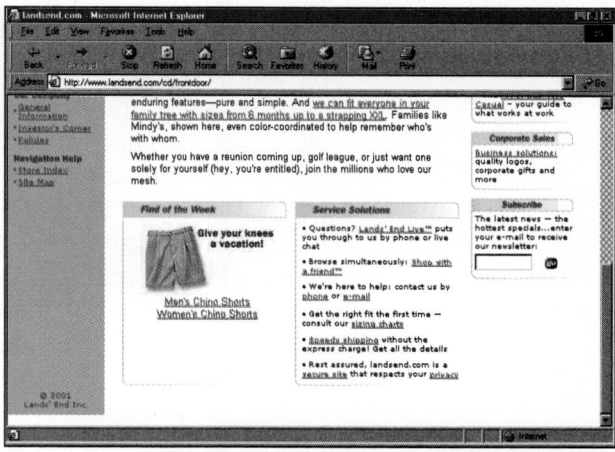

*The Lands' End Service Solutions area provides several ways for customers to contact the company.*

one of their drawbacks is that it is not possible to walk or drive down to the store where an item was purchased to make an exchange or obtain a refund. With an e-commerce purchase, an item has to be repackaged and mailed back to the shipper, a time-consuming and annoying process for the customer. For that reason, most reputable e-commerce firms attempt to appease their customers by offering very reasonable return policies and by paying for the return shipping. The return policy should be prominently displayed and clearly stated. Unhappy customers are unlikely to pay a return visit to any store, and e-commerce sites are no exception.

## Security Elements of an E-commerce Site

Both parties in any online financial transaction need to feel secure. Customers worry about the security of their credit card transactions and the honesty and reliability of the e-commerce retailer. E-commerce retailers worry about fraudulent credit card transactions. In response to these concerns, e-commerce sites have adopted elements dealing with security issues, for their own protection and that of their customers.

There is a significant amount of credit card fraud (from 8 to 20 percent for startup companies) on the Web, just as there is off the Web. Merchants are most often the victim. If you claim that a purchase is unauthorized the merchant has little defense, as it is costly and difficult for them to prove otherwise. There are expensive and elaborate screening systems for merchants, and there are third-party transaction services where a merchant can outsource this authentication process. However, small- and medium-sized companies find it cost prohibitive.

Web site elements dealing with issues of trust must be supported by methodologies and technologies that will enable the site to back up statements regarding trustworthiness, such as those dealing with encryption and authentication.

## Secure Sockets Layer

The way you legally bind agreements and disburse funds on the Web is both similar to and different from doing business off the Web. When you transact business electronically rather than face-to-face, all agreements and payments must be as secure as if you were physically there to verify the transaction. Using a credit card is still the most popular method of paying for something purchased on the Web, and there are now encryption technologies that all but guarantee that a credit card transaction will be secure. **Encryption** is the process of encoding data to prevent unauthorized access.

The most common protocol used for a secure server is called **Secure Sockets Layer (SSL).** If you see *https://* in the address text box at the top of the page and a yellow padlock icon in the status bar at the bottom of the Web page, you are on an SSL encrypted site. (**HTTPS** stands for **Hypertext Transfer Protocol Secure.**) SSL works by employing a private key that is used to encrypt data transmitted over the Web.

Although invented by Netscape, most major browsers in use today, including Internet Explorer, support SSL. Unfortunately, a 1998 study by the Computer Security Institute showed that only 12 percent of small- and medium-sized businesses on the Web implemented the SSL. With all of the attention given to secure systems—over the Internet and otherwise—the percentage of SSL servers has increased steadily.

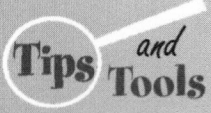

**Order Information** An efficient e-commerce site will send a confirmation message with a confirmation number and a thank you for your order. It is a good idea to keep this message in case you need to trace items that do not arrive in a timely fashion, or if charges mysteriously appear on your credit card bill.

## Hackers

A company that issues Internet keywords for search engine inclusion was a victim of a hacker. The hacker penetrated the computer system, forwarded the inbound traffic to another URL, and tried to penetrate the personal credit card data of the customers. In this case, the invasion of privacy had a criminal motivation. The true company site shut down for three days until it could secure its servers. Most invasions of privacy are not for criminal reasons, but for marketing reasons. Nevertheless, they are violations of your right to be left alone and can hurt your pocketbook.

## Digital Cash

**Digital cash** is cash equivalency purchased from a bank and transmitted over the Web. The vendor deposits your certificate number in a bank or transfers it to another vendor, just like currency. It can be likened to purchasing traveler's checks. A person "buys" the digital cash in various denominations from a participating bank and transfers the serial numbers to the vendor who then "cashes" the numbers from the participating bank or retransmits it to another vendor. Like traveler's checks, the vendor does not obtain information from the buyer, and the digital cash is reusable by the vendor. In this way, digital cash can replace a credit card transaction. Digital payment schemes are safer because they do not send your credit card number over the Web with each purchase: instead, they send your personal code. Digital cash can be kept in some of the virtual wallets mentioned earlier in this chapter. Although it holds promise, using digital cash is still not as convenient as using credit cards, and has yet to catch on with the average online customer.

## Authentication Technology

Authentication allows you to prove that you are who you say you are. Authentication technology permits the signing of contracts and service agreements online, eliminating the need for signing paper documents and transmitting them by mail. **Digital signatures** are the most common method of authentication.

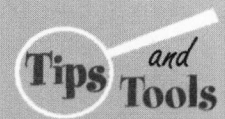

**Keeping It Secret** Don't ever leave a computer terminal without logging off, and don't leave your machine unattended for long. Never give your password to others so that they may have access to your account; this is a violation of your host server's rules that can be punished by termination of your account. It is the epitome of a security violation, and it is foolhardy as well. Although remembering passwords is one of the features of Windows, having it do so is unwise. If you see a box asking you if you want Windows to remember your password, you should ignore it.

The legal barriers that once stood in the way of using electronic technology to form and sign business contracts were removed when **e-signing** became law in October 2000. The ability to use digital identification and digital signatures will save billions of dollars in administrative costs and many days of processing time and eliminates reams of paper. Digital IDs and signatures are coded and encrypted representations of a person. These are not the same as the e-mail digital signatures that you can design in Outlook Express or your ISP mail service. These are certified; you must apply for them with a **certifying authority**. Certification authorities include Verisign (Microsoft's preferred provider), Entrust Technologies, RSA Security, Baltimore Technologies, GlobalSign, or Digital Signature Trust Company (the first licensed certification authority).

**Verisign** http://www.verisign.com
**Entrust Technologies**
http://www.entrust.com
**RSA Security**
http://www.rsasecurity.com
**Baltimore Technologies**
http://www.baltimore.com
**GlobalSign** http://www.globalsign.net
**Digital Signature Trust Company**
http://www.digsigtrust.com

Once you have a digital signature or ID, it is binding, and you may use it for financial transactions. Digital IDs and signatures are invisible. Most stock brokerage houses and banks that are online accept digital signatures and IDs. The recipient is assured that the electronic message it has received is from the person that claims to have sent it. A date/time stamp is applied when it is sent and when it is received. The sender receives notification of its arrival as well. The only snag with digital signatures so far is the date/time stamp. If a server is operating in Daylight Savings Eastern time, and the sender is on Mountain Standard Time, there needs to be an agreement as to which time to record.

The potential for even better authentication methods is in **biometrics**, such as voice recognition and retinal scans. Because human voices and retinas are unique, for authentication purposes they provide the same function as fingerprints. These techniques are already in use in some non-Internet settings, but it is only a matter of time before they will be ready to assist with Internet identification.

### Disabling the Windows Remember Password Feature

1. In Internet Explorer, click Tools on the menu bar and then click Internet Options from the drop-down menu to display the Internet Options dialog box.
2. Click the Content tab and then click on the AutoComplete button.
3. You can indicate whether or not you want Windows automatically to complete Web addresses, names, passwords, and forms. Click in the appropriate check boxes to enable your desired options.
4. Click OK, and then click OK to close the Internet Options dialog box.

## Password Controls

Just as the weakest links in your home security system are the individuals who have access to the dwelling, the most vulnerable spot in personal computer systems and their Internet host sites is the key to the front door—the password needed to get in. Choosing a secure password, keeping it private, and changing it periodically (some systems require changes at regular intervals) are common sense measures. Taping a password to a computer or leaving a password in a desk drawer defeats the purpose of having a password, yet surprisingly many people do just that. Security experts suggest that you choose a password that has no traceable connection to you. Names of pets or children, phone or house number, and so forth, are not good password choices.

Choose something that does not spell anything and includes one or two numbers; B376M and TWZ84L are examples of good passwords.

Some experts recommend thinking of a catchy phrase or saying, then extracting letters and numbers to come up with a password. The result will be a password that is easy to remember, but not obvious to others. Many systems require a combination of letters and numbers. Although it makes it easier to remember if you use the same password on several different systems on which you have an account, it is not a wise thing to do; someone who cracks one of your accounts could feasibly crack them all!

## Advantages and Disadvantages of Buying Online

Although only one percent of overall retail sales in the world are Internet sales, e-commerce is growing daily and will almost certainly become a significant force in the future. More men than women buy on the Internet, and most are in two age ranges: the younger (25 to 34 years) working adults who have little time, and the established, well-educated working population (45 to 54 years) who have more disposable income, earning between $35,000 to $75,000 a year. Together, these two groups make up 57 percent of Internet buyers. Amazon.com, which began as a book sales site and now is a major e-commerce portal, has more than twelve million visitors a month. The advantages of buying online are sometimes obvious; the disadvantages are not.

Time constraints are a major reason for the success of e-commerce. The asynchronous nature of the Internet allows **ATAP** (any time, any place) purchasing. E-commerce locations are open 24 hours a day, 7 days a week, every day of the year—as long as the server and your computer are up and running. You can sit at a computer at midnight to find a book on Amazon.com, order it, and have it delivered within 48 hours.

Not only is buying online convenient, it is frequently less expensive than conventional shopping. Online retailers can afford to sell products for less because they do not have many of the expenses that traditional retailers have, such as the need to lease stores in expensive shopping malls, hire employees, and the other operational expenses of a physical location. These savings can be passed on to the online buyer. Some items on the Web are as much as 30 percent less than comparable items at retail stores. You can peruse online inventory, compare prices, and get extensive information about products. Unless the e-commerce site has a physical location in your state, you are usually not charged sales tax for your order. With e-commerce your purchases are totaled, and shipping charges are included, letting you know exactly what you are spending before you finalize the order. E-commerce sites compete with physical locations, so they make purchasing user-friendly, easy, and inexpensive.

If you are adverse to mail-order catalog or telephone shopping, you will not find Internet buying much more enjoyable. Yes, you can see the item in the screen. You can even "try on" clothes virtually, place furniture items in a virtual living room—with all of the colors and patterns you have chosen—but you do not have a true hands-on examination. You are viewing items on a flat, two-dimensional screen, regardless of the resolution and color depth. You must do everything yourself, from choosing the item, to filling the shopping cart, to submitting the order. You must "jump through all the hoops," performing tasks exactly in the order required, or the purchase will not be completed. A major complaint of online buyers is the level of customer service they receive. E-tailers have a reputation for avoiding customer contact. Many firms spend millions on marketing and getting online and not nearly as much on making sure their order processing runs smoothly. They may have one person assigned to customer support, and your inquiry is processed "in the order in which it was received." Trying to fix an incorrect order, or trying to trace a lost one via the e-tailer's e-mail contact is frustrating at best. Auction sites have the worst reputation for purchase problems.

One of the unanticipated problems of purchasing online concerns bandwidth. Web hosts offer extremely quick T-1 connections to their business clients. They in turn develop memory-intense, multimedia e-commerce pages with sound, complex animations and multimedia enhancements. However, if the purchaser logs on with a 28.8Kbps modem, the site takes far too long to load, the navigation is sluggish, and the graphics are distorted. The potential purchaser will wait about thirty seconds before clicking the Stop button on the toolbar and the sale is lost. Web users will not wait for a long site load; they are less patient when shopping than surfing.

Another disadvantage of e-commerce is behavioral. The social nature of shopping online changes. The habit of "walking the mall," interacting with sales personnel and shoppers, and examining the goods is gone. Regardless of the disadvantages of e-commerce, it is popular, and the number of responsible, well-managed shopping sites increases daily.

## To Tax or Not to Tax?

As of this writing, most out-of-state purchases over the Web are not taxed. If you live in a state that has a sales tax, but you order an item from a company that does not have a physical presence in your state, your purchase may be exempt from sales tax. However, as Web sales grow, the prospects of additional revenue have state tax auditors salivating. It is only a matter of time before all purchases over the Web are taxed. The U.S. Congress passed the Internet Tax Freedom Act in 1998, which places a moratorium on Internet taxes until 2001. Anti-tax proponents have tried, unsuccessfully, to extend the deadline to 2006. In the meantime, efforts are being made to unravel the problems inherent in e-commerce. What state tax rate should be imposed upon an e-commerce Web site that is hosted on a server in Maine, maintained by a Netrepreneur in Minnesota, owned by a corporation in Florida, and physically managed by a company in North Dakota?

This problem is not unique to the United States. European nations, who depend more heavily upon taxes than the United States, are also concerned. In 2000, the European Commission proposed a value added tax scheme that would include all Web transactions. Since the United States dominates the e-commerce market, this would place an extra tax burden on U.S.-based companies selling products in Europe. The proposed schedule would add taxes to the transaction every step along the way. The product or service would be taxed as it left the point of origin, as it passed through distributors, and at the final point of sale.

**Source:** "Creative Web Taxes in Europe," *New York Times,* September 28, 2000.

E-commerce is riskier than some other Web functions. When purchasing goods and services online you must give personal information about yourself, and you must use credit cards or digital cash. Web transactions for the most part are safe and extremely convenient. The tips listed in Table 5.3 are warnings for e-commerce, designed to protect you from having a bad e-purchasing or selling experience.

## Comparison Shopping

1. In Internet Explorer, find several brand-name products on an e-commerce site and note the price, including shipping.
2. Now locate those same products in a local department or discount store. Note the price, making sure to add on any sales tax due.
3. Compare the prices. Is the price of the product the same? How much would you save by not paying sales tax? Would you buy online or would you rather shop locally? Why? Do you think it is wrong to avoid sales tax in this way?

*Table 5.3* **Guidelines for Buying Online**

- Shop with well-known companies if possible.
- Sites on portals, clearinghouses, and directories may be safer to use as they have been reviewed before placement.
- Look for and read the Security and Privacy Statement on the e-commerce site.
- Never give your credit card number if you are not making a purchase.
- Look in the address text box for the https:// protocol that identifies a secure server.
- Look for a seal of approval, like the TRUSTe symbol.
- Use common sense with your private information.
- E-commerce sites directed to children under 13 legally must require a parental consent as well as the child's.
- Keep your confirmation number and a tracking number for any purchase you make.
- Read the Return Policy and any guarantees and know who pays for shipping of returned items.
- If there is not a contact number on the e-commerce site, YellowPages.com and phone information can help you with direct phone numbers.
- If you do not receive delivery within 30 days and have contacted the vendor, take action. TRUSTe, User Feedback sections, dispute solution services, and even your local Better Business Bureau can help.

# Popular E-commerce Activities and Services

It is now possible to purchase almost anything on the Web. The Web is ideal for some types of items, but not so ideal for others. Auction sites have done very well, but sites selling groceries are struggling. The following listing is not intended to be comprehensive, but should provide an idea of some of the more popular e-commerce activities available on the Web. Using a directory or search engine can quickly and easily put you in touch with whatever you are looking for. You don't have to buy; you can have as much fun by virtual window shopping.

## Banking

Most large banks offer online bank sites where customers can check account balances, pay bills, order traveler's checks, exchange currencies, and even log on to document safe deposit boxes. Interestingly, banks were one of the slower institutions to set up a Web presence. Security was an issue; security and privacy on the Web lagged behind the other developments like multimedia and interactivity. There have been remarkable advancements in the last decade, and now that digital signatures are just as valid as hand-signed ones, the public accepts Web banking as both safe and convenient.

Banks initially thought that there was not enough demand for Web banking, and that it would be expensive and quickly obsolete. They were wrong on all counts. Ten percent of Wells Fargo Bank customers now use online banking. The Small Business Banking Survey predicts that banking online will double within a year—mainly due to the approval of electronic signatures.

**Tips and Tools**

**Web Banking** Find out if your bank offers Web banking. Go to the Online Banking Report at http://www.onlinebankingreport.com/resources. This is a resource for the one hundred largest banks in the United States.

## Books

Amazon.com pioneered the selling of books over the Web. Amazon's large-volume purchases mean that it is able to offer deep discounts that local booksellers cannot match. Buying books on the Web offers a number of conveniences. You can quickly and easily search for books that interest you, and then read descriptions of those books as well as professional reviews and reviews by other customers. The larger online bookstores have far larger catalogs than do smaller or local bookstores, so the chances of finding the book you want are better. Many people do not live near large cities with populations that can support large bookstores, so using the Web to purchase books provides a service that would otherwise be lacking.

Despite these advantages, there are some disadvantages to buying books through the Web. Many people miss the ability to browse bookstore shelves. They enjoy holding a book in their hands and perhaps sitting down to read portions of the book before they make a purchase decision. Many bookstores now try to make the shopping experience as pleasant as possible, offering comfortable chairs and coffee to their clients.

**Amazon** http://www.amazon.com
**Barnes and Noble** http://www.bn.com
**Booksmith**
http://www.booksmith.com
**Powells** http://www.powells.com

While many feared that Amazon would drive smaller bookstores out of business, many smaller stores have adapted, and have set up their own Internet presence. It seems likely that consumers will still have a choice between buying books online and buying through a retail store.

## E-auctions

Online auction services have proven to be extremely popular. EBay, the granddaddy of online auctions, claims 12 million users and over 4.5 million bids on any given day. Online auctions act as clearinghouses for buyers and sellers. When individuals have something to sell, they list it on the e-auction site for a given period of time. Bidders submit bids, and the highest-running bid is displayed on the e-auction site. Bidding continues until the time limit is up. The highest bidder is awarded the item, and completes the purchase.

**Proxy Bidding** One of the dangers of auctions is that bidders can get swept up in the excitement and end up in a bidding war. The result is that they may end up paying far more than they wanted to for an item. To prevent such scenarios eBay employs what they call *proxy bidding*. Proxy bidding eliminates the need to sit and watch an auction in order to outbid any competitors. Would-be buyers can decide the maximum amount they wish to bid, and enter this as their bid. EBay keeps this maximum bid amount secret, and bids only enough to outbid the previous high bidder. This continues automatically until the bidding exceeds the maximum amount or the bidder is successful. If the bidding does not reach the maximum amount, winning bidders won't even have to pay their maximum bid amount.

Buying and selling using online auctions is easy and part of the attraction. On eBay a customer must register and leave a credit card number on file. The next step for potential sellers is to write a description of the item they wish to sell and decide what category it should be sold under. They can then click on the Sell Your Item button and fill out the form online. If they wish to provide a photo of the item, they need to place it on a Web page and provide the URL to eBay, who will automatically link it to the listing. Sellers are charged an insertion fee ranging from .30 cents to $3.30, and if their item sells they are charged an additional 1.25 to 5 percent, depending on the amount of the successful bid. There are additional fees to certain services, such as bold type or prominent placement.

**Fraud** Illegally listed items and fraud are handled by a safety resource called SafeHarbor. Despite precautions, online auctions have generated the most fraud cases on the Internet. The Internet Fraud Complaint Center, a joint venture established by the Federal Bureau of Investigation (FBI) and the U.S. Justice Department, logs an average of 1,000 complaints per week.

Bidders on eBay must also fill out a registration form and receive an identification number. If they wish to bid on an item, they fill out a bid box on the listing page, enter their identification number, and click on the Place Bid button.

## Shopping on eBay

1. In Internet Explorer, log on to eBay at http://www.ebay.com.
2. Choose a category you like, or search to find the type of item in which you are interested.
3. Browse through the listings. Did you find anything you liked? What did you think about the prices? Do you think you can trust the people selling the items? Would you use an online auction to buy something? Why, or why not?

E-auctions are more interactive and social than shopping on a traditional e-commerce site. There are types of e-auctions for regular new items, specialty items, art, antique furniture, autos, and almost any product you wish.

## Flowers

Ordering flowers online has proven to be popular. Consumers now have more choices than they did when they had to depend on the corner flower shop. Because the Web allows customers to view floral arrangements before making a purchase, it is a superior method to ordering over the phone, which was the only alternative for those too busy to visit stores.

Online florists offer additional features that attract and keep customers. One such feature is a reminder service. Customers can enter important dates such as birthdays and anniversaries into a database. They will then receive reminders by e-mail in time to order flowers for those occasions. Some sites offer detailed information about the types of flowers they sell and instruction on how to care for them, including the symbolic meaning of certain types of flowers and the kinds of occasions for which they are appropriate.

One of the benefits of buying flowers online versus a phone order is that you can see a sample of your order.

**EBay** http://www.ebay.com
**Squaretrade** http://www.squaretrade.com
**Priceline** http://www.priceline.com
**Biddingtons** http://www.biddingtons.com

## Gift Certificates and Coupons

Coupons have been a successful marketing technique and they are successful on the Web as well. Usually coupons can be printed directly from a Web page and taken to the local store, or the verification number can be used to purchase the discounted item online. That way, the vendor knows that its Web site is the source of sale. Redemption of coupons is a more accurate means of tracking customer visits than counters.

Gift certificates are also available from major e-commerce sites. The recipients of the gift certificate must visit the e-commerce site to redeem them. They receive notice of the gift via e-mail, giving them a gift certificate claim code that is stored on the e-commerce server. They may then redeem the certificate at the site. Businesses like gift certificates because they provide another source of information, build their online customer database, and increase sales. Research has shown that recipients of gift certificates spend an average of 35 percent more than the value of the gift certificate.

**FTD** http://www.ftd.com
**Online Florists** http://online-florists.4-800-florals.com
**Cliffords** http://www.cliffords.com

**Coupon Clearinghouses**
http://www.coupons.com
http://www.coolsavings.com
http://www.ecoupons.com

## Insurance Coverage

Like home and auto loans, the world of insurance sales has changed tremendously since companies established Web sites. Quotes for coverage of all types are available by keying the correct information into an application form. There are even FAQ (frequently asked question) sections for common questions. It is

possible to shop for most types of insurance, obtain premium quotes, and purchase policies on the Web. Although almost all types of insurance can be obtained on the Web, auto insurance sales are the most active.

## Travel

A number of Web travel sites allow you to look for the best prices on fares, hotels, rental cars, and all of the other big-ticket items that make a vacation expensive. Once you have found the best price, you can usually make a reservation and conduct the transaction over the Web.

An additional benefit from doing travel research over the Web is that these sites provide a great amount of background information and usually have links to other sites that will help you decide what to do once you reach your destination.

Some people miss the personal interaction of dealing with the staff of a travel agency, and there are many who prefer to let travel agents do the work of sorting out of all their travel arrangements. However, those who are comfortable making their own travel arrangements can often save money by making reservations doing it over the Web.

Online travel agencies and travel information sites can help you even if you are planning to use a regular travel agent to help with your travel plans. Before going to your agent you can go online to find out about alternative arrangements and the price ranges available. Armed with this information, you will be in a better position to get the best deal from your travel agent.

# Summary

➤ E-commerce is the fastest-growing component of the Web.

➤ The demands of business have contributed to making the Web a much more exciting, multimedia environment.

➤ E-commerce is really Web commerce, and has its roots in EDI (electronic data interchange).

➤ Most e-commerce Web sites share common elements.

➤ For many, the advantages of shopping online outweigh the drawbacks.

➤ Web shoppers who follow basic rules can successfully do all of their shopping online. The growing popularity of e-commerce is testimony to its place in our society.

**Key Terms**

**ATAP**  Any time, any place.

**biometrics**  Authentication and security techniques that measure such things as fingerprints, voice recognition, retinal scans, and so on.

**certifying authority**  Certifying authorities that issue digital signatures for authentication purposes.

**digital cash**  Cash equivalency purchased from a bank and transmitted over the Web. Digital cash can be used instead of a credit card to purchase items from e-commerce sites.

**digital signature**  An identification code created using encryption software that can be attached to e-mail messages as a means of securely identifying the sender. The use of digital signatures, also known as e-signing, became as legally binding as regular signatures with the passage of the Electronic Signatures Act in October 2000.

**e-commerce**  The sale of goods and services via an electronic medium.

**electronic data interchange (EDI)**  Systems where distributors, vendors, and consumers are networked to complete transactions using computers instead of traditional methods.

**encryption**  The process of encoding data to prevent unauthorized access.

**e-signing**  See **digital signature**

**e-tailer**  Companies using the Internet to sell goods and services directly to consumers as opposed to other businesses. The term was created by combining **e**lectronic and re**tailer**.

**electronic funds transfer (ETF)**  The transfer of money by electronic means.

**Hypertext Transfer Protocol Secure (HTPPS)**  The protocol used for SSL transactions. When accessing an SSL server, the address text box on the browser will begin with *https://*.

**portal**  A Web site that functions as an entry point to e-commerce sites. Portals contain categorized links to other e-commerce sites.

**Secure Sockets Layer (SSL)**  An encryption technology used to protect Web credit card transactions.

**virtual wallet**  A program function allowing the storage of identification and credit data for use when shopping on the Web.

 # Navigating and Exploring the Web

## Working the Web

**Project 1**  Go to http://www.clickthebutton.com and check the price for the latest version of Quicken by Intuit.Inc. What does the star rating system signify? What is the best price with at least a four-star rating? What is the best price without a rating?

**Project 2**  Go to http://www.webcrawler.com. Click on the _Auto_ hyperlink and scroll down to the Blue Book Prices section. Click on the _New Car Pricing_ hyperlink, and then find your "dream car"—the car you would buy if money were no object. (Suggestion: BMW Series 7.) List a few of the specifications and the price of your dream car.

**Project 3**  Go to http://www.travelocity.com. Once you have registered to use the site, find the cheapest airfare from where you live to London, England. Next, go to http://www.1travel.com and do the same thing. Are the prices and airlines the same? Does one site come up with a better fare than the other? How do the sites differ? Which one would you prefer to use, and why?

**Project 4**  Someone just gave you a dog. Go to http://www.petSmart.com and print a coupon for dog food that you can redeem at a local PetSmart.

**Project 5**  Go to http://www.amazon.com. Find the Browse section at the left of the screen. Click on the _Books_ hyperlink. In the Search text box, key a subject (for example, key **nature, rock climbing, mystery,** etc.). Click on Go. How many total matches are listed? List the titles that are most popular. Do all of the titles listed have the subject word you selected included in the title?

## Are We Connecting?

### Exercise 1

_Answer the following questions. Questions can be answered individually or assigned as small group discussion_

1. What is the definition of e-commerce as it relates to the Web?
2. What is an e-commerce portal?
3. Some argue that digital signatures are paving the way to a cashless society. Do you agree or disagree? Why? Explain the concept of a digital signature.
4. How do standard e-commerce Web sites and e-auction sites differ?

## Exercise 2

*Indicate whether each of the following statements is True or False. Rewrite the false statements to make them true.*

1. The TRUSTe logo on a Web site guarantees that it is safe to do business on that site.
2. Typically, e-commerce sites have been responsive to customer complaints.
3. E-commerce is a subset of e-business.
4. A sizeable percentage of people decide not to make purchases when they begin filling out the order form.
5. Marketers use e-commerce sites to gather information about their customers.
6. With a virtual wallet you must enter your credit card ID number every time you make a purchase.
7. More men than women purchase online.
8. Amazon.com has never had an unprofitable year.

## Exercise 3

*Write a short answer for each of the following.*

1. List four standard elements of an e-commerce Web site.
2. What statement or policy should you be sure is available before you buy from a Web site?
3. List two advantages of buying online?
4. What is offered by business Web sites to their purchasing customers as an incentive to return to their e-commerce sites?
5. List five guidelines for buying online.

# Creating Web Pages
## Putting Your Mark on the Web

**6**

### Objectives

➤ Plan and design a Web page.

➤ Understand various navigation schemes.

➤ Build a Web page.

➤ Become familiar with HTML and programming languages.

➤ Create a Web page using Notepad.

➤ Create a Web page using Word.

➤ Understand how to upload and publish a Web page.

**Free Web Page Hosting**
http://www.webjump.com
http://www.tripod.com
http://www.freeweb.com

Although it is no longer necessary to know how to program with Hypertext Markup Language (HTML) to create a Web page, it is useful for anyone who wants to become knowledgeable about creating and maintaining Web pages. A **Web page** is a document that consists of an HTML file, with associated files for graphics and scripts, and is identified by a URL (Uniform Resource Locator), or address. Understanding HTML provides you with greater flexibility as you can easily repair, modify, and update pages, as well as borrow code from other pages for your own use. This chapter will take you through the Web page design process, and then will teach you how to build a simple Web page using HTML. You will also learn how to create Web pages using an HTML converter, in this case Microsoft Word. When you are finished, you will have the basic skills necessary to create and maintain your own Web site.

Once you have created the page or pages that will comprise your Web site, you will need to upload all of these files to be hosted on a server. Then your site will be live and viewable by anyone with Internet access. As with most things on the Web, professional Web page hosting service is available for a fee or for free. Most Internet service providers allocate limited space, measured in megabytes, at no extra charge for personal Web pages. The most common allotment is 5MB, which is more than enough for a one- or two-page personal Web site.

There are also Web hosts that will provide you with free service if you agree to allow advertising banners to appear on your pages. Some hosts offer as much as 100MB of free space. These services are an especially good value for newcomers because they offer complete instructions on creating and maintaining your Web site.

To help you understand Web page construction, this chapter will take you through the steps necessary to create your first home page. A home page is an entry page for a series of pages on a Web site. Once you have used a text or HTML editor to code a typical Web page, tested it locally in a browser, and then uploaded the working page so it is "live" on the Web, you can progress to building more sophisticated pages.

**Domain Names** Some individuals host their own Internet domain name servers, allowing them as much room as the disk space allows. They can register and use any domain name that has not been taken. For a list of accredited registrars of domain names, go to the ICANN (Internet Corporation for Assigned Names), Web site: http://www.icann.org/registrars/accredited-list.html. You can use any one of these registrars to obtain a domain name.

You will be amazed at what you can do with a Web page. Web page design takes some experimenting and the more you enjoy working with layout and being creative, the more enjoyable this will be. You can branch out into designing novel backdrops and background colors, sound, images, animation—the possibilities are nearly limitless.

## Planning Your Web Page

To create a successful Web page (or pages) you need to do some planning. Unlike the *Field of Dreams* movie theme, "Build it and they will come," Web site authors must first decide what their Internet presence will consist of, and how they can attract Web surfers to their sites. Users do not just come to Web sites: they either know a specific URL, see URLs returned in a search's results list, or chance upon them by linking from other pages. In this chapter you will learn tactics to help attract viewers.

### Netrepreneurs: From Tumbleweed to Tundra

The Kansas prairies and the Canadian tundra are not often associated with global enterprises. The Web is changing that. Take the example of Prairie Tumbleweed Farm, www.prairietumbleweedfarm.com. A rural Kansas community decided to provide Internet access to all area farmers. Most put up simple Web pages and used the Web for e-mail and for managing their accounts.

One family decided to have some fun. Instead of putting up a typical home page showing photos of the farm, they decided that they would use their page as a parody of the Kansas climate. They named their site Prairie Tumbleweed Farms, after the ubiquitous weeds that covered their land. Tumbleweeds were always a nuisance and routinely had to be cleared from fence lines. One day they took photos of the family clearing the tumbleweeds and loading them onto trucks. They placed the photo on the Web and labeled it "harvesting tumbleweeds." Then they took a photo of their tractor plowing a field. They labeled that photo "planting tumbleweed." They decided, just for fun, to offer tumbleweed for sale on the Web. Imagine their surprise when the orders started coming in! They sold tumbleweeds to customers in Japan and Europe, and all across the United States. The Web turned their family joke into a profitable venture.

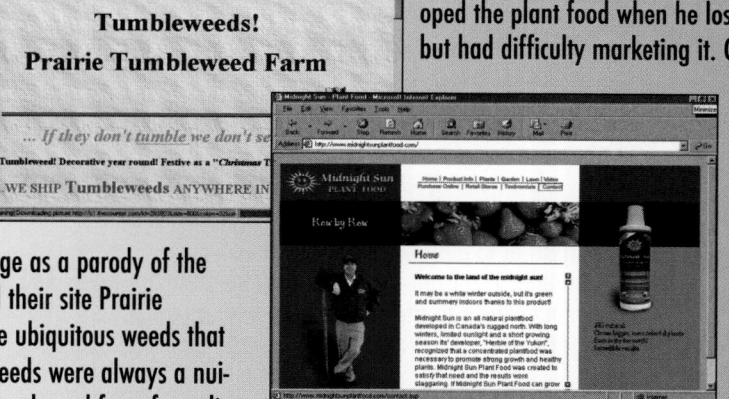

Another success story occurred in the Yukon. The Canadian government wired parts of the Yukon territories for Internet access. These communities were few and far between and were plagued by bad weather and severe winters that limited their access to outside communities. Unemployment was high, and many of the youth were leaving to seek a better life elsewhere. Herbie Croteau, a resident, decided to try selling his locally made plant food using the Web. Croteau had developed the plant food when he lost his job at the local mine, but had difficulty marketing it. Croteau promoted his Midnight Sun Plant Food on his Web site and carefully built links to other sites to promote the product. Sales grew slowly, but by the first three months of 2000 Croteau had sold over 7,000 bottles, and he expected sales to reach $100,000 for the year.

With the Web, individuals in both of these isolated communities were able to start new ventures and improve their access to goods and services. These experiences have been replicated around the world as the Internet makes the world a smaller place.

**Source:** "Cold Comfort," by David Freedman, *Forbes*, May 29, 2000.

Like any project, a Web page requires planning and design before actual production; even if it is a one-page site. Your Web site planning should address the following issues.

- target audience
- Web page content
- navigation scheme
- page design
- accessibility

## Research Your Target Audience

Although your Web page is part of the public domain and anyone can view it, think about the visitors that you want to attract to your site. Whom do you specifically want to view your site? In other words, who is your **target audience**? This can make a difference in your overall design. The more specific you can be, the better. An understated Web page tastefully done to attract potential employers is planned differently from an informal, very colorful, and complex page with sound and/or animations intended to attract young Web surfers and showcase your multimedia skills. The more specific you can be about age range, gender, economic level, viewer interests and habits, nationality, education, lifestyle, and so forth, the more precise your planning can be. Once you have pinpointed the target audience, the rest of your planning will be easier.

### Looking at Web Sites

1. In Internet Explorer, go to www.rei.com and browse the site.
2. Who is REI's target market? How does the company use pictures and design to attract visitors to the site? Are the colors and "feel" of the site appropriate for the target audience? What other elements give you clues about the target market?

## Plan Your Web Page Content

The content of your Web page is what you want to "say." It may take the form of text, graphics, sound, video, or animation. If you are creating a Web page for someone else, a **subject matter expert**, or **SME**, provides the content.

Titles and headlines also make up content. Decide on titles that are precise, meaningful, and that accurately reflect the content on each page. The words you select are important because title words and metatags are used by search engines to index your site. The home page, or the first page users see when they navigate to your site, must be named index.htm or index.html. (Older browsers read Welcome.html as the home page, and all of the new browser versions read either file name—index or welcome—as the home page.)

## Plan Your Navigation Scheme

Before you sit down in front of the computer to enter HTML code and create the page(s) that will eventually make up your Web site, you need to think about how your target audience will move around (navigate) your site. The best way to do this is to lay out the best pathways to information on your pages, with the goal of making it easy for your target audience to find the information they are looking for on your site.

The simplest type of **navigation scheme** operates in a linear or *sequential* fashion (see Figure 6.1). A home or first page leads to a second page, the second page leads to a third, and so on. Suppose your Web site deals with instructions on how to cook a casserole. Cooking a casserole involves a logical sequence of steps (select ingredients, prepare, cook, serve), so a sequential arrangement might be ideal. But if your site deals with a number of recipes, viewers would soon get tired if they had to navigate sequentially through all of the recipes on your Web site to reach the one they wanted.

Another navigation option is a *hierarchical* navigation scheme (see Figure 6.2). In a hierarchical scheme, pages are linked in outline form. The home page provides links to main topic pages, and each main topic page may in turn have links to other subtopic pages. People looking for information on the site do not have to click through a series of pages to find what they look for, as they would in a sequential layout. Instead, they can click the topic heading dealing with the type of information they want, link to that page, and then view subtopic pages, and so on until they arrive at what they are looking for.

 **Technology Tip** Most Web design experts say that when designing your site, you should use the "3 Click Rule." That means that anything a viewer wants to find should be no more than two mouse clicks away. Any more than that, and viewers get bored and move on to another site.

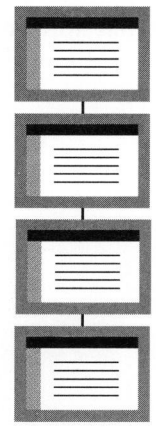

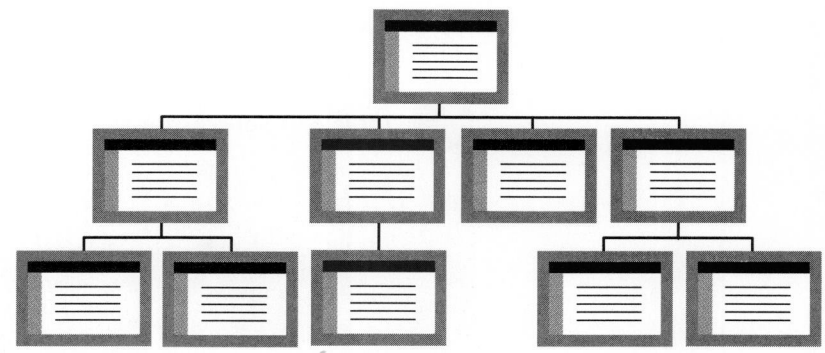

*Figure 6.1*
**Sequential Navigation Scheme**
*A sequential navigation scheme organizes pages in linear form.*

*Figure 6.2* **Hierarchical Navigation Scheme**
*A hierarchical navigation scheme organizes pages in outline form.*

Although there are other types of navigation schemes, the majority of Web sites use a combination of sequential and hierarchical schemes. The way you structure the navigation of your Web site depends on both the needs of your target audience and the content of the pages that make up your site. Your scheme may allow users to navigate in several different ways. The overall goal is how to facilitate your target audience's access to the information on your site.

## Plan Your Design

The layout of material on a Web page is more problematic than the content. Deciding how to structure content and how to place it on the page requires some familiarity with various media, the way other Web pages appear, an elementary sense of layout, and a little aesthetic sense.

The interface, or public appearance, of the content you present is crucial. Plan your design using standard interface conventions. Your Web page(s) should be similar to what users see on other Web pages. You can experiment if you want to, but you may confuse viewers who are used to more conventional pages.

The more pages you view (although many may be poorly designed), the easier designing and creating a Web page becomes. Start with simple text and graphics and concentrate on building links to other pages; once you are successful with a "starter" page, you can branch out into more sophisticated Web authoring. There are many help sites to assist you in authoring your Web pages, as well as sites offering images and other material to add to your pages. Table 6.1 shows helpful sites for authoring Web pages.

**Choosing the Design Features You Like** Before you start planning your Web site, surf the Web and look for sites that you like. Take note of design elements that you found attractive or useful and record the URLs for these pages. You can refer to this list when designing your own pages. You can even look at the source code to see how the elements you liked were coded into the page.

**Design for Limitations** Know the limitations of the Web. There are limited palettes of Web colors and a limited number of fonts that can be displayed. A **font** is a complete set of letters, numbers, and symbols that appear in a particular typeface (i.e., Ariel or Times Roman), type size (i.e., 10, 14, or 32), and typestyle (i.e., bold or italic). They are different from browser to browser, and even

 *Table 6.1* **Sources for Web Page Authoring**

| learn HTML | http://www.werbach.com/barebones/barebones.txt |
| | http://www.html.digitalsea.net |
| | http://www.davesite.com/webstation/html |
| | http://www.members.aol.com/htmlguru/about_html.html |
| | http://www.jmarshall.com/easy/html |
| WebSavant | http://www.websavant.com |
| Yale Web Page Design Principles Manual | http://www.info.med.yale.edu/caim/manual |
| Weinman's Creative HTML Design | http://www.htmlbook.com |

from computer to computer (Windows versus Mac). Each browser contains a select palette of available background and foreground colors and a set of font styles and sizes. This is not to discourage you from experimenting with using color. The Web is perfect for color and graphics. Remember that Web pages are a screen-oriented medium, so a Web page you make may not look exactly like a page you create to print, and may even look different on someone else's computer screen than it looks on yours.

Although Web multimedia authoring programs like Dreamweaver, Flash, and Toolbook enable you to achieve remarkable results with a minimum of programming, the reality of slow connections limits multimedia delivery. Streaming audio and video are being successfully delivered over high-speed lines, but this service is not available everywhere. That day will come, however; we are still in the infancy of the Web, which has been around less than a decade.

Although this chapter does not cover the specifics of authoring animation, video, and sound, much of it is surprisingly simple. Most Web authoring is simple **graphical user interface (GUI)**—authoring without need for formal programming knowledge. If you do know programming and also have a good aesthetic sense, you can become very proficient in a short time. As with anything else, the way to master Web authoring is to *begin*. If you include a contact (your e-mail address) on your Web pages, you can ask your viewers for feedback on your design.

**Media Design options**
www.macromedia.com
www.alienskin.com
www.artbeats.com
www.smartsound.com
www.sonicfoundry.com

**Design for Differences in Media** Even if you wisely decide that your first page(s) will be mostly well-designed text, you should note that text presented electronically and text on the printed page (as in this textbook) are two entirely different things! The symbol system of characters and numbers might be the same, but effective text on the Web follows the law of minimums: *More is not better when authoring Web pages.* Text on the screen is more difficult to read than on the printed page, therefore you compensate by presenting less text on a Web page than on a printed page. Phrases are preferred over complete sentences; paragraphs of straight, unbroken text are almost nonexistent. There is much more surrounding white space. Two basic styles of fonts are used: sans serif and serif. **Sans serif** fonts have no trailing tails on the letters or characters. **Serif** fonts have curls or nubs on the letters. In print material, the serifs help the reader's eyes follow the flow of the text and thus can be easier to read. However, computer screens often use sans serif fonts. Figure 6.3 illustrates examples of sans serif and serif fonts using two different point sizes.

When designing a Web page you should use larger font sizes than you would on a printed piece of paper. While text set in 10 **points** (a size measurement for type) is standard in print, Web designers recommend using 12-point type and avoiding anything smaller than 11-point type.

Besides the type size and font style, there are other contrasts between printed text and electronic text. For example, fewer fonts are available for use on the Web than there are for word processing or desktop publishing. The readability of your Web pages will be increased if you avoid using ornate or flowery fonts.

Arial is a sans serif type font. This example is set in 10-point type.

Arial is a sans serif type font. This example is set in 12-point type.

Times New Roman is a serif type font. This example is set in 10-point type.

Times New Roman is a serif type font. This example is set in 12-point type.

 *Figure 6.3* **Comparison of Sans Serif and Serif Type Fonts and Point Sizes**

Graphic images appear differently on the Web as well. All of the lovely high-resolution bitmap (.bmp), Encapsulated PostScript (.eps) and Tagged Image Format (.tif) files that reproduce well on paper must be converted for the Web. You are limited to Graphic Interchange Format (.gif) and Joint Photographic Experts Group, or JPEG (.jpg) file types. Each of these can vary in bit depth (the number of pixels per inch) and color resolutions, but generally JPEG files are better quality. **Pixels** are the basic building blocks of a display screen; the number and color capacity of the points in a screen affect its resolution, or the clarity of the image. *Pixel* is short for *picture element*, a measurement 1/72 of an inch wide. Figure 6.4 shows an example of the same image at different resolutions.

The better the resolution of the graphic you have to begin with, the better your display will be, but it will still not look like it would if it were printed on paper. Choose graphics with less detail. Scanning photos and other graphics at higher than 72 dots per inch (dpi) is unnecessary because the difference will not show up on computer monitors.

 *Figure 6.4*
**A Low-Resolution and High-Resolution Graphic**
*Pixels are almost invisible in high-resolution images.*

## Plan for Accessibility

Although simple Web pages are surprisingly small files, Web access is still limited by low bandwidth. While connection speed is improving daily, someone who visits your Web site might have a 14.4bps connection, a monitor that displays only 256 colors, a slow-speed processor, and limited RAM—regardless of what *you* have! Design for the lowest common denominator when you design Web pages for the general public. High-resolution graphics, large streaming media files, fancy backdrops, and animations that require plug-ins like Java applets increase the amount of time it takes to download and appear in a user's screen. Users will wait an average of ten seconds for a page to appear in its entirety. If it takes longer, they tend to click the Stop button on the toolbar and go elsewhere. **Progressive graphics** appear in layers and get richer and clearer as they download. They are nicer than **interlaced graphics** that leave users staring at a blank square while waiting for an image to download completely.

Don't limit your design to one browser. Pages that support only one browser can inconvenience Web users. If you design your pages to look comparable in Internet Explorer and Netscape Navigator, and to appear similar on Windows and Mac computers, you will have designed for about 95 percent of the Web users. In short, if you want Web users to view your page, make it accessible.

## How Did We Get There: Is Seeing Believing?

In the past, a photograph was considered incontrovertible evidence. Today, digital editing of photographs has changed that. With a digital camera, or with a scanner and an editing program like Adobe Photoshop, anyone can change photographs to produce images of alternate realities. Tabloid newspapers regularly run such photographs, presenting them as "proof" that aliens landed in Kansas City, or that Elvis is alive and well in Argentina, or that someone is raising winged pigs, or other examples of pseudojournalism. Political campaigns have been known to use digitally edited photographs of opponents in print and television ads. A typical tactic is to alter a photograph to make the candidate appear stressed or disheveled. Another tactic is to combine a photo of the candidate with images to which voters might be expected to have a negative reaction, such as dirty, congested streets or crime scenes.

These may be extreme examples, but the fact is that digital editing is regularly used in print, on television, and on the Web. Nowhere is this practice more common than in advertising. Consider, for example, a typical advertising graphic of a model applying spray cologne. The chances are good that the photo as

it appears has been digitally enhanced: teeth appear whiter, skin blemishes are removed, the body may be reshaped to add more or less of a contour, pupils are enlarged, and legs appear longer than they are. *Trompe l'oeil* (art that fools the eye) is alive and well.

On the positive side, digital editing simplifies the process of preparing photographs for publication. Scratches or dust on prints or slides can easily be corrected with editing, and the editor can correct out-of-focus images, make them lighter or darker, or alter a color scheme. In the same way, parts of images can be cut and pasted to create totally new images.

In short, in this digital age, seeing is not believing. To the old saying "Don't believe everything you read" you could add, "Don't believe everything you see."

# Building a Web Page

Once you have planned carefully and know your content and design, you can begin constructing a Web page. Most Web pages are constructed in HTML, although they could be composed in other Web **scripting languages,** or even in a word processing or spreadsheet application, and then exported to HTML through a utility program.

Web languages, like HTML, are called scripting or "markup" languages because of the tags and attributes that define the way the page content is viewed. **HTML tags** are the commands inserted into a document that specify the style and placement of text, graphics, and links (for instance, <b>, <p>, <img>, etc.). **Attributes** are additional parameters used to format elements called for by an HTML tag. For example, an HTML <body> tag may have the attributes bgcolor="blue" text="white" inserted <body bgcolor="blue" text="white"> to indicate that the body of the Web page should display a blue background with white text. HTML tags and attributes make up the **source code**, or the programming behind the Web page.

To create your Web page you will learn two methods of using HTML. You will use the first method to code the page from scratch in the text editor Windows Notepad. With the second method, you will use Microsoft Word 2000 for automatic conversion to HTML. There are other methods of producing HTML-coded Web pages, shown in Table 6.2.

## HTML and Programming Languages

HTML and most of the other Web authoring languages are **interpreted programming languages**, meaning that each line of code, or instruction, is executed as it is read by the processor, one line at a time. This is less efficient than **compiled languages** in which the entire program, or set of instructions, is converted to a body of executable code that the processor does not have to stop and convert at run time. Interpreted languages are much easier to program than compiled languages. For instance, with the languages listed in Table 6.3 you can edit a hyperlink or an image without having to recompile the whole Web page.

One Web programming language, **Dynamic Hypertext Markup Language (DHTML)**, allows Web content to change each time it is viewed on the client, or user, machine. For example, if Japanese users set a language preference to Japanese, their computers will show a Japanese City Hall Web page (www.city.fujiyoshida.yamanashi.jp) in Kanji characters while a U.S. computer will show the same page in English (see Figure 6.5).

**Viewing Source Code**

1. In Internet Explorer, go to http://www.emcp.com.
2. Click View on the browser menu bar and then click Source.
3. You will see the code that is written to display the page as it appears in the browser.

 *Table 6.2* **Four Ways to Create HTML Documents**

| Method | Sample Applications | Pros | Cons |
|---|---|---|---|
| text editor | Windows Notepad, SimpleText | Free, best way to learn HTML code. | Must type HTML codes by hand; time-consuming to make complex pages. |
| HTML converter | Microsoft Word | Familiar programs; simple way to make basic pages; very easy to make Web pages of existing files. | Not all formatting features will convert to HTML—some formatting may be lost when saved to HTML. |
| HTML editor | FrontPage, GoLive, Dreamweaver | These powerful tools allow you to make HTML pages without knowing HTML. Web page will look just like you create it (WYSIWYG). | Programs are more expensive; new software to learn; requires some HTML knowledge for advanced functions. |
| view source code | Web browser plus any of the above editors | Easily reuse content and features from pages you like. | May include code that is hard to understand or requires additional software to use on your site. |

 *Table 6.3* **Web Scripting Languages**

| Language | Description |
|---|---|
| ActiveX/Visual Basic | Used for authoring controls consisting of self-contained objects that can be activated by HTML; developed by Microsoft to create interactive Web pages. |
| Common Gateway Interface (CGI) | Used to transfer information between the Web and a CGI program. Program can be written in C, Perl, Java, or VB. |
| Dynamic Hypertext Markup Language (DHTML) | Allows content to change each time it is viewed on an individual computer. |
| Extensible Markup Language (XML) | Standardized language to ensure Web authoring uniformity. Uses DOM (Document Object Model) interface. |
| Java | Sun Microsystems Web programming language that uses object-oriented construction to create classes and collections for interactivity. |
| Java Applets | Small programs designed to be executed within another Web application. |
| JavaScript | Netscape scripting language that can be included in HTML source code. |
| Practical Extraction and Report Language (Perl) | Programming language especially designed for reports or for processing text on the Web. |
| Standard General Markup Language (SGML) | ISO Standard for any markup language. |
| VBScript | Subset of Microsoft's Visual Basic language used extensively in Windows applications. IE browser scripting language. |
| Virtual Reality Markup Language (VRML) | To present animation, special effects, and 3-D. |
| PHP Hypertext Preprocessor (PHP) | An HTML-embedded scripting language. Most often used to tie together dynamic Web sites and databases of content. |

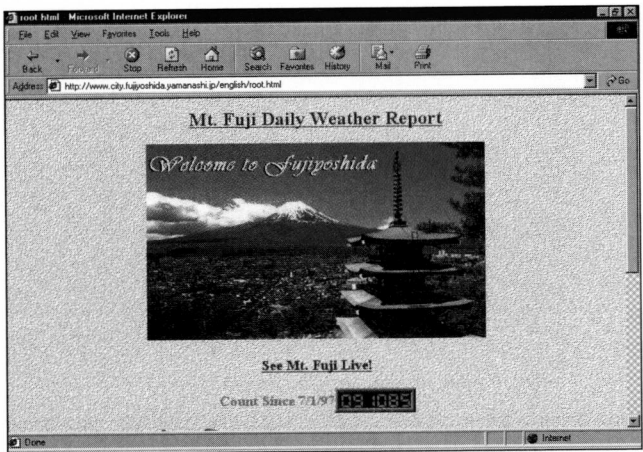
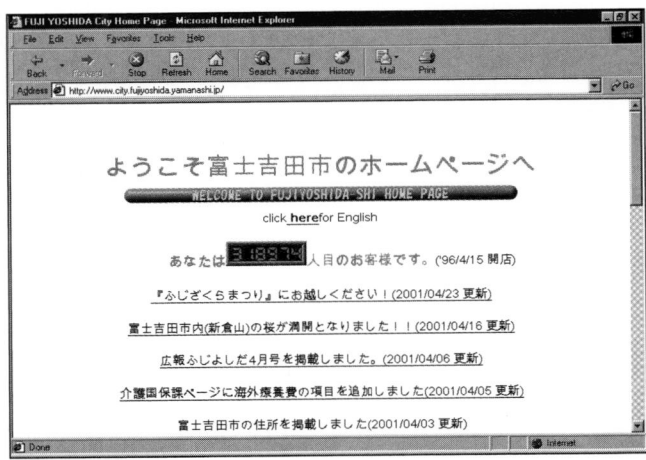

***Figure 6.5*** **DHTML Coded Web Page**
*This page can be viewed in either English or Japanese.*

Another version of markup language, **Extensible Markup Language (XML)**, is part of a larger program and attempts to standardize structured Web documents so there will be a uniform way to add markups. XML uses the Document Object Model (DOM) interface and is termed an open **metalanguage**, or a language used to describe other languages, but is independent of other Web languages. **Standard General Markup Language (SGML)** is a markup language developed by the International Standards Organization (ISO), which sets international standards for all areas of computing and telecommunications. SGML sets requirements for any markup language, whether Web based or not.

Other programs listed in Table 6.3 have specialized applications. **Java applets** are small applications (programs) contained in larger programs that are designed to be executed within those programs. For example, a Java applet may be embedded in a Java program within a Web page that displays a fill-in form. The applet assists that program so you can correctly complete the form. Netscape Navigator and Internet Explorer are considered to be Java-compatible browsers or Java "interpreters" and should be able to process Java applets.

Unfortunately, all browsers do not support all Web authoring languages. If you see an error window indicating a "JavaScript Error" when you are navigating the Web, you are probably not using a Netscape-compatible browser. If you see an "Object not found" window when using a page with an ActiveX control or a page coded in DHTML, you are probably not using an Explorer-compatible browser. There are two browser standards in the Web world, IE and Netscape Navigator. Each browser is continually being revised to support the other's Web scripting languages. That is why you should plan your Web page design to accommodate both browsers.

**Tips and Tools**

**W3C** The World Wide Web Consortium (W3C) oversees all standards for HTML, XML, and other Web code formats. They are the authority on the way these systems work because they write the standards. Some of the pages are highly technical, but they are invaluable as a reference.

World Wide Web Consortium home page http://www.w3.org
HyperText Markup Language home page http://www.w3.org/MarkUp
HTML 4.01 Specification http://www.w3.org/TR/html401
Extensible Markup Language (XML) home page http://www.w3.org/XML

## HTML Tag Commands

Every HTML document consists of multiple objects—text, graphics, movies, sounds, and so forth. They are incorporated into the Web page by the use of HTML tags for labeling each element. Most tags come in pairs, with an opening tag and a closing tag for each element. The tag names are enclosed in angle brackets with < > around the opening tag and </> around the closing tag:

<tag name>text</tag name>

## Tags: From Visible to Invisible

Tag definition is not a new development in computing, nor is it exclusive to the Web. In the 1980s, when microcomputers were at a very early stage of development and before there were **WYSIWYG** ("What You See Is What You Get") applications, the most popular word processing program was WordStar, which showed all of the tags in the screen. Today, you do not see the tags in the screen unless you enable a command that reveals format codes.

For example, if you want a headline that reads "Grand Opening," the HTML coding could look like this: <h1>Grand Opening</h1>. The opening tag—for example, the Header tag <h1>—turns on the header formatting, and the ending tag—</h1>—turns off the header formatting. Header formatting controls the size of the text. Note that the closing tag name is preceded by a slash. If you forget to include an ending tag, in this case </h1>, the rest of the document will continue in the large H1 header size! Or if you turn on Bold with <b> and forget to turn it off with </b>, the rest of the page would appear in bold text from that point on.

There are hundreds of HTML tags used to format and link information in a Web page. Many tags are paired, such as <title></title>. Some tags may be used alone, appearing only in opening tag form. When you create a personal Web page in HTML using a text or HTML editor you will use many of these tags.

Browsers may display formatting a bit differently. Fortunately, Internet Explorer and Netscape Navigator display HTML tags similarly enough that small differences are not crucial. The tags you will use to build your home page in the following examples are supported by both IE and Netscape Navigator. If you choose to use Netscape Navigator for the following exercises, some buttons and menu items may have different labels, but the pages will display and work in the same way.

## Building a Web Page Using Notepad

Out of all the different HTML tags available, only four are required in all HTML documents. Every HTML document must begin with an HTML opening tag <html>. The next set of required tags are header and title tags. The header section contains descriptive information, usually a title for the document, and this descriptive information must be entered between title tags, which are in turn contained between the header tags:

<header><title>Descriptive Information</title></header>

All material on the page after the header section is contained between an opening body tag <body> and a closing body tag </body>. The HTML document ends with a closing HTML tag </html>. Since all HTML documents must contain these tags, it is a good idea to code them into any HTML document right from the start.

**Creating a New Web Page** Pre-entering HTML code into a document so that you can insert other code, text, and graphics later is known as creating a shell. You will start your own home page by creating a simple shell containing the four sets of required tags, with a title for your Web page. To build your home page using HTML you will use Windows Notepad. After creating your new Web page, you can see how your Web page will look in a browser by following the steps in the next Try It Out exercise.

## Creating a New Web Page

1. Click on the Windows Start button. Then click Programs, Accessories, and Notepad to open the Notepad text editing program.
2. Click File and then click Save As to display the Save As dialog box.
3. In the Save as type text box at the bottom of the dialog box, click the down-pointing arrow to change the file type to All Files (*.*).
4. In the File name text box, key **index.htm** to name the file. In the Save in text box at the top of the screen, select the location on your computer in which you wish to save the file, and then click Save. Write down the location of the file so you don't forget it.
5. Click Edit on the menu bar, and then click Word Wrap, which places a check mark in front of the option. (If there already is a check mark, the Word Wrap feature is already activated.) This prevents the text you enter from going off the screen. If you don't click Word Wrap, your data will be entered as one long line. It will still work, but you will have to keep scrolling right to find it. Make sure the Word Wrap feature is activated every time you open and use Notepad.
6. Key **<html>** at the beginning of the document and press the Enter key to move the cursor to the next line.
7. Key a set of header and title opening and closing tags: **<header><title></title></header>**.
8. Using the mouse, position the cursor between the two title tags and key **My First Web Page** and press Enter to move the cursor to the next line.
9. Using the mouse, position the mouse after the closing header tag and press Enter to move the cursor to the next line.
10. Key **<body>** and press Enter to move the cursor to the next line.
11. Key **Welcome to My Web Page!** on the line below the opening body tag and press Enter to move the cursor to the next line.
12. Key the closing body tag **</body>** and press Enter to move the cursor to the next line.
13. Key the closing HTML tag **</html>**.
14. Click File and then Save. Figure 6.6 shows what your Web page index.htm file should look like. Do not close Notepad.

## Viewing Your Web Page

1. In Internet Explorer, click File on the menu bar and then click Open at the drop-down menu. Use the browse function to find the index.htm file. When you have located the file, click Open and then click OK.
2. The browser will show the Web page (see Figure 6.7). The title of the page, "My First Web Page," displays in the title bar at the top of the screen. In the Window browser you see the text "Welcome to My Web Page!"
3. If you want to see the source code for the Web page, click View on the browser menu bar, and then click Source. Notepad will automatically open and display the file, showing the source code you entered to create the page.

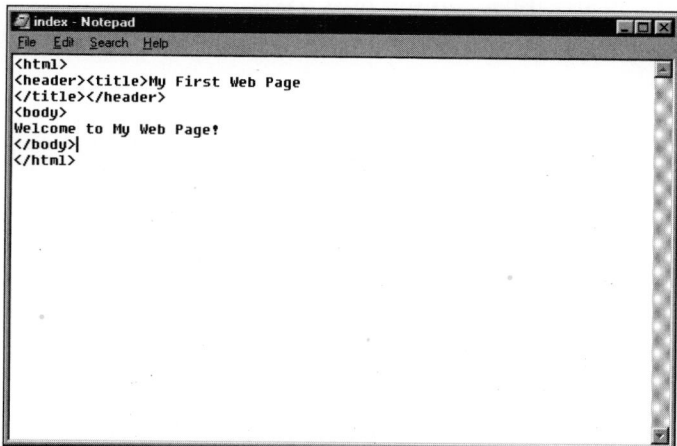

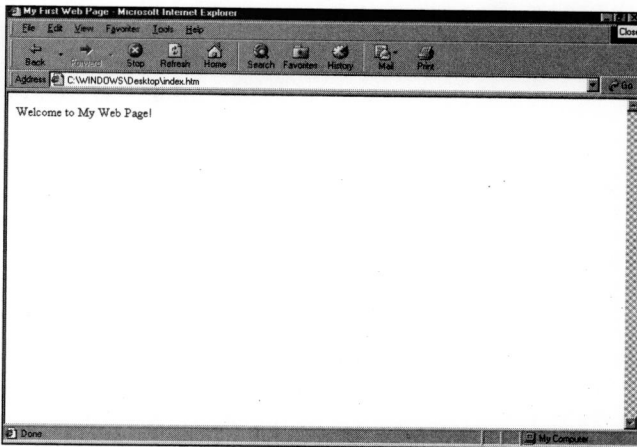

*Figure 6.6*
**The Source Code Entered to Create the Web Page**

*Figure 6.7*
**The Web Page Displayed in Internet Explorer**
*Notice that the browser does not display the HTML code.*

**Capitalizing HTML Tags** HTML tags are not case sensitive. That means they will work whether or not they are capitalized.

**Using Cut, Copy, and Paste** You can use the cut, copy, and paste function to copy code in Notepad, HTML converters, or HTML editors. This can save lots of time and effort. For example, if you need to enter five lines of code with different text but the same formatting, you can code the first line, copy it, and then paste it and change the text for each succeeding line.

**Setting Font Style and Size**   So far, your Web page contains only one line, in black text. The font (type size) is very small, so you will probably want to make it a bit bigger. Table 6.4 shows the six different header levels, from largest to smallest. The header level will determine how the content of your page is displayed. Now follow the steps in the "Changing Header Size" Try It Out exercise.

Your Web page should display "Welcome to My Web Page!" in a much larger font size. Look at the opening and closing header tags, <h1> and </h1>. Opening tags begin a command, while closing tags signal the end of a command. In this case, the opening <h1> tag indicates that the font size for any text following the tag should be the largest size possible, while the closing tag </h1> indicates the end of the command. Any text following the closing tag will be in the normal text size. In most cases, if you do not enter a closing tag, the opening tag command will be in effect from that point on. In the example above, if you do not enter a closing header tag </h1>, all text following the opening header tag <h1> will display as this header size. Now follow the steps in the Try It Out exercise "Opening and Closing Tags" on the next page.

 **Table 6.4** Headers for HTML Documents

| Opening Tag | Closing Tag | Resulting Visual Effect |
|---|---|---|
| <h1> | </h1> | # This is Header 1 |
| <h2> | </h2> | ## This is Header 2 |
| <h3> | </h3> | ### This is Header 3 |
| <h4> | </h4> | #### This is Header 4 |
| <h5> | </h5> | ##### This is Header 5 |
| <h6> | </h6> | ###### This is Header 6 |

## Changing Header Size

1. In the Notepad file, with index.htm open, key an opening header tag **<h1>** just after the opening body tag <body> and a closing header tag **</h1>** just after the exclamation point in "Welcome to My Web Page!"
2. Click File, then Save, and then click the Refresh button on the browser toolbar to see the results.

## Opening and Closing Tags

1. In the Notepad file, with index.htm open, position the cursor just after the closing header tag </h1>, press Enter to move the cursor to a new line, and key **This is a test**.
2. Click File and then Save, and then click Refresh on the browser toolbar. What size is the text that you just keyed?
3. Select View again on the menu bar, and click Source from the drop-down menu.
4. Delete the header closing tag </h1> and reenter it just after "This is a test."
5. Click File, then Save, and then click the Refresh button on the browser toolbar. What changes occur?
6. Delete any changes you made in this exercise, then resave the index.htm file so that you can continue to follow the instructions on building your home page.

**Centering Text** Since "Welcome to My Web Page!" is the opening line of your home page, it would probably look better centered on the page. The exercise on page 172 provides these steps.

**Creating a Horizontal Line** A horizontal line just below the title would help to set it apart from the rest of your home page. Follow the steps in the exercise on page 172.

**Adding Background Color** Your home page is coming along, but a little color in the background will really make it stand out. By following the steps in the "Adding a Background Color" Try It Out Exercise on page 172, add an attribute to the <body> tag that defines which color to use.

There are many background colors you can use. Some of the basic colors are shown in Table 6.5. You can enter the color or its code when you enter the data for your home page.

**Changing Text Color** Black text on a blue background may be difficult to see. Change the text color by following the steps in the exercise on page 173. If you don't like these colors, you can experiment and find colors that you do like.

**Nesting** HTML tags can be nested together. For example, if you wish to have the line "This is a test." display in italic H2 header size, the coding would be <h2><i>This is a test.</i></h2>. The <i> tag is used to italicize text. You could also underline it by using the underline tag <u>. With nested tags the order in which they appear is not important, but they should be symmetrical. That is, if the opening <h2> tag appears first, the closing </h2> tag should appear last, and so on for each tag pair. For example, <i><h2>This is a test.</h2></i> would display the phrase in italic H2 header size, but <i><h2>This is a test.</i></h2> might not be recognized by some browsers and the phrase would not display in italic H2 header size.

**Table 6.5** Common Colors Hexadecimal Codes

| Color | Code |
|---|---|
| black | #000000 |
| cream | #FFFFCC |
| cyan | #00FFFF |
| fuchsia | #FF00FF |
| green | #99CC99 |
| lime | #00FF00 |
| pink | #FFCCCC |
| red | #FF0000 |
| yellow | #FFFF00 |

## Centering Text

1. In Notepad, with index.htm open, key **<center>** just before the opening tag <h1>, and key **</center>** just after the closing tag </h1>.
2. Save the file and refresh Internet Explorer to see the results. The opening line should be centered on the page (see Figure 6.8).

## Creating a Horizontal Line

1. In Notepad, with index.htm open, place the cursor after the closing heading tag </h1> for "Welcome to My Web Page!" and press Enter to create a new line, then key **<hr>**.
2. Save the file and refresh IE to see the results (see Figure 6.9).

## Adding Background Color

1. In Notepad, with index.htm open, place the cursor after the *y* in the opening body tag <body>.
2. Type a space, then enter **bgcolor="darkblue"**.
3. Save the file and refresh IE to see the results.

*Figure 6.8* **Center Tag Applied to Web Page**
Center tags instruct the browser to move the opening line from the left of the screen to the center.

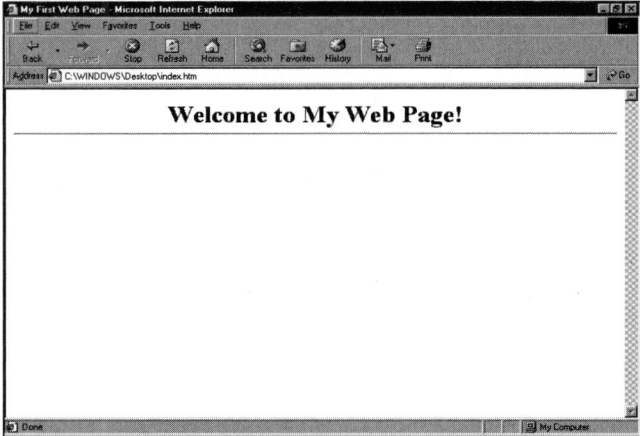

*Figure 6.9* **Horizontal Line Tag Applied to Web Page**
The <hr> tag displays a horizontal line across the browser screen.

## Changing Text Color

1. In Notepad, with index.htm open, in the section of code beginning with the opening body tag <body>, edit the code so that it looks like this:
   <body bgcolor="darkblue" text="white">.
2. Save the file and refresh IE to see the results (see Figure 6.10).

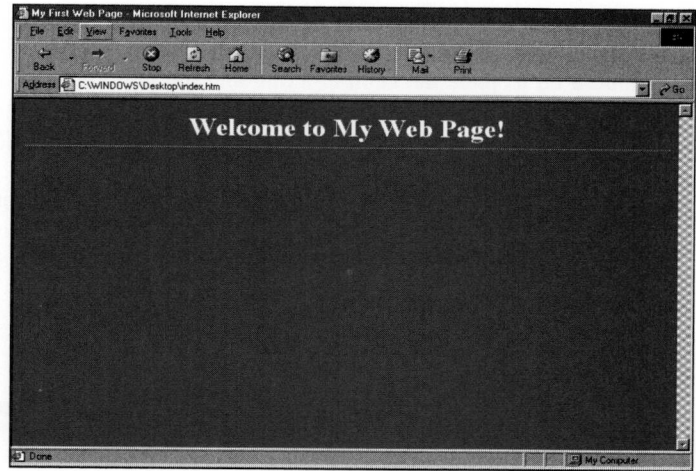

*Figure 6.10* **Background Color Applied to Web Page**
*The Web page now has a dark blue background with white text.*

**Changing the Spacing** Your Web page is starting to look better, but it is time to add some more text to the page. If you enter more text below the "Welcome to My Web Page!" line in the index.htm file, the browser will display this text on the same line as "Welcome to My Web Page!" Even though Notepad displays the two codes on separate lines, the browser will display them on the same line. With HTML, you must indicate line breaks and spaces by using tags. The break tag <br> will end a line, so that any new text will display in the browser below the text that preceded the <br> tag. The paragraph tag <p> at the beginning of a line will display a linespace above the line in the browser, and a <p> tag at the end of a line will display a linespace below the line in a browser. Neither the <br> nor the <p> tags require closing tags. If you enter code for a name, address, and phone number using the <br> tag after each line (e.g., Bob Smith<br>121 Main Street<br>555-9871<br>), the browser displays the information like this:

Bob Smith
121 Main Street
555-9871

Without the <br> tags, the browser displays the following:

Bob Smith 121 Main Street 555-9871

The following exercise shows how to enter line breaks between the title of your Web page and the body text.

## Adding Line Breaks

1. In Notepad, with index.htm open, position the cursor after the horizontal rule tag <hr> and press the Enter key to move the cursor to the next line.
2. Key **I am going to enter a space after this line.<p>** and press Enter to move the cursor to the next line.
3. Key **There should be a space between this line and the line above.<p>** and press Enter to move the cursor to the next line.
4. Key **This line should appear above<br>this line.** Press Enter to move the cursor to the next line.
5. Save your file and refresh the browser. The text you entered should display in the browser with the spaces indicated by the <p> and <br> codes (see Figure 6.11).

**Good Coding Technique** It is a good idea to enter codes in logical segments. This will make it easier to decode (figure out) later on if you experience a problem. If all of your code is jammed together it will be difficult to locate the source of any problem. Code should be separated into segments by function. For example, you can enter a line of code that will display a line in italic H1 header size <h1>text here</h1>, and then press the Enter key twice to create a space before you begin entering code on a new line. This will keep lines of code separated in the Notepad file, but the text will not display on separate lines in the browser screen. Special tags must be entered for breaking sentences or beginning new paragraphs, which will be described later in this chapter. As you gain experience, you will become more adept at entering code to make the tasks of decoding and debugging easier.

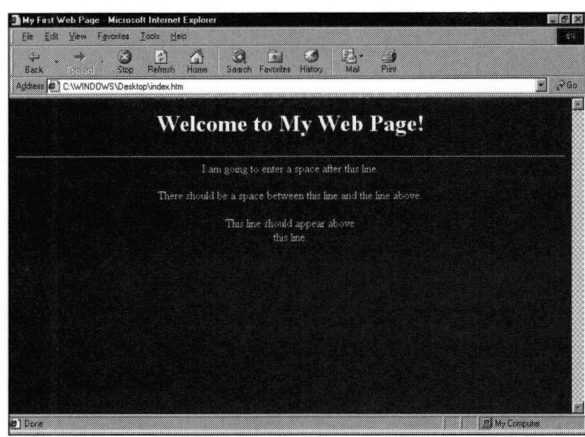

*Figure 6.11* The <p> and <br> Tags Applied to the Web Site

**Inserting an Image on Your Web Page** Placing images on your Web page is a sure way to dress it up and make it interesting to others. Before you can do this, you must have an image ready. It must be in either .gif (Graphics Interchange Format) or .jpg (Joint Photographic Experts Group) format. You can use an image that you saved from the Web, but if you do that you must make sure that the image is not copyrighted or protected. Once you have an image, name it, and save it to the same folder as your index.htm file. For this exercise, name the file image1 (for example, image1.jpg). After you save the image, you will be ready to place the image on your Web page.

## Saving an Image from a Web Page

1. In Internet Explorer, go to the Web page of your choice.
2. Find an image that you would like to save.
3. Position the cursor on the image and the cursor will turn into a pointing hand.
4. Right-click the mouse and a shortcut menu appears. The menu has choices such as Save Picture As, Set as Wallpaper, Set as Desktop Item, Copy, Add to favorites, and so on. Click Save Picture As to display the Save Picture dialog box. (Be careful; if you click Set as Wallpaper, that item immediately becomes the background for your desktop display. If this happens, you can undo it by clicking on the Start menu, and then clicking Settings, Control Panel, Display, Background, and OK.)
5. In the File name text box, key the file name (image1.jpg, for example). In the Save as type text box, make sure JPEG (*.jpg) displays. (Most images are JPEG files; however, the image you pick may be a TIF, PDF, or GIF, for example. Make sure the file extension matches the type of image you pick.)
6. In the Save in text box at the top of the screen, select the location in which you saved the index.htm file. Click Save. The image will be stored in this location, ready for you to use at a later date.

## Inserting an Image on Your Web Page

1. In Notepad, position the cursor just after the horizontal rule tag <hr> and press Enter to move the cursor to the next line.
2. Key **<img src="image1.jpg" alt="new image" border="0" align="center">**. (If the image you picked was not a JPEG image, make sure to use the appropriate file extension.) Table 6.6 explains these tags in detail.
3. Key a **<p>** tag at the end of the line to display a space between the image and the text below it in the browser screen.
4. Save the file and refresh the browser. The image you selected should appear on your Web page (see Figure 6.12).

 *Table 6.6* **HTML Tags**

- img: HTML tag for inserting an image.
- src: Required attribute. Indicates the location of your image file. The file name and extension (.gif or .jpg) must be within quotation marks.
- alt: This is the text that will display if the graphic cannot load on the visitor's screen. Specifying alternative text for a graphic helps convey content to visually impaired users, those who use speech synthesizers, and those on computers that cannot display graphics.
- border="0": Indicates no border around the image. If a border is desired, indicate the thickness by changing 0 to a number. The greater the number, the thicker the border.
- align: Set the alignment of the graphic on the page. Without this attribute, the graphic will align left.

**Using Comment Tags** Comment tags allow you to attach comments that can be helpful to anyone who needs to decode or troubleshoot the program. A large file can contain hundreds of lines of code and even if you have made an effort to arrange it in logical sections, it can be difficult to determine what each section concerns. Any text placed between comment tags <!— xxx —> will not appear in the browser. You can therefore leave instructions explaining what a section of code deals with, such as <!— This is the section that defines the page characteristics —>. You can also leave reminders for future work or modification, such as <!— Insert image Automobile.gif here when ready —>. Using this feature will make it easier to repair or modify code you have written.

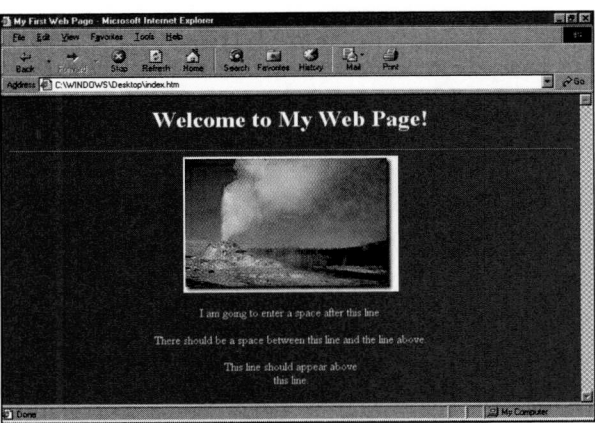

*Figure 6.12* **The Web Page Displaying an Image**

If you want to make the picture larger or smaller, go back into Notepad, with index.htm open, and change the width and height dimensions. Experimenting with different values will give you a feel for how these translate into image size on the browser. If you do want a border, you can indicate the thickness of the border by changing border="0" to a positive number, "1", "2", "3", and so on. The greater the number the thicker the border.

*Figure 6.13* **Web Page with Table Listing Contact Details**

**Creating Tables** Tables are helpful for arranging data. For your home page, you will create a table with your street address, city, state, and phone number. Follow the steps in the exercise on page 177. Once you refresh Internet Explorer, you should see a bordered table in the center of the page, with address, city, state, and phone number headings in the left-hand column, and the details in the right-hand column (see Figure 6.13).

**Creating Lists** You can create bulleted or numbered lists just as you can in a Word document. The Unordered List tag, <ul>, is used to create bulleted lists, and the Ordered List tag, <ol>, is used to create numbered lists. In the "Creating a List" Try It Out exercise, you are going to create a bullet list of five of your favorite hobbies. After completing the steps, you will see your five favorite hobbies listed as a bulleted list (see Figure 6.14). If you want to change the bullet style, just go back into Notepad, with index.htm open, and change the name of the bullet from disc to circle or square.

**Metatags** You may recall metatags from chapter 3 which covered search engines. Metatags provide keywords for search engines, but are not displayed in the browser. Metatags are not paired; the keyword listing for a Web page about breakfast foods might be <meta name="keywords" content="cereal, bacon, eggs">. Some search engines ignore metatags and look for keywords in the body of the page, or apply formulas to determine how much consideration they will give the metatag information. The reason they do this is because the metatags may provide a false idea of the content.

## Creating a Table

1. The opening tag for tables is <table>. In Notepad, with index.htm open, place the cursor at the end of the line containing the code for the image file (just after <p>), and press Enter to move the cursor to the next line.
2. Key **<table**, press the spacebar once, and key **width="80%" border="2" cellpadding="0" cellspacing="0">**. Press Enter to move the cursor to the next line. (Width indicates the width of the table; border indicates the thickness of the border lines. If you do not want a border, change the value to "0". Cellpadding and Cellspacing indicate how much empty space there will be between the cell contents and the cell borders.)
3. Key **<tr>** to start a new table row, and **<td>** to start a new table cell. After **<td>**, key **Address**, followed by the closing tag **</td>**, and press Enter to move the cursor to the next line.
4. Key **<td>** and enter your address. Close the cell by keying **</td>** and then **</tr>** to end the row. Press Enter to move the cursor to the next line.
5. Repeat steps 3 and 4 for **City**, followed by the name of your city, **State**, followed by the name of your state, and **Phone Number**, followed by your phone number (area code is not needed).
6. On the line below your phone number, key the table closing tag **</table>**.
7. Enter a **<p>** after the closing table tag so that there will be a space between your table and the following text.
8. Save the file and refresh IE to see the results.

## Creating a List

1. In Notepad, with index.htm open, key **<p>** at the end of the last line of text (the line reading "This line should appear above<br>this line").
2. Place the cursor after the closing center tag </center> and press Enter to move to the next line. The list will automatically align flush left. If you want the list centered, you can use the <center> tag we used previously by placing the list before the closing center tag.
3. Key **These are my five favorite hobbies:** (be sure to key the colon). Press Enter to move the cursor to the next line.
4. Key **<ul type="disc">** and press Enter to move the cursor to the next line. (You can also indicate circle or square if you prefer those bullet styles. Keying "disc" creates a solid circle, while keying "circle" creates an outline circle.)
5. Key **<li>** and then key the five items on your list. (Be sure to key **<li>** before each item, and press Enter after keying each item to move the cursor to the next line.)
6. After your last item, enter **</ul>** to close the list. Save the file and refresh IE to see the results.

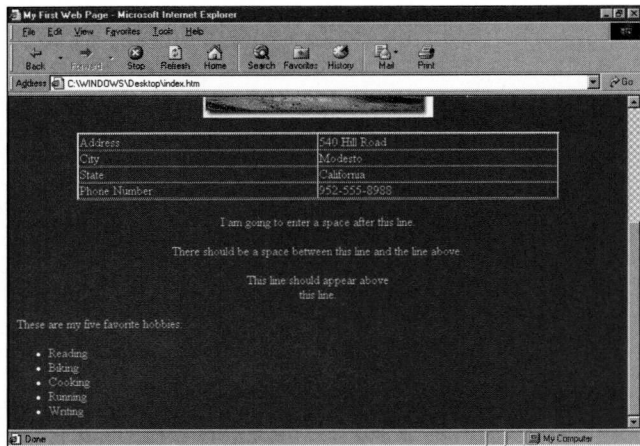

*Figure 6.14* **Bulleted List Created Using the Unordered List Tag <ul>**

To change the bulleted hobby list to a numbered list, all you need to do is change the Unordered List code <ul type="disc"> to an Ordered List code <ol>. Be sure to change your closing tag to match by changing it to </ol>. Save the file and refresh the browser. Your list will be numbered from 1 to 5.

**Creating Links**  You can link your home page to other Web pages you have created, or to pages created by other people. In the next Try It Out exercise, you will be creating a second page using Microsoft Word, but you will establish the link now for later use.

The opening tag <a href=" "> marks the beginning of a hypertext reference, which indicates a link to connect to another object (text, image, and so on). The link can be internal, to the same document, or it can be external, to another Web page or server anywhere in the world. The quotation marks (" ") enclose the address of the object or URL being linked to. The text between the opening and closing tags is what will show, usually blue and underlined, on the Web page as the link. When the users click that link text, they will open and view the linked item. The familiar pointing hand icon will appear when users move the mouse over a hyperlink. The closing tag for the hyperlink is </a>.

"My Second Page" will appear as an underlined link at the bottom of your home page. The link will not work right now, since you have not yet created a file named 2ndpage.htm. Once you have created a second page using Word, you will revisit your home page and check to see if the link works.

### Creating a Link

1.  In Notepad, with index.htm open, key **<p>** just after the last item in your list and press the Enter key to move the cursor to the next line.
2.  Enter **<a href="2ndpage.htm">My Second Page</a>**. Save the file and then click Refresh on the browser to see the hyperlink you have just inserted. Then close Notepad and close Internet Explorer.

## Other HTML Tags and Commands

You have now built a very basic Web page with an image, a table, and a numbered list. Using these basic skills, you can modify your home page and create new pages. You might want to experiment with some of the other basic HTML tags listed in Tables 6.7, 6.8, and 6.9.

*Table 6.7* **Common Paired Tags Used in HTML Coding**

| Opening Tag | Closing Tag | Resulting Effect |
|---|---|---|
| \<html\> | \</html\> | **Required.** Begins and ends the Web document. |
| \<head\> | \</head\> | **Required.** Opens and closes the header section of the page. |
| \<title\> | \</title\> | **Required.** Displays a page title, centered and formatted. |
| \<body\> | \</body\> | **Required.** Opens and closes the body; defines the screen. The content of the page lies between these tags. |
| \< a href="#name"\> | \</a\> | Activates a hypertext link on the same page. |
| \< a href="http://url"\> | \</a\> | Gives location of hyperlink to another page. Activates a hypertext link. |
| \<address\> | \</address\> | Contains the address of the author. Displays the information in italics. |
| \<h1\> | \</h1\> | Defines the first-level header. |
| \<h2\> | \</h2\> | Defines the second-level header. Six levels are allowed. |
| \<b\> | \</b\> | Displays enclosed text in boldface type. |
| \<i\> | \</i\> | Displays enclosed text in italics. |
| \<u\> | \</u\> | Underlines enclosed text. |
| \<em\> | \</em\> | Emphasizes enclosed text (usually in italics). |
| \<strong\> | \</strong\> | Emphasizes enclosed text (usually in boldface). |
| \<blockquote\> | \</blockquote\> | Indents left and right paragraph margins so text doesn't run up against edge of browser frame. |
| \<center\> | \</center\> | Centers the enclosed text or image horizontally. |
| \<ol\> | \</ol\> | Begins and ends an ordered list. |
| \<ul\> | \</ul\> | Begins and ends an unordered list. |

 *Table 6.8* **Single HTML Tags** *These tags do not require matching closing tags.*

| Tag | Resulting Effect |
|---|---|
| \<br\> | Adds line break. |
| \<hr\> | Adds horizontal line. |
| \<img src=" "\> | Inserts an image. The image file name is placed within the quotation marks. |
| \<li\> | Precedes each item in an unordered \<ul\> or ordered \<ol\> list. |
| \<meta\> | Gives keywords for search engines to index by; doesn't appear in screen. Inserts information not defined by other HTML tags or properties. |
| \<p\> | Adds paragraph break. |

 *Table 6.9* **Common HTML Tags Attributes**

| Tag | Resulting Effect |
|---|---|
| align= | Optional attribute for the paragraph and table cell tags, to align the text in a paragraph as left, center, or right. |
| alt= | Attribute for the image tag; displays text if the image cannot be displayed by the browser. |
| bgcolor= | Used with body and table cell tags; adds background color. |
| link=color | Used with body tag only; the color of all unvisited links. |
| text=color | Used with body tag only; the color of all text in the document. |
| src= | The source file of the online image. |
| type= | In lists, specifies type of bullet used for displaying each item \<li\> in the list, as circle, disc, or square. |

The best way to learn more about HTML is by trial and error. You can very easily check your work by saving your source file (index.htm) and then refreshing Internet Explorer. If what you were trying to do didn't work out, take another look at the code you entered and experiment until you get it right.

## Building a Web Page Using an HTML Converter

You have seen how to create a Web page by using a text editor and coding it yourself. Now you will learn how to use an HTML converter. The HTML code is created automatically when you save the file. With an HTML converter program you can point, click, drag, and drop the desired formatting as you key the content of the page. You will use Microsoft Word (Word 2000 or newer version) as your HTML converter.

**Creating a New Web Page**  Creating a Web page using Word is just as easy as creating an ordinary Word document. To build a Web page, all you need to know are some of the special features and commands that will allow you to convert the Word document to an HTML document at the click of the mouse.

Instructions for the Try It Out exercises in this section are written for Word 2000. Instructions for completing the exercises using Word 97 are contained in an appendix at the end of the book.

Follow the steps in the "Creating a New Web Page" Try It Out exercise. You have now completed the linking process between your home page and this new Web page. Before continuing to create a new Web page, test the link to see if it works by following the exercise on page 181.

You can create a Web page in Word using many of the Word formatting commands that you are already familiar with. HTML coding is added automatically and invisibly. You can still click View on the browser menu bar and then click Source to see the code, which will be displayed in a Notepad file. You can also view the code you have created automatically in a Word file. To do this, open the 2ndpage.htm file in Word (make sure All Files is showing in the Files of type text box), click View on the menu bar, and then click HTML Source from the drop-down menu.

As you work on your Web page, you may want to check to see how it is developing by previewing it through the browser. To do this, click File on the menu bar and then Web Page Preview, or click the Web Page Preview button on the Standard toolbar. If the Web Page Preview button is not on your toolbar, you can add it by following the steps in the Try It Out exercise at the bottom of page 181.

**Tips** *and* **Tools**

**ToolTips** If you want to know what a toolbar button does, just move the cursor over any toolbar button you want to know more about. Holding the cursor over the button will cause a small yellow box to appear, describing the function of that button. You can continue to move the cursor around the page to explore other button functions. This is a good way to familiarize yourself with all of the one-click formatting commands at your fingertips. Clicking a button from the toolbar is faster than going to the menu bar and then clicking a command from the drop-down menu.

## Creating a New Web Page

1. In Microsoft Word 2000, click File on the menu bar and then click New from the drop-down menu to display the New dialog box.
2. With the General tab displayed, select the Blank Document icon and click OK.
3. Click File on the menu bar, and then click Save as Web Page from the drop-down menu.
4. The link you made on your Web page was to a document named 2ndpage.htm, so in the File name text box, key **2ndpage** to name the file. (Note that the *.htm* extension will be entered automatically, so you do not need to key it as you did in Notepad.)
5. In the Save in text box, save this file to the same folder in which you saved the index.htm file. When you are finished, click Save.

## Testing the Link

1. In Internet Explorer, click File on the menu bar and then click Open from the drop-down menu to display the Open dialog box.
2. Locate the index.htm file using the browse command. When you have found it, click Open and then OK.
3. Scroll down your home page until you come to the link you created at the bottom of the page. Use the mouse to click on the link.
4. The browser should open to the 2ndpage file you created. Because you have not entered any text or graphic images the browser screen will be blank, but "2ndpage" will display in the browser title bar. If you view the source of this page, you will notice that you do not need to enter any of the required HTML tags such as <html>, <header>, and so on. The GUI editor also automatically creates a title for your page, using the name you chose for the file, in this case 2ndpage.

## Customizing a Toolbar

1. In Microsoft Word 2000, click the down-pointing arrow at the right of the Standard toolbar, then click Add or Remove Buttons; click Customize (at the bottom of the drop-down list); and then select the Commands tab.
2. With File selected in the Categories list box, scroll down through the commands until Web Page Preview appears. Using the mouse, click on the icon, drag it to where you want it to appear on the Standard toolbar, and then release the mouse button.

**Setting Font Style and Size**  Now you are ready to enter text and use formatting commands to build your second Web page. Follow the steps in the following exercise.

### Setting Font Style and Size

1. In Microsoft Word 2000, open 2ndpage.htm.
2. Key an introductory line or phrase for the second Web page.
3. Using the mouse, highlight the text you just entered. On the Formatting toolbar, to the right of the font text box, you will see a large *A* and a small *A*. (If you do not have these buttons on your toolbar, add them by following a procedure similar to the one used above to add the Web Page Preview button. Select Format in the Categories list box.) Clicking on the large *A* will enlarge the text you highlighted, while clicking on the small *A* will make the text smaller. You can bold, italicize, or underline text by using the **B**, *I*, and <u>U</u> buttons on the Formatting toolbar. You can left align, center, right align, or justify the text by clicking on the alignment buttons on the toolbar. The justify feature creates flush margins left and right. You can change the color of text by clicking on the Font Color button on the Formatting toolbar.
4. When you are finished choosing the desired formatting options, save the file and then click the Web Page Preview button to see what you have created.

**Creating a Horizontal Line**  Creating a horizontal line is easy with Word. Click the Enter key to move the cursor down the page. The spacing you create in this file will be automatically converted to HTML paragraph <p> and break <br> commands.

### Creating a Horizontal Line

1. In Microsoft Word 2000, with 2ndpage.htm open, position the cursor where you would like the horizontal line to appear.
2. Click Format on the menu bar, then Borders and Shading. Select the Borders tab, and then click the Horizontal Line button near the bottom of the screen.
3. You can choose from a number of colorful and decorative horizontal lines (see Figure 6.15). Scroll down to see the various lines; click Keep Looking to view even more choices. Click the line you want, then click the Insert Clip icon. The horizontal line will appear where you placed the cursor.

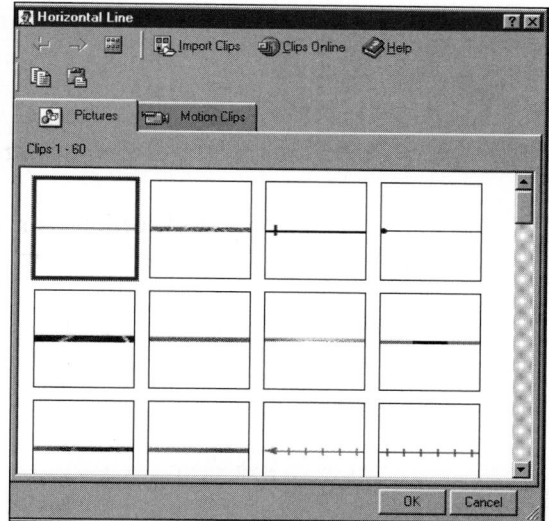

 **Figure 6.15 Horizontal Line Dialog Box**
*The horizontal line feature provides a number of colorful line choices.*

 **Using Undo** Don't forget that you can use the Undo feature on the Word Standard toolbar, just as you would in a regular Word document. If you make a mistake or choose a color you don't like, click the Undo button and try another color.

 **Figure 6.16 Web Page with Background Texture**
*This Web page features white marble as the background texture.*

**Adding Background Color** The background color feature in Word allows you quickly and easily to select a variety of background colors and color combinations as wells as patterns and textures.

 **Adding Background Color**

1. In Microsoft Word 2000, with 2ndpage.htm open, click Format on the menu bar and then point to Background from the drop-down menu.
2. A drop-down menu appears showing 40 color choices. You can click More Colors and choose colors from a palette as well. Clicking on Fill Effects allows you to choose from among a variety of realistic effects, including White Marble, Woven Mat, and Recycled Paper. Click on the color of your choice.
3. Save the file and then click the Web Page Preview button to see how your Web page looks now (see Figure 6.16).

**Inserting an Image**  Inserting images is easy when using Word to create a Web page.

**Creating Tables**  You can create a table just as you did in your home page file.

**Creating Lists**  The list function works exactly the same way it does when creating a normal Word document.

### Inserting an Image

1. In Microsoft Word 2000, with 2ndpage.htm open, position the cursor where you would like an image to appear.
2. Click Insert on the menu bar, then Picture. If you then click Clip Art, you will be able to choose a picture from over 50 categories of images. Select the picture you want, then click the Insert Clip icon. If after clicking Insert, then Picture, you click From File, you can browse to select any image you have previously saved.
3. The image you inserted will appear on the page. Right-click the image and a shortcut menu appears that will allow you to format the picture and align it. You can resize the image by clicking on it and then clicking and dragging one of the corner or side boxes to the size desired (see Figure 6.17).
4. Save the file when you are finished, and then click the Web Page Preview button to see how your image looks on the Web.

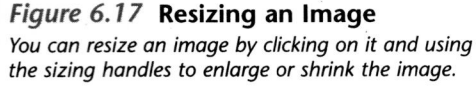

**Figure 6.17  Resizing an Image**
*You can resize an image by clicking on it and using the sizing handles to enlarge or shrink the image.*

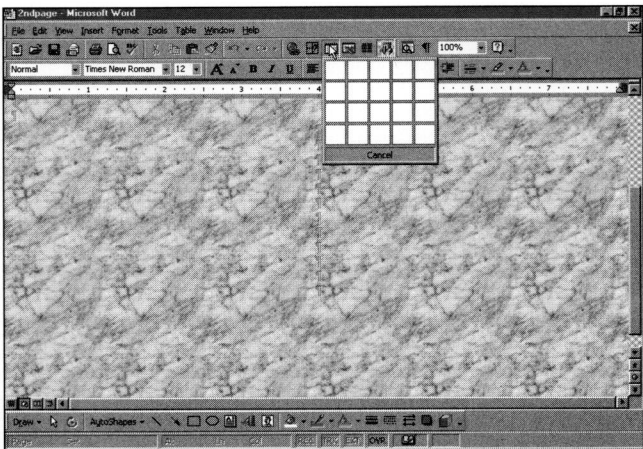

**Figure 6.18  Table Drop-Down Grid**

## Creating a Table

1. In Microsoft Word 2000, with 2ndpage.htm open, position the cursor where you would like to place the table, then click the Insert Table button on the Standard toolbar.
2. A grid box opens just below the button. Moving the cursor over the grid boxes turns the boxes dark blue. The description of the table layout appears at the bottom of the box, indicating the number of rows and columns you have chosen (e.g., 4 x 5 table, or 5 x 5 table). Select the table size you want by highlighting the appropriate number of boxes and then clicking the mouse button once (see Figure 6.18). The table will be inserted into your Web page.
3. To format the table, click Table on the menu bar, click Select, and then click Table from the drop-down menu.
4. Once the table has been selected, click Format on the menu bar, and click Borders and Shading from the drop-down menu to display the Borders and Shading dialog box.
5. Click Grid, find the width of the border you want by clicking the down-pointing arrow in the Width text box and selecting a line, and then click OK. In the Preview box, you will see that the new line width has automatically been applied to the outside border of the table. If you also want to change the grid lines inside the table, click on them in the Preview box and the new line width will be applied to them. You can format a table with any combination of lines by choosing a width and then clicking on the lines you want changed to that width. When you have finished formatting the table, click OK.
6. Fill out the table by keying any text you wish in the boxes.
7. Save the file, and then click the Web Page Preview button to view the table on your Web page.

## Creating a List

1. In Microsoft Word 2000, with 2ndpage.htm open, position the cursor several spaces below the image you placed on the page.
2. Click the Align Left button on the Formatting toolbar so that your list will appear flush left on the page, rather than in the center. If you center the list, the margins will appear ragged on both sides as each line will be a different length.
3. Key a title for your list and press Enter.
4. Enter each list item, pressing the Enter key after each entry.
5. When you are finished keying the items, use the cursor to highlight the listed items.
6. Click Format on the menu bar and then click Bullets and Numbering from the drop-down menu to display the Bullets and Numbering dialog box.
7. You can click the Bulleted, Numbered, or Outline Numbered tab to select the bullet or number style you want. Click on your selection and then click OK.
8. Save the file, and then click the Web Page Preview button to view the list on your Web page.

**Creating Links** The various pages on a Web site are connected using hyperlinks. Hyperlinks can also link to different sections of the same document, or they can link to documents on other Web sites on the Internet. To show you how this works, you will create a link back to your home page.

You can move back and forth between Word and your home page using the links you established, or by using the Back and Forward buttons on the browser. You are not limited to using text links. You can create a link that is activated by clicking on an image just as easily. To do that, click once on the image you wish to establish as a link, and then follow the same procedure that you used to create the text link. When you are finished, you will see that placing the cursor over the linked image changes it into a hand, revealing it as a hyperlink. Clicking on the image will link to whatever file, URL, or location you chose when you created the link.

## Creating a Link

1. In Microsoft Word 2000, with 2ndpage.htm open, position the cursor at the bottom of the page.
2. Key **Return to My Web Page**.
3. Using the mouse, highlight the text you just entered and click Insert on the menu bar. Click Hyperlink from the drop-down menu to display the Insert Hyperlink dialog box (see Figure 6.19). You have a choice of creating a link to another file or URL, or you can link to another section or object in the file you are working on. Because you want to link to another file, click File under Browse for.
4. In the Link to File dialog box that displays, locate the index.htm file and then click OK. Click OK again to close the Insert Hyperlink dialog box.
5. You have created a hyperlink to your home page. The link text you entered is underlined and in blue. You can reformat the link just as you would any other text. Be careful not to click it when you are highlighting it, or you will link to the other file or URL. Save the file, and then click the Web Page Preview button to view the hyperlink on your Web page.

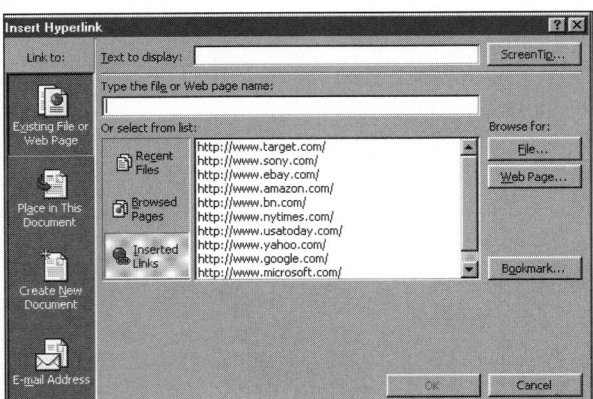

***Figure 6.19*** **Insert Hyperlink Dialog Box**
*The Insert Hyperlink feature in Word allows you to create links to different files, URLs, or even locations within the same file.*

**Creating a Link to Text or Objects within the Same Page** Before you can create a link within the same document, you must name it as a bookmark. Highlight or select the text or object (an image or other nontext item) that you wish to establish a link to. Click Insert on the menu bar, and then click Bookmark. In the Bookmark dialog box that displays, key a name for the bookmark (Topofpage, Image1, etc.). (Notice that there are no spaces between words in a bookmark. If you space between words, you cannot save a bookmark; it is part of the required naming conventions used with the Internet.) When you are finished naming the bookmark, click Add and then follow the instructions for creating a hyperlink (see the previous exercise). This time you will click on Bookmark under Browse for. Select the bookmark you created, and click OK. Click OK to close the Insert Hyperlink dialog box. You have now created an internal link on your Web page.

## Recycling Web Pages

Many Web pages reside in public Internet directories on servers and are not locked or protected from copying. You are able to look at the source code in pages coded in HTML and you can save the code, the images, and the links for reuse. However, some pages have **digital watermarks**, insignia that "stamp" the material's source, and other identifying characteristics embedded electronically that allow the origin of the material to be traced. These marks protect a creator's copyright and result in restrictions on the reuse of those pages.

You can use the cut, copy, and paste function to reuse code on your own pages, unless there is a copyright restriction. Create a simple HTML shell as described earlier in this chapter and try the exercise on page 188.

Research information can be printed from Web pages. Areas can be selected, copied to the Windows Clipboard, and pasted elsewhere. Results of Web searches may be used for manuscripts and reports. The Internet is just as public as a text-based library, and the same rules of plagiarism and proper citation apply. It is a "virtual library" with a massive catalog. It is there to view and share. Misrepresenting material as original is never correct, but recycling another's image or re-tweaking another's HTML code to prepare a first Web page is acceptable. Those who do not want their work recycled will indicate that on their Web pages, or they will take measures to lock their material so that it cannot be grabbed electronically or only viewed for a period of time before purchasing.

## Evolution of Watermarks

When paper was first made and very scarce, the heavy iron presses that produced the sheets of paper had seals on them, identifying the printer. These seals were transferred to the pieces of paper as they came through the press and the water was squeezed out of the pulp to produce the finished paper. These distinguishing "watermarks" became an identifying seal for source of the paper. Through the ages, high-quality paper always contained faint identifying watermarks, even though the presses of earlier times were no longer used. Thus, today the term "watermarks" applies to digital stamps that identify and authenticate the true source of an electronically written Web page.

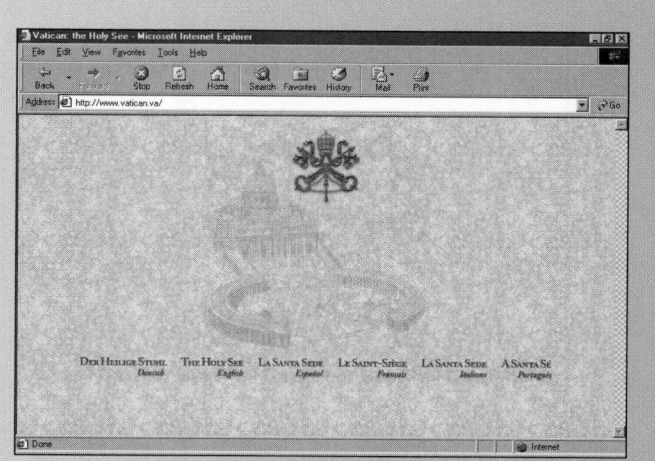

## Recycling a Web Page

1. In Internet Explorer, log on to a Web page of your choice.
2. Click View and then Source on the menu bar to find the source code for a section of the Web page you want to reuse, and copy it.
3. Open the shell you created and paste the copied code between the two <body> tags.
4. Save the file as an .htm file.
5. Open the file using the browser. Does it display just as it did on the original Web page? If it did not, it could be because there was other formatting code that you did not copy. See if you can find any missing code and insert that into the shell file and try again. If graphics are missing, it probably means that they are linked relative to the original page's location. Since you have saved the page in a different location, you will have to save the image from the original Web page to the folder that contains the saved HTML file and relink to it.

# Publishing Your Web Page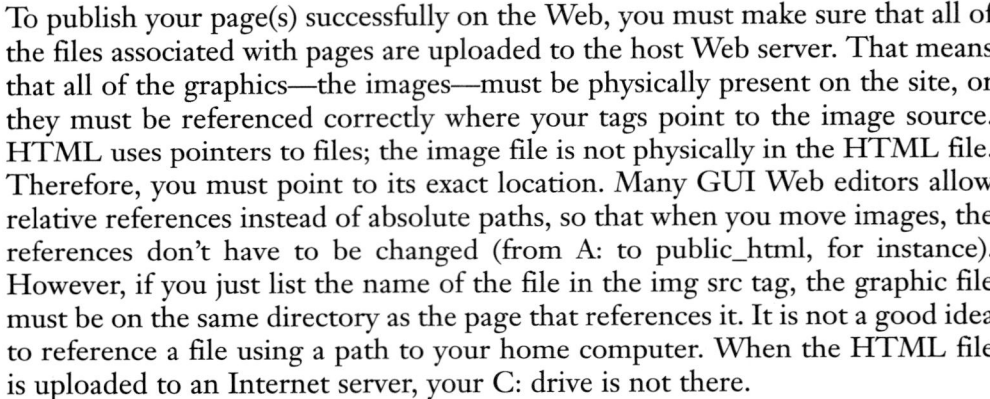

To publish your page(s) successfully on the Web, you must make sure that all of the files associated with pages are uploaded to the host Web server. That means that all of the graphics—the images—must be physically present on the site, or they must be referenced correctly where your tags point to the image source. HTML uses pointers to files; the image file is not physically in the HTML file. Therefore, you must point to its exact location. Many GUI Web editors allow relative references instead of absolute paths, so that when you move images, the references don't have to be changed (from A: to public_html, for instance). However, if you just list the name of the file in the img src tag, the graphic file must be on the same directory as the page that references it. It is not a good idea to reference a file using a path to your home computer. When the HTML file is uploaded to an Internet server, your C: drive is not there.

Once you have an ISP with a directory where you can place your Web pages, and you have composed and **debugged** (checked it to make sure there are no errors) the HTML files, you are ready to load them on your site. Just like formally publishing a book, the pages are published, or placed upon a Web server. You will learn how to **publish** an HTML file to a Web server using the FTP (File Transfer Protocol) function of the Internet Explorer browser. Once you have mastered this process you can use any of the other FTP programs that are available for a fee or as shareware. The Internet Explorer FTP functions are very basic. Other FTP programs offer additional features that you may find useful as you progress to a full-fledged Web page designer.

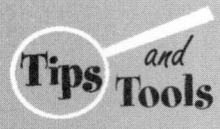

**Tips and Tools**

**Uploading Files** If you are uploading your files to a UNIX server with an FTP utility you may have to create a public directory and set the folder and file protections yourself. Usually, you will get instructions on how to create and name these folders from your ISP. If you work with a school server, check with your instructor to find out how to publish your pages on the server.

## Uploading and Downloading Using FTP

Before you begin, you will need the FTP address of the Web server or the site where you wish to upload or download files. The FTP address looks like a typical URL, but begins with "FTP." You use the FTP protocol instead of HTTP protocol. You will also need to know the name of the folder or directory that your Web host has designated for your use (see Figure 6.20).

Depending on the permission rules of the FTP site, you can cut or delete materials posted on the FTP site by highlighting a folder or file, right-clicking the mouse, and clicking Cut or Delete from the shortcut menu that appears. Be careful not to delete somebody else's material. If there are restrictions, the cut and delete features will appear but be inoperative.

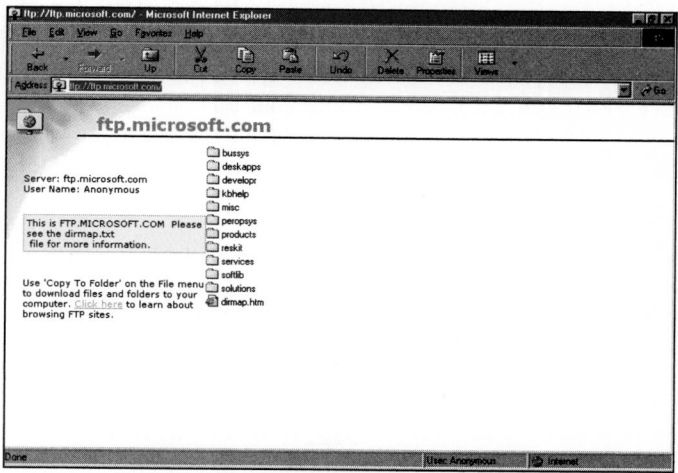

 *Figure 6.20* **Example of an FTP Site**

 **Uploading a File**

1. From your instructor, get the address of your school's FTP site. In Internet Explorer, key the FTP address in the Address text box near the top of the browser and click Go.
2. If the FTP site requires permission to enter, your instructor will supply a password and user name.
3. Once you are logged on to the FTP server, you should see yellow folder icons. You may need to upload your file to one of these folders, or even to a subfolder contained in one of these folders. If that is the case, you can navigate by double-clicking the folder icons to see their contents and locate the directory where you want to upload your files.
4. Once you have located your destination folder, use the Windows Start button to open Windows Explorer (click Start, Programs, then Windows Explorer). Locate the file you wish to upload using Explorer (e.g., the index.htm file). When you have found it, right-click the mouse and then click Copy from the shortcut menu that appears. Use the taskbar at the bottom of the screen to return to the browser and the FTP site.
5. Now click once on the destination file icon on the FTP site, highlighting it in blue.
6. Right-click the mouse button, and then click Paste at the shortcut menu. The file you copied from Explorer will be pasted into the destination file on the FTP server.

### Downloading a File

1. In Internet Explorer, log on to the FTP site again.
2. Locate the file you wish to download and click it once.
3. Right-click the mouse and select Copy to Folder from the shortcut menu that appears.
4. Locate the folder you wish to download the file to, and then click OK. The file you selected will be downloaded and stored in the location you chose.

**Web Links**

**Absolute FTP**
http://www.vandyke.com/products/absoluteftp
**Coffee Cup Free FTP**
http://www.coffeecup.com
**Queue FTP**
http://www.eesoft.com/qftp
**SmartFTP** http://www.smartftp.com
**WS-FTP Pro**
http://www.ipswitch.com

## Maintaining a Web Site

The Web is dynamic—it changes constantly. That is good news and bad news. Unlike printed material, you can edit and update Web pages as much as you'd like. If you want to upgrade graphics or add content, it can be done quickly and simply. You edit the file, make the changes, and then refresh the screen. The changes take effect immediately. This means you have an *obligation* to perform regular maintenance on your site. You are expected to be up to date always; your pages are live and may be viewed at any time. When you make a change, update the date on the page, so Web users know your page is current. (Some GUI editors do this for you when you load the HTML files in the program.)

Routinely update your external links. Continually verify the links, and change them if they become obsolete. Nothing is so frustrating as to click a hyperlink that results in a long wait, only to see a "Page Cannot be Found" error message. Remember to keep your e-mail link current as well. If an e-mail address changes, it should be changed on every Web page.

When you successfully create, publish, and maintain your own Web pages, you will be part of the Web community. You will be an active member of the Global Village—not just a Web surfer, but a Web publisher as well.

Once a Web page is designed, composed, and saved as an .htm or .html file, it can be opened in any text editor or Web page editor. To make corrections, you could open the file in Notepad, Word, HomePage, or FrontPage. (Remember to change the file types to "All Files" so the file will display in the Open window.) However, if you resave a Web page in a different editor than it was created with, it may insert its own tags and comments throughout the code. A program will sometimes "translate" the code into a style that is unique to that program, but the file will still be readable by the Web browsers. The resulting codes can be confusing to read and difficult to edit. For this reason, we recommend editing and printing in a plain text editor, like Notepad.

**Tips *and* Tools**

**Listing Your Web Site** To get help listing your Web site and to see how various search engines will view it, visit the Northern Webs site which has a Search Engine Tutorial for Web designers (www.northernwebs.com). While you are there, check out the excellent learning site for Internet beginners called *Beginners Central*. It contains information about downloading files, using e-mail, newsgroups, newsreaders, FTP basics, telnet, and so on.

 # Summary

➤ Designing and composing your own Web pages is relatively simple.

➤ A rudimentary knowledge of HTML and some basic design principles is enough to begin the publishing process.

➤ Planning and designing a Web page encompasses determining a target audience, and then planning the page content, layout, navigation scheme, and page design.

➤ Web pages can be composed on a plain text editor, using HTML, using an HTML converter like Word, on a GUI Web page editor like FrontPage, or by modifying code from existing Web pages.

➤ The general template of a Web page includes the HTML title, header, and body tags. Other tags are added as needed.

➤ Before publishing your Web pages you should check their accessibility to viewers using different browsers.

➤ Previewing and debugging Web pages is a final step before uploading for publication.

➤ To publish your Web pages, you need an ISP that hosts Web pages, and an allotment of storage on the Web server. This could be on your personal account or through your school (if available). Once your Web pages are live, regular maintenance ensures that they remain current.

 # Key Terms

**attributes** Additional parameters used to format elements called for by an HTML tag. For example, an HTML <body> tag may have the attributes bgcolor="blue" text="white" inserted into the tag: <body bgcolor="blue" text="white"> to indicate that the body of the Web page should display a blue background with white text.

**compiled language** Programming languages in which the entire program, or set of instructions, is converted to a body of executable code that the processor does not have to stop and convert at run time.

**debugging** Checking Web pages to make sure that they function as intended.

**digital watermarks** Insignia that "stamp" the material's source, and other identifying characteristics embedded electronically that allow the origin of the material to be traced. These marks protect a creator's copyright and result in restrictions on the reuse of those pages.

**Dynamic Hypertext Markup Language (DHTML)** A programming language that allows Web content to change each time it is viewed on the client, or user, machine. It is commonly used to allow identical Web pages to appear in different languages.

**Extensible Markup Language (XML)** Part of a larger system that attempts to standardize structured Web documents so there will be a uniform way to add markups.

**font** A complete set of letters, numbers, and symbols that appear in a particular typeface (i.e., Arial or Times Roman), type size (i.e., 10, 14, or 32), and typestyle (i.e., bold or italic).

**graphical user interface (GUI)** The layer of software where the user and computer interact; the presentation layer provided to computer users that allows them to point and click and drag and drop icons to perform computer operations.

**HTML tags** Commands inserted into a document that specify the style and placement of text, graphics, links, and other Web page features (e.g., <b>, <p>, <img>, etc.).

**interlaced graphics** Web page graphics that appear on the page only after the entire pixels group is in client computer RAM.

**interpreted programming languages** Programming languages in which each line of code, or instruction, is executed as it is read by the processor, one line at a time.

**Java applet** Small applications (programs) contained within larger programs that are designed to be executed within those programs. For example, a Java applet may be embedded in a Java program within a Web page that displays a fill-in form.

**metalanguage** A programming language used to describe other languages, but independent of other Web languages.

**navigation scheme** The path by which users can move around a Web site. Typical navigation schemes include sequential schemes (linear—from one page to the next) or hierarchical (like an outline, with index pages leading to topic pages, leading to subtopic pages).

**pixel** The basic building blocks of a display screen; the number and color capacity of the points in a screen affect its resolution, or the clarity of the image. Short for picture element, a measurement 1/72 of an inch wide. Used to specify image size.

**point** A measurement of text or font size.

**progressive graphics** Graphics that appear in layers and get richer and clearer as they download to the browser window.

**publishing** The process of placing Web page files on a host server so that they are accessible through the Internet.

**scripting language** Programming language used for scripting (writing) Web pages, such as HTML, Java, XML, and so forth.

**serif/sans serif** Serif fonts have short tails or trailing characters, sans serif do not (e.g., a serif *A* looks like this [A], while a sans serif *A* looks like this [**A**]).

**subject matter expert (SME)** When designing commercial or professional Web sites, a subject matter expert is often employed to advise Web designers and programmers about the content of the pages.

**source code** The programming behind any Web page. HTML is one example of a source code.

**Standard General Markup Language (SGML)** A master markup language developed by the International Standards Organization (ISO), which sets standards for computing areas. SGML sets requirements for any markup language, whether Web based or not.

**target audience** The people or groups that a Web page or Web site is designed to attract.

**Web page** A document on the World Wide Web that consists of an HTML file, with associated files for graphics and scripts, identified by a URL, or address.

**WYSIWYG** What You See Is What You Get applications refers to programs for creating Web pages that allow users to see how the pages will display as they are created, rather than as code.

 # Navigating and Exploring the Web

## Working the Web

**Project 1** Take a look at the Web page below. Use Notepad to recreate an identical Web page.

> ### Joe's Malt Shop
> _____
>
> _____
>
> **Visit *Joe's Malt Shop*, where every 5th malt is free!**
>
> Joe's is on the corner of Main and 5th Avenue, next door to the bowling alley. There is free parking in the alley.
>
> Kids 12 and under, guess where the hidden beach ball is, and win a free cookie!
>
> **Five Good reasons to visit *Joe's Malt Shop*:**
>
> 1. Friendly, fast service
> 2. Always a lunch special under $5.00
> 3. Games for the kids
> 4. Live entertainment Saturday nights
> 5. A malt a day keeps the doctor away!
>
> | Here are the daily specials for Tuesday: | |
> | --- | --- |
> | Mushroom Cheeseburger, with fries | $4.50 |
> | Chocolate Malt | $2.25 |
> | Peach Pie | $1.25 |

**Project 2** Surf the Web and download two images from a Web site. Insert the two images into the Web page you created in Project 1. You can change the title of the page, and change or add any text that you'd like to the page.

**Project 3** Save a copy of the Project 1 Web page you created and give it another name (use Save As to rename it). Link both pages so that users can click a hyperlink to go back and forth between the pages. Create one of the links using one of the images you placed on your second Web page, so that clicking on the image will link to the other page.

**Project 4** Surf the Web and find the URLs of five Web sites that you like. Copy or write down the URLs for each page. In one or both of the pages you have created in Projects 1 and 3, create links to the five URLs you found on the Web. Save the file and log on to the Internet to check that the links work.

**Project 5** Upload the files you have created to a host server. Check that all of the links to the pages you created work, as well as the URL links to other pages that you created.

# Are We Connecting?

## Exercise 1

*Answer the following questions. Questions can be answered individually or assigned as small group discussion.*

1. What makes a Web page effective? Discuss guidelines for using text, graphics, and white space.
2. How would you plan a page if your target audience were teenagers? How would plan a page if your target audience were older workers planning for retirement? Discuss differences in graphic elements, text, types of links, and page appearance.
3. Within this chapter you were able to use Notepad and Word to create Web pages. Which method did you prefer? Why? Which method will you choose to create your own personal Web page? Would you use the same method if you were creating a Web page for a local business?

## Exercise 2

*Match the acronym or term with the description.*

a. sans serif
b. HTML
c. pixel
d. Java applets
e. tag
f. .gif or .jpg
g. <u>

1. a common Web scripting language
2. the HTML tag used to underline text
3. a typestyle that does not have a trailing character
4. the two image formats that can be displayed on the Web
5. an HTML label that tells the program what to do
6. a unit of measure equal to 1/72 of an inch
7. small programs designed to be executed within another Web program

## Exercise 3

*Compose a short answer for each of the following.*

1. What is the file name usually assigned to the beginning, or home page, of a Web site?
2. List two Web page navigation schemes.
3. Name three different elements that might be placed on a Web page.
4. What are two of the four ways to create an HTML document?
5. What are the beginning and ending characters around tag names?
6. What HTML tags do you use to include comments in your source code?
7. What is the required HTML tag that goes at the beginning and end of text on the page?
8. What HTML tag is used to create a paragraph break?

## Exercise 4

*Indicate whether each of the following statements is True or False. Rewrite the false statements to make them true.*

1. HTML tags are not always paired.
2. Java applets are small apples that appear when you save a Web page.
3. All HTML documents must begin and end with a <body> tag.
4. To publish your Web pages you must download them to a host server.
5. HTML is an interpreted programming language.
6. Metatags provide keywords for search engine indexes.
7. It is never acceptable to copy or use source code from another Web page.
8. HTML shells are used only for Web pages with images.
9. Index.htm files are index files for home pages.
10. *HTML* stands for Hypertext Markup Language.

## Appendix A
## Computer Hardware and Software: A Review

# Microcomputer Hardware

A computer is an electronic tool used for the storage, manipulation, retrieval, and transmission of data. The hardware components of a personal microcomputer system can be divided into input, output, processing, and storage.

## Input Hardware

The mouse, the keyboard, and the scanner are the three major input devices for microcomputers. The mouse and the keyboard are always present with a modern personal computer system, although they may take many different forms. A scanner is helpful, but not required.

**Mouse**  The mouse is an electronic pointing device that operates by the use of a ball embedded underneath a palm-sized, maneuverable unit that is attached to the computer system. You direct the mouse pointer by rolling the mouse along a mouse pad until the indicator (a cursor) reaches the desired selection in the screen. Then you press (or click) a mouse button to confirm the selection of the highlighted item. You may have a track ball or touch pad instead of a mouse, which is basically the mouse without its housing. Newer mouse models have three selection areas—left mouse button for standard selection clicks, right mouse button for context-sensitive pop-up menus (termed Intellisense by Microsoft®), and a scroll wheel to quickly scroll Web pages in both directions. Your mouse may have a cord connecting it to your system unit, or it may be cordless.

**Keyboard**  The keyboard allows you to enter text and numbers much as you would on an ordinary typewriter. The computer keyboard allows key combinations that let you access hot keys (predefined menu choices), change a specific character in the character set, and perform some general editing operations. There are many styles of keyboard, many with Web access function keys and ergonomic designs.

**Scanner**  Scanners allow you to digitize (convert to 0s and 1s) a hard copy of a document or graphic and save it to a file. It operates like a copy machine, capturing an image. Then you can upload (copy a file from your PC to your host computer) the file, or attach it to an e-mail to send to someone else who has Internet access.

You may have some other input peripherals attached to your computer, such as a Webcam (camera) for live videoconferencing, or a microphone headset for Internet phone conversations or speech recognition. These are becoming more common with the beginning of Internet2 standards mentioned in chapter 1. Internet2 will redefine the standards for Web pages; multimedia will be the rule, not the exception.

## Output Hardware

Output hardware refers to the physical devices that allow the computer to display the results of input and processing. The most common output devices in personal computer systems are monitors and printers.

**Monitor**  The monitor is a visual display unit, resembling a television screen, that is attached to the system unit of the computer. Whether it contains a cathode ray tube (CRT) like a television screen, or a liquid crystal or gas plasma display as in notebook computers, the monitor allows you to see the result of your input. The number and quality of pixels, or picture elements, in a screen affect its resolution, or the clarity of the image.

The screen resolution is measured by the number of pixels horizontally and the number of pixels vertically. For example, a lower resolution screen would be 640 pixels horizontally by 480 pixels vertically. A high-resolution monitor available today is 1,600 by 1,200 pixels. The color resolution can be from 256 colors to millions of colors (true color 32 bit).

**Printer**  Printers are used to produce hard copies of your messages, downloaded research files, bulletin board information, individual Web pages, and so forth. A wide range of printers is available. In the mid-range are ink-jet printers, which operate by ink ejected from a nozzle to form a character. Ink-jet printers are moderate in price and produce good print quality. On the high end are the very sophisticated laser printers, in which characters are transferred to the paper by heat and pressure from a drum that contains toner that adheres to the paper by electrostatic charge. Laser printers combine copier technology and printer technology. Most personal computer laser printers handle about eight pages a minute. Ink-jet and laser printers produce typeset-quality print. Color printers are available for both laser and ink-jet technology. The color ink-jet model is by far the most popular and affordable color printer used with personal systems.

## Processing Hardware

Processing hardware is the equipment that accepts your input, stores it, and then performs various operations on it prior to output. It is what does the "computing." All computers, from mainframes to micros, are digital processing devices. To describe the process somewhat simplistically, a computer operates in a bistable, or two-state, mode. The two states of the electronic circuits that are etched into the silicon chip are *on* and *off*. Because the computer cannot read our language, we must tell it what to do using its two states to represent our language. The binary number system, which uses only two numbers (0 and 1), is the chosen method to program computers. A coding scheme is used for the 0s and 1s to represent characters; for example, an *A* in the ASCII (American Standard Code for Information Interchange) coding scheme is 10000001. To create the *A*, the relevant computer circuits would turn on, off, off, off, off, off, off, and then on. It seems very time consuming, but remember that computers operate extremely fast. A cycle, or execution of one instruction by the processing unit, is measured in time units called megahertz—1 million cycles per second. The 0s and 1s are known as *bi*nary dig*its*, or bits. Collectively, the eight bits that make up one character are known as a *byte*, the term used for all computer measurement of memory and storage. For example, 64 megabytes (MB) of RAM is 64 million bytes; a 1-gigabyte (GB) hard drive holds 1 billion bytes of data.

The heart of all computer systems is the central processing unit (CPU). Personal computers use a microprocessor for their central processing unit. A microcomputer contains many integrated circuits on a tiny, 0.25-inch silicon chip. It is mounted on a motherboard (main circuit board) and connected to other components by a bus (path) that is 16 or 32 bits wide. The actual computing processing is done in the CPU. Most PCs today have Pentium processors that operate at speeds of 300 to 800MHz, or 800 million cycles per second. When purchasing software, the software companies will often suggest minimum requirements for their software to run.

## Storage Hardware

There are two types of storage hardware used by a computer, primary and secondary storage hardware.

**Primary Storage Hardware**  The primary storage in computers is referred to as Random Access Memory (RAM). RAM provides temporary storage of programs and data while the computer is turned on. Data must be stored in memory before they can be processed; no computing can be done without such a storage area in which to place instructions and information. Memory is immediately accessible to the CPU; data that are in secondary storage (discussed below) must be moved to RAM before they can be processed. RAM is volatile, limited, and relatively expensive. You probably have at least 64 megabytes (MB) (1 megabyte = 1 million bytes) of RAM, although the newer PC models often have up to 128MB (the equivalent of about 128 million characters). Cache memory is a small amount of extremely fast RAM that lies between main memory and the CPU. It stores copies of recently read instructions and other data and thus increases the processing speed of the computer.

Read only memory (ROM) is an area of primary memory that is unchangeable. It is programmed with each system unit. ROM is loaded when the operating system boots, remains unchangeable throughout the computing session, and terminates when the computer is turned off.

**Secondary Storage Hardware**  Because of the volatility and limited capacity of RAM, you cannot permanently store new data for eventual reuse without using an alternative medium. Writing information to such a medium requires storage hardware. Disk drives and optical storage devices allow for secondary storage by allowing you to write to and read from disk or CD/DVD.

- **Floppy Disk Drives**  Most personal computers have at least one disk drive that allows information to be written permanently to a floppy disk (also called a diskette). They transfer information in memory to a more permanent, reliable form on a magnetic or optical medium. It is designated as the A: drive.

- **Hard Disk Drives** Most personal computers sold today also include a hard disk drive. (I-Openers® basic Web access computers do not have hard disk drives.) A hard disk drive allows high-speed, large-capacity secondary storage. A hard disk in a typical system usually holds from 1 to more than 12GB of data (1 gigabyte = 1 billion bytes). It is most commonly designated as the C: drive

- **Optical Disk Drives** CD-ROM drives use a laser-generated compact disk with information already permanently written on it. Compact disks can store many times the quantity of information of a floppy diskette; the standard storage for a CD is 650MB. CDs are the common medium for installing a software application, and for multimedia programs as well. A CD-RW allows you to write to a CD as well as read one. DVD (digital video disk) drives are much more common today, and are finally standardized and affordable. The storage media use the same optical media technology as the CD, but have a much greater capacity (from 4GB to 17GB with a dual-sided, dual-layered variation), so better quality movie-length multimedia can be stored. Just as CDs were first used for audio CDs, DVDs were first used for videos only. Independent DVD players have been popular for some time; now this same technology is available on your PC. DVD Writers (writable DVDs) are also available for microcomputers, but they are not standardized and not as affordable. DVD drives for PCs also read CDs, so you do not need both kinds of optical drives on your PC.

- **Zip Drives and Super Drives** Other mass secondary storage devices include ZIP® and Super Disk® drives. Their media can store from 100MB to 1GB, depending on the model. The advantage of these drives is that both the drive and the media are portable. You write to them just as you would a floppy disk, without the hassle of "burning" a CD or DVD, and then simply carry the disk, and the drive if necessary, to another PC where it can be read by connecting the drive to an available port (explained below). These mass storage devices are necessary for making very large Web downloads (in excess of 1MB) or for authoring multimedia programs (which consume huge amounts of memory), unless you have a CD-RW and can produce CDs.

- **Ports and Expansion Slots for Peripheral Devices** Ports, which are like sockets, are located at the rear of the system unit of a personal computer; they allow you to plug in peripherals (external components such as a printer, scanner, ZIP® drive, or a mouse) to the unit. Ports can be either serial (transporting data one bit at a time), or parallel (transporting data 8 bits, or 1 byte, at a time). A mouse uses a serial port; a printer typically uses a parallel port. Your personal computer probably has several available expansion slots, or openings, where you can insert extra components such as cards with more memory, an Ethernet (hardware for a local area network connection) card for a cable modem Internet connection, a Fax, a scanner, or other peripherals. Expansion slots allow your computer to grow along with your expertise and needs.

# Microcomputer System Software

System software is the software that is necessary for any computing to take place. In order to run, all computers must have an operating system. System software is concerned with your computer's system operations—the operations of the computer that allow the hardware to perform essential tasks. There are several types of system software; operating systems is one of them. Operating system tasks include reading from or writing to disk, storing certain data in a specific memory location, managing the way information is sent to the printer, the input/output (I/O) of data, the allocation of memory, and the locations of many files on a disk. The operating system is the first software to be loaded into memory, and it must be present in memory during the entire computing session. The operating system underlies all application software, which depend on it to perform the functions already mentioned. There are several kinds of system software, but the operating system is the type we are concerned with here.

The Windows operating system (there are several versions of Windows, including NT, a network version, and XP, a single-user version) is a group of programs that perform basic functions of computing by interacting directly with the hardware. All operating systems allow standard operation tasks, such as preparing a disk for use or deleting files. Windows performs many other tasks in the background that you are never aware of, nor need be concerned about. The operating system manages your computing session so that application programs do not interfere with each other.

Windows keeps track of where each item is stored in memory by assigning it a separate "address," or memory location. The Windows operating system combines the user interface (what you see in the screen, and the part with which you interact) and the operating system into one program. You use Windows to copy and delete files from diskette to hard disk, manage folders of files, create backup files, install software, or add new hardware.

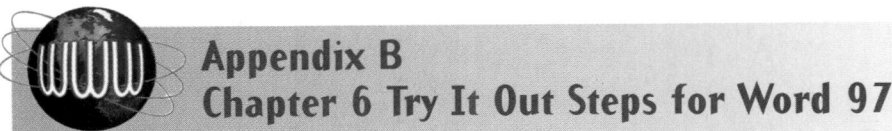

# Appendix B
# Chapter 6 Try It Out Steps for Word 97

The Try It Out exercises in chapter 6 assumed that the user was using Word 2000. Here are the same Try It Out exercises, only written for Word 97.

*Chapter 6, page 181*

## Creating a New Web Page

1. In Microsoft Word 97, click File on the menu bar and then click New from the drop-down menu to display the New dialog box.
2. With the General tab displayed, select the Blank Document icon and click OK.
3. Click File on the menu bar, and then click Save As HTML from the drop-down menu.
4. The link you made on your Web page was to a document named 2ndpage.htm, so in the File name text box, key **2ndpage** to name the file. (Note that the *.htm* extension will be entered automatically, so you do not need to key it as you did in Notepad.)
5. In the Save in text box, save this file to the same folder that you saved the index.htm file. When you are finished, click Save.

*Chapter 6, page 181*

## Testing the Link

1. In Internet Explorer, click File on the menu bar and then click Open from the drop-down menu to display the Open dialog box.
2. Locate the index.htm file using the browse command. When you have found it, click Open and then OK.
3. Scroll down your home page until you come to the link you created at the bottom of the page. Use the mouse to click on the link.
4. The browser should open to the 2ndpage file you created. Because you have not entered any text or graphic images the browser screen will be blank, but "2ndpage" will display in the browser title bar. If you view the source of this page you will notice that you do not need to enter any of the required HTML tags such as <html>, <header>, and so on. The GUI editor automatically creates a title for your page, using the name you chose for the file, in this case 2ndpage.

Chapter 6, page 181

## Customizing a Toolbar

Word 97 does not have a Web Page Preview button, but if you want to add a button to a toolbar, this is how it is done.

1. In Microsoft Word 97, show the toolbar you want to add a button to.
2. Click Tools on the menu bar, click Customize, and then click the Commands tab.
3. In the Categories list box, click a category for the command you want the button to perform.
4. Drag the command from the Commands list box to the displayed toolbar.

Chapter 6, page 182

## Setting Font Style and Size

1. In Microsoft Word 97, with 2ndpage.htm open, if the file is in HTML Source view, click the Exit HTML Source button at the top of the screen to reopen the file in Word.
2. Key an introductory line or phrase for the second Web page.
3. Using the mouse, highlight the text you just entered. On the Formatting toolbar, to the right of the font text box, you will see a large *A* and a small *A*. Clicking on the large A will enlarge the text you highlighted, while clicking on the small *A* will make the text smaller. Because you are working in HTML there are only six different header sizes, just as when you were working in Notepad. You can bold, italicize, or underline text by using the **B**, *I*, and <u>U</u> buttons on the Formatting toolbar. You can left align, center, right align, or justify the text by clicking on the alignment buttons on the toolbar. The justify feature creates flush margins left and right. You can change the color of text by clicking on the Font Color button on the Formatting toolbar.
4. When you are finished choosing the desired formatting options, save the file and then click Refresh on your browser to see what you have created.

Chapter 6, page 182

## Creating a Horizontal Line

1. In Microsoft Word 97, with 2ndpage.htm open, position the cursor where you would like the horizontal line to appear.
2. Click Insert on the menu bar, and then click Horizontal Line from the drop-down menu bar to display the Horizontal Line dialog box.
3. You can choose from a number of colorful and decorative horizontal lines. Clicking on the More button will let you see even more options. Click the line that you want, and then click OK. The horizontal line will appear where you placed the cursor.

Chapter 6, page 183

## Adding Background Color

1. In Microsoft Word 97, with 2ndpage.htm open, click Format on the menu bar and then point to Background from the drop-down menu.
2. A drop-down menu appears showing the color choices. You can click More Colors and choose colors from a palette as well. Clicking on Fill Effects allows you to choose from among a variety of realistic effects, including White Marble, Woven Mat, and Recycled Paper. Click on the color of your choice.
3. Save the file and then click the Refresh button on your browser to see how your Web page looks now.

Chapter 6, page 184

## Inserting an Image

1. In Microsoft Word 97, with 2ndpage.htm open, position the cursor where you would like an image to appear.
2. Click the Insert Picture button.
3. In the Insert Picture dialog box that displays, use the down-pointing arrow to locate any graphic file that you wish to insert. Once you have selected an image, click Insert.
4. The image you inserted will appear on the page. Right-click the image and a shortcut menu appears that will allow you to format the picture and align it. You can resize the image by clicking on it and then clicking and dragging one of the corner or side boxes to the size desired.
5. Save the file when you are finished, and then click the Refresh button on the browser to see how your image looks on the Web.

## Creating a Table

1. In Microsoft Word 97, with 2ndpage.htm open, click Table on the menu bar and then click Insert Table.
2. A grid box opens on the right-hand side of the menu. Moving the cursor over the grid boxes turns the boxes dark blue. The description of the table layout appears at the bottom of the box, indicating the number of rows and columns you have chosen (e.g., 4 x 5 table, or 5 x 5 table). Select the table size you want by highlighting the appropriate number of boxes and then clicking the mouse button once. The table will be inserted into your Web page.
3. To format the table, click Table again on the menu bar. At the drop-down menu, you have a number of choices, including adding or deleting rows or cells, merging or splitting cells, adding a border, and so on. Position the cursor in the row or column you wish to modify. Then click Table on the menu bar and click Select Table from the drop-down menu. *(Note: Merely highlighting the table or a portion of the table you wish to modify is not enough. You must select the function from the Table drop-down menu.)*
4. Once the table has been selected, click Table on the menu bar, and then click Borders from the drop-down menu to display the Table Borders dialog box.
5. Click Grid, find the width of the grid you want by clicking the down-pointing arrow, and then click OK.
6. Fill out the table by keying any text you wish in the boxes.
7. Save the file, and then click the Refresh button on the browser to view the table on your Web page.

## Creating a List

1. In Microsoft Word 97, with 2ndpage.htm open, position the cursor several spaces below the image you placed on the page.
2. Click the Align Left button on the Formatting toolbar so that your list will appear flush left on the page, rather than in the center. If you center the list, the margins will appear ragged on both sides as each line will be a different length.
3. Key a title for your list and press Enter.
4. Enter each list item, pressing the Enter key after each entry.
5. When you are finished keying the items, use your cursor to highlight the listed items.
6. Click Format on the menu bar and then click Bullets and Numbering from the drop-down menu to display the Bullets and Numbering dialog box.
7. You can click the Bulleted or Numbered tab to select the bullet or number style you want. Click on your selection and then click OK.
8. Save the file, and then click the Refresh button on the browser to view the list on your Web page.

Chapter 6, page 186

## Creating a Link

1. In Microsoft Word 97, with 2ndpage.htm open, position the cursor a few spaces below the list you just created.
2. Key **Return to My Web Page**.
3. Using the mouse, highlight the text you just entered and click Insert on the menu bar. Click Hyperlink from the drop-down menu to display the Insert Hyperlink dialog box. You have a choice of creating a link to another file or URL, or you can link to another section or object in the file you are working on. Because you want to link to another file, click Browse next to the Link to file or URL text box.
4. In the Link to File dialog box that displays, locate the index.htm file and then click OK. Click OK again to close the Link to File dialog box.
5. You have created a hyperlink to your home page. The link text you entered is underlined and in blue. You can reformat the link just as you would any other text. Be careful not to click it when you are highlighting it, or you will link to the other file or URL. Save the file, and then click the Refresh button on the browser to view the hyperlink on your Web page.

Chapter 6, page 188

## Recycling a Web Page

1. In Internet Explorer, log on to a Web page of your choice.
2. Click View and then Source on the menu bar to find the source code for a section of the Web page you want to reuse, and copy it.
3. Open the shell you created and paste the copied code between the two <body> tags.
4. Save the file as an .htm file.
5. Open the file using the browser. Does it display just as it did on the original Web page? If it did not, it could be because there was other formatting code that you did not copy. See if you can find any missing code and insert that into the shell file and try again. If graphics are missing, it probably means that they are linked relative to the original page's location. Since you have saved the page in a different location, you will have to save the image from the original Web page to the folder that contains the saved HTML file and relink to it.

Chapter 6, page 189

## Uploading a File

1. From your instructor, get the address of your school's FTP site. In Internet Explorer, key the FTP address in the Address text box near the top of the browser and click Go.
2. If the FTP site requires permission to enter, your instructor will supply a password and user name.
3. Once you are logged on to the FTP server, you should see yellow folder icons. The file you need to upload to may be one of these folders, or it may be in a subfolder contained in one of these folders. If that is the case, you can navigate by double-clicking the folder icons to see their contents and locate the directory where you want to upload your files.
4. Once you have located your destination folder, use the Windows Start button to open Windows Explorer (click Start, Programs, then Windows Explorer). Locate the file you wish to upload using Explorer (e.g., the index.htm file). When you have found it, right-click the mouse and then click Copy from the shortcut menu that appears. Use the taskbar at the bottom of the screen to return to the browser and the FTP site.
5. Now click once on the destination file icon on the FTP site, highlighting it in blue.
6. Right-click the mouse button, and then click Paste at the shortcut menu. The file you copied from Explorer will be pasted into the destination file on the FTP server.

Chapter 6, page 190

## Downloading a File

1. In Internet Explorer, log on to the FTP site again.
2. Locate the file you wish to download and click it once.
3. Right-click the mouse and select Copy to Folder from the shortcut menu that appears.
4. Locate the folder you wish to download the file to, and then click OK. The file you selected will be downloaded and stored in the location you chose.

# Glossary

## A

**.com** The designation for Web-based commercial enterprises. Pronounced "dot com."

**Address Book** A simple, personalized database of names and e-mail addresses usually stored in alphabetical order. Typically part of a mail editor.

**Address/Netsite** In browser context, the drop-down list in the Address (IE) or Netsite (Navigator) text box that keeps a history of the sites visited during the current session and past sessions; a URL is an address.

**agent** See avatar

**analog** Signals that are continuous waveforms—such as the human voice. Converting an analog signal to a discrete binary signal requires digitizing the signal by recording samples of the waveform at a specific frequency, or speed, per second.

**ARPANET** An experimental, wide-area computer network initiated by the U.S. government in the early 1960s. Its purpose was to allow government contractors to share expensive, scarce computing resources. It spanned the United States, and was the precursor to the Internet.

**asynchronous** Refers to communications where there is a time delay between the sending and receiving of a message that prevents simultaneous (synchronous or real-time) dialog.

**ATAP** Any time, any place.

**attributes** Additional parameters used to format elements called for by an HTML tag. For example, an HTML <body> tag may have the attributes bgcolor="blue" text="white" inserted into the tag: <body bgcolor="blue" text="white"> to indicate that the body of the Web page should display a blue background with white text.

**automatic mailing list** Type of Internet asynchronous group communication where postings are distributed to members via e-mail. Automatic mailing lists existed long before the Web.

**avatar** A graphical image representing the user with sound and animation properties. In some new programs, the avatar reads the e-mail to the recipient. Also called an agent.

## B

**bandwidth** The capacity of the conduit to transmit and receive data; the number of bits that can be transmitted at one time over a specific medium.

**banner** Web graphic used for advertising purposes, hyperlinked to a product.

**baud** Measurement of the capacity of a transmission line to change states.

**biometrics** Authentication and security techniques that measure such things as fingerprints, voice recognition, retinal scans, and so on.

**bookmark** A copy of a Web page is cached in the Internet Temporary Files folder on the hard drive; it provides a quick way to navigate to a URL in a Web session.

**Boolean operators** Search operators (qualifiers) such as AND, NOT, NEAR, and OR that are used in advanced searches.

**bot (robot)** See spider

**bps (bits per second)** Measurement of the speed at which data travels over a communication line.

**browser** A Web software program such as Microsoft Internet Explorer or Netscape Navigator that provides the interface for the Web portion of the Internet. The browser allows navigation of Web pages.

## C

**cable modem** Hardware that allows digitized information to be transmitted from a remote site to a local computer, using existing television cable lines. Cable modems emulate a local area network and use fiber optic lines for transmission.

**CD-ROM drive** Computer hardware mass storage drive that uses a laser-generated compact disk with information already permanently written on it.

**Central Processing Unit (CPU)** The CPU is the brains of the computer, the hardware component in which all processing occurs.

**CERN** The Centre Européen pour la Recherche Nucléaire (European Laboratory for Particle Physics) where the World Wide Web was developed.

**certifying authority** Certifying authorities that issue digital signatures for authentication purposes.

**chat** See Internet Relay Chat (IRC)

**chat sessions** Synchronous computer communication sessions where participants hold a conversation, typically by keying their messages which display in the screen in real time, and reading what other participants have to say.

Voice-driven chat sessions are usually referred to as Net meetings.

**client-server** A type of computer network relationship where a server stores, or hosts, material that is accessed by a connected computer (client) that in turn may also serve as a host for other connected clients.

**coaxial cable** High-capacity fiber-based transmission cable for telecommunications.

**compiled language** Programming languages in which the entire program, or set of instructions, is converted to a body of executable code that the processor does not have to stop and convert at run time.

**cookie** A small text file containing user information that is downloaded to the user's computer when he or she first accesses some sites.

# D

**database** An organized arrangement of data that can be retrieved by field or record; a self-describing collection of integrated records.

**debugging** Checking Web pages to make sure that they function as intended.

**decompressing** Returning files that have been condensed to their original size.

**digital cash** Cash equivalency purchased from a bank and transmitted over the Web. Digital cash can be used instead of a credit card to purchase items from e-commerce sites.

**digital signature** An identification code created using encryption software that can be attached to e-mail messages as a means of securely identifying the sender. The use of digital signatures, also known as e-signing, became as legally binding as regular signatures with the passage of the Electronic Signatures Act in October 2000.

**Digital Subscriber Line (DSL)** Conditioned telephone line that adjusts transmission capability for much higher bits per second than originally possible, resulting in faster transmission.

**digital watermarks** Insignia that "stamp" the material's source, and other identifying characteristics embedded electronically that allow the origin of the material to be traced. These marks protect a creator's copyright and result in restrictions on the reuse of those pages.

**directory (index)** A manual entry (human-maintained) database system; use if you want to search deeper within a topic in a hierarchical fashion.

**domain address** Each participant of TCP/IP has a unique 32-bit IP address, such as 144.440.35.6. The unique digital address of a domain server. Also called Internet address.

**domain name** A registered Web site name. This name is included in the unique URL following the www. part of the URL.

**download** To transfer files from an Internet or host source to the user's personal client computer.

**Dynamic Hypertext Markup Language (DHTML)** A programming language that allows Web content to change each time it is viewed on the client, or user, machine. It is commonly used to allow identical Web pages to appear in different languages.

# E

**e-commerce** The sale of goods and services via an electronic medium.

**electronic data interchange (EDI)** Systems where distributors, vendors, and consumers are networked to complete transactions using computers instead of traditional methods.

**electronic funds transfer (ETF)** The transfer of money by electronic means.

**electronic mail (e-mail)** The computer transmission of text messages asynchronously between individuals.

**emoticons** Keyboard symbols used to express emotion or mood in text correspondence. Examples include :) for smiling, happy, and :-O for shocked.

**encryption** The process of encoding data to prevent unauthorized access.

**e-signing** See digital signature

**e-tailer** Companies using the Internet to sell goods and services directly to consumers as opposed to other businesses. The term was created by combining **e**lectronic and re**tailer**.

**Extensible Markup Language (XML)** Part of a larger system that attempts to standardize structured Web documents so there will be a uniform way to add markups.

**external search engine** A search engine that searches the entire Internet, or at least a portion of it.

# F

**fiber optic** Transmission medium that uses thin glass fibers to transmit signals as pulses of light.

**File Transfer Protocol (FTP)** A software standard of transmitting data from one computer to another. FTP allows the user to "put" and "get" files to and from remote computers and save downloaded files to the user's computer.

**firewall** Computer systems—both hardware and software—that are used to put an intervening fireproof layer between the outside user and the vulnerable inside computer system.

**flaming** To engage in rude or insulting behavior in an e-mail message.

**font** A complete set of letters, numbers, and symbols that appear in a particular typeface (i.e., Arial or Times Roman), type size (i.e., 10, 14, or 32), and typestyle (i.e., bold or italic).

**forum** A means of public asynchronous communication where individuals may read and post comments on various topics, organized by threads.

**frame** Separately functioning panes, or independent areas in one screen with their own horizontal and vertical scroll bars. Navigation in one frame can be done without affecting the other frame(s) in the screen.

**freeware** Copyrighted software available free of charge. Freeware can often be downloaded from sites on the Internet.

**full duplex mode** A type of audio capability, meaning two individuals can speak at the same time, in real-time.

# G

**graphical user interface (GUI)** The layer of software where the user and computer interact; the presentation layer provided to computer users that allows them to point and click and drag and drop icons to perform computer operations.

# H

**hardware** The computer system's physical components.

**history** A record of the pages visited during a Web session so that you can return to them using Back, Forward, and History buttons.

**home page** The first of a series of pages for a specific address on a Web site.

**host computer** A mainframe or minicomputer that stores individual e-mail accounts.

**hot word** A hypertext selection that allows you to jump directly to the subject on a Web page.

**HTML tags** Commands inserted into a document that specify the style and placement of text, graphics, links, and other Web page features (e.g., <b>, <p>, <img>, etc.).

**hyperlink** Nonlinear associated links to other URLs embedded within the source code; hot words or graphics. Hyperlinks are often referred to as "links."

**hypermedia** A system of relating by association, regardless of media type.

**HyperTerminal** One type of software program that allows modems to communicate with each other.

**hypertext** A nonlinear way of handling text so that words are linked and/or associated with each other, not by their position in an article or by chronological or other order, but instead by a system of pointers.

**Hypertext Markup Language (HTML)** The primary coding system for Web pages.

**Hypertext Transfer Protocol (HTTP)** The default Web protocol for Web page access.

**Hypertext Transfer Protocol Secure (HTPPS)** The protocol used for SSL transactions. When accessing an SSL server, the address text box on the browser will begin with https://.

# I

**image map** Graphic equivalents of hypertext links; can be sections of a main image connecting to different anchors, or URLs.

**instant messenger** A service that allows users to communicate in real-time with other users who are logged on to the Internet at the same time.

**Integrated Services Digital Network (ISDN)** Special high-speed, high-capacity digital lines for multimedia transmission offered by telecommunication companies.

**interface** Computer software that allows users to interact with the underlying computer hardware and software.

**interlaced graphics** Web page graphics that appear on the page only after the entire pixels group is in client computer RAM.

**internal search engine** A search engine that searches only for material contained in its home site.

**Internet** An infrastructure of networks connecting many smaller networked computers in a global client-server environment. Also known as the Net.

**Internet Message Access Protocol (IMAP)** A popular mail protocol in which mail remains on the ISP's server until the user deletes it.

**Internet Relay Chat (IRC)** A real-time (synchronous) way of communicating with text on the Internet. It predates the establishment of the Web.

**Internet service provider (ISP)** A provider of access to the Web or the Internet in general.

**interpreted programming languages** Programming languages in which each line of code, or instruction, is executed as it is read by the processor, one line at a time.

**intranet** A network based on TCP/IP protocols (an Internet) belonging to an organization, usually a corporation, accessible only by the organization's members, employees, or others with authorization.

# J

**Java applet** Small applications (programs) contained within larger programs that are designed to be executed within those programs. For example, a Java applet may be embedded in a Java program within a Web page that displays a fill-in form.

# K

**keywords** Words in a Web site that are included in the title and the metatags and in the text of some search engines. They form the basis of Web searches.

# L

**link** See hyperlink

**LISTSERV** Type of Internet asynchronous group communication where postings are distributed to members via e-mail. Listservs existed long before the Web.

**local area network (LAN)** A group of computers physically wired or connected to each other in order to share programs, data, and peripherals, and to allow communications within the group.

**lurker** A silent participant in an automatic mailing list or chat room who reads all, but chooses not to actively participate in the discussion.

# M

**mail editors** Simplified word processing programs that allow the user to key and edit an e-mail message.

**mail servers** A type of computer with software dedicated to storing and routing e-mail.

**mailbox** The area where mail is indexed in a mail editing program.

**mailstations** Dedicated low-cost Internet e-mail devices that allow the sending and receiving of e-mail without using a conventional computer.

**metalanguage** A programming language used to describe other languages, but independent of other Web languages.

**meta-search engine** Search engine that searches multiple directories and multiple search engines, all from one location. Maintained by both humans and spiders or robots.

**metatag** HTML deliberately created to attract the attention of a search engine.

**modem** From modulator-demodulator, computer hardware that has a special device that allows computer data to be sent in waveform over phone lines, then demodulated back to digital form for reception by the target computer system.

**MPC3** Stands for Multimedia Personal Computer, level 3 hardware and software standards. These are minimum requirements that allow enough main memory and a powerful enough processor (CPU) to handle the data coming in from Web pages and hardware to hear sound files and view video files.

# N

**navigation scheme** The path by which users can move around a Web site. Typical navigation schemes include sequential schemes (linear—from one page to the next) or hierarchical (like an outline, with index pages leading to topic pages, leading to subtopic pages).

**netiquette** Short for network etiquette. Rules for good behavior when communicating by e-mail.

**network** Two or more computers connected to each other by some means.

**network cards** A hardware peripheral that allows computers to be networked.

**newsgroup** E-mail discussion group, also know as Usenet.

**newsreader** A software application that allows the user to read newsgroup articles that are posted by thread, or topic.

**nonlinear** Words that are linked and/or associated with each other (hyperlinked), not by their position in an article or by chronological or other order, but instead by a system of pointers.

## O

**offline** Working on interface programs, such as composing e-mail messages, when not logged on to the Internet.

**operating system** System software necessary for a computing session; it manages the session and performs the primitive computing functions. The most common OS for microcomputers is Windows.

## P

**phone modem** Internal analog modem installed in one of the available slots on the main circuit board of a computer.

**pixel** The basic building blocks of a display screen; the number and color capacity of the points on a screen affect its resolution, or the clarity of the image. Short for picture element, a measurement 1/72 of an inch wide. Used to specify image size.

**plagiarism** Taking someone else's ideas and passing them off as your own.

**plug-in** Helper applications introduced to enhance the capability of the browsers to display Web pages.

**point** A measurement of text or font size.

**pointer** Variable that stores addresses, or locations, of other data to be linked.

**portal** A Web site that functions as an entry point to e-commerce sites.

Portals contain categorized links to other e-commerce sites.

**Post Office Protocol (POP)** A popular mail protocol in which mail is downloaded to the computer and then deleted on the ISP's server.

**POTS** Plain old telephone system; voice lines that were originally designed to transmit at a maximum of 9600 baud rate.

**progressive graphics** Graphics that appear in layers and get richer and clearer as they download to the browser window.

**protocol** Set of rules or software standards governing handling of data.

**publishing** The process of placing Web page files on a host server so that they are accessible through the Internet.

## Q

**quota** The amount of server disk space an ISP allows the user to access for Web pages, for personal workspace, and for e-mail storage.

## R

**Random Access Memory (RAM)** A type of computer memory that can be accessed randomly. RAM is the most common type of memory found in computers and other devices, such as printers.

**Real Time Streaming Protocol (RSTP)** A set of software standards for transmission of live video and audio feeds via the Internet using caching and simultaneous playback.

**relational operators** Symbols describing the chronological (time-related) relationship between keywords and numbers.

## S

**scripting language** Programming language used for scripting (writing) Web pages, such as HTML, Java, XML, and so forth.

**search conventions** Rules to sort information, utilized by search engines and directories. For example, one rule is do not include articles and prepositions in a search.

**search engine** Internet software program that makes finding information on the Internet easier by

using database queries to indexed material and returning a results list.

**search operators** Boolean operators (AND, NOT, NEAR, OR) and relational operators (+, -, >, <, =>, <=) and others used to further qualify a search.

**Secure Sockets Layer (SSL)** An encryption technology used to protect Web credit card transactions.

**serif/sans serif** Serif fonts have short tails or trailing characters, sans serif do not (e.g., a serif A looks like this [A], while a sans serif A looks like this [A]).

**server** Computer that hosts the information on the Internet.

**software** Computer programs or coded stored instructions that drive computing sessions.

**source code** The programming behind any Web page. HTML is one example of a source code.

**spam** Unsolicited e-mail sent in bulk.

**spider** Software tools for sifting through written material on the Web to scan Web content and update the search engine's index automatically. See also bot

**Standard General Markup Language (SGML)** A master markup language developed by the International Standards Organization (ISO), which sets standards for computing areas. SGML sets requirements for any markup language, whether Web based or not.

**streaming** A video or audio file is "streamed," or downloaded in small increments, to the cache memory. It is buffered, or stored, until there is enough of it downloaded to start playing the file. While file is being played, the next block is being downloaded, resulting in a constant stream of data.

**subject matter expert (SME)** When designing commercial or professional Web sites, a subject matter expert is often employed to advise Web designers and programmers about the content of the pages.

**synchronizing** An option of the Favorites feature (IE) that allows you to save Favorites offline. Then, when you go online these pages are automatically refreshed or updated.

**synchronous** Communications where the time delay between the sending and receiving of a message is so short that two-way or real-time dialog (conversations) can be held.

## T

**tags** Tags are the building blocks of formatting and hyperlinking in Web pages. Tags are commands inserted in a document that specify how the document should be formatted, what graphics should display, or to what other location it should be linked. They form the basis of markup languages. Also called metatags.

**target audience** The people or groups that a Web page or Web site is designed to attract.

**tele-immersion** The perceived immersion into computer-based virtual reality environment—the illusion of immersion into a distant environment.

**telephony** The use of the Web for telephone conversations.

**telnet** An Internet functionality that allows accessing a remote computer from within a computer logged on to another network, using the target computer's IP address.

**thread** Specific topics of discussion used on forums and Usenets. They are hierarchical, or treelike, in their structure. In outline format, participants respond to each other's comments.

**tooltips** Text aids inside pop-up rectangles used to orient users or to explain or identify something on-screen.

**Transmission Control Protocol/Internet Protocol (TCP/IP)** A set of software standards that is required for Internet access; developed by V. Cerf and R. Kahn.

## U

**Uniform Resource Locator (URL)** A unique identifier that provides the global address of documents or other resources on the Web. There cannot be two identical URLs.

**upload** To transfer files from a personal computer to a remote computer on a network, usually via FTP protocol.

**Usenet** Type of Internet asynchronous group communication where users may read and post comments on specific topics in a "bulletin board" fashion. Unlike LISTSERVS, Usenets do not use e-mail for transmission, but instead use newreaders.

**user interface** Computer software layer that allows users to interact with the underlying hardware and software. What the user sees in the screen; the place where the user and computer interact.

## V

**virtual library** In Web context, specialty collection maintained by human experts in an area.

**virtual wallet** A program function allowing the storage of identification and credit data for use when shopping on the Web.

**virus** A program that searches for and copies itself to other programs. When these programs are executed the virus program is executed as well, thus spreading the "infection." The effects of a virus can range from harmless to catastrophic, depending on the nature of the virus.

## W

**Web page** A document on the World Wide Web that consists of an HTML file, with associated files for graphics and scripts, identified by a URL, or address.

**whiteboard** A display area in a chat room participants can use without leaving the chat session to input other than text of conversation.

**wide area network (WAN)** A network that spans a wide distance and connects two or more LANs (local area networks).

**wired** A computer network where nodes are connected by private or public physical lines, such as telephone or coaxial lines, or Ethernet cabling.

**wireless** A computer network where the connected computers are not physically connected, but rely on infrared, radio, or satellite transmission.

**World Wide Web** The total collection of information available on that portion of the Internet that contains hyperlinked documents. Also referred to as www, or the Web.

**WYSIWYG** **W**hat **Y**ou **S**ee **I**s **W**hat **Y**ou **G**et applications refers to programs for creating Web pages that allow users to see how the pages will display as they are created, rather than as code.

# Index

## A

About, 72
 Web site for, 69
Absolute FTP, 190
Acrobat Reader, 61
Active e-mail, 6
ActiveX/Visual Basic, 165
Address bar, 38
Address book, 107–109
 adding names from e-mail, 109
 creating groups, 108
 deleting names from, 109
 entering new names and addresses, 108
 sending e-mail using address book, 109
 tips for, 107
Address/Netsite, 39
 using to show history, 48, 49
Adobe Acrobat Reader, 61
Advanced Research Projects Agency (ARPA), 16
Agent, 120
AltaVista, 70
 Web site for, 69
Amazon, 147–148
 greeting cards, 9
 Web site for, 13
American Greetings, 9
American Heritage Dictionary Online, 11
America Online (AOL)
 browser, 27
 Instant Messenger, 6, 122–123
Analog, 22
AND, Boolean operator, 78–79, 81
AOL. See America Online (AOL)
APA Publication Manual, 85, 86
Applets, 59–60
Argus Clearing House, 74
 Web site for, 69
ARPANET, 16
Articles, search operator and, 81
Ask Jeeves, 73
 Web site for, 69
Asynchronous, 94
ATAP (any time, any place), 144
Atkinson, Bill, 51
Attachments, 112–114
 adding, 113
 compressing, 112
 opening, 114
Attributes
 commonly used, 179

defined, 164
Automatic mailing lists, 116–118
 disadvantages of, 118
 joining, 117
 leaving, 117
Avatar, 120

## B

Back button, 47
 using to show history, 48, 49
Bandwidth, 21, 22
Banking, e-commerce, 147
Banners, 85, 132
Baud, 22
Berners-Lee, Tim, 18–19
Better Business Bureau (BBB)
 Code of Online Business Practices, 139
 Web site for, 140
Bezos, Jeff, 132
Biddingtons, 149
Biometrics, 143
Bitmap files, 162
Blind carbon copy, 102
Blue Mountain, 9
Bookmarks, 55–58. See also Favorites
 benefit of, 48
 function of, 55
 organizing, 58
 saving search engines as, 71
Bookstores, e-commerce, 147–148
Boole, George, 78
Boolean operators, 78–81
Bots, 68
 Web sites for, 68
BotSpot, 68
Brin, Sergey, 70
Browser, 38–58
 creation of, 18
 Favorites/Bookmarks, 55–58
 file management functions, 54–55
 frames, 59
 function of, 4, 38
 help menu, 58
 home pages, 40
 home sites, 40
 hot words, 44
 image maps, 45–46
 Menu Bar commands, 51–53
 navigation options, 38–46
 plug-ins, 60–62
 selecting, 39
 software, 27
 toolbar shortcuts, 46–50
 tools menu, 58

Uniform Resource Locators (URLs), 41–44

## C

Cable modems, 24
 Web sites for, 25
Capitalization
 in e-mail, 105
 HTML tags, 169
 search operator and, 80–81
Carbon copy, 102
CD-ROM drive, 20
Censorship
 China and Internet, 5, 6
Centering text, 171
Central Processing Unit (CPU), 19
CERN (Centre Européen pour la Recherche Nucléaire), 19
Certifying authority, 143
 Web sites for, 143
Chain letter, 111
Chair, computer, 10
Charles Schwab, 13
Chat, 120–122
 chat screen name, 122
 defined, 6
 participating in, 121
 private chat warning, 122
 system requirements for, 121
 whiteboards, 120
Checksum, 26
Chicago Manual of Style, 85
China, People's Republic of
 attempts to control access to Internet, 5, 6
Citations, 84–87
Client-server, 22
Client-server networks, 17
Cliffords, 149
Closing tag, 167, 170, 171
CNet, 69
CNN, 12
Coaxial cable, 24
Codewallet, 137
Coffee Cup Free FTP, 190
Color
 adding background, 183
 changing background, 171, 172
 changing text color, 171, 172
 common color codes, 171
 limitations on Web pages, 160–161
Comment tags, 176
Common Gateway Interface, 165
Communications software, 26–27
 HyperTerminal, 26

# T

Tables, creating, 176, 177, 184, 185
Tagged Image Format files, 162
Target audience, 158
Taxes
  e-mail and, 145
  filing taxes on Web, 14
TCP/IP (Transmission Control Protocol/Internet Protocol), 26
Tele-immersion, 20
Telephone lines, phone modem and, 22–24
Telephony, 123
  Web sites for, 15, 123
Television, virtual broadcasting, 14–15
Threads, 7, 118
Title tag, 167
Toolbar, 38
  customizing, 181
  Internet Explorer, 46
  Netscape Navigator, 47
  shortcuts, 46–50
  tips for, 180
Tools menu, 58
  Internet Explorer, 52
Tooltip, 45
Travel arrangements, e-commerce, 150
TRUSTe, 140
Try It Out
  e-commerce
    checking business practices, 140
    comparing e-commerce home pages, 133
    comparing e-commerce site, 136
    comparison shopping, 146
    disabling Windows Remember Password feature, 143
    reviewing contents or site maps, 133
    shopping on eBay, 148
  e-mail
    address book, adding names to, from e-mail, 109
    address book, creating groups, 108
    address book, deleting names from, 109
    address book, entering new names and addresses, 108
    address book, sending e-mail using, 109
    announcing new mail, 98
    attachment, adding, 113
    attachment, opening, 114
    automatic mailing list, joining, 117
    automatic mailing list, leaving, 117
    automatic signature to outgoing mail, 110

    blocking incoming mail, 104
    composing and sending message, 102
    copying and pasting text into e-mail message, 104
    default setting for message reply, changing, 110
    folders, creating new, 115
    folders, organizing messages in, 115
    forwarding message, 111
    mail preferences, setting, 98
    newsgroups, reading, 119
    newsgroups, setting up new account, 119
    newsgroups, subscribing and unsubscribing to, 119
    responding to message, 111
    selecting Outlook Express as default mail program, 100
  general Internet activities
    chat room, participating in, 121
    checking today's news, 12
    financial information, finding, 14
    forums, using, 8
    game, playing, 10
    greeting card, sending, 9
    learning more about "father of Web," 18
    online dictionary, using, 12
    searching, 11
    shopping at auctions, 13
    telephony, finding out about hardware and software requirements, 123
    understanding elements of Web page, 5
  information retrieval
    asking Jeeves a question, 74
    copying and pasting using taskbar, 83
    copying text from Web site to word file, 82
    job, finding, 78
    job, looking for, 76
    limiting results list and searching for exact words, 77
    operators, using, 79
    saving image from Web site to word file, 83
    search engines, comparing, 72
    search engines, understanding how search engines view each other, 71
  navigation tools
    changing default home page, 40
    domain names, learning about, 42
    domain names, understanding, 43
    downloading forms, 61

    favorites, adding, 56
    favorites, creating personalized file folder for, 57
    favorites, deleting or renaming, 57
    favorites, organizing, 57, 58
    finding flight, 40
    finding text, 54
    history, selecting number of days to store, 50
    history, using Address/Netsite to show, 49
    history, using Back button to show, 49
    history, using History button to show, 50
    hyperlinks, 46
    icon size, changing, 48
    shortcut buttons, 47
    understanding Web page elements, 57
    using help, 59
  Web page design
    background color, adding, 172, 183
    centering text, 172
    customizing toolbar, 181
    downloading file, 190
    header size, changing, 170
    horizontal line, creating, 172, 182
    image, inserting, 175, 184
    image, saving from a Web page, 175
    line breaks, adding, 174
    link, creating, 178, 186
    list, creating, 177, 185
    new Web page, creating, 168, 181
    opening and closing tags, 171
    recycling Web page, 188
    setting font style and size, 182
    source code, viewing, 165
    table, creating, 177, 185
    testing link, 181
    text color, changing, 173
    uploading file, 189
    Web page, viewing your, 169
    Web sites, looking at, 158

# U

Undo button, 183
Unicast transmission service, 20
Uniform Resource Locators (URLs), 38–39
  access protocol of, 41
  defined, 19
  domain name, 41–43
  number of, 41
  parts of, 41–44